On March 29, 2017, the United Kingdom gave notice under Article 50 of its intention to quit the European Union.

You're the British Prime Minister. You now have just two years to negotiate the unpicking of an alliance that's been built up over four decades. And that's not the only minefield you're going to have to cross. Your cabinet is unruly, your party is splitting itself apart, and the country remains bitterly divided over the whole issue.

Can you hang on and bring Britain safely into harbour? Forge new trade deals around the globe? Juggle popular support at home with the goodwill of your former EU allies? Stop the economy from spiralling down the plug hole? And all the while keeping an eye on those Parliamentary colleagues whose knives are ever-ready to plunge into your back?

This is a gamebook in which the outcome is decided by the choices you make. You know the kind of thing. You'll need a pencil to keep track of how you're doing on the Brexit Memo Pad, which you'll find at the back of the book.

Anything else? Oh yes, you start at section **1**. Seems obvious, but these days we can't take anything for granted…

WHO'S WHO

Armand Alprèves	EU Commission chief negotiator
Bill Appleby	Presenter of the BBC show *Now Then*
Jay Arthur	Health Secretary
Leslie Barkwell	International Trade Minister
Ron Beardsley	Downing Street chief of staff
Dave Deadpool	US chief strategist
Dennis Dent	Secretary of State for Exiting the EU
Amelia Dimple	Environment Secretary
Harvey Doggerbank	Chairman of the 1922 Committee
Bob Fobber	Leader of the Liberal Democrats
Willy Franjeboom	Chief negotiator for the EU Parliament
Colin Fungale	Sometime leader of UKIP
Crispin Gorm	Attorney General
Ingrid Käsen	Chancellor of Germany
Yalayip Kulübe	President of Turkey
Jonathan Leonine	Former Tory grandee
Douglas Mac	President of the European Council
Martin Mugglemore	Presenter of the TV show *Feeding Time*
Gervais Noysom-Reek	Conservative backbencher
Bob Owlbear	Deputy leader of the opposition
Jaume Pandillero	President of the Philippines
Kirstin Pike	First Minister of Scotland
Lemmi Puukaasu	Prime Minister of Finland
Tiffany Rufus	Home Secretary
Barry Scraggle	Leader of the opposition
Chloe Stoat	Business Secretary
Alan Stollard	Chancellor of the Exchequer
Bill Strait	Father of the House
Peter Strewel	Foreign Secretary
Jean-Jacques Terlamen	President of the European Commission
Thomas Tode	Prominent Leave campaigner
Terri Trough	Downing Street Press Secretary
Dumpster P Windrip	President of the United States

It was a game played for no reason but to keep playing.

Toss two coins. If both are heads, turn to **403**. Otherwise, turn to **313.**

9

Strewel was expecting you to fight him on either a Leave or Remain ticket, both of which he was prepared for. The one tactic he never anticipated was that you would refute the factious politics of the last three years.

The British people, by nature moderate and conciliatory, seize at your proposals as the life preserver that could save the country from going under. More importantly, the Tory party members who will decide this contest see which way the wind is blowing. Polls suggest that the less extreme of them are beginning to appreciate the wisdom of supporting a concordant solution, without which the party was always in danger of winning a Pyrrhic victory.

You have Strewel on the ropes. Can you finish him off? If your Popularity score is 53% or higher, turn to **519**. If your Popularity is 52% or less, turn to **347**.

10

'Ever had a near miss, Wilkins?' you ask as he draws back the curtains to reveal a sky of dazzling sunlight.

'I got four out of five numbers on the Euromillions once, only it turned out to be an old ticket.'

'I mean a near disaster. A piano crashing to the pavement two steps behind you. A gas leak, only you were woken by the cat. Escaping death by a whisker, so to speak.'

'Can't say I have, Prime Minister.'

'This is like that. I feel as though I'd just driven through a ten-car pile up, burning wreckage and screaming on all sides, only I sailed right through and came out without a scratch. I'm living a charmed life, Wilkins. Untainted by a campaign that could have ended my career.'

He opens the wardrobe. 'On with the job, then?'

> On your Brexit Memo Pad:
> ❖ Mark Second EU Referendum as complete.

Then turn to **450**.

11

'Your real Death Star there is the whole legal issue of international trade talks. Then there's the shaky position of existing trade deals, or those that are being negotiated by the EU at the moment. We might not inherit those automatically. There's the time it takes to negotiate trade deals, too – we can move faster than a monolithic bloc like the EU, but we've got to do lots of bitty deals and meanwhile the pressure is mounting and the national debt is climbing.'

'I don't think your father would agree with you on any of those points.'

'You're kidding, right? He knows all right. Haven't you noticed that glassy look in his eyes? It's fear. Constant, blood-curdling, ball-shrivelling fear.'

'Oh, come on. Britain has faced worse threats before.'

'The Dunkirk spirit, yeah? We're all in it together? Except those voters who wanted their country back aren't going to like the country they actually get.'

⇒ 'What do you mean by that?' Turn to **224**

⇒ 'What legal issues are you talking about?' Turn to **211**

⇒ 'I don't think it will take too long to hammer out a few simple trade agreements.' Turn to **198**

⇒ 'Let's not focus on the negative.' Turn to **700**

12

Appleby laughs at that, but the audience don't laugh with him. And behind them you sense the British people. They believe you. Conditioned by half-remembered history lessons when they gazed in boredom at the red maps of Empire, and with contempt for foreigners and clever-clogs bred into the bone, they really do imagine that the rest of the world will beg Britain's forgiveness.

> On your Brexit Memo Pad:
> - ❖ +1% Authority – MPs respect an audacious leader.

You leave the studio with renewed confidence. If you have the keyword NYLON, turn to **193**. If not, turn to **726**.

13

To call an election before 2020, when the current Parliamentary term ends, you need two thirds of MPs to vote for one. The notepad on your desk is covered with doodles of the Commons benches, all of which show your own party having less than 55% of the seats.

The LibDems have nothing to lose from an election, having been punished by their supporters last time for entering a coalition with the Conservatives. This time round, with their policy of strong support for Remain, they might hope to pick up a dozen seats. The trouble is, even with LibDem support in a vote, you don't have the necessary two-thirds majority. And that's assuming you don't have any dissenters in your own ranks.

Look at your Brexit Memo Pad. If your Goodwill is 60% or more, turn to **271**. Otherwise turn to **796**.

14

Sterling is falling faster than Wile E Coyote carrying an anvil. People are angry that their shopping bill gets more eye-wateringly expensive every week.

Check your Brexit Memo Pad. If Economy is less than 50% turn to **502**. Otherwise turn to **311**.

15

'Give them time. In many of the areas that voted to leave the EU, the proportion of immigrants has increased very rapidly – tenfold or more in the last decade. Other regions, like London, have had more time to get used to a high number of foreign-born residents and were in favour of remaining in the EU. You've travelled through the more rural areas of your own country. How do locals react to strangers? It takes them a while to grow accustomed to change. The days when elitists could order their people around are gone. We are democracies and we must accept the democratic will. None of us here wants a bad outcome in these talks, and you know I must uphold the decision of my electorate, so let us hear no more insults, please.'

It's good. Statesmanlike. You notice several of the ministers exchanging glances of approval – or maybe envy, either will do.

> Record on your Brexit Memo Pad:
> - +1% Authority – that speech will play well at home.
> - +1% Goodwill – the EU ministers respect your candour and like the veiled hints of a soft Brexit strategy.

Turn to **453.**

16

Despite your announcement that EU nationals will not retain their rights following Brexit, the EU decides to let UK ex-pats stay in Europe anyway.

'Are we the baddies?' the Home Secretary asks you. Her wry smile suggests it's some pop culture reference, but you have no time for such frivolities.

> On your Brexit Memo Pad:
> - -10% Goodwill – you haven't made any friends in Europe.
> - Mark Residency Rights as complete.

Then turn to **200**.

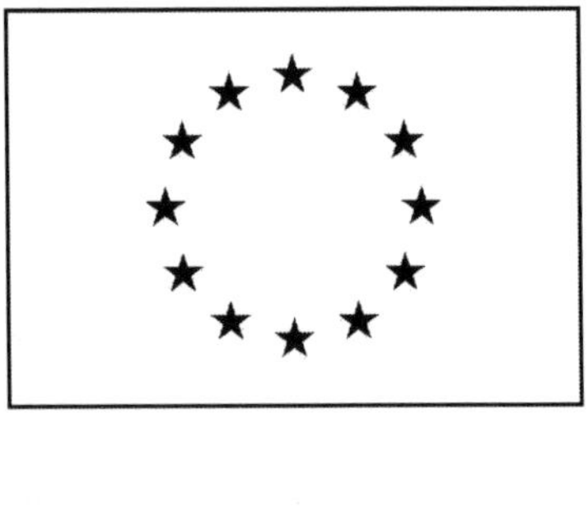

17

The discussion is about whether to apply for membership of EFTA within the European Economic Area alongside Norway, Iceland and Liechtenstein.

⇒ 'But would Norway block our membership?' Turn to **42**

⇒ 'Let's consider the free movement question.' Turn to **237**

⇒ 'What would EEA membership cost?' Turn to **601**

⇒ 'Would Britain have any influence in EFTA?' Turn to **330**

⇒ 'What will it mean for the UK services market?' Turn to **579**

⇒ 'How about the Swiss model?' Turn to **2**

⇒ 'Let's review all our other options again.' Turn to **703**

18

As you're coming into Penzance station, a thought occurs to you. 'What am I going to say about the bus?'

The aide chews her lip in thought. 'Risk of roadworks. Showing support for intercity rail. The need to stick to a tight schedule. And it's a four hour drive to Penzance. The train was really the only option, Prime Minister.'

'I meant the Brexit bus. The £350 million a week that isn't going on the NHS or on Cornish industry either.'

You know the press are bound to ask you about how much of the money that used to be spent on EU membership will now go on regional development. What will you tell them?

⇒ 'The government will guarantee every penny that Cornwall used to get from EU funding.' Turn to **755**

⇒ 'It's too early to talk about numbers, but the government remains committed to promoting Cornish industry and innovation.' Turn to **840**

⇒ 'That claim on the Leave bus didn't have anything to do with me.' Turn to **696**

19

It's make or break. You can't point to many useful achievements over the last two years of Brexit talks, but you still have the instincts honed by two decades at the hustings. You pull out all the stops to make yourself look like the reliable candidate and the others like self-deluding incompetents.

If your Popularity is 59% or more, turn to **489**. Otherwise turn to **377**.

20

You meant it half-jokingly, but you'd underestimated the depths of his laziness. 'Actually, that's a wizard idea,' he says. 'You're on!'

> On your Brexit Memo Pad:
> ❖ Mark the keyword YELLOW.

When Strewel announces he's backing you, Dent sees there isn't room for both of you and withdraws from the race. Soon after Alan Stollard declares his support for Tiffany Rufus, shoring up her base on the moderate wing of the Party. That leaves the ultra-Brexit candidate – and one more round of MPs' voting before it goes to the Conservative membership.

If you have the keyword NYLON, turn to **193**. If not, turn to **726**.

21

'Everyone aboard?' says the driver. As soon as he's counted you all, he taps instructions into the bus's dashboard and then jumps off just before the doors close.

'He's not coming with us?' you say, watching as the bus lifts off and the waving figures in the parking lot dwindle into the distance.

Beside you is a man with a glazed smile like a Jehovah's Witness who's succeeded in converting a pensioner. 'He can't come. It's not for him.'

The person in front swivels in their seat. The same demented satisfaction, the same beatific tone. 'Only the truly hopeless deserve the ultimate cure.'

'We used to send a fortune to the Evil Union,' says the man behind you. He's the one with the saline drip. 'Now we're spending it on our NHS.'

'Our NHS…' intone the others.

On the dashboard a red display is counting down. You're so high above the city now that its lights have been swallowed in the murk of pollution. You push past your neighbour and stagger to the front of the bus. Under the steering column is a large metal canister with wires leading into it. The last few seconds tick away.

You turn to the other passengers, all staring past you with wondering, tear-filled eyes at the imminent rapture.

'But I'm only here because of my bear – '

The blossom of flame opens to accept you all. Turn to **368**.

22

'Canada has the Comprehensive Economic and Trade Agreement…' begins Stollard.

'"Comprehensive", really? A bit like calling it the World's Greatest Trade Plan of 2017, isn't it?' snorts Strewel. 'You mean it doesn't stand for Canadian-European Trade Agreement?'

'That's a useful mnemonic,' concedes the Chancellor with studied patience. 'And then there's EUSFTA – '

'Don't tell me. It's the, um, excellently useful, stonkingly fantastic – '

'It's the EU-Singapore Free Trade Agreement,' says Stollard drily. 'Both these agreements remove or phase out tariffs between the parties. In Singapore's case there are still quotas in some products, while the CETA deal is much more comprehensive and will give Canada tariff-free access to 98% of EU goods. There are some restrictions on agricultural products, as you might expect. And Canada and Singapore must both be compliant on rules of origin, of course.'

⇒ 'Rules of origin being what?' Turn to **667**

⇒ 'Tell me the pros and cons of this kind of deal.' Turn to **303**

⇒ 'How long did it take to get CETA and EUSFTA agreed?' Turn to **276**

23

A relative boom in the economy serves to reassure the public that it was the right decision to quit the EU. Polls show a surge in support for Leave.

'It's all fuelled by credit cards, is my worry,' moans the Chancellor. 'The underlying wealth of the country is not in good shape.'

'Perception is reality,' you tell him, not for the first time. 'We're just here to hold the wheel and pretend we're steering.'

Look at your Brexit Memo Pad. If your Goodwill score is 40% or higher, turn to **864**. If it's 39% or lower, turn to **207**.

24

A close call. So you campaigned for a soft Brexit and instead the public want a hard one. They're deluded, of course, but you won't get anywhere by worrying about the rights and wrongs of it all now.

'What now?' call the reporters waiting for you in Downing Street.

You turn to face the barrage of popping flashlights. You have never felt more certainly the wind of destiny in your sails.

'Now,' you tell them, 'I get on with the job.'

> On your Brexit Memo Pad:
> - -5% Popularity – your misjudgement in the campaign will take some living down.
> - Mark Second EU Referendum as complete.

Then turn to **450**.

25

'What part of our customs union arrangement do you think will bring down the government?'

'Oh heavens. Well, I don't think it'll go that far. But a lot of MPs in both major parties would prefer a closer relationship with the EU than that.'

'That's not going to be what they get to vote on, though. It will be the customs union or the restore-to-factory-settings option, namely WTO rules. They'll take the lesser of two evils, believe me.'

You're right. The Commons votes almost unanimously for the deal you have struck with the EU, and although there is some criticism in the Lords you can safely ignore that.

Turn to **806**.

26

Your ministers return with fixed grins that strike a sense of foreboding into your heart. 'We laid down the law, eh?' chortles Strewel, as usual with the air of having swiped an extra cream bun from the tuck shop.

'What did you tell them?' you say in a carefully controlled tone.

'That it's our way or the highway,' says Dent brightly.

The imbecile. You don't know which is more to be deplored, his incompetence at even the simplest task, or his hopelessly muffed attempts at using catchphrases.

> Record on your Brexit Memo Pad:
> - ❖ -2% Goodwill – the only outcome is to irritate the other EU members
> - ❖ Mark Negotiation Strategy as complete.

Turn to **580.**

27

So the contest is now between you and three others.

Tiffany Rufus, the Home Secretary, is perhaps the least of your worries. She's said enough rational, adult, fact-based things in the last few years to get herself tarred as a secret Remainer. She's even on record as saying that a hard Brexit may not be in the UK's interests – the sort of heresy for which the medieval Church would burn somebody alive. Of course, many of the MPs sympathize with that view, but she'll get short shrift from the party faithful.

Dennis Dent is a more serious contender. He cleaves to his own vision of Brexit, which is about as soft as a Glasgow kiss, but two years across the table from the EU negotiators have forced him to face facts. He drops occasional hints regarding Britain's future relationship with Europe that fall far short of Colin Fungale's sniggering hatred.

And then there's Fungale himself. So far you've been selling yourself as the crusader for a bare-knuckled Brexit, but it's hard to outdo Fungale's track record in that respect.

'So where do you stand now, Prime Minister?' asks one of the reporters outside Number 10. 'Are you as committed to Brexit as Colin Fungale?'

⇒ 'More so. While Mr Fungale has been talking the talk, I've been walking the walk. He really has no conception of how strong and uncompromising a Brexit we've got planned.' Turn to **268**

⇒ 'Brexit is a bit of an obsession of Mr Fungale's, and like most people with a bee in his bonnet he doesn't have patience for the details. We intend to deliver Brexit on schedule, but we don't want to make an enemy of the EU. They will continue to be a valued ally and trading partner.' Turn to **852**

28

You're seen as someone who will do whatever it takes. A lot of MPs like that.

But is it enough? The next vote will decide. Toss a coin. If you get heads, turn to **377**. If you get tails, turn to **349**.

29

'The EU tariff quotas protect orange growing, particularly November through April which is the peak season for Mediterranean countries. But since Britain imports a quarter billion's worth of oranges every year and doesn't grow any, we could afford to drop those quotas.'

'Yes indeed. That might add a little "juice" to our negotiations with places like South Africa and Egypt, eh?'

'That's basically it, just South Africa and Egypt. We get half our oranges from them, and the other half from the EU. Mostly from Spain.'

⇒ 'A great opportunity there. What else?' Turn to **260**

⇒ 'You sound dubious. If we offer to free up orange imports for trade deals, what could go wrong?' Turn to **557**

30

'So it is – slowly. Right after the referendum we had about forty experienced trade negotiators. The EU has nearly six hundred. And these trade wonks don't come cheap. Most of them are paid more than you are, do you know that?'

'It doesn't do to dwell too much on monetary compensation in politics. Service is its own reward.'

She gives a yelp of laughter that sounds like a fox finding an open dustbin. 'Right. Not to mention the book advance, after-dinner speeches and non-exec positions once you finally get shoved overboard.'

'Your school... It's not St Trinian's, by any chance?'

'Point being that Brexit was sold to the public as a money-saver. But when you've hired a few hundred experienced negotiators and all the civil servants needed to support them then you won't have much change out of a quarter billion. Never mind that the whole point of the exercise was to cut red tape, not wrap us up in it like an Egyptian mummy.'

'Don't let your daddy hear you talk that way.'

Turn to **700.**

31

In the early hours the results come in and it's like all your Christmasses. Labour have lost the seat! Soon you'll have a fresh-faced new Tory MP arriving to swell your majority.

'Send him a crate of champagne,' you tell an aide.

'He's a devout Muslim, Prime Minister.'

'Might as well make it a box of fruit and a card, then. Forget the bubbly. No, on second thoughts, have it delivered to Number 10. I feel like celebrating.'

> On your Brexit Memo Pad:
> ❖ +2% Authority – you make sure to claim the lion's share of the credit.

Turn to **350.**

32

'Such as what?' he snaps back. 'Getting into a pointless scrap with the Spanish over Gibraltar? That's not going to help us get a good deal with the EU, is it? Even the Chief Minister of Gibraltar described it as Britain's biggest diplomatic cock-up since Suez.'

When did interviewers get so rude? The rot set in with punk rock, and now the public expect their politicians to be treated given as short shrift as Christians being herded into the Roman arena. And manners cost so little, after all.

The interview goes south from there. Everyone on your staff has seen your humiliation. You sense it the next morning as, waiting for the vote, none of them can meet your eye. You're reminded of a man who, encountering Cromwell in Regent's Park shortly before his death, said that it was like passing the time of day with a ghost.

Turn to **377.**

33

'I don't like it. Politics is not a game.'

There's no answer, of course. It's not that kind of conversation. But you sense an amused and gently chiding smile turned upon you from the unseen reaches of the infinite.

'Also I made a promise. No general election before 2020.'

Still silence. You press your knuckles to your forehead and think.

'I suppose I could make an appeal to unity, say that Parliament needs to come together behind Brexit the way the country is. It's not true, but repeat it often enough and with absolute conviction and people will believe it. Well, You don't need me to tell You about that, Lord.'

⇒ Continue to seek spiritual guidance Turn to **177**

⇒ Enough of this. God's in His Heaven but you have a country to run. Turn to **666**

34

What now? Strewel portrays himself as a merry, bumbling Humpty Dumpty character, and his act goes down well with the party members who still laugh at xenophobic jokes and wonder why jam jars don't have golliwogs on the side any more. Every gaffe just makes him seem more human to them.

But you've seen his true nature – the ruthless calculation, the compulsive dishonesty, the vicious streak, and the sullen bad temper that bubbles up whenever he's thwarted.

⇒ Dig up some dirt to use on him. A scandal will show them what he's really like. Turn to **71**

⇒ Talk to one of his old cronies; they might suggest a way to undermine him. Turn to **470**

⇒ Rise above it. Show everyone a better example of leadership. Turn to **752**

35

You know the answer to that without any advice from on high. The Fixed-Term Parliaments Act of 2011 sets a period of five years between elections.

There are two ways an election can be triggered before the five years are up. The first is if Parliament passes a motion of no confidence in the government. That just requires a simple majority. It would be so humiliating, though. You'd have to tell your own MPs to vote against your government. After saying that politics isn't a game, you'd be gaming the system to the hilt. Just imagining the cartoons in the rebel press makes you cringe.

'The other way is if two-thirds of the Commons agree to an election,' you remind the Lord. 'But Labour wouldn't go along with that, would they?'

The Lord puts the answer in your heart. They just might. The Labour leader, Barry Scraggle, is obviously lukewarm at best about the EU. In his heart of hearts he'd like to abolish it and NATO and go into alliance with Russia.

Also, Labour's leadership is rooted in the old internecine struggles of the 1980s, when their hard-left wing saw the real enemy not as the Conservatives but the centrist faction of their own party. They know that a general election might cut Labour down to the bare stubble, but they could see that as a marvellous opportunity to rebuild it as a party of hairy radicals in Lenin caps.

You know that God wouldn't be callous enough to laugh at that thought, so you laugh for Him.

⇒ 'Is there any threat from Labour, or are they a spent force?' Turn to **626**

⇒ 'The Liberal Democrats are campaigning hard for Remain. They could pick up a lot of seats.' Turn to **784**

⇒ 'We're wiped out in Scotland. No chance of gaining ground there.' Turn to **3**

⇒ 'What do I stand to gain from calling a snap election, though?' Turn to **725**

⇒ 'Amen, Lord. Your humble servant thanks You.' Turn to **666**

36

'You're lucky,' remarks Jean-Jacques Terlamen, the European Commission President, over an informal dinner. 'You have just enough friends on our side of the table to get a trade deal pushed through.'

'Is it friendship? Maybe it's self-interest?'

'The two can be in accord. You know the expression "doing well while doing good"? Only a fool imagines that every gain must be bought with someone else's loss.'

Whatever the reason, the EU is receptive to whatever deal you want to propose. Will you ask for a EEA-like relationship such as Norway has (turn to **82**) or a slightly more distant Swiss-style model (turn to **417**)?

37

Just for a moment it seems to quell her perpetual nervous energy. 'That's good to know,' she says thoughtfully. 'Obviously I'm behind you all the way.'

'Don't breathe a word of this. I need to weed out the nutcases first.'

'Of course not. My lips are sealed. Well, I'll leave you to get on with your meeting, Prime Minister.'

> On your Brexit Memo Pad:
> ❖ Tick the keyword OPAL.

Then turn to **507.**

38

'You aren't allowed to have one, that's the thing. MFNs, I mean – not muffins, "most favoured nations". Got to be a level playing field, you see. So you have to apply the same market access, tariffs and what have you, to all nations equally. Unless you have a free trade agreement, of course, but we're just talking about WTO rules at the moment, unless I missed something.'

'But we could drop our EU tariffs to zero?'

'Have to do the same for everybody in the world in that case. Cheap foreign goods, lovely. But queues of the great unwashed at the gates of closed-down factories – bad news that. Even Scraggle and the Labour mob might manage to claw back a few votes with unemployment going through the roof.'

'Also we'd forfeit our ability to close trade deals,' admits Barkwell. 'If we're tariff-free, we don't have much to offer.'

Strewel nods emphatically. 'And the EU couldn't drop tariffs on our stuff, even if they still wanted to after this fiasco, without having to drop them for every johnny foreigner and his dog.'

'Whose side are you on, Peter?' asks Stollard with a wry smile.

'Ours, of course. Right or wrong. *Pro patria mori.*'

⇒ 'What about quotas and schedules?' Turn to **61**

⇒ 'You mentioned non-tariff barriers.' Turn to **383**

⇒ 'Those are details we can look at another time.' Turn to **454**

39

Rufus falls at the next round of voting. Seeing himself pitted against two of the big beasts of Brexit, Stollard realizes he has little chance and withdraws rather than lose more of his influence by a defeat.

So now you and Peter Strewel go through to a ballot of the membership. Turn to **67**.

40

Peter Strewel arranges a clandestine late-night meeting at a kebab shop in north London. Two teams of protection officers cram into the shop. You see them hungrily eyeing the sweaty plugs of meat rolling behind the steamed-up glass. Strewel himself is wedged behind a tiny table stuffing a greasy-looking pitta sandwich into his mouth. He waves you to the seat opposite.

'Do you want to be Health Minister, Peter?'

He gives an explosive laugh that sprays half-chewed bits of kebab meat onto the formica top. 'Funny. Although, joking aside, what I had in mind was Chancellor of the Exchequer.'

He's quite serious. 'Put you in charge of the country's finances, you mean?'

'Not that difficult, is it. I had a piggy bank when I was a nipper. Handled the pay-offs to disgruntled restaurant owners when I was in the Bollinger Club. Dreamt up a wizard wheeze involving taxi expenses when – well, better forget that one. But I can handle the moolah. The important question is whether you want to be the one who gets to decide who is Chancellor.'

'A deal?'

'Even cardinals do it, you know.' He dabs ketchup off his chin. 'Handshake and a wink, you get my support, and when all this has blown over you remember whose back to scratch. Don't say right now. Sleep on it.'

On returning to Number 10 you sit up late into the night pondering Strewel's offer.

If you accept, turn to **607.** If not, turn to **792.**

41

Lucy Tooth dives in and saves Tode from self-inflicted drowning. 'Most of the people you're talking about, Thomas, are legitimate refugees, not illegal immigrants.'

'That's all very well, Lucy, but the lady there has made a legitimate point. Immigrants claiming benefits are a real drain on the nation's resources.'

⇒ See where this goes. Turn to **229**

⇒ Find a different question. Turn to **405**

⇒ Turn it off and get some sleep. Turn to **125**

42

'Norway?' says Strewel. 'One of our closest allies. Send us a Christmas tree every year. Heroes of Telemark and all that. They'd never veto us.'

Dent isn't convinced. 'The Norwegian industry minister is on record as saying they might not welcome us. The EEA has had twenty years to evolve along its own lines. They're bound to worry about us coming along and wanting to start moving the goalposts on things like agriculture and fisheries, which aren't currently covered as part of their deal with the EU.'

Stollard nods. 'And you know what their prime minister said just before the referendum last year, when a lot of people were proposing "the Norway model"...'

⇒ 'What did she say?' Turn to **114**

⇒ 'Let's not get sidetracked.' Turn to **17**

43

Your deal to allow visas to Turkish workers gave a boost to the economy, but now you're paying the cost in the form of excoriating headlines from the right-wing press. Too many people remember the Leave poster campaign about 80 million Turks flooding into Britain.

> On your Brexit Memo Pad:
>
> ❖ -2% Popularity – voters expected you to turn to the clock back to an all-white Britain that exists in their imagination.

Then turn to **300.**

44

> On your Brexit Memo Pad:
> ❖ Tick the keyword EIGER.

As the first referendum was an open vote, you naturally have to offer the same freedom to your ministers now. To your surprise, Peter Strewel stays out of the campaign. 'I think the public would appreciate a holiday from my voice,' he guffaws in front of the cameras, calling on his usual groundhog-woken-early act. The truth is surely that there's no gain for him in it this time. A seat in Cabinet within grasping distance of Number 10 was his goal all along, and now he has that.

The big guns of Remain are either out of Parliament now or else reluctant to air their views in case another win for Leave scuppers their careers for good. The notable exceptions are Bill Strait, who in his seventies and Father of the House doesn't give a fig for your authority, and Lord Leonine, who is even older and more obdurate.

'The problem with old ministers,' you remark to Wilkins as he brings in your late-night Horlicks, 'is that there's nothing you can promise them. Nothing you can threaten them with.'

'What about your own opinions, Prime Minister? Will you be joining the campaign?'

⇒ 'Good lord, no. I'm sitting this one out.' Turn to **293**

⇒ 'Of course, I shall be leading the fight to Remain.' Turn to **64**

⇒ 'I intend to give my support to the Leave campaign.' Turn to **841**

45

The Spanish prime minister has not forgiven or forgotten your bombastic response to his suggestion of sharing sovereignty over Gibraltar. At the next summit he gives you the cold shoulder, and then makes a point of disputing control of Gibraltar's airport, which lies on reclaimed land between the two countries.

> On your Brexit Memo Pad:
> ❖ -2% Goodwill – it seems you can't count on Spain's support during negotiations with the EU.

Now turn to **300**.

46

Growth is uneven, but on the whole the economy is doing a lot better than the old Project Fear predictions. Those industries that don't need to import components or raw materials, and that aren't reliant on foreign workers, are ticking along. Inflation is not too high for those who fill their supermarket trolleys with ready meals and don't care about exotic foreign foodstuffs. And the draining away of financial services can be sold as telling the fat cats of overseas investment firms to pack their bags and clear out.

Staffing essential services will mean bringing in more immigrants, but you can massage the figures by pointing out that immigration from the EU has dwindled almost to nothing. Eventually the old populist boils will break out again, when the people who voted Leave start to notice and resent the new wave of workers from India, the Caribbean and South America. But that's a headache for another day.

Turn to **210**.

47

'The country now has a rock-solid government with clear and definite vision and the ability to see it through.'

> On your Brexit Memo Pad:
> - +2% Economy – the markets are optimistic that the future is less uncertain now.

If you have ticked the keyword YELLOW on your Brexit Memo Pad, turn to **670**. If not, turn to **163**.

48

Despite the ever more strident thundering of the hard right press, there are signs that people are heeding your warnings. Brexit in some form still seems likely, but maybe you can stave off the worst.

Toss two coins. If both come up heads, turn to **173**. Otherwise, turn to **403**.

49

'And all about reel shadows of indignant desert birds…'

Doggerbank surprises you by getting the reference. 'Slouching our way towards Brexit, is it? I wouldn't say that if I were you, Prime Minister.'

'Then I'll forget that you said it, Sir Harvey.'

You look again at the letter he has brought. It only confirms what he's just told you. Fifteen percent of your MPs have informed him, as chairman of the 1922 Committee, that they no longer have confidence in you as leader.

He grips the arms of his chair as if fearing you have a Blofeld button under your desk.'You know what this means?'

You cast a brief gaze out of the window. A few reporters are shuffling about in the drizzle. In an hour they'll be packed like factory farm chickens, flashes popping, shouting questions at the door. You don't want to sit quietly and quote Yeats. You feel like herding these fifty-odd MPs into a truck at gunpoint and screaming, 'Really? *Now?*'

You drop the letter on the desk. 'It means a leadership contest. That's if anyone decides to stand.'

Doggerbank seems to take it as a hint. He gets up and gives you a stiff little nod of the head. You can imagine the executioner giving Charles I that same final signal of respect.

'I shall inform you of the list of candidates in due course,' he says.

An hour later you know the name of your first challenger: Dennis Dent. That smarmy little turncoat! How often have you dreamt he was a pug puppy you had to drown? If only you could.

'He's broken cover too soon,' is the opinion of your press secretary.

'Terri's right,' says Ron Beardsley. 'Dent isn't the one we have to watch out for.'

Check your Brexit Memo Pad. If you have the keyword NYLON, turn to **406**. If not, turn to **734**.

50

The rank and file have made their choice. You're out, and Gervais Noysom-Reek is the new leader of the Party. Inevitable, really. His views seem locked in some ivy-covered time warp of the mid-1950s. He makes the members imagine they can go back to those endless summers of cake and ginger pop. And rationing. And conscription. And teddy boys with flick knives.

'What will you say to the new incumbent, Wilkins?' you ask as he oversees the removal men carrying your belongings.

'I shall say what I have always said. "Welcome, Prime Minister." But first...'

You wait. 'Yes?'

'Goodbye, Prime Minister.'

THE END

51

There has to be a way to scotch Peter Strewel's gains among the party faithful. Your eye travels along the bookshelf seeking inspiration. Machiavelli, Sun Tzu, Nelson Mandela, Clausewitz, Dale Carnegie... Do any of them have a lesson for you in this fight to the finish?

⇒ Try talking to Strewel's old colleagues. Turn to **470**

⇒ Issue a statement of intent that's even more ultra-Brexit than anything he's been saying. Turn to **738**

⇒ Rise above the petty squabbling. Show people a better kind of leadership. Turn to **752**

52

'Certainly we can lower them. The average import tariff under WTO rules is just over 2%, but it varies by industry. The tariff on cars is 10%. So cars being bought from Germany will be 10% more expensive. This gets even worse when it's a car being assembled in components. An engine comes into the UK, there's a tariff. It goes back to Germany, now with something else fitted – another tariff. Automotive parts can go back and forth like this half a dozen times, and the tariff on those is only 5% but it stacks up. And when the parts come back in a car, the 10% tariff gets whacked on yet again.'

'Oh, come on,' scoffs Barkwell. 'We don't have to stay on default WTO rates for long. We'll be making new regional trade agreements.'

'We can,' agrees the Chancellor. 'So you're proposing a tariff-free trade agreement with the rest of Europe?'

'Yes.'

'We've already got that. It's called the European Union.'

'Just on cars, I mean.'

'No good. Under WTO rules, any free trade agreement must apply to "substantially all trade", not just to one sector.'

'So we lose out a bit in trade with Europe. We'll more than make it up with new trade deals with the rest of the world.'

'We're party to numerous trade deals right now through our membership of the EU,' says the Chancellor. 'And in all cases where there isn't a trade agreement, we already operate under WTO rules. So I'm struggling to see where tearing up those existing trade deals gives us any kind of an advantage.'

⇒ 'But we can threaten to raise tariffs, can't we?'
Turn to **338**

⇒ 'All right, let's drop this for now.' Turn to **454**

53

President Terlamen lays it on the line for you over a private dinner. 'Britain should make a goodwill gesture. Something to win friends on this side of the negotiating table.'

'What do you have in mind?'

He spoons a little mustard onto his steak. Dijon, you notice, not English. 'Everyone is very concerned about the rights of EU nationals currently living in your country. They should not be pawns in this process. So if you were to look into the question of continued residency...'

If you agree to that, turn to **320**.

If not, you have the option to pursue a customs union like Turkey's arrangement (turn to **674**) or else a bespoke free trade agreement (turn to **294**).

54

'Your representative owes you, not his industry only, but his judgment; and he betrays, instead of serving you, if he sacrifices it to your opinion.'

'Ah wahted hoo ho uf – '

The dentist withdraws the instruments of his trade from your mouth and tilts the light away. 'Don't you agree, Prime Minister?'

'I wanted to know if I need a filling in that tooth. Not your thoughts on governance.'

He nods to his assistant. 'Number seven amalgam, please, Hilary. Yes, we'll need to drill and fill. That sweet tooth is your Achilles heel, isn't it? Not my thoughts, by the way. Edmund Burke's.'

'Burke lost his seat for opposing popular opinion.'

He nods. 'Well, that's one lesson you could take away. Open wide.'

'Hang on. Since you've brought it up, you might as well say what you're driving at.'

He peers at you, momentarily distracted. 'We might want to give those front teeth a polish if you're going on television. I was just thinking, the Article 50 deadline coming up, negotiations drawing to an end, country still divided, all that – whether you'd given any thought to a second referendum?'

It can be useful to find out the views of ordinary people. Preferably polite, well-spoken, ordinary people in a hygienic environment. And seeing as you're here anyway, why not?

Turn to **376.**

55

'Exactly,' says Barkwell. 'The British people voted for us to have complete freedom in our international trade relationships.'

Dent nods vigorously, looking more than ever like a henna-stained walnut with a tuft of cotton wool glued on top. 'What's the use of squirming out of the clutches of the EU only to fall into the quicksand of EFTA, where we'd be obliged to adopt a whole tranche of trade deals we never had any say in?'

'And let's not forget future deals,' says Barkwell. 'Would we have to do those through EFTA too?'

'In fact, no,' says Stollard, obviously surprised that as Minister for International Trade he doesn't already know that. 'EFTA member states are free to make independent third-country deals. Whether we'd want to do that rather than team up and spread the workload is another question.'

'They're not independent when it comes to dealing with the EU, in any case,' puts in Dent. 'We'd want to tailor the deal between the EU and EFTA to suit our own requirements, and the bare fact is that Liechtenstein, population forty thousand, would have power of veto over Great Britain, population sixty-five million.'

'Cornwall isn't free to do its own deals in clotted cream,' points out the Chancellor. 'Wales doesn't get to set the tariffs on imported lamb. The achievements of the United Kingdom demonstrate the value of compromise. Everything's a trade off.'

Barkwell sets his jaw. 'Absolute sovereignty!' he declares. 'Nothing less will satisfy the people.'

⇒ 'Would we have much of a say in EFTA?'
Turn to **793**

⇒ 'Sovereignty is important. Would our courts be subservient to the EU?' Turn to **161**

⇒ 'Time out. This is getting us nowhere.' Turn to **17**

56

'I think that's my area,' says Barkwell.

Dent shakes his head. 'Not a bit of it. You can scurry about the world doing all these "jumbo deals" with the likes of Turkey that Peter likes to boast about. My department deals with the EU.'

'It's international trade, so it's mine. Once we're out of the EU that makes it international.'

'Once we're out. But we're doing this deal before we get out, aren't we, Leslie?'

'Unless the talks blow up,' you remind them both. 'In which case we fall into the WTO's safety net and start building up new deals from there.'

'Ideally it won't come to that,' says the Chancellor. 'We'd really like to conclude a free trade agreement with the EU along the lines of Canada's or Singapore's.'

⇒ 'Tell me a bit about those' Turn to **22**

⇒ 'How quickly can we get a deal like that?'
Turn to **276**

⇒ 'What are the pros and cons?' Turn to **303**

⇒ 'Let's review the World Trade Organization rules.'
Turn to **826**

57

'Welcome to the ER,' announces an automated, American-accented voice as the door slides open.

The room is filled with people watching a wall-sized television. The screen shows endlessly looping adverts for a much nicer, shinier hospital where everyone is healthy and smiling. You step up to a desk where a harassed looking intern is playing Minecraft.

'Premium service or standard?' she asks.

'What's the difference?'

She sniggers, but doesn't look up from her phone. 'About two months' income.'

'It's for my teddy.'

You hold him up. Poor Abednego. He should be propped among plump cushions looking at a toy tea set, not hanging around in this medical limbo.

'Do you love him?' She pronounces it to rhyme with nerve.

'Well... Of course.'

Still not looking, she pushes the card reader across the counter. 'Swipe it, and then the docs can take a look. Or you can take a seat.'

There must be two dozen people waiting here, most of them displaying swollen sprains or streaming cuts. 'It's not so bad,' says a man with a cotton wad over one eye. 'They bring you a cup of tea every four hours.'

⇒ Swipe your card — Turn to **202**

⇒ Join the queue — Turn to **218**

⇒ Try a different department — Turn to **76**

58

To your relief and amazement, the Labour leadership supports the motion and most of their MPs go along with that. Thus the vote carries in spite of those quislings in your own ranks. You allow them to feel the iciness of your stare as they return to their seats. A deeper chill will come in which many of them are destined to wither.

Turn to **428.**

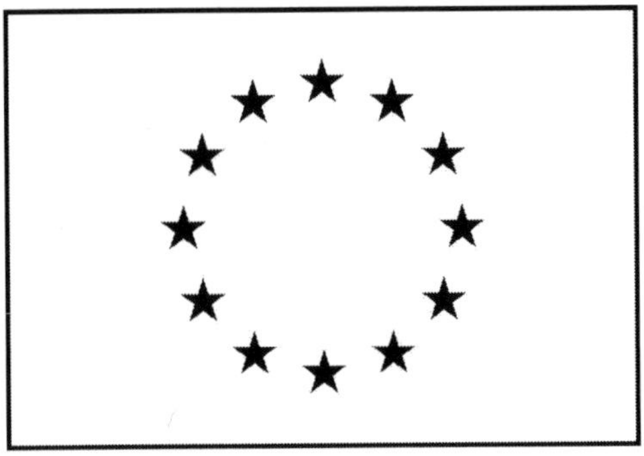

59

'This is going to be hard to sell,' says your chief of staff, Ron Beardsley, when you explain it to him later. Typically he gives nothing else away.

'It's the only sensible way forward. By incorporating the current EU legislation on free movement into UK law we can make sure we stick to the letter of the rules, no more and no less. And over time we can prune away some of the liberties the European Court of Justice has allowed to creep in – things like welfare benefits and rights of non-working spouses.'

'Will the rest of the EU go along with that? Push it too far and they'll start pruning away our single market access too.'

'We're not the only country in Europe to find the *table d'hôte* free movement rules a bit hard to stomach. I think we'll continue to lead the way even outside the EU, and we'll start to see the other states arguing for reform along the same lines.'

'The big question, then, is whether the hardcore Leave vote will stand for it.'

On your Brexit Memo Pad:

- -5% Authority – your whips report open stirrings of revolt.
- +5% Economy – the financial prospects look less risky now.
- +5% Goodwill – the EU feel that you're trying your best to seek a compromise.
- -5% Popularity – the right-wing media are up in arms at your betrayal of the cause.
- Tick the keyword MAPLE.
- Mark Immigration as complete

Now turn to **150.**

60

You throw yourself into a heated debate in which you argue the case for staying in the EU.

The ubiquitous Martin Mugglemore is chairing the debate. 'So, Prime Minister,' he asks, 'do you really think it's possible for us to turn back now?'

'I don't see why not, Martin. The other EU states have repeatedly said they're willing to welcome us back into the fold. And Article

50, which let us remember was only intended to be used in the event of a coup, can be legally rescinded right up until the two-year limit.'

'I don't mean that. I was thinking that the big problem that Britain has had with the EU is that we've always seen it as something we have no control over. Instead of working to change the things we didn't agree with, we just went into a characteristically British passive-aggressive sulk. It's like being shipwrecked. Somebody suggests banding together to build a shelter. But there's one person who gripes about where the shelter is, what it's made of, who does what. And when we don't get everything our own way we swan off in a huff.'

'Are you asking me a question?'

'Is there any point in Britain remaining in the EU if we're so unable to act as team players?'

⇒ 'We can be a team player. But not all members of a team are identical. The EU needs to recognize that Britain has unique skills to bring onto the field. Our military expertise, our financial sector skills, our international diplomatic reach. So this last two years will hopefully have taught both sides something.'

Turn to **48**

⇒ 'If your child makes a noise in class and pulls another child's pigtails, is that any reason to give up on them? I think the country has learned its lesson from the sharp shock of Brexit. We'll be better behaved in future.'

Turn to **212**

61

'Well, quotas – obviously that's how much you can take of something before another tariff rate cuts in. So if it's a thousand containers of inflatable sex dolls – '

'Oh please!' cries Dent, going slightly pinker even than his usual radishy complexion.

'Could be anything. Cucumbers, then. First thousand containers, 1% tariff. Next thousand, 2%, whatever. Thing is, that's stuff that's being sold across the whole EU. When we come out, what bit of it is our quota? Got to be agreed. How many calories do you think that éclair was, by the way?'

'What about schedules?' says the Chancellor, plainly astonished.

'Cripes, even more complicated. It might be different tariffs on goods that the rest of the EU wants more than we do, or the other way round. And regulations like how much of a domestic financial institution can be held by foreign investors. But nobody in Russia wants a Greek bank and they'd all like a British one, so when we break our schedules out of the EU, what ends up where? So you can see how frightful it all is.'

⇒ 'What about most favoured nations?' Turn to **38**

⇒ 'You mentioned non-tariff barriers.' Turn to **383**

⇒ 'Those are details we can look at another time.' Turn to **454**

62

Dennis Dent is knocked out. That leaves you, Colin Fungale and Tiffany Rufus for the win. After one more round of voting by the Parliamentary party, the remaining two candidates will go to a ballot of the rank-and-file membership.

'If you can win against Fungale,' says Ron Beardsley, 'you're a shoo-in against Rufus. The members regard her as an England-hating technocrat Europuppet.'

'I don't want to be up against Fungale, that's for sure. Most of our members are Kippers at heart.'

'Right. So in this next round you need to knock Fungale out. Quite a few of our MPs would as soon give a loaded gun to a toddler as give him control of the party. Just stick to a Brexit-for-grown-ups position.'

'Maybe. Another argument is that neither I nor Fungale will attract many of the votes on the soft-Brexit wing of the party, so actually I have to vie with him for the crown of mad prophet of *Brexit impavidus*.'

'Just for God's sake don't use any Latin,' says Ron, narrowing his eyes warily. 'One thing the members hate more than a moderate is an intellectual.'

What's it to be?

⇒ Maintain a policy of rational Brexit with allowance for dialogue and compromise. Turn to **353**

⇒ Go full throttle – show that your Brexit zeal is even more vehement than Fungale's. Turn to **552**

63

'India, for instance. They want Mode IV access to UK markets for their service suppliers.'

'Meaning?'

'It's the World Trade agreement allowing workers from one country to move to another WTO country in order to provide a service. So we're not talking about Delhi call centres. These are boots on the ground – or sandals, I guess. The point is they'll need to send people over here. And they want us to ease up on visa restrictions for students and business personnel. And your Leave voters aren't going to like it. Not to sugar-coat it, they don't want to see more brown faces on their way to the betting shop, do they?'

'That's pretty offensive, I must say.'

'The whole referendum campaign was offensive. Talking of which, it'll be the same with Turkey. Remember that Leave poster – "the Turkic horde is about to arrive in Britain, eek"? Well they weren't, but they are now.'

Turn to **700**.

64

A few days later, you and the Chancellor are working together into the evening.

'You're taking a risk,' he says, a rare confessional mood coming upon him as you press a whisky into his hand.

'I'm surprised to hear you say that, Alan. Isn't the risk that Britain falls off the cliff of a disastrously negotiated Brexit?'

'We've spent two years talking about the gory details. Now you're turning round and telling everybody it was all a mistake. They're bound to say that we've put too much into negotiating Brexit to back out now.'

'That makes no sense. It's arguing from the basis of sunk costs.'

He stares into his glass, swirling the ice cubes thoughtfully. 'I hate to admit it, but people aren't rational. Worse, as the reality of Brexit comes home to them they start to panic. And that makes them even harder to reason with.'

'You're a ray of sunshine.'

'Looking on the bright side, if you muck this up I'll get a crack at the top job, eh?' That brings a brief, wintry smile to his lips. He knocks back the whisky at a gulp and says goodnight.

On your Brexit Memo Pad:
❖ Tick the keyword GAZELLE.

How will your own stance sway the public? To find out, check your Brexit Memo Pad. If your Popularity score is 51% or higher, turn to **388**. If it's 50% or lower, turn to **766**.

65

Look at your Brexit Memo Pad.

If you have either of the keywords BLEAK or HEMLOCK, turn to **476**. Otherwise turn to **863**.

66

'Services are more important to Britain than goods,' says Strewel, looking for a pen to jot it down on his shirt cuff. 'Mustn't forget that. I'm on *News Talk* tonight and bloody whasisname might try and trip me up.'

⇒ 'Are the European Economic Area's financial service agreements as good as full EU membership?' Turn to **72**

⇒ 'We can depend on the EU to accommodate us when it comes to financial services, surely?' Turn to **327**

⇒ 'Jog my memory; what are financial passports?' Turn to **318**

⇒ 'Presumably financial services only really affect London, not the rest of the country.' Turn to **807**

⇒ 'Let's talk about other service industries.' Turn to **418**

⇒ 'We'll leave this discussion for another day.' Turn to **17**

67

This promises to be a battle-royal. Despite a stompingly insensitive public persona beside which Prince Philip comes across as the poster boy for liberal enlightenment, Peter Strewel is the darling of the grassroots members.

If your Goodwill score is 33% or less, turn to **78**.
If your Goodwill score is 66% or more, turn to **783**.
If your Goodwill score is in the range 34% to 65%, turn to **415**.

68

'It's only a half-hour appointment, I'm afraid.'

'Make a stab at it. Not literally,' you add, noticing the gleaming steel prong in his hand.

'First of all, referendums at best simply vote on an objective. They don't give a weighting of desired outcomes, or any basis for compromise.'

'Good government isn't about compromise. It's about doing what is right.'

For that he drops your chair a few inches. 'Sometimes compromise is what's right, isn't it. Suppose that the referendum had actually spelled out the kind of Brexit people wanted. "Stay in the EU, or move to a Norway model?" And the Norway model won out. But then on day one you find out there's a cost to the Norway model. Perhaps the EU27 want Britain to pay twice Norway's per capita contribution. Or perhaps that model is simply too much of a fuss for all concerned and it's not on offer.'

'Then we'd walk away. No deal is better than – '

'Would you walk away today with a sucking hole in your tooth right now if I said I only had gold amalgam to stick in the filling? Sometimes no deal is the very worst that can happen. More to the point, in this example the public didn't give you a mandate to walk away. They gave you a mandate to move us to a Norway trading model. No wriggle room.'

'That's ridiculous.'

'Of course it is. The referendum only gives you a goal to aim at, not – ' He pauses. 'But maybe you don't have time for this?'

⇒ 'Go on.' Turn to **356**

⇒ 'Never mind that, why do you say a second referendum is acceptable if you don't think they produce good government?' Turn to **571**

⇒ 'You're right, I don't. Just give me a temporary filling and I'll book an appointment with another dentist.' Turn to **425**

69

Look at your Brexit Memo Pad.

If General Election is marked as complete, turn to **743.**

If General Election has not been completed, turn to **862.**

70

Your opponents are quick to point out that you've vacillated between Leave and Remain. 'The Prime Minister has been spinning faster than the weathervane on the village steeple,' says Noysom-Reek, who bizarrely chooses to be interviewed in red trousers in front of a gastropub. He turns to the wrong camera. 'Whereas I know exactly where I'm headed.'

'Yes – the dustbin of history, you ridiculous popinjay!' you screech at the screen.

For his TV spot, Stollard picks a desk in front of a shelf of pristine leather book spines. 'I have always been clear about my position,' he says. 'I want what's best for the country, and I don't mind speaking some hard truths to get there. I've never been one for saying what people want to hear.'

'If that was an interview for somebody to do the annual accounts, I'd hire him,' you remark to Wilkins.

'I wasn't sure whether you wanted tea or coffee, Prime Minister, so I've brought a pot of each.'

Look at your Brexit Memo Pad. Have you ticked the keyword UNCTION? If so, turn to **251**.

Otherwise turn to **460**.

71

The chief whip dumps an armful of folders on your desk. Funny how these fellows still prefer paper documents, but given all the hacking that goes on during elections nowadays it may be just as well.

'Are all of these about Peter Strewel?'

'Oh no.' He raises an eyebrow. 'I'd have needed a trolley for his amorous peccadilloes, and all they'd achieve is to paint him as more of a jack the lad. So I just brought the escapades that might actually, you know, tarnish his reputation.'

You leaf through the files. 'I didn't know you could do that with a turkey... Remind me never to have Christmas dinner with him. Burning £50 notes in front of tramps. Well, who hasn't? Ah, now what's this?'

He glances at the grainy photo that has Strewel leering into the camera while a naked man streaks past behind him.

'That was after a Bollinger Club dinner. They stripped a

homeless man and chucked him in Mercury Fountain.'

'Doesn't sound too bad.'

'It was midwinter. Nine below zero. The bloke got pneumonia and nearly died.' He waits. 'What do you think, Prime Minister? Shall I throw it to a tame paper and let them run with it?'

⇒ 'Yes. It's time people got to see what a callous bastard Strewel really is.' Turn to **89**

⇒ 'No, smearing is no good. The man's Teflon. I need a better plan.' Turn to **51**

72

Stollard looks around the table, but the others all busy themselves in notes or on their phones. 'That one's mine as well, is it? All right, there are three drawbacks to the EEA version of the passport. First is regulation. This is a big issue for all our service industries, in fact. To trade services you must be able to show that they meet the market requirements and standards. Within the EU that's automatic. Once outside the EU our institutions must submit to the relevant supervisory bodies.'

'Just paperwork, isn't it?' says Barkwell.

'It would be, except that there's no one to send the paperwork to. The EU supervisory agencies governing banking and insurance are not part of the existing EEA agreement.'

'So we'd have to hit the ground running, get those agencies incorporated into the new improved EEA. It's in everyone's interest to get that sorted out quickly.'

A drawn-out silence suggests that not even Barkwell himself believes it will be as easy as all that.

⇒ 'You mentioned two other problems, Alan?' Turn to **466**

⇒ 'OK, let's not get bogged down in the details.' Turn to **66**

73

The next round pits you against Dennis Dent the Brexit Secretary, Tiffany Rufus the Home Secretary, and Gervais Noysom-Reek, twittish hope of the back benches.

To your relief, Noysom-Reek is eliminated. He was the favourite among the grass roots of the party, and would have been a hard opponent to go up against once the voting was opened up to the membership.

'The double barrel who fired a blank, that's how I shall always remember him,' you tell Ron Beardsley. 'I think a lot of the members like him because they imagine he's an aristocrat. They're such forelock-tuggers. Whereas you and I, Ron, know that he's from a long line of posh farmers.'

'Let's not focus on yesterday's fight,' warns Ron. 'We've got a new problem. The Chancellor has entered the contest.'

'What? Can he? I mean…'

Ron shrugs. 'He's got the support of a sizeable fraction of the Parliamentary party. Maybe 40% of the MPs are Remainers at heart, and he's the only one who gets up and uses terms like damage limitation when referring to Brexit.'

Turn to **339**.

74

The Business minister Chloe Stoat mentions in an interview that you've always had a sensible view on Brexit. Luckily she doesn't say any more than that, seeing as you actually told her Brexit was a catastrophic mistake.

'Well, that's a relief,' you confide to your press secretary. 'It's not often a skeleton jumps out of the closet, does a tap dance with top hat and cane, and then offers you a golden ticket to the chocolate factory.'

'Don't worry, Prime Minister,' she says, furrowing her brow. 'It'll be over soon.'

Chloe Stoat's revelations carry weight with the moderate wing of the Party, who now see you as the last hope for a rational outcome. Turn to **489**.

75

'A hard Brexit is what this country needs,' says Tode. 'Will there be tough times ahead? Yes. Will it be hard to bear? Oh yes. Austerity will have to shift up a gear. Some of Britain's cherished institutions may not survive. But it will be worthwhile because out of these hardships we will forge a new and stronger Britain, in much the way that Mao took the creaking feudal edifice of China and turned it into a white-hot powerhouse nation that bestrides the world like a colossus.'

He draws himself up to his full height of five foot ten. You continue to studiously ignore the fleck of spittle that has been nestling in the corner of his lip throughout the tirade.

Then it occurs to you that he's waiting for your reply.

⇒ 'Perhaps I wouldn't go quite that far...' Turn to **308**

⇒ 'Come now, Thomas. High-flown speeches might win votes, but you and I need to consider the practicalities.' Turn to **423**

⇒ 'You took the words right out of my mouth.' Turn to **633**

76

You return to the hospital foyer to make another choice:

⇒ Geriatric unit Turn to **413**

⇒ Miracle cure facility Turn to **133**

⇒ The Innovative Medicines Initiative Turn to **273**

⇒ Casualty Turn to **57**

⇒ Wake up before it's too late! Turn to **368**

77

You step out of the contest and give your support to Peter Strewel, enabling him to sweep to victory. It's like electing Scaramouche. Still, that's not your problem. You can put your feet up at the Treasury.

Or so you thought. Strewel phones with a lot of flowery self-congratulation before dropping his bombshell. 'There's a bit of a hitch, I'm afraid. Better book that removal lorry for the shires after all.'

'What? You promised.'

'I thought long and hard about it over a plate of linguine. Sorry, and all that, but it's not exactly the first promise to escape back into the wild, eh? Remember that red bus? Well, just picture it with "You will be Chancellor" painted on the side.'

THE END

78

'Brexit should have been a smooth road,' says Peter Strewel in an interview, 'but the EU didn't want it that way. They're like the scorpion that stings the dog that's taking them both across the river. Frankly, every time I sit down opposite those chaps I'm waiting for my chair to flip back SPECTRE-style and drop me in a vat of acid.'

'Good idea there for the next time we redecorate the Cabinet Room,' you remark to Ron Beadsley.

'In the fable it's a frog, not a dog,' he points out, always needled by an inaccuracy.

'Strewel knows what he's saying. It's a better image for the British people, isn't it. The trusty bulldog.'

When asked by reporters for a statement on Strewel's remarks, how will you respond?

⇒ 'It's not as black and white as Mr Strewel makes out. Negotiation isn't a zero-sum game. We and the EU can find a deal we're both happy with.' Turn to **243**

⇒ 'I don't need Mr Strewel to tell me the EU are the bad guys. I'm the one who has to try and hammer out a deal with them on a daily basis.' Turn to **496**

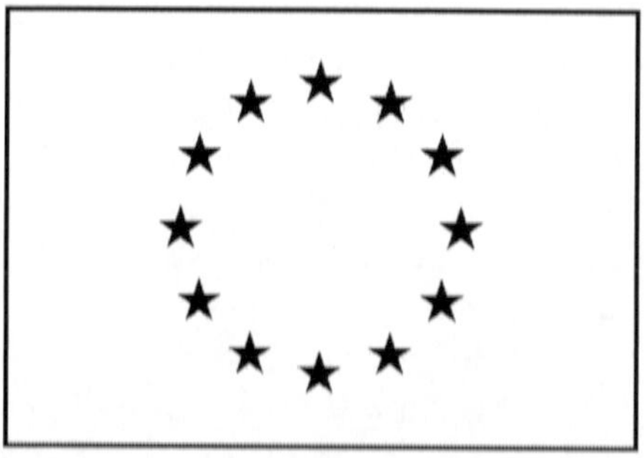

79

Even if the status quo isn't ideal, it's not always a good idea to throw everything away and start again. You can't be sure you won't end up with something worse.

> On your Brexit Memo Pad:
> ❖ Mark Second EU Referendum as complete

Now turn to **450.**

80

'What are my chances of beating Colin Fungale?' you ask your closest advisors.

Ron Beardsley turns his pipe in his hands as if expecting to find the answer written on the side of it. He doesn't say you have no chance. He doesn't have to.

'To most of the members he's a cheeky chappie,' says Terri Trough. 'They imagine him leading them back to a magical time when Morecambe and Wise are on the telly and the butcher measures out cuts of meat in pounds and ounces.'

'Poetic. You ought to write a novel, Terri.'

'I might have to.'

If you have both the keywords HEMLOCK *and* BLEAK, turn to **713**.

If you have only one of those keywords, or neither, turn to **366**.

81 ☐

If the box above is empty, put a tick in it and turn to **756**.

If the box was already ticked, turn to **666**.

82

'So it's a case of the only way is Norway,' says the Chancellor when you discuss the outline of the deal in Cabinet.

'It's a damnable compromise,' fumes Barkwell. 'We have to track standards laid down by European courts, use informal channels to try and influence regulations, and – worst of all – they'll still be sucking money out of us year on year.'

'Parasites,' chimes in a little voice from the far end of the room, reminding you that Thomas Tode is here.

'But compromise is the very soul of politics,' you point out.

At that Peter Strewel produces a meaty laugh. 'Yesterday's politics, that! We're on the other side of history now. People have lost patience with negotiation and compromise. They're demanding easy answers.'

'Politics is complex,' says the Chancellor. 'There are no easy answers.'

'Really?' chortles Strewel. 'Religion has been riding the high hog on exactly that promise for four thousand years.'

You look at the febrile light in the eyes of Barkwell and Dent and the other hardline Brexiters and you know he is right. This isn't politics any more; it's blind faith.

On your Brexit Memo Pad:

- -5% Authority – many of the hardcore Brexiters in the party are furious that you're keeping such close links with the EU.
- -3% Economy – even with EEA-level access to the single market, there will be some degree of disruption to trade in services on which the UK depends.
- +5% Goodwill – the EU27 may be hoping that in time Britain will return to the fold.
- -10% Popularity – after all the *sturm und drang* of negotiation, the voters resent such an undramatic conclusion.
- Tick the keyword CLARION
- Mark EU Trade Talks as complete.

Then turn to **666.**

83

'You'd have thought people would be sick of Strewel's brand of custard by now,' says Ron Beardsley, chewing at his unlit pipe as he stares ferociously at the television in the corner of the room. 'The naughty-boy grin, the blokeish manner, the mussed-up coiffure.'

'He's not the first son of privilege to sell himself as a man of the people, Ron.'

'Of course. Nero, for example. Is Strewel just fiddling because he likes the music, or does he want to see things burn?'

Strewel's influence actually seems to be nudging the voters towards a moderate Brexit, but he's the master of fudging and in any case nothing is certain until the ballot papers are counted.

Toss two coins. If both come up heads, turn to **127**. If both come up tails, turn to **403**. Otherwise, turn to **173.**

'So it's a case of the only way is Norway,' says the Chancellor when you discuss the outline of the deal in Cabinet.

'It's a damnable compromise,' fumes Barkwell. 'Our courts will be obliged to track standards laid down by European courts, we'll have hardly any influence over regulations, and – worst of all – the fangs of the EU will still be sucking money out of us year on year.'

'Parasites,' chimes in a little voice from the far end of the room, reminding you that Thomas Tode is here.

'But compromise is the very soul of politics,' you point out.

At that Peter Strewel produces a meaty laugh. 'Yesterday's politics, that! We're on the other side of history now. People have lost patience with negotiation and compromise. They're demanding simple answers.'

'Politics is complex,' says the Chancellor. 'There are no easy answers.'

'Really?' chortles Strewel. 'Religion has been riding the high hog on exactly that promise for four thousand years.'

You look at the febrile light in the eyes of Barkwell and Dent and the other hardline Brexiters and you know he is right. This isn't politics any more; it's blind faith.

On your Brexit Memo Pad:

- -5% Authority – many of the hardcore Brexiters in the party are furious that you're keeping such close links with the EU.
- -3% Economy – even with EEA-level access to the single market, there will be some degree of disruption to trade in services on which the UK depends.
- +5% Goodwill – the EU27 may be hoping that in time Britain will return to the fold.
- -10% Popularity – after all the *sturm und drang* of negotiation, the voters resent such an undramatic conclusion.
- Tick the keyword CLARION
- Mark EU Trade Talks as complete.

Then turn to **666**.

85

Nobody can accuse you of being a friend of the EU. Over the last two years you've gained the kind of reputation in dealing with them that a Confederate bushwhacker would have had with United States homesteaders. And whenever one of your ministers has failed to adhere to pure Brexit doctrine you've slapped them down hard.

Against anybody else that would be enough, but Fungale is the mad clown of English nationalism. One of his former UKIP allies gives a speech in which he rants about 'scurrying hordes of migrants' and ends with the words, 'The EU is laying out the red carpet for these so-called refugees. "Welcome to Eurabia" – but what kind of future is that for our wives and kiddies, eh?'

'Ugh.' You turn off the TV. 'Goering himself would have puked. That's exactly the sort of scumbag the Nazis got rid of in the Night of Long Knives.'

But it isn't long before Fungale is giving an interview in which he denounces the speech. Or does he? 'We don't need inflammatory language,' he says, as sweetly reasonable as a stiletto in the ribs. 'Nobody is in favour of stirring up hate. But come on, we can all see what's going on around us. There are a lot of people coming here who do not share our British values.'

Now there's pressure on you to make a statement.

⇒ 'No comment.' Turn to **827**

⇒ 'I'm as worried as the next person about all these immigrants. We're going to put a stop to it.'
Turn to **594**

⇒ 'We're leaving the EU, we're securing our borders, and we will tackle terrorism with renewed vigour. I'm just saddened that many are using the situation to promote views that are divisive, unhelpful and racist.'
Turn to **28**

86

'There was a big payout for the rollout of super-fast broadband. About £132 million spent on that. Then there's improvements to the railway lines.'

'I thought this track felt smoother than the last time I came to Cornwall. Go on, what else?'

She shows you an image on her phone.

'The new *Star Trek* movie? I honestly haven't had time.'

'I know it looks like a spaceship, but it's actually it's the reception centre of the Penryn campus near Falmouth. Believe it or not, there was also going to be a *bona fide* spaceport at Newquay as part of EU investment in the UK aerospace industry. And then there was Project Eden, of course. That's quite sci-fi. Again, EU funding.'

⇒ 'It all sounds far too positive. Give me some horror stories. Mad bureaucratic waste, that sort of thing.' Turn to **236**

⇒ 'Never mind, we're nearly there.' Turn to **203**

87

While trying not to appear too fulsome, they are obviously encouraged and even pleasantly surprised by your proposals.

> Record on your Brexit Memo Pad:
> - ❖ +3% Economy – sterling shows a modest improvement as news of the good temper of the talks gets out.
> - ❖ +10% Goodwill – the other EU states are relieved that the talks have got off to a hopeful start.
> - ❖ Mark Negotiation Strategy as complete.

Turn to **150.**

88

Almost every EU state has a list of amendments they want to the draft trade agreement. And all have power of veto if they don't get what they want.

'It's whack-a-mole,' says the Chancellor. 'Half of these amendments contradict the others. We concede to one, it opens a fresh argument elsewhere among the EU27.'

'The devil is in the detail. How long will it take?'

He shrugs. 'There's a good chance Turkey will have been made an EU member by the time we've unpicked this tangle.'

In the meantime you can limp on with an interim agreement signed off by the EU Parliament, but the storm clouds of uncertainty will hang over Britain's businesses for years to come.

Turn to **865.**

89

No matter what stories are leaked in the press, they don't so much as dent Strewel's reputation. It defies all logic. He's posh, entitled, arrogant, buffoonish, and can barely open his mouth without insulting great swathes of the population.

'How can he be so popular?'

Ron Beardsley shrugs. 'Alf Garnett was the most popular character on *Till Death*. Dive far enough into an appalling comic shtick and you come out the other side, star of the show.'

It's too late to try anything else. The members have cast their votes. Nervously you wait for the results.

If your Popularity score is 70% or more, turn to **519**.

If your Popularity is 33% or less, turn to **782**.

If your Popularity is in the range 34% to 52%, turn to **727**.

If your Popularity is in the range 53% to 69%, turn to **528**.

90

Perhaps easier said than done. Fungale follows up by announcing his intention to stand as a Parliamentary candidate if the Conservatives will have him. He's picked a clapped-out East Anglian seaside town where the current incumbent is a forlorn hope of the Remain wing of the party.

The local constituency are fawning over Fungale already. They think they have a superstar offering to represent them, so it's not going to be easy to block his membership.

What kind of sway do you have in the party these days? Check your Brexit Memo Pad. If your Authority is 86% or more, turn to **789**. Otherwise turn to **758**.

91

You reap the reward of backing the winning side with a surge in both your public approval rating and your control within the party.

'What now?' call the reporters waiting for you in Downing Street.

You turn to face the barrage of popping flashlights. You have never felt more certainly the wind of destiny in your sails.

'Now,' you tell them, 'I get on with the job.'

> On your Brexit Memo Pad:
> - +5% Authority
> - +10% Popularity
> - Mark Second EU Referendum as complete.

Then turn to **450**.

92

A strong lead for Leave leads to the obvious question for the second heat: do the British people want to quit the single market in a hard Brexit, or are they in favour of something more like the so-called Norway model?

'Given that the old referendum came out 48% for Remain and 52% for Leave, I think we could have spared ourselves all this bother,' says the Chancellor. 'It's pretty obvious that the overall public mood will be for a soft Brexit.'

'It's politics, Alan. Nothing's obvious till long after it's happened.'

Toss two coins. If both come up heads, turn to **157.** Otherwise, turn to **637.**

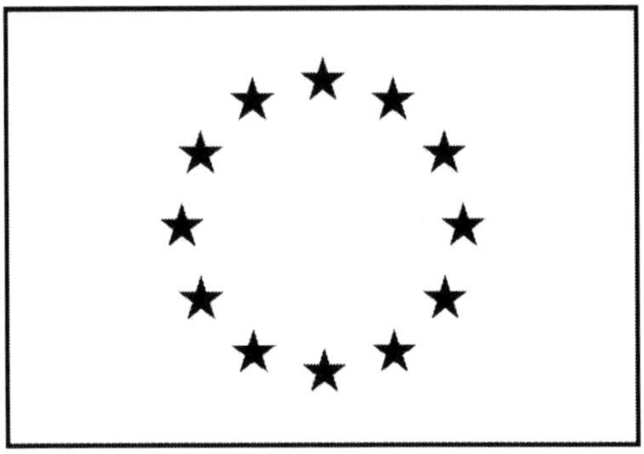

93

It would be impossible to outdo Fungale in Brexit zeal. The man has devoted his entire life to caustic mockery of any attempt to forge a united future for Europe. He's the very epitome of end-of-the-pier nationalism, beer glass in hand, contempt for liberal values dripping from his rubbery jaws.

He'll go down a storm if this ever gets to the party members, most of whom have spent the last two decades wondering why Conservative policies weren't more like UKIP.

Your one advantage is that Fungale hasn't had much time to build up support in the Parliamentary party. You must try to portray him as the smirking mask over the hate-contorted face of far-right populism.

If your Authority score is 61% or more, turn to **708**.

If not, turn to **283**.

94

'It's all about who the public trusts to deliver the Brexit they voted for,' you tell a radio interviewer. 'If you sent Peter Strewel out to buy a paper, he'd come back a week later with a sheepish grin, a three-legged greyhound and lipstick on his collar. The voters know there's nothing to choose between us when it comes to our faith in Brexit, I'm just saying that at a time like this you need the strong and stable leader you can depend on.'

Reminding the MPs of your authority is always risky. They might imagine they'd get an easier ride under Strewel. Most importantly, can you convince them you are the person to oversee Brexit?

If you have the keyword FOG or LEAF, turn to **534**.

If you have neither of those keywords, turn to **565**.

95

'IMI was a partnership of public and private medical research,' says the scientist. 'Private companies on their own tend to avoid the long-term research programs needed for really advanced new medicine. Shareholders haven't got the patience, you see.'

'So what do I do about my teddy bear?'

'Is he eligible for EU citizenship? A lot of sick teddy bears have moved to the continent. If he has an Irish grandparent, for example...'

'What are you saying? He's an English teddy through and through.'

'Better fly over to the States, then. You'll need to take out a second mortgage, though.'

'No,' groans Abednego. 'Let me die in my own bed.'

It's the first time you've ever heard him speak.

Turn to **368**.

96

Look at your Brexit Memo Pad. If you have the keyword UNCTION, turn to **645**. If not, turn to **778**.

97

'I don't see that the EU can afford to ice us out,' says McKay. 'But there are going to be some bumps in the road.'

'Such as?'

He unfolds his massive hand and starts counting off points on his Havana-sized fingers. 'Weapons, for starters. Planes and missiles and that are getting more expensive to design and make, and that takes a continent-wide budget and all the boffin skills to go with.'

'We'll just have to ramp up the armaments industry here in Britain.'

'Still got the declining R&D budget to worry about, though. Got to hand it to the EU, science and tech is one thing it does well.'

'Two things,' you snap back. 'What else?'

'Well, we mostly get our weaponry from the US, and the drop in sterling is going to make that hurt. Maybe Windrip will mess up the American economy, though, in which case we might get a wholesale deal.'

'Anything else?'

'Trident's an issue if Scotland splits off, eh? And there's the refugee jungle at Calais. Will the French be happy to police our border once we're out?'

'The Le Touquet agreement is between us and France. It's not an EU matter.'

He keeps that finger extended. 'I suppose we'll soon find out, Prime Minister.'

⇒ 'How are joint EU forces currently organized?'
Turn to **217**

⇒ 'Tell me about the European Defence Agency.'
Turn to **296**

⇒ 'What do you see as the implications of Brexit for policing and counter-terrorism?' Turn to **314**

⇒ 'That'll be all. Thank you, McKay.' Turn to **666**

98

'Services are definitely the most important issue for us. That's 80% of our economy. Now, the future favours us here – perhaps, a little bit anyway. The usual drop-off of trade with distance might not be such an issue in an era of tele-working and international consultancy. But people like to see a face, and not just on a crackly Skype call either. You still hear people in the City saying, "Don't do business until you've been to their office."'

'Europe will still be just over there. So you're saying we need a deal that prioritises services. There aren't off the shelf models for that?'

'Raw European Free Trade Area rules don't make any provision for access to EU service markets. It wasn't designed for that purpose.'

'But Norway has free trade in services with the EU.'

'Because it's in the European Economic Area, not because it's in EFTA.'

'And Switzerland – '

'Has limited access for services, because it's negotiated that deal specially, and with no provision for passporting in financial services. That's why a lot of Swiss banks trade through London. And financial services are 12% of our GDP, by the way, so unless you just want to stuff it to London and Edinburgh you really need to focus on those.'

'We may need a solution outside of the EEA. I'm not sure I can sell freedom of movement even at the Swiss level.'

'Potentially we might be able to do a free trade deal for services that works out well for Britain and the EU yet satisfies the EU Commission that we're not getting an overall better package than membership itself. That would be good, but hard to pull off under WTO regulations because free trade agreements must remove "substantially all" trade restrictions between the parties. In practice that means 90% of restrictions at least. A sectoral deal that just covered services could be challenged by any WTO member.'

⇒ 'Other than the general free-for-all of the WTO, what are the other risks of going it alone?' Turn to **588**

⇒ 'Let's pick this up later.' Turn to **666**

99

Your attacks on Tiffany Rufus will certainly damage her chances in the membership vote that decides the eventual winner. But at the moment she is uncontested on the moderate wing of the Party, while you are one of two advocates for strong Brexit – and only one of you can win through to the final round.

If you have the keyword NYLON, turn to **193**.

If not, turn to **726**.

100

To be briefed on the issues you're facing, turn to **125**.

Briefings are a distraction. It's time to do something! Turn to **150**.

101

Look at your Brexit Memo Pad.

If you have ticked the keyword TIGHTROPE, turn to **178**.

If you have ticked the keyword KOALA, turn to **16**.

If you have ticked the keyword WELTER, turn to **764**.

If you have none of those keywords, turn to **4**.

102

You know it's hollow, this fighting talk, and Bill Appleby knows it too. His lip curls in scorn. 'You gonna bark all day, little doggie?'

Wait. No. He wouldn't say that. He didn't. You can't even remember what he said. You panicked. The rest of the interview passed in a blur and now you lie tossing in your bed, half awake. In twelve hours the next round of voting will take place, but in the sweat-soaked chill of the night you already know the result.

Turn to **377**.

103

Who better than Thomas Tode, who stood shoulder to shoulder with Strewel in front of every poster-sized falsehood put out by the Leave campaign, from the claim that Turkey was about to join the EU – and by implication send hordes of Turks flooding through British ports – to the exaggerated figure for Britain's EU membership painted along the side of their battle bus.

After the referendum, Tode surprised everybody – most especially Strewel himself – by knifing his erstwhile colleague in the back. At the time he said it was because he suddenly realized that Strewel was incapable of unifying the party. Of course, everybody else already knew that, and probably only Tode still thinks that you have to unite the Tory party in order to lead it.

'Things a bit strained between you and Peter, eh?' you ask Tode, having cornered him coming out of a select committee meeting. 'Some bad blood there.'

'That was my fault for being unclear,' he says gnomishly.

'He hasn't changed in the last few years, has he? Still opens his mouth only to stick his foot in it. Divisive. Lazy. Badly organized.'

'You want my help to see off his leadership challenge.'

There's the steel-trap mind you were looking for. What will you say to convince him?

⇒ 'You ought to have a better Cabinet position, Thomas. Something closer to the head of the table.'
Turn to **402**

⇒ 'My real worry is that Peter just isn't as committed to Brexit as you and I are.' Turn to **861**

104

The court's decision is an eye-watering €60 billion. It's not only a blow to the Treasury but to you personally, as the press are blaming you for handling the matter incompetently.

> On your Brexit Memo Pad:
> - ❖ -5% Authority – there's a sense in the party that you're making this up as you go along.
> - ❖ -10% Economy – this is going to leave a big dent in Britain's finances.
> - ❖ Mark the Exit Fee as complete.

Then turn to **400**.

105

The leadership contest now pits you against three heavyweights of the party: Tiffany Rufus, the Home Secretary; Alan Stollard, the Chancellor of the Exchequer; and Peter Strewel, the clownish but formidably popular Foreign Secretary.

'Which of them should I concentrate my fire on? Which of them is the most dangerous?'

'Prime Minister,' says your chief of staff. 'Those might be two different questions.'

As you approach the next round of voting, which of your opponents will you single out to attack?

⇒ Tiffany Rufus Turn to **751**

⇒ Alan Stollard Turn to **657**

⇒ Peter Strewel Turn to **744**

106

True, a second referendum could backfire on you. However carefully it was phrased, it would leave a yawning chasm of ambiguity to be filled by whichever party mustered the most cynical, opportunistic and hollow arguments.

⇒ Better not, then. Turn to **79**

⇒ You're confident you have the qualities needed. Go for it! Turn to **845**

107

It comes out that in an unguarded moment you let slip to Chloe Stoat, the Business minister, that you were opposed to Brexit.

'But why, Prime Minister?' says your press secretary, almost in tears.

'I also told her to keep it buttoned as I needed to weed out the nutcases first. So what does she do? Wait till the biggest fruitbat in the Party is standing for the leadership, and then blurt it all out.'

'Speaking of which…' Ron Beardsley points at the television. You turn up the sound.

'I would characterize this as a betrayal equivalent to the Albigensian heresy ,' Noysom-Reek is telling a reporter. 'Does the Prime Minister spit on the cross? The people's will is being treated with contempt.'

'Meanwhile,' says Terri Trough, scanning a website on her phone, 'Ms Rufus is saying you're a political weathervane.'

You call an impromptu press conference to put your side of the story. What do you tell them?

⇒ 'I only said what I did to Mrs Stoat to find out her true colours. Well, she's revealed them now.'
Turn to **287**

⇒ 'My job all along has been to act in the public interest. When I spoke to Mrs Stoat nearly two years ago, Brexit wasn't looking like a sensible option, but now we're on course for a good outcome.' Turn to **461**

108

Revenues are falling, growth rates stalling, and unemployment is creeping up. Some sectors are already in recession. The ship of state is heading for the reefs of Brexit, and with you at the helm it is ill prepared.

'BROKEN BREXIT,' some of the newspapers are calling it. What did they expect? They demanded a manure delivery and now they're griping about the stink.

'Is there an upside?' you ask the Chancellor. 'I can't help thinking that a large part of the referendum result was an anti-austerity vote, and what's coming now is going to make that look like a holiday in Willy Wonka's chocolate factory.'

He spreads his hands. 'If there's a bright side, it's that an extended recession will probably reduce inequality in Britain. Everyone will be impoverished, naturally, but the richest will flee abroad – or stow their money there, anyway – and the middle classes will have to cut back.'

Perhaps he's right. You can cling on through the dark days ahead by appealing to the disaffected white working class voters whose rallying cry was a rejection of business, wealth and privilege. The history books may not be so forgiving, but by then you'll be past caring.

Turn to **210**.

109

You feel that your arguments have helped swing the result, but nothing is certain till the votes are counted. You settle down in front of the television with a glass of milk and a plate of sandwiches and wait to see which way it will go.

Toss two coins. If both come up heads, turn to **403**. Otherwise, turn to **313.**

110

You call in the Health Secretary, Jay Arthur. 'As this is an unpopular policy,' you tell him, 'I'm afraid you'll have to head it up.'

'Er…' You can almost see his mental gears churning as he weighs up his career. 'Of course, Prime Minister. What I thought we could do is dump a load more responsibility onto local surgeries. GPs won't be able to cope, but then we can say that it's their fault for running an inefficient service.'

'Good.' You'd better watch him. He's displaying all too devious a way of thinking for a stooge.

> Record on your Brexit Memo Pad:
> - -3% Popularity – you can't fool all of the voters, and the smarter ones see through the attempt to blame GPs.

If you have ticked the keyword DODO, turn to **431**. Otherwise, mark the NHS as complete on your Brexit Memo Pad and then turn to **450**.

111

Check your Brexit Memo Pad.

If you have the keyword HEMLOCK, turn to **851**.

If not but you have the keyword ZEBRA, turn to **399**.

Otherwise turn to **761**.

112

Check the keywords list on your Brexit Memo Pad.

If you have the keyword APRICITY, turn to **485.**

If not but you have the keyword BLEAK, turn to **126.**

Otherwise turn to **722.**

113

'That's a good point, your majesty – I mean, Prime Minister. See, the EU budget can't be used for military purposes. Some rule made up by old geezers with tweed jackets and pipes back in the seventies, no doubt. But if there's one thing the EU know how to do it's make a fudge. So they set up this funding mechanism called Athena that pays for joint operations.'

'And countries pay into Athena an annual sum based on Gross National Income. That's separate from their official EU contributions. I know. I have to sign the cheques, remember.'

'Only it doesn't cover more than 15% of real military costs, so the rest of the bill has to be met by whichever state is actually deploying troops. Oh, and "in kind".' He sees you don't get it. 'Providing expertise, training. That's where Britain gets to do more than pull her weight, as you'd expect. We stop their amateur hour squaddies from falling over their own unlaced boots.'

'How much is all this costing?'

'More than it's worth, I bet. There's been a 12% decline in spending on joint defence by all the EU states over the last ten years. That's 22 billion euros in hard cash.'

'Do you think the EU should have its own army?' Turn to **474**

'Let me ask you something else.' Turn to **432**

114

'That if Britain adopted their model we wouldn't like it. Though probably what she meant was that she didn't like it.'

'Why does she put up with it, then?' says Barkwell.

Stollard looks at him as if he's landed from outer space. 'Referendums. She knows Norway would be better off in the EU, but the Norwegian people are more at home in a shack on the edge of a glacier.'

Barkwell drums his fingers on the table. 'The simple fact is, Norway has to pay a sizeable proportion of EU membership fee, and it has to accept the four freedoms, and its courts have to abide by ECJ rulings – and after all that it gets no say in how the bloody EU is run.'

⇒ 'We'd be worse off than we are now.' Turn to **709**

⇒ 'Even so, let's not rule it out just yet.' Turn to **17**

115

'The merits of the proposal would be seen over several years,' says the German Chancellor. 'Let this nationalist wind blow over. Meanwhile, we in the EU will debate the terms of free movement and agree a new treaty. Many feel that there are unfairnesses in the current system, and while I don't personally believe it is fundamentally flawed I am open to discussion.'

'I still don't see what difference this will make to Britain. What you're talking about will take a decade. You know how long it takes the EU to make up its mind about anything. And we won't have a vote anyway, as we'll be out.'

'I'm sure that many of the EU27 will consult with Britain – off the record, of course – in order to find a wording of the free movement rules that you could sign up to.'

She means Britain could rejoin the EU. It's a proposal to rework some terms of freedom of movement to make it acceptable to the British electorate of 2028. Is that daringly radical, or hopelessly utopian?

⇒ 'It's not going to happen. Britain is quitting the EU and we're never coming back.' Turn to **636**

⇒ 'I can't go home with such a wishy-washy proposal. We need clear immigration controls right now, in the form of a visa system.' Turn to **839**

116

Eh? What's this YouTube video? Oh, heh! Look at that pet meerkat stealing the dinner guest's food off her plate! Hilarious! Hah, hah! Oops – she's coming back. Hah, the meerkat looks as guilty as hell, like Tode the day after the referendum when he stabbed Strewel in the back. But he's still wolfing that chicken down, come what may, just like Tode, hah, hah!

No, no. Enough distractions. You have to get back to work. You retype 'single market' into your search engine, this time spelling it correctly.

Turn to **190.**

117

'That's the usual line, but since we're talking freely I can't see it making up the difference. Not even close. For one thing, the EU is our natural trading partner in terms of both proximity and in the nature of its markets. New deals will take time, and our ability to strike those deals is affected by our negotiating strength. Our economy will be a sixth the size of the EU's post-Brexit, and in many cases they'll be chasing the same contracts as us.'

'Let's hope you're wrong.'

'It's like climate change, isn't it? The data are saying something many politicians can't allow themselves to hear. But I'm old school, as you know. I still have faith in experts.'

'OK. Tell me what the experts say.'

Turn to **772.**

118

'They won't want to set a dangerous precedent either,' Stollard points out. 'Whatever package we get, the EU can't let it seem a sweeter deal than full membership or the whole thing would fall apart.'

'It will anyway,' says Dent with a gleeful little grin.

'Maybe, but that doesn't help us. The point is that we can be sure the Commission won't say, "Fine, keep your financial passports and tariff-free trade. We're happy that you won't accept free movement, automatic compliance with EU trade law, or pay anything into the EU budget." Something has to give.'

Strewel suddenly booms out in a richly resonant voice: 'Across the Channel, intellects cool and unsympathetic are regarding this island with envious eyes, and slowly and surely drawing their plans against us.'

Everyone looks at him in astonishment.

'My Richard Burton impression,' he says. 'Used to go down a treat in the Union bar. Anyway, whether it's Martians or Krauts, the fact remains they will all want to carve a piece off Britain's financial rump if we let them get hold of the knife. We've got to watch out for that.'

⇒ 'When it comes to the negotiations, what have we got in our favour?' Turn to **495**

⇒ 'I think that will do for today, gentlemen.' Turn to **81**

⇒ 'What's likely to happen if we can't get a deal? Then it's WTO rules, am I right?' Turn to **826**

119

'Armand Alprèves. Europe's "most dangerous man" if you listen to the *Tomahawk*. They also say he nurses a grudge against Britain because of a vote that cost him his job years ago.'

'They've been watching too many James Bond movies. I do wonder about the mental health of these leader writers. When a train is late or it starts to rain and they forgot their umbrella, do they immediately think conspiracies and vendettas?'

'To be fair, even some LibDems said that Alprèves' appointment as chief negotiator set off alarm bells. He's a close friend of the President of the Commission too, so we've got to see it as a signal.'

'Game playing, is it? We're supposed to be intimidated.'

'He's come out swinging, that's for sure. His initial estimate of our Brexit bill is about twice what we might hope for.'

'Hmm. Assuming there's wriggle room, that's potentially quite good. Knock it down to a fair sum and we'll look like we've come out on top.'

Turn to **374.**

120

'It just means that the treaty automatically updates to reflect changes in EU legislation. Normally the Swiss would have to formally rubber-stamp any new rules coming from Brussels, but doing that every time slowed things up. The dynamic clauses mean they've already agreed to changes in advance. Really, after all the fuss and bother, the Swiss have gone a long way round the houses to end up with a kludgier version of the standard EEA deal.'

⇒ 'But it's still technically sovereignty.' Turn to **509**

⇒ 'Hardly ideal. We don't want to look like we're subservient to EU jurisdiction.' Turn to **378**

121

A few days before the final vote you agree to be interviewed in one of the Sunday papers. At the Ivy you meet a girl who's so carefully made-up that she could be the prototype of a race of perfect androids. You don't catch her name, but after some questions prepared by Ron Beardsley to present your caring, domestic side, you launch into the main pitch.

'Politics has become divisive. Being passionate about our views is important, but we mustn't let that sour into contempt for other opinions. Democracy is not a battle between football teams, where one side goes home singing and the other is sunk in despair. We mustn't let it turn into that.'

A steely flicker in her eye suggests she'd give the Voight-Kampff test a run for its money. 'Are you saying we should try to get out of Brexit?'

'Not at all. We voted to leave the EU. We are going to leave. But very nearly half of the country like being EU citizens, and we can't leave them behind. We British have a reputation for being good losers, now we need to show we can be good winners too. We need to find a way to reflect the will of *all* the people.'

'A soft Brexit?' The little catch in her voice means she's sensed this might be the scoop that gets her off the lifestyle pages.

'A compromise. We cannot have the kind of Brexit that alienates half the country and threatens the future of the United Kingdom. The Conservative Party I know stands for tolerance and magnanimity. We're not the nasty party. We don't rub people's noses in the dirt the way the left like to. That's why I'm confident that we're going to come together now behind the candidate who can unite the country.'

There's quite a bombshell for the readers to find among their toast and marmalade. It's a gamble. Now to see if it pays off.

If you have either of the keywords APRICITY or TIGHTROPE, turn to **665**.

If not but you have the keyword YELLOW, turn to **815**.

If you have none of those keywords but your Popularity is 66% or more, turn to **519**.

Otherwise, if your Popularity is between 36% and 65%, turn to **801**.

Failing all of the above, turn to **50**.

122

'An agreement is mixed if it includes things that the Commission isn't authorized to sign off on. For example the Canada agreement was mixed because it covered more than just trade in goods, which meant that okaying the terms wasn't solely within the competence of the EU Commission. With a mixed agreement like that, every state gets to vote, and in this case the Wallonians – '

'Ridiculous, they sound like something out of Gulliver's Travels!' sneers Barkwell.

' – The Wallonians very nearly scuppered the whole Canada deal because they objected to the power it gave private corporations to sue national governments. The situation with the Singapore deal looks to go the same way. The European Court of Justice has ruled that EUSFTA – the EU/Singapore free trade deal – is a mixed agreement and must therefore be signed off by all the member states.'

⇒ 'That won't apply in our case, though.' Turn to **550**

⇒ 'If we can't get a deal we'll just have to resort to World Trade Organization rules.' Turn to **826**

⇒ 'It's a lot to take in. Let's call it a day.' Turn to **81**

123

All right, you've researched some of the rules and regulations that the single market requires. If Britain wants continued access after 2019, we'll have to keep some of those rules and regs. And then there are the EU regulatory bodies we are signed up to. What's going to happen to those? For example, we're currently part of the Single European Sky, an air traffic control regulator for the EU, Norway and Switzerland. If we're not signed up to the EU-wide air traffic control rules after Brexit, all our flights to and across Europe would be unable to fly. Other regulatory bodies that we probably will have to recreate or replicate if we want access to the single market include:

European Research Council
European Maritime Safety Agency
European Railway Agency
European Food Safety Authority
European Aviation Agency
European Fisheries Control Agency
European Safety at and Health at Work
European Medicines Agency

And many more. Take the European Medicines Agency. Without complying with their rules, British medicines and drugs could not be exported to the EU. And that's just one agency of many. It's going to get complicated.

What do you want to take a look at now, if you haven't already?

⇒ EFTA. Turn to **346**

⇒ Freedom of movement. Turn to **414**

⇒ You've had enough, and it's time for bed. Turn to **441**

124

At least it should be fairly straightforward, you think. After all, Britain is already trading with South Korea, it's to everyone's advantage, business is booming, and they won't want to lose that market when the UK and the EU part company.

In practice it's not quite that simple. A lot of South Korean exports go through Britain to reach the single market. Now that's cut off we may not look so attractive a trading partner – or at any rate it gives them an excuse to tweak the terms of the agreement.

'Look on the bright side, Prime Minister,' says your chief of staff. 'We can't legally sign a new trade agreement with Korea until after Brexit anyway.'

'How is that a bright side?'

'It means that whatever extra concessions they manage to squeeze out of us aren't yet part of the narrative. All we need to announce is that Korea is open to affirming the existing arrangement. It's a success story once you remove the fiddly details.'

As it turns out, the success is so meagre that the EU doesn't even object.

On your Brexit Memo Pad:

- +5% Popularity –voters buy into the notion of Britain forging exciting new deals across the globe, even when the deals are actually old ones.
- Mark International Trade Deals as complete.

Then turn to **666**.

125

So many problems, so little time. There are plenty of experts clamouring to advise you, of course, but more reliably you have your own experience, social media, and a legion of paid sycophants to fall back on.

What pressing issues do you want to take a closer look at?

⇒ To find out about immigration and freedom of movement, turn to **162**.

⇒ To consider the status of EU citizens already living here, turn to **612**.

⇒ To bone up on negotiating strategy, turn to **384**.

⇒ What is the single market anyway? Turn to **362**.

⇒ Take a trip to Cornwall to find out about development funding: turn to **267**.

⇒ Enough talk. Actions speak louder than words. Turn to **150**.

126

Look at your Brexit Memo Pad. If the Exit Fee is marked as complete, turn to **722**. If not, turn to **334**.

127

'BRITAIN COMES TO ITS SENSES,' says Wilkins, reading from the headlines the morning after the vote.

'Yes, but that's – '

'The *Daily Heil.*' He puts it on the breakfast table. The rest of the front page is taken up with the exhortation, 'NOW LET'S GET OUT OF EUROPE!'

And what of your own political career?

Look at your Brexit Memo Pad. If you have the keyword FOG, turn to **91**. If you have the keyword GAZELLE, turn to **434**. If you have the keyword SANCTION, turn to **24**.

If you have none of those keywords, turn to **10**.

128

The polls all show a strong lead for the Remain campaign. Some of the politicians who were reluctant to get behind it now jump on the bandwagon. But much will depend on how the average voter feels the country is being treated by the EU27. Will they go along with the *Heil*'s headlines, which portray a plucky, blokey Britain standing up to sinisterly well-groomed foreign bullies? Or will they listen to the internationalist propaganda of the BBC who, with their treasonously even-handed and disinterested reporting, paint the EU negotiators as no less reasonable than the UK team?

Look at your Brexit Memo Pad. If your Goodwill score is 40% or higher, turn to **811**. If it's 39% or lower, turn to **204**.

129

The deal is done. But it's not going to look that good back home.

> On your Brexit Memo Pad:
> - -2% Authority – your critics are calling you a weak negotiator.
> - +5% Economy – the UK economy needs those EU nationals, and it helps not to be handed back a million pensioners from Spain.
> - Mark Residency Rights as complete.

Then turn to **200**.

130

'I've moved mountains,' is Willy Franjeboom's first remark when you next meet him.

He's smiling, so you let the self-congratulation pass. 'And?'

'We conceded that Britain should have special status with the European Defence Force. We'll call it Most Favoured Ally, something like that. Details to be drafted.'

'But there'll be an EDA security council, and Britain will have a seat on it?' You give him your won't-back-down stare – indeed, it's the only kind of stare you know. Some have likened it to Winston Churchill on crystal meth.

He nods. 'You'll have equal input into joint military ventures.'

> Record on your Brexit Memo Pad:
> - +5% Authority – you have robustly asserted Britain's status as a major independent military force.
> - Mark Security & Defence as complete.

Turn to **269**.

131

Stollard folds his hands and glances around as if he's about to give you all a tax audit. 'I don't know if you remember a story that did the rounds in the *Heil* and the *Outrage* a few years ago. "EU bans the Union Jack from British beef."'

'How soon they forget,' snarls Barkwell. 'Yet few of them complained when the tanks and planes marked with that same flag liberated them from the yoke of Nazi tyranny.'

'On the surface it's a clear case of the EU pointlessly pushing us around. But actually it was no such thing. The directive simply stated that meat packaging should show the genuine country of origin. So a company couldn't import beef from France, stick a Union flag on it and claim it was British.'

'The EU may not have been the villain of the piece,' puts in Barkwell, 'but it's pretty typical of their love of red tape.'

'Ah,' says Stollard. 'That's my point. The red tape in this case came not from the EU, but from the World Trade Organization's rules of origin. The EU legislation was just bringing us into line with international standards. And here's another example...'

⇒ 'All right, Alan, tell us the other example.'
Turn to **537**

⇒ 'So you're saying the best way to get heard is to directly lobby the WTO.' Turn to **684**

⇒ 'This is just raking over old coals. What other issues do we have to consider?' Turn to **17**

132

Ron searches through his sheaf of notes and extracts a much smaller piece of paper with a few bullet points on it. 'The Commission is starting with an eye-wateringly high figure of €60 billion. Even some of the other member countries are a bit startled at that. If we can argue it down quite a bit...'

'It needs to be half. €30 billion would be the magic number. Then I've got a story to tell to the Eurosceptics.'

'That's a best case. Obviously it depends on other factors – and whether the negotiations go well.'

'*Whether* the negotiations go well. Quite. You always have a bucket of cold water handy, don't you, Ron?'

'We do have some legal grounds for resisting the Commission's estimates. For example, the EU exists as a separate entity. It could be argued that as long as we pay our dues up to the point of departure, we can't be held responsible for overspend and development commitments thereafter.'

'Some good news.'

'Unfortunately, the EU could turn to the precedent we established ourselves prior to the Scottish referendum. The Treasury made it clear that, in the event of the UK breaking up, Scotland would continue to be financially responsible for a "fair and proportionate" share of debts and liabilities.'

'Bugger.'

'And if we tear that one up now, what happens if the United Kingdom breaks up in a few years' time? Scotland could say, look, you squirmed out of paying the EU for spending you'd agreed to, so why should we cough up now.'

'We'll cross the Union Bridge when we get to it. Let's just get ourselves out of this thing in one piece first. Anything else going for us?'

'It's not all flowing out. Some of the cohesion budget was earmarked for impoverished regions of Britain, meaning pretty much everywhere that voted Leave. If we pay our whack, we're also entitled to a share of that.'

'Not a lot, though, I'm guessing.'

'Along with Britain's share of EU assets, maybe as much as €10 billion. Not all of that is for regional infrastructure projects, but…'

'I get it. Like £350 million a week, it just needs to make a good headline.'

Turn to **374.**

133

Panels on the floor light up to guide you to a parking bay at the back of the building. Patients are hobbling or being carried aboard a large red vehicle that looks like a hovering plastic maggot.

'Terminal case?' asks an attendant. You assume she's an attendant, anyway, though she's dressed in a shocking pink rave outfit and glittering mirror glasses.

You look at Abednego. 'I don't know if it's terminal. He hasn't been diagnosed.'

'Looks hopeless to me,' she says, staring off bored into the blankness of the night sky. 'Terminal and desperate cases only.'

'Let me aboard,' cries a man wired up to a saline drip that he's rolling along beside him. 'I need the miracle cure.'

'Miracle cure sounds good,' you say to the attendant. 'How much?'

'Special treatment bus, innit? It's paid for by the proceeds of Brexit. No cost to the customer.'

That sounds good. But is it *too* good?

⇒ Get on the bus	Turn to **21**
⇒ Try a different hospital department	Turn to **76**

134

Try as you might to position yourself as the strongest candidate for a pure Brexit, it won't wash. Your track record causes too many to doubt your sincerity. The hard Brexit vote is split between two and you emerge the weaker.

Turn to **377**.

135

'If they're all paying so much in taxes,' demands the questioner, 'how come our trains and hospitals are overcrowded?'

Ah, the public. With their drab George at ASDA clothes and their piggy little eyes darting about in fear that somebody's getting one over on them. Thank God they aren't bright enough to figure out who that somebody is.

Owlbear has leaned forward like Buddha in a bad suit. 'First of all, you've got to remember that immigrants help to keep those hospitals going. And as for why the tax benefit of immigration wasn't passed on to the public in the form of new building and infrastructure – well, you can blame Tory austerity for that. That's what half the Leave voters were really incensed by. The Brexit vote was a vote against divisive Tory policies.'

A sigh of indrawn breath. Ha, you fat fool. The electorate don't appreciate being told they fell for a bait and switch. Especially when it's true.

⇒ Try another question. Turn to **405**

⇒ Give up and get some sleep. Turn to **125**

136

You wait until the following day to get the other ministers' verdict on your proposal.

If you have the keyword KOALA, turn to **846**.

Otherwise turn to **183.**

137

The notepad in front of you is covered in underlined words, jotted graphs, and random doodles. It looks like Einstein's blackboard without the eureka moment. 'So what we're after is a free trade agreement that gives us everything we like about EU membership with none of the bits we don't.'

'That's it exactly,' says Dent, nodding his head vigorously like an over-excited chipmunk.

⇒ 'What can we learn from similar agreements the EU has done in the past?' Turn to **22**

⇒ 'What are the pros and cons?' Turn to **303**

⇒ 'How long would a deal like that take?' Turn to **276**

⇒ 'And if we can't get a deal we can always fall back on World Trade Organization rules, is that right?' Turn to **826**

⇒ 'I think that'll do for today.' Turn to **81**

138

'Our membership of 5 Eyes gives us an edge. We're the only European nation in that particular club, so the EU needs us. Unless – '

'Unless what?'

'The others, America and Canada and the Kiwis and Aussies,

they might decide it needs to be 6 Eyes. Get an EU seat on the bench there. Let's hope not, because we need the ace up the sleeve that gives us. See, we'll be outside the European Court of Justice, won't we?'

'Of course. That's the whole point.'

'Right. But that means we're not actually subject to EU data protection laws. Remember how the ECJ struck down the Safe Harbour agreement with the US on account of it gave a third country access to information covered by EU privacy laws? It'll be like that.'

'And data laws matter why?'

'Tracking terrorists, getting intelligence from our spooks watching out for radicalization, and so forth. And the EU won't let us get hold of information that might get passed on to the US, not now Windrip has been muttering about torturing suspects and killing terrorists' families.'

'Yes, the EU would inconveniently view those acts as criminal.'

'Not just the EU. The Court of Human Rights too.'

You nod so emphatically that McKay takes a step back. 'That's why we'll be getting out of that one too. All these rules. They make it impossible for us to defend ourselves.'

'Anything else, Prime Minister?' he asks nervously.

⇒ 'What about extradition? Turn to **773**

⇒ 'You say that day-to-day police cooperation shouldn't give us any problems?' Turn to **315**

⇒ 'Let me ask you something else.' Turn to **432**

139

You make your announcement the next day: 'EU nationals currently living in Britain will be permitted to stay.'

The press go wild. No change there, then. The *Hypsterion* editorial calls it 'doing the right thing' while also putting pressure on the EU to reciprocate.

The *Daily Heil* headline? They're not happy, naturally. 'Sold for a Song!' blares the headline.

The *Klaxon*? 'It's Brussels Hold 'Em and the Prime Minister folds!'

And so on. Encouragingly, the *Tomahawk* thinks it's risky but might work. 'The High Road' they call it.

The EU are very pleased. The EU chief negotiator tells you he'll do his best to reciprocate but he has to get agreement from the Council of the European Union.

On your Brexit Memo Pad:

- ❖ +5% Economy – those three million EU nationals are a considerable net benefit to UK finances.
- ❖ Tick the keyword TIGHTROPE

Now turn to **150.**

140

A few days later you find out that the press have learned where you're going on holiday. OK, well, nothing to hide there. But it seems someone's picked up on something you said when one of your aides booked your holiday. "PM SNEERS: 'I'M SLUMMING IT IN SUSSEX!" is the *Klaxon*'s headline. Even the *Daily Heil* has gone with it: "'I'D RATHER BE IN FRANCE,' PM TELLS AIDES."

When did you say that? You can't remember, although it does sound perfectly plausible. You'll really have to be more careful in the future. It's like a sieve, this office.

The rest of the article goes on about how you've snubbed the hard-working vineyard workers of southern England, and that maybe you're a secret Remainer, or if you like your fine wines that much, you should have just come out and said so.

It's not fair, but then again, what can you expect? It's the British tabloid press. The broadsheets, though, seem to be saying that it's OK to like good wine and go on holiday to Europe – after all, you're supposed to be a posh Tory PM – but you should have had the guts just to be up front about it.

Record on your Brexit Memo Pad:

- ❖ -1% Authority – you're the PM, you should have the courage of your convictions and just gone where you wanted.

You shake your head. You just can't win, can you? Still, it's really slow news day stuff, the damage is minor and it will be soon forgotten.

Now turn to **125**.

141

'Could it be sunspots? Something in the water supply? The Roman Empire fell because of lead pipes, I heard.'

'Is this a routine for *Have I Got News For You?*, Prime Minister?' asks Wilkins.

'I'm just wondering why the world is going stark staring mad. The United States has a President who makes the Punisher look like a left-wing peacenik. Turkey and Russia embrace their dictators as if they were rock stars. Actual Nazis are getting elected to some European parliaments. And now people are falling for Fungale's brand of custard.'

'I believe the term in most of the better restaurants is *crème Anglaise*.'

Luck plays a real part in politics, and always has. Toss two coins. If both come up heads, turn to **349**. Otherwise turn to **377**.

142

'Except I don't know if they will. Oh, don't get me wrong. I'm a great believer in British pluck and ingenuity. But this isn't like rebuilding Germany after the War. The people weren't sold Brexit as a hard road. Quite the reverse. Chaps like Strewel and Fungale offered them easy street – a vision of accelerating prosperity, a huge fiscal windfall. Are we supposed to say now, sorry, got that wrong, you're all going to have to work longer and harder for the next ten years while we fight for our new place in the world?'

'I can see why you became an accountant rather than a football coach.'

'I know, it all sounds like "project fear". But if you're sending an army into a battle zone it's no use saying everything will be fine. We've got to at least consider the worst so as to be ready for it.'

⇒ 'All right. Anything else?' Turn to **188**

⇒ 'We'll talk about this again some other time.' Turn to **666**

143

'A vote of no confidence, Prime Minister?' says your Chief Whip, looking as if you'd offered him a choice of hemlock or arsenic.

'We need an election, and because of the Fixed Term Parliament Act...'

'I understand. But the media will worry it like a pit bull with a kitten. People are going to say we're treating politics like a game.'

'Never mind what they say. I'll worry about what they say. You just get those zombies shambling into the right lobby.'

The vote carries. 'This House has no confidence in Her Majesty's Government.' On reflection, you needn't have raised the idea with Scraggle. You could have done it without Labour, and it's gruelling to see their smirks as they march back into the Commons.

Worse still the next day's headlines: PM ORDERS AN OWN GOAL and the caricatures that depict you as a contortionist, a card sharp, and a sneering puppeteer. Still, you've got what you wanted. A general election will be held in six weeks' time.

> Record on your Brexit Memo Pad:
> - -5% Authority – even a sham vote of no confidence has emboldened some of your critics.
> - -5% Popularity – many voters dislike these Parliamentary games; fortunately the dimmer ones don't understand it.

Turn to **428.**

144

You've managed to steer a judicious middle course in your dealings with the EU. You've compromised in some areas and played hardball in others. Mostly, that's worked out. They aren't happy about all aspects of the post-Brexit arrangements, but you have won a measure of their respect and they see you – and the UK as a whole – as somebody they can still do business with.

It bodes well for the future, as you've managed to maintain a working relationship with the EU without looking like you're kowtowing to their every demand. Whether you can hang on as Prime Minister depends on other factors, but at least you won't go down in history as the leader who took a wrecking ball to the best and noblest aspirations of post-war Europe.

Turn to **351**.

145

The country's future is on the line here. And, more importantly, your own future.

> On your Brexit Memo Pad:
> - Tick the keyword FOG.

Then turn to **302.**

146

Predictably squirming out of responsibility for setting an exact figure, the court rules that Britain should pay "not more than €40 billion". It's a blow, but the way it's phrased means you can drag things out a little longer. Every day above ground is a good day, as the saying goes.

> On your Brexit Memo Pad:
>
> ❖ -6% Economy – this is going to leave a big dent in Britain's finances, but not right away.
>
> ❖ Mark the Exit Fee as complete.

Then turn to **400**.

147

'You heard Monsieur Terlamen just now. The article clearly makes provision for a situation where the member state is experiencing societal difficulties.'

'Oh, and where is the societal difficulty?' asks the French president.

'You don't call Brexit an emergency?'

That gets a laugh – with you, not at you. But the French president isn't going to drop it there. 'The emergency brake was designed as a temporary measure,' he insists, 'to allow an EEA member to recover stability. If you wish Britain to trade freely within the single market, may we know how long you expect to remain deranged?'

He's a graduate of the École Nationale d'Administration, so you're quite sure he understands how *déranger* sounds in English. How will you answer his question?

⇒ 'Let's say we'll enforce the brake for five years and then review the situation.' Turn to **336**

⇒ 'The fact is the brake must be applied indefinitely. I have a commitment to the British people to reduce annual immigration to five figures.' Turn to **497**

148

'The poison that was festering has been sucked from the wound. Now I sense the country coming together to wholeheartedly support everything we are doing to make Britain great again.'

> On your Brexit Memo Pad:
> ❖ +2% Popularity – the people are always happy to be told there's nothing to worry about.

If you have ticked the keyword YELLOW on your Brexit Memo Pad, turn to **670**. If not, turn to **163**.

149

You almost laugh out loud at the sight of Labour MPs tramping through the Lobby in support of the motion. Do they think they stand any chance of winning an election? This vote will give you the opportunity you need to crush them forever.

And then, with Britain as effectively a one-party state, perhaps it will be time to switch to an executive presidency. You must have a chat with Mr Erdogan soon to see if he can give you any tips.

Turn to **428**.

150 ☐ ☐

If both of the boxes above are already ticked, turn to **580**. Otherwise, *don't* tick one yet, just read on.

You only have limited time to oversee areas of the Brexit talks in person. Other negotiations are left to your deputies. The issues that need to be dealt with now are listed below, and you will only be able to deal with *two* of them personally.

When you choose an issue to oversee, you'll be asked to tick one of the boxes above:

⇒ Deal with the Exit Fee (only if it is not already marked as complete on your Brexit Memo Pad)
tick a box above and then turn to **768**

⇒ Deal with the rights of EU citizens already living in Britain (only if Residency Rights is not already marked as complete on your Brexit Memo Pad)
tick one of the boxes, then turn to **494**

⇒ Deal with the question of immigration and border controls (only if Immigration is not already marked as

complete on your Brexit Memo Pad)
tick a box and then turn to **622**

⇒ Agree a framework with the EU for how talks should proceed (only if Negotiation Strategy is not already marked as complete on your Brexit Memo Pad)
tick a box and then turn to **558**

Incidentally, if you need a rest from running the country, this is a good place to take a break and come back later. Just make a note that you're on the first phase of talks at section **150** so you can find your way back here.

Once you have dealt with two of these issues (indicated by having ticked two of the boxes at the top of this section) turn to **580.**

151

'Agree to the exit fee quick and we've bought time and some goodwill,' says Stollard.

Dent gives an angry snort. 'Roll over and let them tickle our tummy, eh? How do you think that'll go down?'

The Chancellor isn't one to rise to easy bait. 'I'm listing the options. Refuse outright to pay and it'll go to the courts. We might even win the case – but only like Pyrrhus.'

Recognizing a swipe at his lack of a university education, Dent gives Stollard his trademark crinkle-cut sneer. 'I may not know much about Ancient Rome, but I know Texas Hold'em, and I say if we call their bluff they'll fold.'

Stollard lets that hang in the air for a few seconds, then turns to you and goes on as if Dent hadn't spoken. 'Or there's the middle ground. Either continue to negotiate the exit fee in parallel with other talks, or reach a quick agreement over the basic principles that will be used to calculate the amount, and come back and revisit it later.'

'Dragging it out is a problem given our lack of negotiators,' you remind him.

'True. Though it does also buy us time to hire in some talent, which God knows we need.'

'That's all for today, gentlemen.'

Turn to **125.**

152

'What's *he* on the news for? Somebody turn the sound up.'

There's a bustle as your aides fall over themselves to find the TV remote. Suddenly it's blaring away.

'Turn it down. I'm not deaf.'

' – the right time for me to rejoin the Conservative Party, yes,' Colin Fungale is saying. 'UKIP has served its purpose. Now I'm looking forward to doing my bit as part of the – '

You seize the remote and stab at the mute button. If only you could erase Fungale from existence with the touch of a button.

'Allow that odious blot into the Tory Party?' you fume. 'Over my dead body.'

'Well…' ventures an aide. 'He is very popular among a certain section of the voters.'

⇒ Regardless, you must block him from rejoining the party at all costs. Turn to **90**

⇒ Maybe it's not a bad idea at that, if he brings a few million voters with him. Turn to **680**

153

'Calamity? What sort of calamity?'

'We need to present a bold and positive front. Remember that it's not just about dealing with the EU. We have a divided nation. Almost a half wanted to stay part of the EU. Of the rest, how many expected a soft Brexit, along the lines of the deal Norway has?'

'What? None. Hardly any…'

You shake your head. 'Right now, maybe two-thirds of voters want either to stay in the EU or are expecting a close relationship that's tantamount to associate membership. And we can't ignore the fact that many votes for Brexit were a reprimand for our previous leader and his austerity policies.'

'You're not thinking of reversing austerity?'

'We still desperately need to make savings. Now more than ever, so that we have some leeway as we start to forge new trade deals around the world. But I have to tell you, Sir Harvey, I've had enough of infighting. This party needs to come together and provide the nation with a shining example as we shape Britain's new role in the world.'

'I see,' he says slowly, mulling over what you've said. 'Well, here's your assistant so I'm sure he's going to shoo me away. Thank you for your time, Prime Minister.'

> On your Brexit Memo Pad:
> - ❖ +1% Authority – he's impressed by your firm stance.
> - ❖ Tick the keyword PEDAL

Turn to **507.**

154

'Quite emphatically, too: 57% on a higher than average turnout. But it seems a lot of them weren't aware that Brexit would mean losing EU funding.'

'Really, that came as a surprise, did it?'

'You have to remember, Prime Minister, that the Leave campaign was promising a cash windfall once we left the EU.'

- ⇒ 'I can't bring that up. Think of something positive I can say.' Turn to **258**
- ⇒ 'Give me more of an on-the-ground view. Who in Cornwall is complaining the loudest?' Turn to **847**
- ⇒ 'What's the EU trying to achieve with these funding programs? Apart from robbing the rich.' Turn to **573**

155

Before you get a chance for an in-depth briefing on defence, you're whisked off on another regional outing. This time it's a drive out to the middle of the Kent marshes to be photographed next to an old coastal fortress, presumably to convey an impression of Britain standing in dignified isolation against the envy of less happy lands. It seems like every day you're having to go somewhere and reassure frightened people that Brexit isn't going to change their lives. Even though that's exactly what it's going to do.

'Slough Fort,' you say, gazing at the ruin with distaste. 'I was expecting better than this. It's not even in Slough, unless they were thinking of Bunyan's slough of despond.'

You turn your gaze across a bleak expanse of sand and wind-flattened grass, where sky and land and sea merge in a migraine-inducing blister of colourless light. The clouds threaten rain, which is no doubt why your advisers are now in a huddle with the TV cameramen. To come all this way and not even get a photo-op. The only thing that slightly warms your heart is the thought that you'll be able to sack a few people when you get back to Number 10.

Your protection officer stands a little way off. What's this one called? They're all the same. Burly, raw-faced men dressed with the professional care of undertakers. No, better to say estate agents – less of an ominous connotation.

You nod to him. 'We'll give it another ten minutes, see if the rain holds off.'

He scans the heavens with an Easter Island impassivity. 'I think it'll brighten up. I'm sorry you don't care for the fort, Prime Minister.'

You give it another glance. Hard to see what use it would be in time of war. It could just as easily be an excavation of a Victorian public lavatory. 'Why is it here? Do you know, McKay?'

A stab in the dark. The gleam of recognition in those thousand-yard eyes says you guessed right.

'Built to stop the French, Prime Minister. Back in the 1800s when they got uppity, and somebody realized there wasn't much to deter them from sailing up the Thames to attack London.'

That gives you an idea. You're here to talk about UK security after Brexit, and right now your MoD adviser is busy working out light levels with the photographers. As a man with real military experience, maybe McKay can give you some pointers.

Turn to **432.**

156

They know full well that you can't shut the door on unskilled workers right away because your own Brexit secretary has already said so at a summit in Latvia. Although it's mostly the lower-skilled immigrants in impoverished areas who raised the hackles of the British electorate, it's going to take time to retrain British workers to handle some of the dirty jobs in farming, social care, and public services that currently only EU citizens from eastern Europe are willing to do.

Privately you doubt that native Brits will ever want to do those jobs, in fact. Each pasty white, lager-drinking, pit-bull-owning Leave voter is a lord of the Earth in his own mind. In ten years African and

Indian immigrants will be doing those jobs instead of Latvians, and otherwise nothing will have changed.

Even so, it's the skilled workers who really matter to the economy. Both Britain and the EU have a vested interest in keeping down barriers to movement in the service sectors – especially financial services. So although they're not happy with you applying a visa system, they'll go along with it.

> Record on your Brexit Memo Pad:
> - ❖ -5% Goodwill – the EU aren't ecstatic, but it could be a lot worse.
> - ❖ +5% Popularity – the visa system sounds to voters like a credible attempt to control immigration.
> - ❖ Mark Immigration as complete.

Then turn to **150.**

157

The result of the second and final round of voting is a majority in favour of a soft Brexit.

'It doesn't tell us very much,' points out your chief of staff. 'Do they mean within the European Economic Area, like Norway, or outside that but still in the single market, like Switzerland?'

'Haven't you said yourself, Ron, that the beauty of the first referendum result was that it was wide open to interpretation? We have to leave ourselves wiggle room with these things.'

He's not listening. The panic of unpredictable events has sent him into a mental tailspin. 'Or do they mean like Turkey? In the customs union but outside the market? Does that still count as a soft Brexit?'

'Perhaps they mean that they want access to the single market without being in it.'

He stares at you. 'But what does that mean? Access to a market but not *in* a market?'

'Ron, Ron. It doesn't matter. It's only advisory, remember. Your job is to figure out what the public want and then explain it to them.'

Turn to **446.**

158

Chloe Stoat's own opposition to a hard Brexit lends credence to the stories you plant in the media of her being a disaffected Remainer trying to stir up trouble.

Turn to **577**.

159

Barkwell suddenly perks up as if somebody has put a shilling in his meter. 'There's Mifid,' he says brightly. 'Just as good as the old passport system only without the EU baggage to go with it.'

You look to the Chancellor for the other side of the story. 'There's something in that,' he says. 'Mifid – it stands for the Market in Financial Instruments Directive – allows third parties to have the same rights as those enjoyed by companies with EU and EEA financial passports. And the new Mifid regulations are due to take effect before Brexit, so at that point UK firms should be established as equivalent to their EU counterparts.'

⇒ 'I'm sensing a but.' Turn to **299**

⇒ 'We're in danger of getting punch drunk on acronyms. Let's recap the effect on services if we were to follow the Norway model.' Turn to **66**

160

You undertake to oversee security discussions personally as soon as you have a window in your schedule.

On your Brexit Memo Pad, tick the keyword REGENT and then turn to **666**.

161

'As I said, that's quite intolerable,' insists Barkwell.

'I've actually looked into this,' says Strewel, surprising himself as much as everybody else. Putting aside a Danish pastry, he shoves his fat, sticky fingers into a briefcase and pulls out an old newspaper with some of the columns circled in red. 'Here we are. EEA states can send legislation back to the EU asking for amendments if it would conflict with domestic laws. Of course, the EU might refuse. "No straight bananas for you, *mein Herr*!" The country in question can then refuse to adopt the legislation. So technically their courts are sovereign. But then they wouldn't be in compliance with EU laws, which would halt trade in bananas or whatever the law applied to.'

The Chancellor leans over and whispers in your ear. 'Not one of Peter's own newspaper columns, obviously.'

'How can you tell?'

'There are actual facts in it.'

Turn to **17.**

162 ❑

If the box above is empty, put a tick in it and turn to **409.**

If the box was already ticked, turn to **828.**

163

That was the final distraction, hopefully. Since the 2016 referendum, British society has been wobbling from one near-crisis to another. It's hardly surprising. Two years to unpick four decades of alliance and cooperation? Promises that can never be kept because they were built on lies? A populace sick of austerity who are about to take a financial hit equal to the 2008 crash? It's a *Darkness At Noon* scenario that was bound to lead to panic, uncertainty and pointless infighting.

You share a brandy with the Chancellor now that the leadership challenge is behind you. 'It strikes me,' he says, 'that the referendum result was like throwing a fox into the henhouse. And it starts slaughtering its way through the chickens but we have to keep saying, that's fine, this is all good, opportunities abound, never mind the blood.'

'You're missing something, Alan.'

'What's that?'

'We're the fox.'

On your Brexit Memo Pad:

- +8% Authority – you prevailed and now your position as leader is unassailable.
- +1% Economy – the markets are faintly encouraged that the period of uncertainty is past.

Then turn to **603.**

164

'It's the pot calling the kettle black, isn't it, Bill? Colin Fungale left the Conservative party because he didn't like what we stand for. He spent his career belonging to a parliament he hardly ever turned up to, other than to collect his pay cheques and grandstand like a child who's being ignored. He kept saying he was quitting, then deciding he'd like to come back after all, and when his own party didn't look like serving his ambitions he jumped ship to us. Quite frankly he might just as easily have joined Labour or the LibDems if he thought they looked like winners. He's the rat who jumps onto the boat that isn't sinking.'

Stern stuff, even when dished out to a knave like Fungale, but if it swings the vote in your favour who cares? Turn to **28**.

165

'There's no time for a second referendum at this late stage,' you tell your ministers. 'That ship has sailed.'

'Probably just as well,' says Peter Strewel. 'Be a bit embarrassing if it went the other way now, eh?'

> On your Brexit Memo Pad:
> ❖ Mark Second EU Referendum as complete.

Then turn to **385.**

166

'I expected as much,' she says, handing you her letter of resignation the moment she's shown into your office.

'Then why? You've torpedoed such a promising career.'

She looks at you as though you'd spoken to her in a foreign language. 'It's the principle,' she says at last. 'The referendum vote didn't say we had to sabotage the British economy by quitting the single market.'

'That's the price of staying in power.' You look back at your computer screen, leaving her to find her own way out.

> On your Brexit Memo Pad:
> ❖ +1% Authority – you acted quickly and ruthlessly, impressing the hardcore Brexiters in the party.
> ❖ Tick the keyword LEAF

Now turn to **275.**

167

Check your Brexit Memo Pad.

If you have the keyword HEMLOCK, turn to **851**.

If not but you have the keyword ZEBRA, turn to **399**.

Otherwise turn to **769**.

168

'Funny, in a way,' says McKay, with a smile that flickers like a match. 'The EU lot are always banging on about wanting a proper military force, and how there's all these conflicts they reckon they should be mucking in around the world. But it's us that's got the real experience, isn't it? Teaching us to suck eggs, I reckon it is.'

A refreshing take, this. You consider what to ask his advice on.

⇒ 'Tell me about joint EU forces.' Turn to **217**

⇒ 'What's your opinion on the European Defence Agency?' Turn to **296**

⇒ 'What about the military situation post-Brexit?' Turn to **97**

⇒ 'What do you see as the implications for policing and counter-terrorism?' Turn to **314**

⇒ 'Can you explain why the EU has so many security and defence acronyms?' Turn to **503**

⇒ 'That's all. Thank you, McKay.' Turn to **666**

169

Dent and Rufus withdraw from the contest, citing the need for party unity.

'Hah! The need for keeping their seats in Cabinet, more like,' you say to Ron Beardsley.

'Planning to dismiss them?'

'Not at all. You've seen *The Godfather*. I'm keeping my beady eye on those two.'

If you have the keyword YELLOW, turn to **670**.

If not, turn to **163**.

170

You recall a heart to heart with the Almighty in which you sought divine guidance on this question.

Turn to **177.**

171

'What did you think?' you ask your press secretary as soon as you've unclipped the mic.

She sucks her teeth. That's one of her tells. 'I'm not sure if the mood is with us. The audience seemed a little sceptical.'

'That's just a bunch of losers who had nothing better to do this evening than take up the offer of free BBC tickets. They don't matter.'

But you feel a pall of unease settling over you all the same.

If your Popularity score is 64% or more, turn to **99**. Otherwise turn to **134**.

172

You've done all you can. Now it's all down to how the MPs vote.

Toss two coins. If both come up heads, turn to **513**. If both come up tails, turn to **534**. Otherwise turn to **377**.

173

The result of the second referendum is –

'Undecided? What?'

'A three-way split, Prime Minister,' says Terri Trough, your press secretary. 'A third of the voters back a hard Brexit, a third are for staying in the EU, and a third think we should adopt the Norway model.'

'How can I govern these people, Terri? They need a slap.'

Turn to **206**.

174

'I suppose it would be quite a homecoming for Britain to rejoin the European Free Trade Area,' observes Dent, 'seeing as we were instrumental in setting it up. Of course, that was because we wisely opted not to join the EEC back in the 1950s. And now the EEC has mutated into the overcooked spaghetti of bureaucracy that is the EU.'

'And the more integrated we remain with Europe, the less of a hit to the economy,' points out Stollard.

'The jury's out on that!' fumes Barkwell. 'Once we're unfettered from the shackles of the EU we might very well be a lot better off.'

'There's the EU, and then there's Europe,' Stollard reminds him. 'EFTA would give us vital access to the latter. And we're going to need that unless you think that trade in Mongolian yurt felt and Nepalese buttermilk is going to make up for the £11 billion in goods and the £88 billion in services we sell every year across the Channel.'

'Closer to Europe, that's good,' says Strewel. 'Not ever closer, mind you. And in a relationship that suits our needs, is what I say. More French maids, fewer sour Krauts, eh?'

Stollard throws you a look that seems to be asking if you have a gun. Barkwell is still seething over the merest hint of concessions with the EU. Dent looks vaguely troubled. And Strewel is reaching with glee towards a plate of biscuits that Wilkins has just brought in. What will you say?

⇒ 'The best option for us might be the Norway model.'
Turn to **492**

⇒ 'I'm leaning towards the sort of semi-independent deal Switzerland enjoys.' Turn to **2**

⇒ 'On due reflection, EFTA membership is a bridge too far. We'll review the customs union option instead.'
Turn to **367**

⇒ 'It's clear we're going to need a bespoke deal after all.'
Turn to **836**

175

You've survived the first six months of Brexit negotiations, but it's still a long road ahead.

Turn to **666** and tick one of the boxes there before doing anything else.

176

As you'd expect having met the current US President, his philosophy is all about the zero-sum. To him, business consists of grabbing whatever the other person has and making sure they're never in any position to claw it back.

Naturally if business really worked like that then human beings would live in lean-tos and eat grubs and fruit. Still, there's no denying that Windrip has done very well for himself considering he started out in the mid-seventies with only a hundred million or so. Not so well as he could have done by investing in a tracker fund, perhaps, but since each dollar he's made has been taken from a rival, he could probably claim to have a put a fair few competitors out of business along the way.

The book ends by reminding the reader that hype trumps facts. An ironically self-reflexive comment by the ghostwriter? As you toss the book aside and settle down to sleep, it's the thought that stays with you. What matters most is not managing the best deal, but being seen to be the best leader. At least that's a simple goal, one far less daunting than pulling in the myriad reins of trade, defence, finance, immigration and diplomacy. Slogans, that's what you must arm yourself with in the coming months.

You drift off with the mental image of Windrip pointing his stubby finger at you and saying, 'You're hired.'

Turn to **482.**

177

Calling a general election is a big gamble. There are so many snares and pitfalls, it makes you feel like Christian in the Valley of the Shadow of Death. But you know you can trust God to give you wise counsel. He may have misled your predecessor about Iraq's weapons of mass destruction, but you know He wouldn't try that with you.

⇒ 'But how would I call a snap election?' Turn to **35**

⇒ 'What about Scotland? We'll win no votes there.' Turn to **3**

⇒ 'At least I can forget about Labour.' Turn to **626**

⇒ 'The Liberal Democrats might be a force to reckon with. They're campaigning hard for Remain.' Turn to **784**

178

Your bold move has seized the moral high ground and leaves the EU little choice. They reciprocate by announcing that UK nationals living in Europe will be allowed to remain after Brexit.

On your Brexit Memo Pad:

- ❖ +5% Authority – you're seen to be setting the agenda.
- ❖ +10% Goodwill – the EU are encouraged that you will have an open and fair approach to negotiations.
- ❖ +5% Popularity – nobody can call you the nasty party now.
- ❖ Mark Residency Rights as complete.

Then turn to **200**.

179

'There are still significant restrictions on trade in energy and capital, for instance. Rome wasn't built in a day, and the EU wasn't built in a decade or two. The thing is, trade tariffs are simple to get agreement on, if you leave product certification and quotas out of the frame. You just say there's no duty on widgets and there you go. That's why the trend has been for lower and lower tariffs worldwide. But the EU is designed to be a lot more than a market in goods.'

'Yes. More like one of those massive Indian idols on rollers that flatten worshippers who don't get out of the way fast enough,' says Strewel.

'It is the slow trundling towards "ever-closer union",' admits Stollard. 'The EU is a work in progress, and arguably the tangle of regulations around any services market means that it can only edge towards completion by way of Zeno's Paradox. But in any case we'll be out by 2019, when the building blocks of the Capital Markets Union are passed into law. Wherever the EU is heading after that, we won't be aboard for the trip.'

'And good riddance,' adds Barkwell.

⇒ 'Will we be able to include financial services in a new free trade agreement?' Turn to **220**

⇒ 'If we have to resort to World Trade Organization rules, what will that mean?' Turn to **826**

⇒ 'Let's wrap up there, gentlemen.' Turn to **81**

180

Finally, as Napoleon knew, it all comes down to luck. Toss a coin. If you get heads, turn to **519**. If tails, turn to **782**.

181

To your fury, none of your advisers goes along with the idea of a snap election. 'We just can't do it,' says one. 'It would be too much of a distraction. We'd look irresponsible, and the voters would punish us for it.'

The Cabinet take the same view. Even the Home Secretary has the temerity to contradict you. 'Right now, with the EU negotiations coming to a head and the two-year deadline on Article 50 almost up…' She spreads her hands.

The others are nodding. Individual treachery you can cope with, but not when they all line up clutching knives beneath their togas. The smiling villains. Inwardly seething, you turn to the next order of business.

> On your Brexit Memo Pad:
> - Mark General Election as complete.

Then turn to **385**.

182

You can't afford to lose those EU citizens. They're a vital part of the British economy. If you sent them packing then the NHS would have to rapidly replace them with immigrants from even further afield, which would soon excite the ire of Middle Englanders. If they don't want a Romanian nurse, still less do they want a brown- or yellow-skinned one.

'Britain applauds your gesture,' you tell Franjeboom, 'and we are happy to demonstrate equal generosity. EU nationals already living here will of course be allowed to remain.'

> On your Brexit Memo Pad:
> - +5% Economy – those three million EU nationals are a considerable net benefit to UK finances.
> - +2% Goodwill – for whatever it's worth at this late stage.
> - Tick the keyword TIGHTROPE
> - Mark Residency Rights as complete.

Now turn to **385.**

183

It's not a bad compromise and they know it. You can go home and announce the introduction of a visa system, which will please the Kippers and the right of your own party. At the same time, the visa guidelines will pretty much replicate the best elements of free movement – the ability of the labour market to respond rapidly, the necessary fluidity of service sector jobs – while removing the ways that some voters perceive, rightly or wrongly, that it is being abused.

Record on your Brexit Memo Pad:

- +5% Economy – the financial markets breathe a sigh of relief.
- +5% Goodwill – the EU see you're trying your best to find common ground.
- Tick the keyword MAPLE.
- Mark Immigration as complete.

Turn to **150**.

184

After weeks of consultation, the other EU states have hammered out a proposal which Willy Franjeboom presents to you.

'This is disappointing,' you say when you've heard him out. 'It doesn't seem to be substantially different from the participatory framework that Norway uses to cooperate with the EU.'

'That makes sense, surely? Why not use an existing template?'

'Because Britain has the most effective armed forces in Europe, whereas Norway's army comprises five husky sleds and a large firecracker.'

'So you are declining the offer, Prime Minister?'

⇒ 'I'll put up with it for now, but by excluding Britain from the strategic planning stage you're sacrificing our experience and commitment.' Turn to **701**

⇒ 'Of course I'm declining it. We can't participate in joint military ventures without having equal input.' Turn to **301**

185

Do you have the keywords TIGHTROPE or WELTER? If so, turn to **471**.

If you have neither of those keywords, turn to **724**.

186 ☐

Your information on international trade comes from a very unorthodox source...

If the box above is empty, put a tick in it and turn to **685.**

If the box was already ticked, turn to **860.**

187

'Now I don't like to contradict a lady,' says Fungale, 'but you really are talking absolute bosh. I'm sure it's all very well living in Hampstead or Richmond or wherever it is. You can pop out to the deli and no doubt you're glad you can get real Polish sausage for your dinner parties. But in the areas of the country that have seen the steepest rise in immigration – I'm talking about places like Boston and Redditch – wages have fallen by a tenth over the last fifteen years.'

His tone in addressing an opponent is a blend of syrup and cyanide, perfectly judged so that a perceptive viewer will see his snide contempt while at the same time it conveys a Brighton seafront lounge kind of charm to any old ladies who may be watching. 'He's so polite,' they'll say, entirely missing the sinusoidal wrinkle in his lip and the thuggish shine in his eye. All the charm of Ronnie Kray offering a guy a cigarette. It's a good job you don't have him on the backbenches to contend with.

Owlbear blunders back in. 'Under the last Labour government –'

'Can anyone here remember that far back?' quips Tode.

The audience roars with laughter, drowning out Owlbear's point about the fund Labour set up to distribute the financial benefits of immigration to the areas that most needed it. You make a mental note to shave a few days off Tode's time in political purgatory for that.

It's time you got some sleep.	Turn to **125**
Watch a little more.	Turn to **405**

188

'The EU has been pretty effective at lowering the costs of trade. Things like shipping, border checks, paperwork.'

'No great surprise. That's what the EU was designed for.'

'Yes, and over the last decade it's brought those trade costs down 40% faster compared with other OECD countries. My point is that we can expect that trend to continue. Even if it halves, by 2030 other OECD countries – and that's now including Britain, remember – will on average have trade costs 25% higher than intra-EU costs. Add all this up, and the bottom line is a hit to household income of between £1000 and £6000 a year. And that's even if we stay in the European Economic Area.'

⇒ 'What about if we stay in the single market?'
Turn to **520**

⇒ 'So what should our highest priority be in negotiation?'
Turn to **98**

⇒ 'Any other risks of going it alone?' Turn to **588**

⇒ 'Let's pick this up later.' Turn to **666**

189

Noysom-Reek is the next to fall. Despite his strong support among the party faithful, the MPs apparently realized it would be like handing the reins of power to Attila the Hun's idiot brother. So that leaves you and Alan Stollard to go on to a vote of the party members.

How unpopular would you have to be to lose to somebody who all but admits Brexit will be a disaster? Let's find out.

If your Popularity score is less than 36%, turn to **782**. Otherwise turn to **244**.

190

Okay, then. The single market. Some say it's just a free trade area, as it gets rid of customs, tariffs, quotas and taxes. But it's more than that because it also includes free movement. Of everything – people, services, goods and capital. Also, there are rules and regulations to create a level playing field for all members of the market. That doesn't happen in a free trade zone. And finally, in a free trade area, some sectors could be excluded by mutual agreement, like cars or wine, or fishing but in a single market everything has to go into the pot, no exceptions.

There are a handful of single markets in the world – the Eurasian Economic Union, one in the Gulf states, and one in the Caribbean – but the EU is the only entity committed to actually completing the concept of a single market. That means full economic integration and the removal of all barriers to trade – a bit like the United States, where individual states vary on product and prices but the market is completely integrated internally in terms of free movement of people, goods, capital and services. The EU really isn't the same as the United States politically, in the sense of the federal Europe warned about by Brexit doomsayers, but it's not hard to spin it like that.

In general, single markets tend to be mutually very beneficial to their members, though some sectors within a given country can suffer when first joining – the UK fishing industry, for instance, in the early days. Whatever happens, it's going to hurt if Britain doesn't continue to have some kind of access to the European single market.

It's also important to remember that the EU and the single market are not the same. The EU runs the single market, but you can be in the single market and not in the EU. However, you can't be in the EU and not be part of the single market, just like you don't have to have the Euro to be in the EU or the single market. Remember, though, if you're not in the EU but you are in the single market, you don't get any say on how that market works. That's the problem faced by the EFTA lot.

⇒ EFTA? What's that? Turn to **346**

⇒ Learn more about free movement Turn to **414**

⇒ Delve into EU regulations and standards (oh, joy!) Turn to **655**

⇒ You've had enough, and it's time for bed. Turn to **441**

191

'The main one will be what's going to happen to it. The EU invests in development through its structural and cohesion funds. Cornwall received £2.5 billion in EU funding over the three funding terms from 2000 to 2020. That's around £250 per year for everybody in Cornwall. They're all concerned about the funds drying up after Brexit.'

⇒ 'But didn't Cornwall vote Leave?' Turn to **154**

⇒ 'Structural and cohesion funds – what's the difference?' Turn to **643**

192

'A second referendum? Is that wise?'

You look up, unaware that you'd spoken out loud. You'd forgotten there was anyone else in the room, in fact. It's a Cabinet meeting. They all gape along the table at you like newly hatched ducklings waiting for something to follow.

'Why would it not be wise, Alan?'

'It might go against us.'

'What do you mean, against us? Leave or Remain?'

'Either. It's uncontrollable. Whatever the result is, it's like drawing a new hand of cards.'

'Russian roulette,' agrees Dennis Dent, nodding vigorously like one of those toy dogs you used to see on car dashboards.

Peter Strewel perks up. 'Mm, sounds tasty, that. Velvety dark chocolate laced with vodka. Oh no, I'm thinking of roulade.'

'A new referendum would be an unknown unknown,' chimes in the Home Secretary. 'Why shake things up? We could be handing Barry Scraggle the keys to Number 10.'

⇒ The panicky fools. Turn to **845**

⇒ No, they're right. Turn to **106**

193

The contest has come down to you, Tiffany Rufus, and Colin Fungale. While Rufus sets her cap at the moderates, emphasizing the need for compromise and a warm relationship with the EU, Fungale becomes ever more evangelistic about EU untrustworthiness and the need for what he calls a True Brexit.

⇒ Try and outdo him for ultra-hard Brexit zeal. Turn to **552**

⇒ Stick to a midway agenda between him and Rufus. Turn to **353**

194

Now that Alan Stollard is in the running, Tiffany Rufus has no chance. The Parliamentary faction that would like to see Brexit watered down if not reversed is not big enough to support two candidates, and Stollard has the stronger backing. Sure enough, Rufus is the next to be eliminated.

'It's irrelevant,' is Terri Trough's judgement. 'No candidate tainted by Remainism could possibly win once the vote goes to the members. So if you can see off Gervais Noysom-Reek you'll walk it.'

'I surely can't lose to that goof. He's a cartoon caricature of fusty right-wing prejudice. Give him a snuffbox and lace cuffs and he'd be an ineffectual villain straight out of *Blackadder*.'

It's with a sinking feeling that you realize that description would also fit a fair proportion of the party members.

Look at your Brexit Memo Pad. If you have the keyword OPAL *and* your Authority is less than 52%, turn to **70**.

Otherwise turn to **544**.

195

'California holds a lot of referendums. They're a way for politicians to duck the blame when things don't work out. And because voters don't need to weigh up alternatives or turn their minds to how to implement any given desire, they often lead to contradictions.'

'Such as?'

'Did Californians want more spending on public services? Yes they did. Did they want higher taxes? Oh no. Have your cake and eat it? Thanks.' He pauses. 'Sorry, I know Peter Strewel is hot on that one.'

'Your argument is exactly why we should only have the one referendum.'

'But then how do we know what people wanted? It's like asking them to vote for whether a bus should go to Bristol or somewhere else. Somewhere else, they tell you. But where? We don't know what they were voting for.'

'They were voting for Brexit. Brexit means Brexit. Strong and stable government getting on with the job of Brexit... What are you doing?'

'Just checking how much anaesthetic I gave you, Prime Minister.'

Turn to **668**.

196

The by-election results in an even bigger majority for the new candidate. Your press secretary is quick to trumpet it as an endorsement of your policies. It is, at least, a better outcome than you feared.

On your Brexit Memo Pad:

- ❖ +1% Authority – you're quite happy to use the result as a barometer of public opinion.

Turn to **350**.

197

Britain is going to need new trade deals. Even if leaving the EU only reduces our trade with Europe by 10%, that's still a £200 million blow to the economy every week. It's not possible to actually conclude or even substantially negotiate new trade agreements before Brexit, but at least you can line them up and bask in the credit.

One option is to look at agreements that the EU is already negotiating with third countries such as Japan. The slowly grinding gears of EU bureaucracy mean that those can take years or even decades to complete. Potentially you could swoop in on a deal like that. And you could close it faster, too. What Britain loses in negotiating strength by going it alone is compensated for by not having to get twenty-seven squabbling states to all sing from the same hymn book. The only snag is that the EU would probably see that as unfairly trading off their hard work. It could make the exit negotiations a lot trickier.

Another option is to go after deals that the EU already has in place with third countries like Mexico and South Korea. As a member state, Britain is a party to those agreements now, so in theory all you'll need to keep them going is a rubber stamp. And the EU certainly can't object as everyone is hoping for Britain to ratify those existing agreements as a sign that the post-Brexit arrangement will be business as usual.

But there's a third option. All-new trade deals would give you something to trumpet about at home without antagonizing the EU too much. Somewhere like the Philippines. The EU has started talks on a free trade agreement there but it's years away from signature. That's where you could nip in and show how the UK is the agile egg-stealing mammal to the EU's lumbering dinosaur.

⇒ Have a go at snagging a big new trade deal from under the EU's nose – with somewhere like the USA, for instance. Turn to **254**

⇒ Focus on repurposing existing deals between the EU and third countries. Turn to **234**

⇒ Start discussions on completely new trade agreements involving countries the EU currently don't have a deal with. Turn to **337**

198

'You ever heard of Mercosur?'

'Isn't that what they're calling diplodocus these days? It's been a while since I did my Biology O-level.'

She gives you the classic OMG round-eyed, slack-jawed look. 'My granny's not that gaga and she's got Alzheimer's. Mercosur is a South American trading bloc. They've been negotiating a trade agreement with the EU since before I was born.'

'We'll do better.'

'We're going to have to, because whatever our final deal with the EU we're likely to end up with a blank sheet of paper as far as the rest of the world is concerned. And incidentally the Mercosur bloc includes Argentina, so get ready to reopen the Falklands question if you want a deal there.'

Turn to **700.**

199

Article 50 of the Lisbon Treaty states:

First, that any member state can decide to withdraw from the European Union 'in accordance with its own constitutional requirements.'

Second, that a member state that decides to leave starts off by notifying the European Council of its intention. The European Union then negotiates a withdrawal agreement with that state, taking account of the framework for its future relationship with the Union. That agreement requires the consent of the European Parliament and is then put to a vote in the European Council, in other words the heads of state of all the EU countries.

Third, the state ceases to be a member of the EU two years after declaring its intention to leave, unless an agreement for a transition period has been made before then. Since you declared Article 50 yesterday, you now have two years to conclude that agreement. Two years. Is that luxurious indulgence, or is it going to be a white-knuckle ride from hell? That's what you'll soon find out.

The lawyer who drafted Article 50 says that he never expected any nation to actually invoke it unless their government had fallen to a coup or something similar. Of course, many critics of Brexit say that's exactly what it is, a populist takeover by the right wing of your party. But so far you're still in charge.

Got all that? It's only going to get more fraught, so if you've got any Valium you might want to pop a couple now. Once you've steeled yourself for the fray, turn to **289**.

200

If this box ☐ is not ticked, tick it now and turn to **101**. Otherwise read on.

If this box ☐ is not ticked, tick it and turn to **14**. Otherwise read on.

To be briefed on the issues you're facing, turn to **225**.

Who has time for briefings? It's time to do something! Turn to **250**.

201

'Forget it, it's good for us,' says Terri. 'Stollard and Rufus will split the soft Brexit vote. And some of them will drift over to back us against Noysom-Reek.'

You can only hope. Turn to **194**.

202

Instantly a frosted glass door slides back and an army of doctors and nurses march out. They whisk Abednego away to a private suite on the top floor of the hospital. While he is given blood tests (well, stuffing tests) and x-rays and CAT scans, you are served a lobster dinner with a very passable bottle of Pouilly-Fumé.

Eventually a senior consultant is called. He goes through Abednego's results while you are treated to a manicure.

He puts his notes aside. 'Hum. Hem. Yes. As I thought.'

'What is it, Doctor?'

'This teddy bear is in perfect health.'

'But what about the bandage?'

He whisks it away. There's a blotch of red ink on Abednego's forehead. The doctor snaps his fingers and a nurse hands him a bottle of stain remover. 'Two drops no more than three times a day.'

He sweeps out as an assistant hands you the bill for Abednego's treatment. And when you see the total, that's when you really need Casualty.

Turn to **368**.

203 ☐

If the box above is empty, put a tick in it and turn to **18.**

If the box was already ticked, turn to **125.**

204

As you approach the day of the vote, campaigning is suspended. The final polls put Remain just ahead. Who knows how much faith you can put in that?

'This is the day of reckoning, Wilkins,' you say. 'Better mix me a stiff G and T.'

Toss two coins. If both come up tails, turn to **429**. Otherwise turn to **221**.

205

'Bill, let's be grown-ups. A policeman doesn't have to dislike someone before he'll arrest them for committing a crime. We don't need to be all fired up with zeal to do our jobs properly. In this country we believe in values like duty and professionalism. So let's not allow the Brexit issue to turn us into a baying mob demanding that politicians bend the knee to dogma. You know where that leads? Look at cults around the world, all run by hypocrites getting rich by gulling their followers. No, I'm here to do a job. I've been tasked to deliver Brexit and that's what I'll do. And I'll do it because I have a creed. Yes I do. But that creed isn't Brexit, it's democracy.'

If you have the keyword UNCTION, turn to **28**. If not turn to **594**.

206

'So what now, Prime Minister?' asks Wilkins as he sets out your afternoon tea. 'Press ahead with Brexit, or not? Oh by the way, jam or clotted cream?'

'Both, obviously, Wilkins. It's a scone. As for Brexit... the people have spoken.'

'Twice now. The will of the people seems a trifle erratic if I may say so. My granny isn't that confused, and half the time she thinks the TV remote is her mobile phone.'

'It is not for us to judge. The public are waiting to be told what they have voted for, and tomorrow I shall tell them.'

⇒ Proceed with Brexit. Turn to **763**

⇒ Announce that you are revoking Article 50 and Britain will stay in the EU. Turn to **255**

207

In the final week, Leave surge forward to take a commanding lead in the polls. Sterling starts to fall against the euro, but not enough to tip the balance. The right-wing press strike a triumphalist note, and it seems the voters are convinced.

'At least it's an end to uncertainty,' you say to the Chancellor as together you watch the results being announced.

'I suppose.' He pats his pockets, forgetting that he gave up smoking twelve years ago. 'A bit like being told that pain in your side is definitely a tumour.'

Look at your Brexit Memo Pad. If you have the keyword EIGER, turn to **92**. If not, turn to **446**.

208

'Well, of course, I've been saying this for years,' Colin Fungale replies in a tone pitched halfway between common sense and self-congratulation. 'With a points system we can have a fairer intake of the immigrants we really need, and we'll be able to turn that tap on and off as circumstances demand.'

Bob Owlbear shakes his head. 'How is it that countries like Canada and Australia that pioneered points systems have had to admit that they don't work? In Australia, take a look at the people who moved there because they were actually offered a job, just like under our current EU system. After five years, only one in a hundred of those immigrants is without a job. Then look at the people admitted under the Australian points system. Fifteen percent of them end up unemployed. It's not very efficient, is it?'

'Anyway, I thought the rallying cry of Brexit was to do away with bureaucracy?' puts in Lucy Tooth. 'The moment you have a points system you have to pump up the bureaucracy to deal with it. Right now EU citizens can come here if they've got a job. So the selection process is outsourced to private enterprise. Your points system will need an army of civil servants – and as Bob just said, points systems haven't even turned out to be fit for purpose. Britain already has a better proportion of skilled immigrants than Australia, France or the USA. The system we have ain't broke.'

The attempt at slang was ill-judged given her polite middle-class accent, but the rest of it wasn't too shambolic. You'd better keep an eye on her in case the next election returns another coalition. Not that you can imagine the Lib Dems ever making that mistake again.

You fast-forward through the rest of the answers. Thomas Tode mentions how points systems are open to lobbying, though even he seems unsure what point he's trying to make there. A man in the audience with a neck full of spidery tattoos is concerned about whether his football team will be able to keep its key members, all of whose names sound like stops on the Stamboul railway. It's the usual stew of misinformation, self-interest and half understood concepts. Not that you're complaining. It's knowing how to stir that stew that keeps you in power.

⇒ Maybe it's time for bed. Turn to **125**

⇒ Skip to the next question. Turn to **405**

209

You're on BBC radio being interviewed by Bill Appleby. Interviewed? Grilled is more like it. Fricasseed, even.

'Now then, Prime Minister,' says Appleby. 'Colin Fungale is saying you point whichever way the wind blows. No conviction, that's the charge. How can you deliver Brexit if you don't believe in it?'

⇒ 'But I do believe in it.' Turn to **816**

⇒ 'What about Fungale's own record?' Turn to **164**

⇒ 'It's politics, Bill, not religion.' Turn to **205**

210

Next let's consider the state of the UK's relationship with the European Union. After the sometimes bitter contest of the divorce settlement, can you stay friends?

If your Goodwill score is 25% or less, turn to **702**.

If Goodwill is 26% to 59%, turn to **144**.

If Goodwill is 60% or more, turn to **848**.

211

'Britain can't actually do any new deals until after Brexit, can we? Remember how my dad blithely announced that a dozen trade agreements would be ready to sign the day after we leave the EU, then two days later he had to be trotted out in front of the cameras to admit that we couldn't even start negotiating? Tragic. The ribbing I took at school for that.'

'There's plenty of room for informal discussions. We can lay the groundwork for future deals.'

'Can you? A bit of a grey area, isn't it? What's the line between formal trade negotiations and a preliminary chat?'

'Wherever that line is, I'm confident we'll be able to talk up the details of treaties without stepping over it.'

'Is that confidence or is it Dunning-Kruger? See, you might think you're within your legal rights but how do you suppose the other 27 states will feel? There's not a lot of goodwill there already, and it only takes one unhappy camper to blow the whole thing up.'

Dunning-Kruger? Is that a German thrash metal band? Better not to ask in case she thinks you're a fuddy-duddy. Turn to **700.**

212

You fight to muster the energy for a last push, but it's been a long road and no one is in a mood to take advice from you now. Your opponents turn your own arguments against you. 'The Prime Minister's heart was never in Brexit,' says Thomas Tode, campaigning for Leave like the strange little lemming of wrangled logic that he is. 'That's why we're in this mess. Because we didn't fully embrace the result of the first referendum.'

You sit down with Ron Beardsley, your chief of staff, to watch the results as they come in. 'The trouble is that the voters have been sold a time machine to return to the promised land of their youth,' he says.

'Whereas in fact it's a euthanasia machine.' You nod. 'I think I saw a science fiction play about that once.'

Toss two coins. If both come up heads, turn to **173**. Otherwise, turn to **127.**

213

The funding you announce is mostly cosmetic, but it's hard for your opponents to criticize any plans to increase NHS spending. They're reduced to saying that it's not enough, which your ministers easily counter by describing it as 'phase one'. All in all, you think you got away with it.

> Record on your Brexit Memo Pad:
> - ❖ -1% Economy – you're having to spend money the Treasury doesn't have.
> - ❖ +2% Popularity – voters applaud any promise of more funding for the NHS.

If you have ticked the keyword DODO, turn to **431**. Otherwise, mark the NHS as complete on your Brexit Memo Pad and then turn to **450**.

214

If you have the keywords CLARION or QUORUM, turn to **264**.

Otherwise turn to **280**.

215

'No, we won't be held over a barrel.'

'Excuse me?' says Alprèves. 'A barrel?'

'As diplomatically as possible, I'd like you tell the Spanish to go and play with their castanets. I'm not giving in to blackmail – not where blameless pensioners are concerned.'

He can see you have a strong case, or at least so it will seem to the media. A day or so later he comes back with new terms. It turns out the Spanish have backed down and agreed to the deal.

> On your Brexit Memo Pad:
> - ❖ +2% Authority – you've shown you can drive a hard bargain.
> - ❖ +5% Economy – the UK economy needs those EU nationals, and it helps not to be handed back a million pensioners from Spain.
> - ❖ Mark Residency Rights as complete.

Now turn to **200**.

216

Your aides are waiting for you when the doors open and the ministers pour out into the sunshine for a buffet lunch.

'What's the verdict, Prime Minister?' your press secretary asks.

'We're putting up the barricades, Lizzie. Crashing out of free movement. Instead we'll have the Aussie-style points system that the Kippers have been banging on about.'

'But...'

'But what?'

'The Kippers are idiots. Points systems cause a bureaucratic snarl-up and they don't even work.'

'Tell me about it. I'm like the CEO of a company whose shareholders are all chimps. Don't repeat that to anyone, obviously.'

Record on your Brexit Memo Pad:

- +10% Authority – the uncompromising approach consolidates your grip on power.
- -5% Economy – the markets see choppy waters ahead.
- -15% Goodwill – your policies aren't making any friends in the EU.
- +10% Popularity – voters welcome the prospect of reduced immigration, even if it's a myth.
- Tick the keyword HEMLOCK
- Mark Immigration as complete.

Then turn to **150.**

217

'Not many people know this,' says McKay, 'but the Common Security and Defence Policy was actually instigated by us and the French. Back in 1998 that was.' He casts an ironic glance at the wreckage of the Victorian sea fort.

'And ever since the EU has been trying to twist it into something it was never meant to be. That's the Commission's thinking to a T.'

'Luckily we've vetoed it,' says McKay, with the look of someone contemplating a narrowly averted catastrophe. 'Can you imagine what a shambles it would be putting our lads in regiments alongside the Belgians, say?'

⇒ Ask him how EU military missions are authorized. Turn to **343**

⇒ Ask him what kinds of mission EU forces undertake. Turn to **632**

⇒ Talk about something else. Turn to **432**

218

Abednego was brought up in a vicarage and you know he wouldn't approve of spending money to jump the queue. Settling in a slippery plastic seat, you wait for an unknown length of time as the same ads play on the screen, the same jingles are repeated, hour after hour, until you almost feel tempted to sing along with them.

'What's the trouble? Tell Dr Happy.'

You do a double take. It's a robot vending machine. Inside it you can see chocolate bars, fizzy drinks, packs of aspirin, and rolls of bandages.

'I'd like to see a real person.'

A child in a nurse's uniform hurries over. 'Here is a person,' says Dr Happy. 'This person works with me.'

The child nods and holds up a syringe. She doesn't seem to speak any English.

'What is the trouble?' repeats the robot.

Abednego looks at the child, then his head turns right around to face you. 'You know what she did?' he says in a horrible voice.

This isn't right. Surely Abednego's never seen *The Exorcist*.

Turn to **368**.

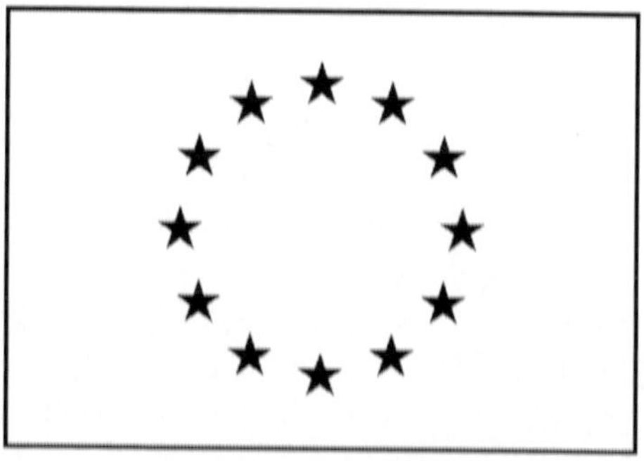

219

'The logical markets to target there are places like India and China. They've got a growing middle class, increasing prosperity, but their service sectors are weak.'

'What kind of services?'

'Banking, accountancy, insurance. Just look at India. They've got a fifth of the world population but they only account for about 2% of insurance premiums. Get in there, the world's your lobster.'

'Oyster.'

She gives you a slow-fuse stare. 'I don't like oysters.'

Turn to **700.**

220

'We have to hope we can work something out,' says Dent. 'Finance has been one of Britain's key strengths for over a hundred years.'

'It's another area where the EU has been a bit slow in achieving full integration,' says Stollard. 'Because of the deep background Dennis just alluded to, we've been the ones really pushing for it.'

'It's nice to hear you both agree on something.'

They look at each like a couple of enemy soldiers who have strayed into No Man's Land by mistake. 'Well, where we probably differ is in how we see it going in future,' says Dent. 'I think our financial institutions will go from strength to strength once unshackled from the stifling regulations of European bureaucrats.'

'Whereas I'm concerned that without financial passports to trade freely with the single market, we stand to lose a lot of business. The Swiss banks in London will all be packing up shop for a start.'

⇒ 'I can't believe the EU will want to lose Britain's financial clout and expertise.' Turn to **118**

⇒ 'What have we got going for us in terms of getting a good deal out of the EU?' Turn to **495**

⇒ 'Let's wrap this up for the day.' Turn to **81**

221

An unexciting campaign ends in a slim but definite majority for Remain, thanks largely to the mobilization of young voters.

Bob Fobber appears on television to talk about how the government will respond.

'As leader of the only major party to oppose Brexit, ' says the reporter, 'you'll naturally be hoping for an upswing in LibDem fortunes as a result of this.'

'This wasn't a general election,' says Fobber, mustering all the statesmanlike gravitas of a travelling salesman. 'It's much more important than that. We were told that 52% was an overwhelming mandate for hard Brexit. Well, what about now the vote has gone the other way?'

It is a good question. Your political future may depend on how you answer it.

Look at your Brexit Memo Pad. If you have the keyword EIGER, turn to **473**. If not, turn to **714**.

222

He returns an owlish blink but says nothing. Saints alive, the man is hard to read.

'So what do you think?'

'An election?'

'That's the idea.'

'And why are you telling me?'

Hard work, this. You give him a big smile – it's that or grit your teeth. 'Because I need your support in the Commons. You know, to get around the Fixed Term Parliament Act.'

'I can propose a vote of no confidence in the government.'

'That would do the trick, I suppose, but I'd prefer a two-thirds majority to wave through a new election.'

You're not sure if he's considering that or not. After a moment he says, 'A vote of no confidence, that's the only deal I'll make.'

Ouch. It's hardly even a deal. You'd need to get a third of your own MPs to vote alongside Labour against your own government.

If you agree to that, turn to **143**. If not, turn to **13.**

223

'I have a suggestion,' says Jean-Jacques Terlamen, the President of the Commission. 'What if the rules restricting a citizen's right to remain in another state were established in a treaty?'

'Could you clarify, please?' asks another of the ministers.

'Well…' Terlamen seems to be thinking on his feet, but he's good at it. 'A citizen can only remain in another state for three months. After that they must be employed, studying, or self-sufficient. The state is not obliged to pay housing benefit or income support to EU citizens who do not have a job.'

You shrug. 'You're not saying anything new. We all know the rules.'

'Yes, but those restrictions are only a matter of case law. They result from rulings by the European Court of Justice. What if they were to be incorporated into the articles of the existing treaties?'

You can see why he's suggesting it. As part of a treaty, the restrictions on free movement would apply as core principles of the EU, not just ad hoc rulings by the ECJ that different states can and do interpret in their own way. What's even more cunning – in debating the new treaty article, there'd be a chance to tighten up the rules. Maybe remove the three-month grace period, for instance. And that could be a neat way to cut the legs out from under secessionist movements like the National Front in France.

They're all waiting for your reply.

⇒ 'How does a new EU treaty make any difference to the UK, seeing as we're leaving?' Turn to **440**

⇒ 'It doesn't go nearly far enough. The mood in Britain is not going to be satisfied with legal tweaks to the rules.' Turn to **115**

224

'Hmm, let's see. Post-Brexit Britain is going to be a very different place, isn't it? Think of immigration. Or the effect on the landscape.'

⇒ 'Landscape? Really?' Turn to **472**

⇒ 'How does international trade have any bearing on the immigration question?' Turn to **63**

⇒ 'That's enough about the threats.' Turn to **700**

225

Who knew quitting the European Union could be so complicated? You have an army of civil servants, ministers, special advisers and consultants who are positively queuing up to give you advice. And even if they fail you, there's always anecdotal evidence and hearsay to fall back on. What do you want to find out about?

- ⇒ For a briefing about Britain's exit payments, turn to **112**
- ⇒ For a discussion about future trade deals with the EU, turn to **651**
- ⇒ To consider the status of EU citizens already living here, turn to **612**
- ⇒ To seek divine inspiration as to the risks and benefits of calling a general election, turn to **69**
- ⇒ To consider security and defence issues, turn to **628**
- ⇒ Who has time for planning? Action is what's needed now: turn to **250**

226

'They ought to be happy that we're staying in the Single Market, then.'

'They might prefer a closer relationship still.'

'Cancel Article 50, you mean? That horse has bolted. If they were to vote against the future relationship, by which I mean the trade deal, we'll still be leaving the EU. So it's a pretty sure bet they'll count their lucky stars.'

And so it turns out. The Commons votes almost unanimously for the deal you have struck with the EU, and although there is some criticism in the Lords you can safely ignore that.

Turn to **806**.

227

Distracted by other issues, you had no choice but to leave the main immigration talks to your deputies. The first you hear as to the outcome is a two-page article by Peter Strewel in the *Tomahawk*. You read it in mounting dismay, barely noticing the marmalade sliding off your morning toast. Ten minutes later you have Strewel on the phone.

'What's the meaning of this? Are you trying to undermine my authority?'

You can almost catch the sweaty reek of his shiftiness over the line. As usual, in a pattern of behaviour that must go back to his top-hatted schooldays, he resorts to bluster at being caught out.

'Mandate of the people,' he says. 'Mere servants, us. No more foreigners shouldering to the front of our chip shop queues. That's the message, loud and clear. Up to us to deliver. Doing my bit, you see.'

'Peter, you have informed the EU that we will not subscribe to any form of free movement. That doesn't strike you as precipitate?'

'Stop them on the beaches and the airports, that sort of thing. Sack me if you want, but 'tis a far, far better thing – '

You hang up.

Record on your Brexit Memo Pad:

- -5% Economy – the markets see choppy waters ahead.
- -15% Goodwill – your negotiators aren't making any friends in the EU.
- +10% Popularity – voters welcome the prospect of reduced immigration, regardless of the cost to the country.
- Tick the keyword HEMLOCK
- Mark Immigration as complete.

Then turn to **580.**

228

'Outside of London and the South East, quite a lot of the UK looks impoverished by the standards of northern Europe. So Wales was allotted £2 billion in the last funding round and the South West got £1.3 billion. Total EU funding for the UK was £9.3 billion.'

'Over seven years. So that's, call it £25 million a week. I can still sell it as the EU tossing us back the small change from our own contributions.'

'It does beg the question of how well we'll redistribute wealth around Britain once the EU funding bodies aren't there to oversee it.'

'Fortunately rhetoric is free, so I can talk up the promise of regeneration programs a bit. And the front page story is that from now on we'll be keeping the cash that was previously being lavished on Polish motorways – stuff that's one rung up the ladder from daylight robbery as far as our supporters are concerned.'

'I'm not sure you can push that too hard,' says the aide. 'Britain is the third largest recipient of research and development funding in the whole EU.'

⇒ 'What sort of things does all this cash get spent on in Cornwall? Turn to **86**

⇒ 'I can't very well tear a strip off research funding while opening a swanky innovation centre. Tell me some really dumb uses of EU funds.' Turn to **236**

229

'It's the old benefits lie,' bellows Bob Owlbear. 'Haven't the wheels fallen off that one yet? I thought you'd parked it where you left the Leave bus. In a junkyard with all the other broken promises, wasn't it?'

'I'm glad you can make light of such a, such a, serious issue, Bob,' says Tode, blinking furiously.

It's no good. Owlbear is like a supertanker. Slow to get started, but once he's moving he'll steamroller a little worm like Tode.

'Why it's a lie is this. EU migrants have no right to claim benefits if they're not in work. The European Court of Justice has been very clear about that. No member state has to pay benefits to an EU citizen if they have no history of work in that country. The EU passport was never a ticket for benefits tourism, whatever the Leave campaign may have said to the contrary.'

'What about them Pakis?' bellows the woman in the audience.

Owlbear looks straight at her. 'That's not the European Union.'

'Well, there ought to be some rules,' she retorts. 'At the moment they're letting just anybody in.'

⇒ See how he answers that Turn to **605**

⇒ Fast-forward to a different question. Turn to **405**

⇒ Switch this off and get some sleep. Turn to **125**

230

It's time you treated yourself to a quick break. You deserve it after all your hard work. So, what holiday did you decide on? France for fine wines and sun-kissed hills? Or will you slum it in Kent and Sussex?

⇒ A wine tasting tour of France. Turn to **735**

⇒ Wine tasting in Southern England. Turn to **140**

231

'Free trade in goods,' says Barkwell.

'Non-agricultural goods,' adds the Chancellor.

'And?'

Barkwell shrugs. 'That's all really.'

⇒ 'What about services?' Turn to **673**

⇒ 'What, they don't even have free trade in agricultural goods?' Turn to **707**

⇒ 'How does Switzerland cope with the EU's rules on free movement?' Turn to **457**

232

It is an ignominious end to the brief, blazing glory of your career. At a critical moment in your country's history you took the rudder, only to founder on the rocks of ingratitude and envy. The helm passes to another and you must take your leave of Number 10, with only the prospect of lucrative book deals and highly-paid after-dinner speeches to console you.

THE END

233

'There are a lot of unknowns. Find me a weather forecaster who'll tell you which days it'll rain even a month from now.'

He's always been cautious. 'Take some wild guesses. General climate, if not specifics.'

'EU members do a lot more trade with each other than with Norway and Iceland. Distance is part of that. Typically if you double the distance you halve the trade, though obviously that applies more to goods than services.'

'All these caveats. I'm not taping the conversation, Alan.'

'All right. If we plug those figures into the UK, allowing for distance and so on, even if we join Norway in EFTA we're going to lose about a quarter of our trade with the EU.'

⇒ 'But we'll have more trade with the rest of the world.' Turn to **117**

⇒ 'All right. Anything else?' Turn to **772**

234

'There's the deal with South Korea,' suggests your chief of staff.

'But, Ron, you don't think it's too lame? I don't want to go in front of the electorate with a plate of crumbs and try claiming it's a whole cake. How much trade do we even do with South Korea?'

'Tricky one, off the top of my head,' he says, sucking at his unlit pipe. 'I know our exports there have trebled over the six years since the EU-Korea free trade agreement was signed. If I had to put a figure on it, probably about a thirtieth the size of our trade with the EU.'

'Ugh. So we need twenty-nine more deals like that.'

He shakes his head. 'We already have a deal with Korea, remember. If we can ratify that deal, we're still just running to stand still.'

⇒ Press ahead with the Korean deal anyway. Turn to **124**

⇒ See if you can steal a march on a deal the EU is already progressing, for example with the US. Turn to **254**

235

It's the gamble of your career, but you've decided to stake everything on campaigning to reverse Brexit.

> On your Brexit Memo Pad:
> ❖ Tick the keyword GAZELLE.

Then turn to **302**.

236

'There was a four metre tall stainless steel dragon statue commissioned in Ebbw Vale as part of an urban renewal project,' she says. 'Locals were up in arms about that.'

'Ha ha, an own goal from the EU Commission there.'

'Not really, Prime Minister. The ERDF – that's the European

Regional Development Fund – invests via the national government and local authorities. So the Ebbw Vale council will have had to make the case that the statue would improve civic pride, tourism, something along those lines. The ERDF doesn't stipulate individual projects like that.'

'Luckily none of that would fit in a headline, whereas EU BLOWS CASH ON STATUE NOBODY WANTED is just what the spin doctor ordered.'

'In that case you could mention the golf course in Morocco.'

⇒ 'What golf course?' Turn to **252**

⇒ 'Another time. We're here.' Turn to **203**

237

'That is a knotty problem,' admits Strewel.

'Is it?' asks the Chancellor. 'Who says the British people were voting against free movement when they ticked that box? The Leave campaign continually held up the Norway model as the most desirable outcome.'

'We also wrote £350 million on the side of a bus,' chortles Strewel. 'Anyway, all that talk of Norway was before Fungale's Nazi posters went up. Hordes of unwashed refugees and terrorists trekking across the green and pleasant land. That's the thrust of the argument now. We have to show we're capable of keeping the beggars out.'

Turn to **17.**

238

You mobilize the full heft of your political machine behind undermining Colin Fungale. Not for nothing those dreary sherry parties at the Union bar, those picnics on a punt with a warm jug of Pimms. While Fungale was selling penny stocks out of his barrow, gormless school-leaver that he was, you were laying the groundwork that will now shore up your power.

Your cronies draw attention to his Nazi-style posters, his tendency to gallivant off on the after-dinner circuit instead of doing the job he's paid for, his hobnobbing with dubious autocrats, his gnat-like attention span, even his barbarously tailored suits.

'It's a brutal business, Ron. Politics.'

He nods. 'It is, Prime Minister.'

You lean back at your desk with a sigh. 'I'd forgotten how much I love it.'

For all your preparation, there's always an element of luck. Toss two coins. If both are tails, turn to **377**. Otherwise turn to **349**.

239

For weeks your ministers are able to talk up the investment program for new hospitals, staff training, and medical research. It may not save any lives or even free up that many beds, but it sounds impressive. And the opposition are reduced to having to grit their teeth and say things like, 'The government's strategy is fine as far as it goes, but it doesn't go far enough.' They might even be right, but nobody is listening.

> Record on your Brexit Memo Pad:
> - ❖ -2% Economy – you're having to spend money the Treasury doesn't have.
> - ❖ +2% Popularity – voters applaud any promise of more funding for the NHS.

If you have ticked the keyword DODO, turn to **431**. Otherwise, mark the NHS as complete on your Brexit Memo Pad and then turn to **450**.

240

You spread your hands helplessly. 'Sorry, Chloe. I'd love to go over all this in detail with you another time, but right now I have an important meeting.

She sets her jaw and marches out. Breathing a sigh of relief, you nod to Wilkins that you're ready for your meeting.

Turn to **507.**

241

Look at your Brexit Memo Pad. If you have any of the keywords CLARION, GAZELLE, SANCTION or TIGHTROPE, turn to **134**.

If you have none of those keywords, turn to **99**.

242

It's less exciting but at least you won't have to decimate the domestic chicken industry just to close one big deal.

'The essential thing is to get the media on side,' your press secretary tells you. 'We don't want them whining about the scale of these deals. "Scraps from the EU table", that sort of nonsense. We need them to see it as a step-by-step process towards building the UK's new role in international trade.'

'That's good, Terri. Show that we're going forward one step at a time. Like those pensioners who make models of the Topkapi Palace out of matchsticks.'

She purses her lips. At times like this it always seems like she's counting to ten. 'Perhaps we can find a metaphor with a higher ardency value,' she says at last.

Look at your Brexit Memo Pad. If your Popularity *and* Authority scores are both 60% or more, turn to **262**. Otherwise turn to **516.**

243

'A wise man once said that a contract is an agreement between friends to make sure they stay friends. It's perfectly possible to do a good deal without the other party losing out. If it wasn't, there'd be no society, no civilization, and no business.' You look around at the journalists, warming to your theme. 'The essence of negotiation, and the reason these talks are so complex, is that we are all striving to find solutions that are in everyone's interest, rather than just trying to grab what we can and run out of there like bank robbers.'

'Good speech?' says Ron Beardsley later. 'Depends on the context. If delivered in the 2008 US presidential campaign, or even the 1997 UK election, then yes. But we're on the other side of the Brexit mirror now. You can't explain things to the electorate with cogent arguments. That just makes them think you're trying to put one over on them.'

You can always rely on Ron to be doggedly honest. Turn to **34.**

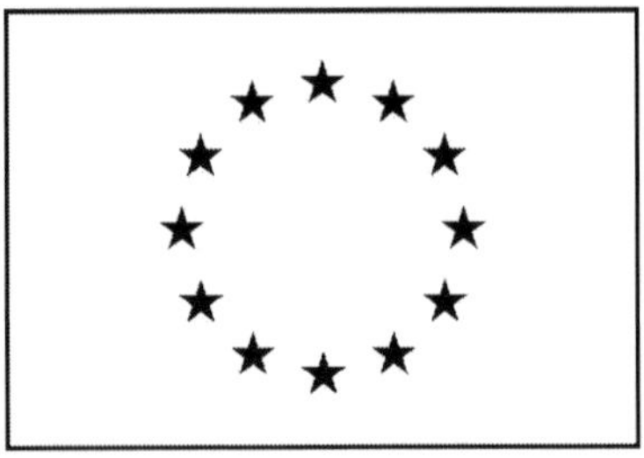

244

'You've won, Prime Minister!'

You don't even look up from your work as Terri Trough comes bouncing into the room. 'Of course I've won. Did you ever imagine the bowling clubs and women's institutes of Britain would rally behind a Remainer with a charisma bypass?'

If you have ticked the keyword YELLOW on your Brexit Memo Pad, turn to **670**. If not, turn to **163**.

245

In such a lacklustre campaign, it's perhaps not surprising that the outcome has come down to the wire. Turnout is low, perhaps reflecting that the public are getting tired of referendums. A pity, as they're so much better an instrument for driving your policies through than old-style Parliamentary democracy is.

Toss a coin. If it comes up heads, turn to **221**. If it comes up tails, turn to **429**.

246

'I'm sorry,' says Terlamen, 'but there's no way to get something like that steamrollered through just for Britain's benefit. Each company has to apply individually. We can't just hand the UK government a stack of blank passports to fill out.'

'Fill *in*,' you snap, terminating the call.

That was just an excuse, of course. France, Germany, Belgium and Ireland all stand to profit from UK-based financial institutions transferring to them. Grudge-harbouring guttersnipe that he is, Terlamen has chosen to favour EU countries' interests over Britain's.

Turn to **857.**

247

Strewel frowns uncertainly. Barkwell puts a hand to his chin and grimaces.

'That's risky, prime minister,' says Dent. 'Very risky. It'd be hard enough to sell to the press, never mind getting the party rank and file to swallow it. Think of the field day Fungale and the kippers would have with a story like that. He'll claim it's a stitch up, and that we're buying time to wriggle out of Brexit altogether.'

'The *Daily Heil* would be right behind him there,' says Strewel,

'The press will be all over you, saying you're trying to subvert the will of the people and all the rest of it. And I should know – it's exactly what I'd be writing for them if I wasn't Foreign Secretary.'

Dent continues. 'And do you want to risk splitting the party, maybe even forcing an election? Admittedly the opposition are in a mess, but on the other hand our majority isn't that robust.'

'And what if they come to their senses and ditch Barry Straggle,' puts in Barkwell. 'Even form a coalition with the Liberal Democrats? They could sweep up if the people see us betraying their sacred right to Brexit.'

You look to Stollard but he is making some notes and studiously avoids catching your eye. What will you say?

⇒ 'We'll worry about how to sell it later, but we really do need to be aiming for single market access along the lines of either Norway or Switzerland.' Turn to **174**

⇒ 'You're right. Perhaps we can get most of the terms we need from a customs union.' Turn to **367**

⇒ 'Let's work on an entirely new and bespoke trade arrangement, then.' Turn to **836**

248

'A lot of use that will be,' she snorts. 'You know that most of our GDP comes from service industries. And even the goods we export – they're not bolts and rivets. They're usually complex components that call for technical expertise, and which may shuttle back and forth between multiple countries as the products are assembled.'

'Clearly we'll need to train our own people. And at the same time we'll develop new supply chains and production lines within Britain. It's the old wartime spirit, Chloe, only without the Blitz this time.'

She gives a yap of bitter laughter. 'Oh, there'll be plenty of devastation, I'm sure of that.'

Enough. It's time for the important meeting of the morning. Turn to **240.**

249

'According to Burke, your duty to voters is to give them your mature judgment and your enlightened conscience. A trust from Providence, he said, which politicians were not to abuse.'

'But the will of the British people is for Brexit.'

'The will of the British people is for toffees, ice cream and sticky buns too. That doesn't mean it's good for them. Isn't your job as a politician to take the time to get fully informed on complex issues on our behalf? Because running the country is a difficult job, after all, and I can't be fully up to speed on all the latest geopolitical developments as well as keeping abreast of orthodontic research.'

'You seem to have very strong views on politics for somebody who claims not to have time for it.'

'I know what I was told during the referendum. That if I voted to leave the EU we'd probably remain in the single market, like Norway. That being out of the EU would give Britain an extra £350 million a week to spend on the NHS – '

'I never made that promise.'

'It was made all the same. Those promises were used to secure my vote.'

'Wait a minute.' You fix him with a sidelong stare. 'Which way did you vote?'

'It's not important.'

Hah, that's rattled him. Turn to **668.**

250 ☐

If the box above is already ticked, turn to **549**. Otherwise read on.

If you need a rest from running the country, this would be a good point to take a break and come back later. Just make a note that you're on the second phase of talks at section **250** so you can find your place again. If you're still raring to go, read on.

So much to do. You're just one person and you've only got two years, so decide which aspect of Brexit you're going to oversee in person. You'll only have time to deal with one of these; when you decide you'll put a tick in the box at the top of this section to remember that you've done so. Your ministers will take care of the rest:

- ⇒ Negotiate the Exit Fee (only if you have the keyword APRICITY) tick the box above and then turn to **720**
- ⇒ Deal with EU Trade Talks (if not already marked as complete on your Brexit Memo Pad) tick the box above and then turn to **688**
- ⇒ Deal with Residency Rights of UK and EU citizens (if not already marked as complete on your Brexit Memo Pad) tick the box above and then turn to **638**
- ⇒ Try to to call a General Election (if not already marked as complete on your Brexit Memo Pad) tick the box above and then turn to **416**
- ⇒ Handle the question of UK/EU cooperation on Security & Defence (if not already marked as complete on your Brexit Memo Pad) tick the box above and then turn to **420**

When you have personally overseen one of the issues there should be a tick in the box above, in which case turn to **549**.

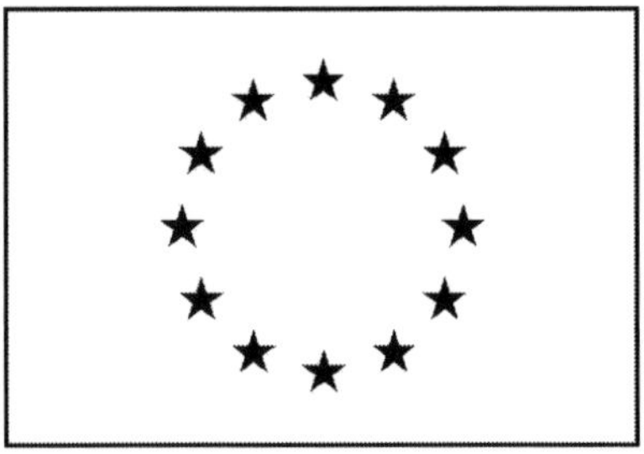

251

'The thing is,' Terri Trough explains, 'you're seen as lacking in firm principles, even unscrupulous, the sort of politician who will do whatever's expedient.'

'You're my press secretary. How did you allow that sort of image to get out?'

'Oh no, Prime Minister, it's perfect. A lot of MPs distrust ideology. You're exactly the kind of leader they want.'

Let's hope she's right.

Toss two coins. If both come up heads, turn to **189**. Otherwise turn to **460**.

252

'About £1 million of EU funds were spent building a luxury golf club in Melilla, a Spanish city on the coast of north Africa. Naturally you had refugees trying to climb the barbed wire to get into EU territory. Which they would have done with or without the golf course, I suppose, but it's hard to justify a swanky nine-hole course as an essential investment.'

'So how did they?'

'The fund commissioner ruled that it promoted sport, helped tourism, and created jobs.'

'For lots of poor Africans with watering cans, sure. Well, we can make hay out of that carefully manicured grass.'

'Except that, like the dragon statue, it wasn't actually the ERDF who allocated those funds. It was a local decision by the Melilla authorities.'

'As John Ford advised, just tweet the myth. Only the *Hypsterion* will bother to fact-check it. The other papers will be happy to blame the EU for throwing money away. They might even find a picture of the Commission President on a golf course.' You turn to the window. 'And here we are.'

Turn to **203**.

253

Scraggle seems hesitant. 'I understand,' you tell him. 'You're behind in the polls. Most of your MPs think they'd do better going into an election with Worzel Gummidge in charge. I'd be worried too.'

'I'd welcome the chance to get our policies across,' he retorts. 'If the public understood the Labour message they wouldn't be so eager to support another five years of Tory austerity.'

'Fighting talk, eh, Barry? Well, you'll never get a better opportunity than an election for getting your message across.'

He nods. 'Very well. We won't stand in the way.'

'You'll vote for a new election?'

'And we'll win.'

You very much doubt that, but if his powers of self-delusion mean you can vote through a snap election, you can take yes for an answer.

Will you first inform the Cabinet of your decision to call an election (turn to **641**) or just announce it at a press conference (turn to **542**)?

254

You fly over to Washington and are then kept waiting a day while President Windrip works on his golf handicap down in Florida. When he finally arrives back at the White House he gives you his usual belligerent scowl, like a pensioner spotting a paper delivery kid on his lawn.

'Great deal. The greatest,' he says slurrily once you've explained that you'd like to accelerate a version of the Transatlantic Trade and Investment Partnership between Britain and the US.

'Oh, absolutely. There are just a few details we'd need some give and take on. For example, we can't throw our health services completely open the US pharmaceutical companies. That would mean effectively privatizing the NHS, and British voters wouldn't stand for it.'

'Huh.'

You notice that he's staring off into a corner of the room but you press on anyway. 'Then there's the matter of allowing private corporations to sue the government. We can't claw our sovereignty back from the European Court of Justice only to hand it over to attribution tribunals. You can see…'

He reaches across his desk and starts playing with a Newton's cradle. *Click clack, click clack*. You decide to take it as a positive sign that he feels so relaxed with you. He wouldn't do that with Chancellor Käsen of Germany in the room, you bet. The special relationship at work.

With a warm glow of mutual respect, you conclude by talking about banking regulations. 'Certainly the current rules are stifling investment, Mr President, and I think you'll agree with me there. But we have to be careful not to go too far the other way. If the regulations are loosened up too far, we'll have all the ingredients for another financial crisis.'

It takes him some time to notice you've finished talking. Fixing you with a puzzled frown, he says simply, 'No.' And then he gets up and leaves.

One of his staff comes over. 'What the President is saying here is TTIP is a take it or leave it type deal,' he says. 'Shall I tell your driver to bring the car round?'

So now what? Going back with no concessions at all will make you look like Windrip's puppet.

⇒ Press ahead with a TTIP-style deal with the US regardless. Turn to **7**

⇒ Give up on this and just repurpose a trade agreement that's already in place between the EU and a third country. Turn to **234**

255

Even the hard-line right of your party greet the news with only token protest. The *Heil* grumbles about U-turns, the *Outrage* mutters darkly about crawling back under the European yoke. But the arguments are muted, the tone grumpy rather than defiant.

'The cause hasn't gone away, of course,' says Dennis Dent as he clears his papers from the Cabinet Room table.

'Of course. You'll be back.'

'Not me. Gardening and an evening pint watching the cricket for me. Leave it to younger men to fight the battle for Britain.'

You feel a little sorry for him. He spent most of his political life campaigning to quit the EU, but you suspect that his time as Brexit Minister has been a sharp shock to those long-held convictions. Over the last two years, the country has been careering towards a terrifying precipice into the unknown, and even the maddest ideological plan does not long survive contact with pitiless reality.

'You think it's not over, then?'

He turns at the door. With his shoulders hunched and his hair in birds-nest disarray he looks like any other disappointed pensioner.

'Fungale will be back. He'll breathe on the embers of UKIP and blow up a firestorm of xenophobia. The British just don't like foreigners, you see. Foreigners make them feel inferior – or just equal, which to a Brit is every bit as bad. The funny thing is, I think we could have made it work. If we'd switched back to a manufacturing economy, turned the country into a tax haven, abolished employment laws, and opted out of foreign aid and human rights, I think we could have made a decent fist of going it alone in the world.'

'I dare say we'll find out sooner or later. This is the era of referendums. What was it Pericles said? The public's moods are like the tantrums of an infant? All that's left for us politicians is to play the indulgent parents.'

'You know, you've reminded me of something I haven't thought about for many, many years. It must have been when I was about three or four years old. I got in a strop with my mother and announced that I was leaving home. Mother got out the loaf and the butter, made me a sandwich, wrapped it up in a handkerchief, and waved me off at the door. I got as far as the end of the road and then came back.'

'Is that some kind of lesson?'

'Wouldn't matter if it was. Nobody learns.'

He shrugs and goes out.

THE END

256

Look at your Brexit Memo Pad.

If you have the keyword MAPLE, turn to **300**.

If not, turn to **45**.

257

You have the distinct impression that the EU negotiators are relieved Britain still wants to be part of the single market.

'It's best for all concerned,' President Terlaman assures you. 'What kind of single market membership are you looking for?'

⇒ The so-called Norway model: a very close relationship within the European Economic Area, giving comprehensive access to trade in goods and services.
Turn to **396**

⇒ The Swiss model: an arrangement outside the EEA with only partial access to trade in goods and services, but with more opt-outs and no contributions to the EU budget.
Turn to **312**

258

Good at thinking on their feet, these graduates. 'You could say that the whole EU funding policy is about rich countries having to support shirkers.'

'I don't think I will say that as it sounds like I'm calling the people of Cornwall shirkers.'

'Oh. No, perhaps not. Well, you could swing it one-eighty – what's the good news about Brexit? A boost to tourism. Or go with all the money frittered away on nonsense projects. The newspapers love to run a story on EU wastefulness.'

⇒ 'All right. What's the tourism slant?' Turn to **562**

⇒ 'Wasting money, yes. The British public lap that up. Let's have some examples.' Turn to **236**

259

The Pugin Room always puts you in mind of a Victorian chapel that's collided head-on with the headquarters of a Zurich bank. Your ministers are waiting for you, along with their army of scrubbed and fresh-faced civil servants. There's Dennis Dent, the Secretary of State for Exiting the EU, looking more than ever like a recently shampooed pug. On either side of him sit Leslie Barkwell, the perpetually astonished International Trade Minister, and the human teddy bear that is Peter Strewel, the Foreign Secretary.

There's a discreet cough behind you. It's the Chancellor, Alan Stollard. One glance at his lugubrious face tells you he's not relishing this meeting any more than you are. Although come to think of it he always looks like that.

'It's time to bite the bullet,' pipes up Dent. 'There's no point in remaining within the single market in any form whatsoever. We can all see that. It'd be just the same situation as we have now, but with no say in how things are run. The people voted overwhelmingly for a good hard Brexit and they won't stand for it.'

For a moment it looks as though he's going to bang his fist on the table, but instead he takes a decisive gulp of coffee.

'The *à la carte* option,' says Stollard, taking his seat. 'It raises a lot of questions. What sort of model are we aiming for? Something like Singapore? Canada? A completely bespoke free trade agreement of our own?'

'If you ask me,' says Barkwell, 'we could do a lot worse than just walk away. Tell the EU we don't have time to get tangled up in their blasted bureaucratic bunting. We just go straight to World Trade Organization rules and get down to business.'

In the middle of the long table are bowls of fruit, trays of sandwiches, and pots of hot coffee. Thank goodness for the coffee. The prospect of spending several hours in one room with this lot is already making you yawn.

⇒ 'Let's talk about the WTO.' Turn to **826**

⇒ 'Some sort of free trade agreement with the EU sounds like the way forward.' Turn to **56**

260

'Here's a big opportunity. A lot of the obstacles to a trade deal with the United States have been down to inconvenient EU regulations on things like food safety, genetically modified crops, and the cost-effectiveness of pharmaceuticals. If we can loosen up in those areas it should be possible to do a deal across the Pond.'

'Not bad. Obviously we'll need to pass all that through the spin doctors. Make it more about cutting red tape, abolishing European bureaucracy, that kind of thing.'

'Perception is reality, that's what our Media Studies teacher says. Still, it all looked a bit rosier before…'

'Before what?'

'Before President Windrip stole the election.'

'I'm sure he's not as bad as he's been painted. He likes cats, I'm told.'

Her mouth twitches. A nervous tic? It looked more like a smirk. 'The hitch is, we need a free trade deal – and ideally one including financial services – but he's protectionist, isn't he. Which makes it a bit iffy, unless we apply to join the USA.'

'You mean become the fifty-first state? You must be joking, young lady. Why would regain our sovereign status only to bind ourselves in thrall to another union?'

'Hey. I'm fifteen. I'm studying to go to university. What do I care about the Suez crisis and Britain's imperial past? Was up to me, we wouldn't be leaving the EU in the first place.'

Turn to **700.**

261

The next round serves to knock out Amelia Dimple. She sinks back into obscurity with the same perplexed expression with which she announced her challenge. Her concession speech is like watching Stan Laurel in drag.

Your press secretary brings bad news. 'Alan Stollard is giving his support to Tiffany Rufus. So that's pretty solidly sewn up the moderate wing.'

'Moderates? Is that what we're calling traitors now?'

'Perfect. Go with that, Prime Minister. Exactly that tone. You've got to out-Kipper Colin Fungale now.'

Ron Beardsley disagrees. 'A lot of the Parliamentary party regard Fungale as not far short of a Nazi. Can't stop himself having a crack at "the Jewish lobby" and all that racist claptrap. I think the sweet spot is to come down strongly for Brexit, but make enough progressive European noises to show you're not a crackpot.'

Which is it to be?

⇒ Try to outdo Fungale's bombastic rabble-rousing. Turn to **552**

⇒ Aim to hold the centre ground as a level-headed Brexit supporter. Turn to **353**

262

The press buy into the story. They focus on the pigheadedness of the EU in trying to prevent Britain from holding trade talks with third countries up until Brexit. Headlines you decide are worth preserving in your scrapbook include BABY STEPS TO A BOOMING ECONOMY and SLOW BUT SURE COURSE TO A BRIGHT BREXIT FUTURE.

On your Brexit Memo Pad:

- -5% Goodwill – the EU disapprove of the UK talking up trade deals while still a member.
- +5% Popularity – voters see you as having a sure hand on the tiller.
- Mark International Trade Deals as complete.

Then turn to **666**.

263

An hour later, invigorated by a shower, you're sipping strong black coffee in the main conference room when Ron Beardsley bustles in.

He just manages to get to the table with the overstuffed card folders and floppy leather briefcase he has wedged under his arm. Papers flutter across the polished walnut veneer. Ron pulls them together in a vaguely tidy heap and looks around the room.

'Am I early?'

'I wanted us to have a chat before the meeting. A bit of background on this bill the EU wants us to pay. Our divorce settlement.'

He tugs a thick document out of the pile. Always exactly the document needed. It's quite a magic trick, like finding the right card in a shuffled deck. Unless he's bluffing and really all of this information is in his head. He barely needs to glance at the document, anyway.

'There are three components to the amount the EU expects from Britain, prime minister – '

'Wait a moment. How much are we talking about?'

'Depends who you talk to. Possibly in the region of €60 billion.'

'Seems rather steep.'

'The member states would largely agree with you there. Other calculations produce a much lower figure, but the Commission has come in hard. There might be some leeway.'

'All right. Break it down for me.'

'Well, the three components are the EU overspend, ongoing projects, and pensions.'

⇒ 'The overspend – what's that?' Turn to **6**

⇒ 'Tell me about funding for ongoing projects.' Turn to **316**

⇒ 'Pensions sound like a problem that won't go away soon.' Turn to **795**

264

You're able to agree a legal framework whereby the data protection rules set by the European Court of Justice automatically update UK law.

'Naturally, British law remains sovereign,' you tell the other heads of state at the next European Council meeting. 'We reserve the right at any time to opt out of the ECJ's rulings.'

'As we reserve the right, should that happen,' says Chancellor Käsen of Germany with a lopsided smile, 'to exclude Britain from the Schengen Information System.'

'But until then,' puts in President Mac hastily, 'everything can proceed as before.'

Now turn to **822.**

265

For years EU nationals have come to live, work and study in Britain, just as British citizens have moved to Europe to work or – more often – enjoy their retirement. For better or worse, the future of those people has now been decided. History will judge the outcome.

Turn to **666**.

266

It's all the most absurd sabre-rattling, of course, but the public lap this stuff up. And that's a useful distraction in these difficult times.

> On your Brexit Memo Pad:
> - +2% Popularity – you stop just short of ending your speech with a rousing chorus of "Land of Hope & Glory".
> - Get the keyword IRIS.

Then turn to **175.**

267

'Would you rather eat a pasty, Prime Minister, or a scone with clotted cream?'

'Is this one of those internet quizzes that tell you what kind of person you are deep down?'

'No, I meant after you open the innovation centre. You'll have to be photographed doing something typically Cornish.'

You gaze out of the train window. Only a hundred yards away waves roar in off the Atlantic, crash into tall outcrops of rock, and are blasted into spume that sinks back into the grey water. It's a stirring stretch of track. Too bad Penzance is at the end of it.

'Something typically Cornish...' you muse to yourself. 'Tin mining? Smuggling? Surfing?'

'Can you surf?' says the aide with sudden interest.

'No. It'll have to be the bloody pasty. Just don't get me a runny one. I don't want to be on the front pages with gravy all over my chin.'

The aide makes a note on her phone. 'The important thing is to give a positive statement about Cornwall's future. International, technological, business focused, that kind of thing. And watch out for questions about development funding.'

⇒ 'What kind of questions?' Turn to **191**

⇒ 'What's this innovation centre?' Turn to **640**

268

You're coming up to the next round of voting, and you're starting to wonder if your strategy of trying to outdo Fungale's Brexit zeal can possibly pay off. This is the moment of truth.

Look at your Brexit Memo Pad. If your Authority *and* your Popularity are both 66% or more, turn to **488**. Otherwise turn to **377**.

269

Look at your Brexit Memo Pad. If you have the keyword REGENT *and* EU Trade Talks are not marked as complete, turn to **333.**

Otherwise turn to **666**.

270

He looks at you darkly. 'Huh. Well, I appreciate your honesty at least. Still clinging to the shattered mast of the good ship Remain, are you?'

'Not necessarily. But we have to be realistic. There are a lot more ways to make a pig's ear out of Brexit than to make a silk purse. My job is to get the best deal for Britain, and I don't think it helps anyone if I pretend that's going to be easy.'

'I see. Well, you have your meeting to get on with so I won't take up any more of your time.'

> On your Brexit Memo Pad:
> ❖ +1% Authority – he may not agree with you, but he's impressed.

Turn to **507.**

271

The Whips don't have good news. Many of the backbenchers are unhappy that you've been treating the EU with kid gloves. Are you a pushover? A closet Remainer? Either way, there's a dissenting element who aren't eager to reinforce your leadership.

'A three-line whip,' you say. It's half a question.

'That's all we can do,' ventures one of the Whips.

'They'll toe the line if they know what's good for them,' growls another.

Another nods. 'The proof of the pudding – '

'Puddings! Don't be soft, man.' You glare at him. 'If you have to make an analogy, gird your loins for battle. No one knows if a shield is strong or brittle until it's struck.'

Look at your Brexit Memo Pad. If your Authority is 61% or more, turn to **543**. Otherwise turn to **407**.

272

'We can't even do them then. We're in a customs union with the EU, so we're bound to the trade agreements negotiated by the European Commission.'

'Er...'

Damn, he's right.

'The upside, of course,' he goes on, warming to his theme, 'is that we get the benefit of the EU's negotiating team. So you can sit back with a pina colada, Prime Minister. Keep bees if you like. The European Commission will do all the work on our behalf.'

As you leave the studio you ask your press secretary how it went, but she can't even meet your eye. Turn to **377**.

273

You're guided to a distant wing of the building where only half the lights are working. Walking down a long corridor, you pass laboratories and wards filled with state of the art equipment, all of it gathering dust. Abednego has nothing to say, but his silence is eloquent.

In the furthest lab you encounter an old scientist in a white coat. He's dripping liquid into Petri dishes and labelling them.

'Have I taken a wrong turn somewhere?'

He looks up. 'Depends what you were looking for. This is the Innovative Medicines Initiative. What's left of it.'

'What is it – or was it?'

'It's the old EU program to fund research into the latest medical developments. We've got departments for stem cell therapies, new antibiotics, cancer treatments, and work on autoimmune diseases.'

'Well, I don't know what's wrong with my friend,' you say, holding up Abednego, 'but it sounds like we've come to the right place.'

He shakes his head. 'It's all closed down since Brexit. No EU funds, you see.'

⇒ 'That's ridiculous. Surely private enterprise would foot the bill?' Turn to **95**

⇒ 'Are you telling me the UK government didn't take over funding?' Turn to **838**

274

As the first referendum was an open vote, you naturally have to offer the same freedom to your ministers now. To your surprise, Peter Strewel stays out of the campaign. 'I think the public would appreciate a holiday from my voice,' he says with a self-satisfied smirk to the cameras. The truth is surely that there's no possible gain for him in it this time. A seat in Cabinet within grasping distance of Number 10 was his goal all along, and now he has that.

The big guns of Remain are either out of Parliament now or else reluctant to air their views in case another win for Leave scuppers their careers for good. The notable exceptions are Bill Strait, who in his seventies and as Father of the House doesn't give a fig for public opinion, and Lord Leonine, who is even older and more obdurate.

'The problem with superannuated politicians,' you remark to Wilkins as he brings in your late-night cocoa, 'is that there's nothing you can promise them. Nothing you can threaten them with.'

'What about your own opinions, Prime Minister? Will you be joining the campaign?'

⇒ 'Of course, I shall be leading the fight to Remain.'
Turn to **64**

⇒ 'I intend to give my support to the Leave campaign.'
Turn to **841**

⇒ 'Good lord, no. I'm sitting this one out.' Turn to **293**

275

It has now been a full year since you gave formal notice to the EU of Britain's intention to leave.

Turn to **666** and tick one of the boxes there before doing anything else.

276

'The Canadians started negotiating their deal in 2007 and it was concluded in 2016,' says Strewel as if recalling the dates of the Punic Wars.

'But – ' puts in Stollard.

You turn to him. 'But we'd be able to fast-track it, you think?'

'Um… Not really, Prime Minister. I was about to say that it hasn't yet been signed into law. Most of it will take effect later this year.'

'Still, we're a bigger economy and closer to Europe. I can't believe any deal we make is going to drag on for ten years.'

He nods. 'We're starting with the advantage of already having the same regulations in place as the rest of the EU, which helps, but agreeing these massive deals calls for large, skilled, and highly committed negotiating teams.'

'Really, I'm getting sick of this defeatist talk,' protests Barkwell. 'We're going to hire lots of brilliant negotiators.'

'I'm sure, but it takes time. More importantly, there have to be two negotiating teams and the EU won't be in any great hurry to recruit theirs.'

'Just as well,' chuckles Strewel, 'since they'll probably be after hiring the same people. Those Kiwis are bloody good at the whole deal-making lark, I hear.'

⇒ 'If it's going to take years, we'll need some kind of transitional deal.' Turn to **790**

⇒ 'Let's look at the broad strokes of a free trade deal we might strike with the EU.' Turn to **137**

277

'It's not the worst deal we might have struck,' says the Chancellor when you tell him the outline of the deal. 'We'll have minimal influence over the regulations we have to abide by, of course.'

'The crucial distinction, Alan, is that we don't *have* to abide by them. British law will track the rulings of the European Court, but with the option to go its own way.'

'If we ever do opt out, that could cut off our remaining access to the single market.'

'The point is we can sell it to the voters as sovereignty regained. Better to rule in an EFTA limbo than get booted out of office by voters who would never be happy with either the economic inferno of a hard Brexit or the bovine compromise involved in the Norway model.'

On your Brexit Memo Pad:

- ❖ -5% Economy – Britain's service industries will find it harder to trade with Europe.
- ❖ -2% Goodwill – the EU are already sick of the complexity of dealing with the Swiss under similar terms.
- ❖ -5% Popularity – the voters are dimly resentful that all the fireworks of Brexit have ended in the damp squib of thoughtful diplomacy.
- ❖ Tick the keyword CLARION
- ❖ Mark EU Trade Talks as complete.

Then turn to **666.**

278

You'd forgotten Terri's nephew, who's here on sufferance because she and Ron thought a kid-to-work day would humanize your public image. He sighs and shuffles out into the corridor without taking his eyes off his phone.

'Sorry about that,' says Terri. 'I forgot you don't like kids.'

'Well, I couldn't eat a whole one. Noysom-Reek has dozens, I suppose, being Catholic.'

'Another point in his favour,' says Ron despondently. 'Family values.'

'Maybe there's some scandal we can dig up,' suggests Terri.

Ron shakes his head. 'I think we need to play on his lack of experience.'

'Alternatively I could beat him at his own game. Show the members I can be as rabid a Brexiteer as the best of them.'

What strategy are you going to focus on?

⇒ Look for dirty secrets your opponent would like to keep hidden. Turn to **856**

⇒ Contrast your track record with his inexperience. Turn to **717**

⇒ Claim the ultra-Brexit ground by outdoing him on anti-EU rhetoric. Turn to **499**

279

'As you know,' says Franjeboom, 'there are existing frameworks that allow countries such as Iceland and Norway to participate in our Common Security and Defence Policy.'

You're shaking your head as he speaks. 'Off-the-peg agreements? Those won't do for Britain. We'd be tied to missions over which we didn't have as much influence as EU member states did.'

'I think that's why they call it Brexit.'

'Britain is on the UN Security Council. We possess nuclear capability – '

'Not independently of the US, however. Unlike France.'

You wave that aside. 'And we still have the best-trained armed forces in Europe. So I think you'll find the other EU states will be very keen to do a special deal.'

'Well, we'll see.' Not for the first time, you find yourself wondering if he plays poker.

Look at your Brexit Memo Pad. If your Goodwill score is 66% or more, turn to **130**. Otherwise turn to **184**.

280

It proves impossible to reach an agreement that would allow Britain full access to EU crime databases. At least you're able to spin it to the voters as a firm stance against the high-handed demands of the EU27.

> Record on your Brexit Memo Pad:
> - ❖ -2% Goodwill – the EU are fully aware that with Britain out of SIS II, everyone is less safe.
> - ❖ +3% Popularity – the public buy into the frankly preposterous idea of SIS II as a leaky sieve of badly handled data.

Turn to **822.**

281

'There's the question of EU nationals already living here,' the Home Secretary reminds you.

'And our citizens living over there. I know, but that's pretty much dealt with under the agreement we've made about free movement.'

She makes a thoughtful gesture as if brushing invisible cobwebs out of the air. 'Sort of. Under the free movement "emulator" we're setting up after Brexit, sure, most of those EU nationals are eligible to stay. But there are still about a hundred thousand of them who aren't either working, studying, or financially self-sufficient. Strictly speaking we could round them up and take them to the airport tomorrow.'

'Save them for a rainy day,' you tell her. 'Next time UKIP are shouting about immigration, we'll announce a tightening up of rules and we can boot out a bunch of freeloaders. The papers will love it.'

'That way we end up looking tough, and the EU can't object because it's within the terms they've signed up to. Masterful, Prime Minister.'

'Don't suck up, Tiffany. I can't abide an upsucker.'

> On your Brexit Memo Pad:
> - ❖ +1% Authority – you can count on the Home Secretary to spread an admiring word through the ranks.
> - ❖ +1% Popularity – having some immigrants to deport whenever you need to is political capital in the bank.

Now turn to **150.**

282

As you squirt a good dollop of maple syrup onto the pancakes, you muse on Canada's trade arrangements. Is there a guide there to Britain's post-Brexit position?

The upside is that by dropping out of the single market, Britain would have no obligation to accept the free movement of people. That's the issue that most sticks in the craw of the diehard Brexiters, though in fact it's inevitable that an ageing country like Britain desperately needs immigrants, and those immigrants bring value to the economy.

That aside, there are other advantages to something like the Canada model. A bespoke free trade agreement would be less of a blow than crashing out to raw WTO rules. But there's probably no future in actually joining Canada and Mexico in the North American Free Trade Agreement. For one thing, America is a lot further away than Europe and distance has a major drop-off effect on trade. On top of that, NAFTA's focus is more on goods than services, which is no use to Britain.

Turn to **747.**

283

You're finding it hard to muster the support you need. Even some MPs who supported the Remain cause are seen huddled over G&Ts with Colin Fungale and his cohorts. It must stick in their craw to deal with the likes of him, but they know how strong his grassroots support is.

'He's taking over, Wilkins. It's like *Invasion of the Body Snatchers*. UKIP is taking control of the Conservative party.'

'If asked to express a preference, Prime Minister, I would choose the 1950s black and white version.'

'You think you're talking about movies, Wilkins, but you could just as well be describing Fungale's vision of Britain.'

Toss a coin. Yes, it's come to that. If you get heads, turn to **377**. If you get tails, turn to **349**.

284

'Currently, all EU citizens are permanent residents, in effect. They can stay as long as they like, and don't have to fill in any forms to do so. We can extradite individuals if we want, or prevent anyone from entering. I'm talking about criminals or terrorists, but actually that applies to pretty much anyone the Home Secretary doesn't want here, as long as she can come up with a convincing enough reason.'

⇒ 'Can an EU national apply for UK residency?'
Turn to **295**

⇒ 'Thank you, that tells me what I needed to know.'
Turn to **666**

285

The only result of that is to rally Stollard's supporters to knock you out in the next round. Turn to **377**.

286

The next thorn in your side is the question of continued access to EU security databases, in particular the second generation Schengen Information System.

'Surely this is straightforward?' you tell Willy Franjeboom over one of many phone calls. 'Police and security forces on both sides need to be open and timely with regard to details about criminals, terrorist suspects and fugitives.'

'They do indeed,' he agrees, 'but to access EU databases you will need to abide by our data protection laws. You'll recall that the European Court of Justice struck down the "safe harbour" agreement between the US and Europe.'

'You can't seriously be suggesting that Britain's own data protection rules are not at least as good as anywhere in the EU.'

'Suppose you access sensitive information and share it with President Windrip. And then he blurts it out to Russian diplomats, or uses it to target the families of terror suspects? No, if you wish to keep SIS II you must submit to ECJ rulings.'

Oh god, the spectre of sovereignty again. Of course, the reality is that all states make trade-offs with their sovereignty all the time. But the referendum has established a new level of knee-jerk popular involvement, and the public's attention span is too short to explain the intricacies of a complex world.

⇒ 'Fine, we don't need access to EU security databases in order to fight crime and terrorism.' Turn to **822**

⇒ 'Close cooperation is essential to people's safety. Let's find a way for Britain to remain within SIS II.'
Turn to **360**

287

No one is convinced. You are discredited, denounced by both the moderate and ultra wings of the Party. Turn to **377**.

288

'Let's not characterize these talks as a severance deal, monsieur. We don't want a divorce, simply a more open relationship. Now, as Article 50 itself states, any negotiations we have about remaining financial obligations must take account of the framework of Britain's future relationship with the European Union. There are many factors that could come into play there – cooperation on defence, the final structure of the new relationship, UK investment in individual states...'

The last is a broad hint that you could get some of the more impoverished countries on board with the promise of handouts. Britain has experience in that, and he knows it.

'So you are proposing...?'

'That the exit fee will be negotiated alongside other talks so that we can converge on a figure that reflects our degree of access to the single market post-2019.'

You can almost hear him grit his teeth. He weighs it up for a few hours, no doubt having stormy words with his advisory team, but the next day he returns to the table to concede that the exit fee discussions will happen in parallel with other talks.

> On your Brexit Memo Pad:
> - ❖ -5% Goodwill – many of the member states resent you getting your own way so early in the talks.
> - ❖ Tick the keyword APRICITY

Then turn to **150.**

289

Hold on. Maybe you've never seen a book like this before? The idea is that you make choices and those choices will direct you on a path through the book.

What are you trying to do? The clue is in the title.

You'll be keeping track of how you're doing on the Brexit Memo Pad, which is at the back of this book. Listed on the Brexit Memo Pad are four metrics that you really want to keep an eye on:

Authority is your control of your own Parliamentary party.

Economy measures the financial health of the country.

Goodwill is how well-disposed the other EU members are towards Britain.

Popularity is what the voting public think of how you're doing.

Those are all measured as percentages, and they all begin at 52%. Contrary to the belief of sports coaches and management gurus, they can't go higher than 100%. Nor can they go below 0%. For example, if you're awarded a bonus of +15 to your Popularity when its score is already at 90%, you should just increase it to 100%.

You'll be keeping notes on the Brexit Memo Pad and also in the book itself, so have a pencil or pen handy.

A very few events will be completely outside your control, and for those you'll be asked to toss a coin. Or you could cheat. Who's going to know? And after all, it is politics.

Now turn to **669**.

290

Support for you and Rufus is neck and neck. This next round of voting will be crucial. As you wait to hear the results, what is your private opinion of your Home Secretary?

⇒ A worthy adversary. Turn to **39**

⇒ A mere distraction before the main event. Turn to **377**

291

Look at your Brexit Memo Pad.

If International Trade Deals are marked as complete, turn to **309**.

If International Trade Deals have not been completed, turn to **186.**

292

You and Lord Elmstead are going over the results you commissioned from his polling company.

'Look at those figures. President Spetsnaz would kill for approval ratings like mine. Quite literally, in fact.'

'You're the envy of the world's leaders,' Elmstead agrees. 'And that includes the dictators who get to set their own popularity at gunpoint. And all without a Twitter account, too.'

Admittedly you've sometimes had to buy these approval ratings at the cost of doing what's right, by pandering to the tabloids and deliberately antagonizing the EU for rabble-rousing effect. But it's put you in an unassailable position. Just let the party try to ditch you now – you're their best chance of winning the next election. And you've done it through the most turbulent times Britain has faced in the last fifty years.

Anything might happen. The economy could collapse. The wind of populism you've sown could become a whirlwind that sweeps the whole of the old order away. Britain could circle the drain for decades, slowly swirling off into irrelevance. But for now, at least, you can bask in the power of the polls.

THE END

293

The new referendum will be a test of your own policies in dealing with the EU. Has the nation become entrenched in an us-versus-them mentality, ready to pull up the drawbridge? Or are people starting to regret turning their backs on Britain's biggest trading partner and ally?

What's your take on it?

⇒ Buyer's remorse is starting to kick in. Turn to **388**

⇒ People are sticking to their guns. Turn to **766**

294

You can't hope to hammer out every clause in a new free trade agreement at one conference. The negotiations could take years. That's why your focus is on laying the broad strokes.

'Why so sad, so serious?' you ask the Chancellor when you get a chance to go over the draft heads of agreement with him.

'I fear it means goodbye to fine wines and the ingredients of an exotic meal. We'll soon be back to boiled cabbage and warm beer.'

'Nonsense. The EU want this deal as much as we do.'

He peers at you lugubriously over the top of his spectacles. 'The EU might, but what is that as an entity? There are twenty-seven separate states, and every one of them gets a veto of every point. This – ' he waves the papers ' – might not be resolved in our lifetimes.'

On your Brexit Memo Pad:

- ❖ +5% Authority – the rest of the party are not as sceptical as the Chancellor.
- ❖ -10% Economy – it's a case of taking the least-worst hit for leaving the single market.
- ❖ -5% Goodwill – most of the EU members regard this bespoke agreement as Britain yet again demanding privileged treatment.
- ❖ Mark EU Trade Talks as complete.

Then turn to **666.**

295

'Certainly they could. Not many bothered before because it wasn't necessary. As EU citizens they weren't technically immigrants, any more than a Californian moving to Utah is an immigrant.'

'Actually the cultural gulf there sounds far deeper than between a Pole and an Englishman.'

'Quite. Anyway, there's been an upsurge in applications from EU citizens since the referendum, as you'd expect.'

You consider your next question.

⇒ 'What happens to EU citizens in Britain if we leave without a deal being struck on residency rights?' Turn to **465**

⇒ 'What are the criteria for residence?' Turn to **438**

⇒ 'All right, I think I've heard all I need.' Turn to **666**

296

'The EDA consists of every EU state except Denmark.'

'Why is that?'

'They had a sort of mini-referendum on it,' says McKay. 'More than one, I think. They didn't go the whole Brexit but they opted out on a bunch of things. Defence, policing, citizenship rights, the euro. You name it. Rejected full-on EU rules by 53% to 47%, I heard.'

'And yet they're still in the EU. Maybe that's the referendum we should have had here.'

'Spilt milk,' says McKay with commendable matter-of-factness. 'Anyhow, Britain vetoed the proposal to set up a single Europe-wide military HQ in Brussels. That was in 2001. So the EDA operates as a sort of sticky label you can put over the national colours when deploying troops. Like the UN, only even less useful.'

⇒ 'And who pays for it? Turn to **113**

⇒ 'What do you think about an EU army?' Turn to **474**

⇒ 'Let me ask you something else.' Turn to **432**

297

The International Trade Minister returns from a trip to the Philippines declaring the shared values of the British government and President Pandillero. Unfortunately Pandillero is on record as claiming to have personally gunned down suspected drug dealers, and his human rights record is barely more liberal than Stalin's. UKIP supporters are delighted by the prospect of vigilante law coming to Britain but everybody else is appalled.

On top of that, the minister overreaches himself by announcing that a UK-Philippines free trade agreement has been substantially worked out and only requires signatures. A few days later he is grilled about it on *News Talk* and forced to admit that detailed negotiations ahead of Brexit would be in breach of international treaty law. Overall, it is a debacle wrapped in a fiasco inside a cock-up, as Churchill would surely have said.

On your Brexit Memo Pad:

- ❖ -5% Authority – you're seen to have no control of your ministers.
- ❖ -5% Economy – the money markets are losing confidence in Britain.
- ❖ -5% Goodwill – the EU disapprove of the UK talking up trade deals while still a member, even when those deals are going nowhere.
- ❖ -5% Popularity – voters are beginning to doubt that Brexit is worth the social and economic cost.
- ❖ Mark International Trade Deals as complete.

Then turn to **385**.

298

Watching the recording of the debate later, you realize that your reply to Mugglemore's point could have been made more smoothly. You gave way to your tendency to lecture. It's too late in the campaign to be emphasizing detail, and the voters are already coming round to the idea that the first result was ill-judged. All you need now is to give them permission to tweak that result a little.

Still, it's one response to one question in a much bigger debate. On the night of the referendum, you sit back with a glass of wine and wait for the results to come in.

Toss two coins. If both come up heads, turn to **173**. Otherwise, turn to **403.**

299

The Chancellor sighs. 'It's all about compliance again. To retain Mifid equivalence, Britain has to show that we're staying in line with EU regulations. But we'd have no say in those regulations – none at all, as these are set at the EU level, not internationally.'

'So there'd need to be regular reviews, to ensure we remain in line with EU laws?'

'And the inevitable delay in signing off on those. But that's not the worst of it. Mifid hasn't been designed as a perfect substitute for financial passports, remember. It's just intended to oil the wheels with third parties. So it covers investment banking, but completely ignores whole areas of vital importance to the City – insurance, asset management, lending, and so forth.'

'I'm sure it's not as sorry a picture as you're painting it, Alan,' mutters Dent.

'How can I put it? You know when you're flying out to your cottage in Provence, and it's bank holiday weekend and it seems like everybody had the same idea? There's an orderly queue that says "EU Passport Holders". Well, we're not in that queue any more. Mifid means, "Sorry, sir, you have to dive into that pack of world travellers and good luck fighting your way to the front." So it's time to sharpen our elbows.'

Turn to **66.**

300

If you have the keyword JEWEL and this box ☐ is not ticked, tick it now and turn to **43**. Otherwise read on.

If you have the keyword IRIS and this box ☐ is not ticked, tick it now and turn to **256**. Otherwise read on.

If you have the keyword VERTIGO, and this box ☐ is not ticked, tick it now and turn to **514**. Otherwise read on.

To be briefed on the issues you're facing, turn to **325**.

Briefings are a distraction – and you don't need distraction, you need action! Turn to **469**.

301

Franjeboom looks disappointed. 'I would have thought, for the mutual security of all our peoples – '

'Come now. The defence of Europe is already handled by NATO. Brexit won't have any effect on that; Britain will stay fully involved. The fact is that, measured against NATO, any EU-level military missions are barely above the level of the Peace Corps. Instead of talking about an EU army, you'd do better to encourage other NATO members to meet their spending commitment.'

> Record on your Brexit Memo Pad:
> - +4% Authority – you've strongly reaffirmed Britain's status as a major independent military force and a member of the UN Security Council.
> - -3% Goodwill – the EU have been put in their place, and they don't like it.
> - Mark Security & Defence as complete.

Turn to **269.**

302

Look at the Brexit Memo Pad.

If your Economy score is 52% or more, turn to **819.**

If your Economy score is 39% or less, turn to **478.**

Otherwise, if it's between the two, turn to **361.**

303

Dent ticks off points on his fingers. 'We're already in sync with the EU on trade regulations, standards and so forth – that's a head start most countries don't have. We won't have to contribute to the EU budget unless we want to. And once outside the single market we've no obligation to accept freedom of movement, which seems to have become the big fear of the age.'

'The big fear of the aged, more like,' mutters the Chancellor.

'Also it's quite an easy matter to arrange tariff-free trade,' Dent goes on, glaring at him like an angry bird. 'So I don't think our negotiating teams will be over-stretched.'

The Chancellor clearly doesn't share his optimism. 'What are the downsides, Alan?' you ask.

'Well, free trade agreements are traditionally not so hot on freeing up trade in services. Restricting freedom of movement could present problems there too. We have to consider behind-the-border trade barriers – product quotas, standards, that sort of thing. Obviously those are less of an issue in Britain's case because currently our regulations are harmonized with the EU's as Dennis just said, but over time there'll be drift. And then there are all the speed bumps that are inevitably going to get in the way of closing a deal.'

'To be quite honest I think you're exaggerating the problems,' says Dent tetchily.

You step in before they start a stand-up row:

⇒ 'What have we got going for us in terms of getting a good deal?' Turn to **495**

⇒ 'What might get in the way of a deal?' Turn to **616**

⇒ 'Why could freedom of movement pose a problem for services?' Turn to **477**

⇒ 'Wait – did you imply we might actually *choose* to pay into the EU budget?' Turn to **608**

304

In a horrifying upset, the seat goes to Labour by a landslide. Accusing glances are cast in your direction from the back benches.

'So how come it's my fault?' you say, venting your feelings to your chief of staff. 'Maybe the public are just starting think Brexit wasn't such a scintillating idea.'

He gives you a lugubrious look which, thanks to his abundant beard, reminds you of a crow peering out of a thicket. 'Don't let anyone hear you say that, Prime Minister, or the jig is most definitely up.'

On your Brexit Memo Pad:

- ❖ -2% Authority – you take the brunt of the blame.

Turn to **350**.

305

'A tall order,' says the Chancellor, rubbing his jaw. 'A lot of the time those interests are pulling in different directions.'

'Negative thinking won't help,' grumbles Dent. 'Can't make a success of Brexit that way.'

'Ever done any DIY, Dennis?'

'Eh?'

'Only usually it's a good idea to sketch it on the back of an envelope first. Otherwise the first time you encounter a problem is when the kitchen floor is two inches underwater.'

You lean forward and fix them both with a freezing stare. 'Nobody said this would be easy. We only have two years to unpick a four decades long association. But that's the job, and it's our duty to do what's best for the country while delivering the mandate of the people.'

Stollard nods, but as he's going out you hear him say to one of his team, 'The mandate of the people. Whatever that is.'

Turn to **125.**

306

The Irish peace process was facilitated by not needing a hard border between north and south because both belonged to the EU. Now that has to be dealt with.

'What are our options?' you ask the Secretary of State for Northern Ireland.

'Other than hand the six counties back to Eire, you mean. Sorry, my little joke. Well, there's a bit of bang-up technology that we could put into play. Cameras that identify vehicles as they come across the border, and even faces, and run automated customs and immigration checks.'

'A bit Orwellian.' You think for a moment. 'I like it.'

'The civil rights lefties might kick up a fuss. But if it's not done with computerized surveillance then it has to be done with physical border checks. Imagine a human hand beeping on a lorry horn – forever.'

What's your decision?

⇒ Computerized surveillance. Turn to **663**

⇒ Physical border checks. Turn to **481**

⇒ Leave it for now. The problem might go away. Turn to **739**

307

Tiffany Rufus gives a speech in which she extols the virtues of sober, considered, diligent and consistent leadership. She doesn't even have to mention Peter Strewel's name for everyone to see that it's an attack on him.

Your own speech later that day dwells on some of the fire-fighting you've had to do in your three years as Prime Minister. Ostensibly you're just laying out your pitch. If most of the examples of damage control you mention happen to be Peter Strewel's gaffes, so much the better.

'And the fat oaf does make it easy,' you remark to your press secretary on the way back to Number 10. 'I just had to decide which of his many blunders to leave out.'

The MPs are starting to think carefully if they really want a leader who is lazy, unreliable and prone to clownish blunders. You think they'll see sense.

Turn to **534**.

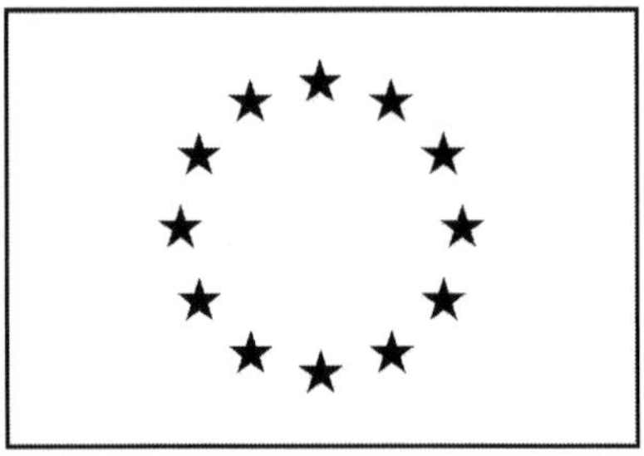

308

He fixes you with a burning stare and, while he may lack any quality of charisma or authority, there's no denying the intensity of his belief.

'I know in my heart that if we are bold and determined we will win through to the shining city on the hill. Our country is the greatest in the world. Our people are better than other people. Our best days aren't in the past. Oh no, they're yet to come.'

'Wait… what? Greater than when we ruled the largest empire in history, with a quarter of the world's population under one flag? And you're saying we haven't peaked yet?'

'We can make Britain better than it was. Better. Stronger. Faster.'

'Oh-kay.' You glance at your watch. 'I have to go now, Thomas, because I'm due back on the planet Earth.'

You can forget about his support, and it's too late to try anything else. Next day the members cast their votes. This is it. The moment of truth.

If your Popularity score is 70% or more, turn to **519**.

If your Popularity is 33% or less, turn to **782**.

If your Popularity is in the range 34% to 52%, turn to **727**.

If your Popularity is in the range 53% to 69%, turn to **528**.

309

Britain's destiny seems to be a return to freewheeling trade and deals done in the shady backrooms of the world. History repeating itself, or just the last protesting gasp of a moribund nation unable to come to terms with the loss of its empire? Hopefully this time round you can do without the gunboat diplomacy and drug wars.

Turn to **666**.

310

With Dent gone you are now the front runner among the hard Brexit candidates – at least as regards the Parliamentary party, although the membership may have entirely different ideas. And the next round brings more good news as Amelia Dimple falls by the wayside.

'And then there were three,' you say, sitting back with satisfaction.

'Your goal,' Terri Trough advises, 'must be to weed out the opponent you wouldn't want to face in a head-to-head with the party members making the choice.'

You nod. 'Tiffany Rufus has a lot of support among MPs, but she wouldn't stand a chance when it comes to the retired colonels, bored housewives and strutting barrow boys who make up the membership. Gervais Noysom-Reek, on the other hand…'

Ron Beardsley rushes in, uncharacteristically flustered. 'Alan Stollard has entered the contest.'

You sit bolt upright. 'Can he even do that?'

Ron gives a shrug. 'So many grey areas. Much of politics these days is make it up as you go, isn't it. We could write a note of protest to the 1922 Committee..?'

⇒ Challenge Stollard's right to put himself forward at this late stage. Turn to **285**

⇒ Let it go. Turn to **201**

311

'Looking on the bright side,' chips in the International Trade Minister, 'the slide in the pound will make our exports more attractive.'

> On your Brexit Memo Pad:
>
> ❖ -1% Popularity – you're getting some flak for the higher price of prosecco, but the majority of voters seem happy to switch to warm beer.

Then turn to **200.**

312

'It's not the worst deal we might have struck,' says the Chancellor when you tell him the outline of the deal. 'We'll have minimal influence over the regulations we have to abide by, of course.'

'The crucial distinction, Alan, is that we don't *have* to abide by them. British law will track the rulings of the European Court, but with the option to go its own way.'

'If we ever do opt out, that could cut off our remaining access to the single market.'

'The point is we can sell it to the voters as sovereignty regained. Better to rule in an EFTA limbo than get booted out of office by voters who would never be happy with either the economic inferno of a hard Brexit or the bovine compromise involved in the Norway model.'

On your Brexit Memo Pad:

- -5% Economy – Britain's service industries will find it harder to trade with Europe.
- -2% Goodwill – the EU are already sick of the complexity of dealing with the Swiss under similar terms.
- -5% Popularity – the voters are dimly resentful that all the fireworks of Brexit has ended in the damp squib of thoughtful diplomacy.
- Tick the keyword CLARION
- Mark EU Trade Talks as complete.

Then turn to **385.**

313

The vote is strongly in favour of staying in the EU. So that was a lot of avoidable pain and bother. Still, the people have spoken. Their latest whim has come across loud and clear. What you have to consider now is your own political future.

Look at your Brexit Memo Pad. If you have the keyword FOG, turn to **805**. If you have the keyword GAZELLE, turn to **775**. If you have the keyword SANCTION, turn to **692.**

If you have none of those keywords, turn to **206**.

314

McKay nods soberly, glancing out over the flat, wind-scoured marshes as if searching for convicts escaped from a prison hulk.

'The way I see it there are three things. Finding out who the criminals are, catching them, and shipping them to where they'll face justice.'

OK so far. You could do with more briefings like this. Brief being the operative word. You give McKay an encouraging nod.

Warming to his subject, he goes on, 'It's actually the first and the last of those that'll give us the most grief, I reckon.'

⇒ 'So not the policing itself?' Turn to **315**

⇒ 'Finding out about criminals – you mean surveillance?' Turn to **138**

⇒ 'So extradition will present us with a problem?' Turn to **773**

⇒ 'Never mind security, let's talk about defence.' Turn to **168**

⇒ 'Enough chit-chat. I need to get back to London.' Turn to **666**

315

'There's a good history of cooperation between police forces internationally, right throughout the West really, so I can't see that Brexit will make a whole lot of difference. We'll just operate alongside Europol the way the US and Australia do.'

⇒ 'What about surveillance? Turn to **138**

⇒ 'But you think extradition will be an issue?' Turn to **773**

⇒ 'Let me ask you something else.' Turn to **432**

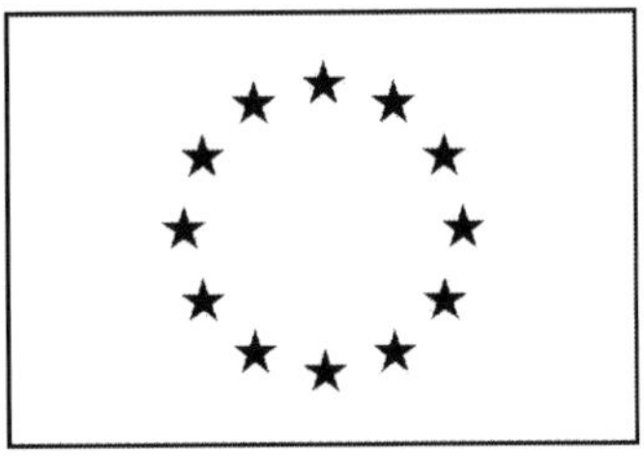

316

'OK, well those are our investment commitments.'

'Scientific research, things like that? Well, we're happy to pay for those because we'll see a benefit from them.'

'No, er…' Ron shuffles his papers around. 'This is principally cohesion spending. Regional development funds and – '

You glance at your watch.

' – motorways in the Czech Republic, housing in Poland. That sort of thing.'

'All their best builders are over here, that's their problem.'

He doesn't crack a smile – not that you'd know under that luxuriant Edwardian cricketer's beard. 'The point of the cohesion spending, prime minister, is to bring the less developed areas of Europe up to an even footing. In the long term it makes sense. Corruption drops off, productivity increases as transport and social conditions improve. Everyone benefits.'

'I sense a but.'

'Less than a third of funds needed for the ESI – that's European Strategic Investment – will have been paid by the time we leave the EU. But we've signed up to the initiative, so the Commission's view will be that we still owe the remainder of our share.'

'And if we don't pay up?'

'Either the richer countries have to dig deeper, or that development has to be scaled back. We'd make no friends over there if we take that tack.'

'What worries me more is losing friends over here if we don't take it. Or at least find a way to sweeten the pill.'

Turn to **374**.

317

Against your chief of staff's advice you stick to your guns, carefully explaining the reasoning behind your policy and putting yourself forward as the sensible candidate who refuses to be swayed by doctrine.

'The British people distrust ideology, Ron,' you tell him just before the first round of voting.

'That was then. Now we're a country of trembling lips and on-tap *EastEnders* sentiment. While you've been talking like a grown-up, your opponents have kept the media spellbound with scripted playroom tantrums. Here's my letter of resignation, by the way.'

Your integrity reaps the usual reward. Turn to **377**.

318

'Having a passport allows a company to market financial products throughout Europe,' explains the Chancellor. 'It's the reason that getting on for 90% of US investment banks operating in Europe have their headquarters in London.'

'Swiss banks too...' says Strewel hesitantly, as if dimly remembering the declension of an irregular verb.

'That's right. Switzerland is outside the EEA, so in order to trade freely with the rest of Europe it has a lot of its financial institutions based here in Britain. They only came for the passports, so without those they're gone. They'd be no better off in London than in Zurich.'

⇒ 'If we lose passporting, what can we put in its place?' Turn to **159**

⇒ 'Fine. What else?' Turn to **66**

319

The next day you discuss the matter with the EU chief negotiator, Armand Alprèves. He accepts it all quite sanguinely. It's standard EU stuff after all, hammering out the give and take of a deal.

'I'll have to consult with all twenty-seven member states,' he reminds you. 'But we all want a win-win.'

You'd like to think that's true, but you're not sure about Spain. They have the most British ex-pats, and they have political goals of their own that could muddy the waters.

> On your Brexit Memo Pad:
> - ❖ +5% Goodwill – at least you've shown willing that you'll guarantee citizens' rights.
> - ❖ Tick the keyword WELTER

Then turn to **150**.

320

'That might be possible,' you concede. 'Subject to the specifics of the agreement, of course.'

'I think you need to look into it personally.'

'If I have the time.'

'You shouldn't leave something so important to your ministers. Most of them are opportunists or zealots. They'd like nothing better than to blow all this up and walk away from the wreckage.'

'You may very well think that. I couldn't possibly comment.'

He smiles. 'Anyway, I'm saying that if you guarantee the rights of those EU citizens, maybe we can reopen the matter of Britain staying in the single market.'

Another thought seems to strike him. He pauses with his fork halfway to his mouth.

'Something else?' you ask him.

'Don't leave it too late.'

Tick the keyword VERTIGO on your Brexit Memo Pad and then turn to **666**.

321

Britain has sacrificed her former close links with the other European Union states, and in doing so has been forced relinquish many of the benefits of being 'closer than allies' as the President of the European Council put it.

Turn to **476**.

322

A busy schedule, but these days they all are. After a packed morning you went into Prime Minister's Questions with only minutes to prepare. Luckily that dunce Scraggle only got up to score an obscure point about the pricing of school dinners. You were able to deflect that one onto your plans for new grammar schools, which should get a few Kippers on side.

As you leave the Chamber you're looking forward to a relaxing half hour on the Westminster shooting range. You want to try out the gold-plated custom Desert Eagle, a gift from President Windrip. It's tricky to handle as you've noticed the grip is a bit small, but maybe you just need more practice. And afterwards perhaps a leisurely lunch out on the terrace.

A junior civil servant comes scuttling across the lobby towards you. You try holding her off with your trademark death stare, but although you see her flinch it doesn't stop her.

'Prime Minister – '

'Go away. I'm taking a long lunch break.'

'But you have your meeting in the Pugin Room.'

'What meeting?'

'With the three Brexiteers – I mean, the ministers in charge of exiting the European Union.'

You'd forgotten. This afternoon has been set aside to thrash out possible trade deals.

'Is there lunch?'

'There's sandwiches, Prime Minister. The Chancellor said that a full meal with wine would just put everyone to sleep.'

So much for a leisurely lunch – unless…

⇒ 'Reschedule the meeting. I have other plans.' Turn to **658**

⇒ 'All right, I'd better see them.' Turn to **259**

323

'We'll just have to hire them from outside the European Union. The rest of the world does have doctors and nurses.'

'Yes, but standards of training vary. We'll need to beef up the relevant accreditation agencies to assess any medics coming to work here. And isn't the aim to get immigration down, not just shift it from Germany to Tuvalu?'

'Let's not worry about the staffing levels a decade from now. What's needed are some headline-grabbing initiatives.'

'Building new hospitals? Investing in medical research?'

'Exactly. The British people have that one little sarcoma of socialism, don't they? They care about the NHS.'

'Interesting analogy. Well, as your economic oncologist I can suggest two courses of action. Expensive therapy is one. The alternative: do nothing.'

⇒ Invest heavily in the NHS. Turn to **239**

⇒ Leave it to muddle along as best it can. Turn to **517**

324

The choice is stark. If you settle the UK's financial obligations, the EU will allow you to remain in the single market.

'But what *are* our "financial obligations"?' thunders Dennis Dent when you tell him about it.

'Substantial. But significantly less of an economic hit than we would suffer if we don't secure access to the single market.'

He fixes you with a look of cold fury such as a desert prophet of ancient times might have given to somebody seen eating pork on the sabbath. And in this moment you realize the gulf between you can never be bridged by rational arguments.

On your Brexit Memo Pad:

- ❖ -5% Authority – the Brexit hardliners are livid at what they see as your capitulation to EU demands.
- ❖ +15% Goodwill – the EU see this move as heralding a close relationship in future.
- ❖ -10% Popularity – the people are suspicious of U-turns.
- ❖ Mark Exit Fee as complete.

The payments to the EU are agreed. Now you must decide the trading relationship you want after March 2019:

⇒ The so-called Norway model: a very close relationship within the European Economic Area, giving comprehensive access to trade in goods and services.
Turn to **82**

⇒ The Swiss model: an arrangement outside the EEA with only partial access to trade in goods and services, but with more opt-outs and no contributions to the EU budget.
Turn to **417**

325

Time is ticking away. You'd bite your nails if you had any left. Luckily you're surrounded by bright people whose job it is to brief you on all the issues you have to deal with. What do you want to find out about?

To weigh up possible models for Britain's future trading relationship with the EU, turn to **651**.

For an update about Britain's exit payments, turn to **112**.

To consider the status of EU citizens already living here, turn to **612**.

To think about security and defence issues, turn to **628**.

To look into possible international trade agreements after Brexit, turn to **291**.

To pray for guidance as to whether you should call a general election, turn to **69**.

Enough talk. Actions speak louder than words: turn to **469**.

326

She holds up her fingers to count off the points. You're amazed that schoolgirls are allowed nails like that. Things were very different when you were at school. Not for the first time, you feel a hundred years old in the face of an onrushing future.

'We'll have reduced bargaining power,' says Miss Barkwell, folding one ornamentally taloned finger. 'We're short on negotiators. And we're turning our backs on our biggest and nearest trading partner.'

'That's only three,' you say as she makes a fist.

'The last one is so dumb that I'm counting it twice.'

⇒ 'Give me some examples of reduced bargaining power.' Turn to **504**

⇒ 'Hiring negotiators is what your father's department is meant to be doing.' Turn to **30**

⇒ 'We're not exactly turning our back on the EU.' Turn to **553**

⇒ 'That's enough about weaknesses.' Turn to **700**

327

'Some member states will want to,' agrees the Chancellor. 'But these are rich pickings. The financial services industry contributes about 12% of Britain's total tax revenue. Other countries might see an opportunity.'

'Such as?'

'Worst case, say we lose passporting. Financial institutions here can no longer sell their services throughout the EU. If keeping their employees means a similar culture and language then they might relocate to Dublin – or, heaven help us, an independent Scotland. But other places will be touting for that business. France, Germany, Luxembourg. Whoever gains, we'll lose out. The only question is by how much.'

⇒ 'What's the significance of passporting?' Turn to **318**

⇒ 'But Norway does have passports, so in what way is their financial arrangement not as good as full EU membership?' Turn to **72**

328

Against all the odds, the economy is doing rather well. Growth rates are up across all sectors despite the Brexit factor. Employment remains high, and wages are finally starting to creep up. That's quite a feat under the circumstances.

But to get there you've had to make some compromises with the EU. The Brexiteers in your party are not happy about it, nor are the tabloids. As long as the economic indicators are sound, though, you can shrug off a hostile press. History will show that you've done right by your country.

That will go into the record books. But for now, best watch your back. Turn to **210**.

329

At least it was a Labour seat, and one with quite a slim majority too. If you could turn that around and swipe the seat for the Conservatives, especially with a candidate hand-picked for loyalty to you – what a coup!

'Get me the list,' you tell your chief of staff. 'Ideally a woman or ethnic, or both. But the main thing is that they're young, impressionable and not already tainted with some demented Ukipperish ideology.'

Look at your Brexit Memo Pad. If your Popularity is 61% or more, turn to **31**. Otherwise turn to **401**.

330

'Arguably with us on board EFTA would have real clout,' says Strewel. 'Who'd have thought it, Vikings and Anglo-Saxons teaming up shoulder to shoulder against the continental scrum? In a way I suppose it was what King Alfred was aiming for once he got out of the bog.'

⇒ 'How much sway would we have against the whole of the EU?' Turn to **793**

⇒ 'But in EFTA we wouldn't be free to do our own trade deals.' Turn to **55**

331

You wake up to the news that Gongtrit's Bank, one of the country's most venerable financial institutions, is moving its main headquarters from London to Frankfurt.

'It's the passporting problem,' says your press secretary. 'Their CEO has been saying that it's like a shopkeeper pulling down the steel shutters and still hoping to do a roaring trade.' She sees your glowering look. 'His words, Prime Minister, not mine.'

'These investment banks were happy to make a killing in the great days of the Empire. It makes me sick to see them turn tail now, like rats leaving – '

'A sinking ship? Let's not say that.'

'What shall we say? Give me some options.'

⇒ 'We could plant a story in the loyal press describing these banks as traitors who will miss out on a great opportunity. It might dent their share price.' Turn to **829**

⇒ 'You could try to get the EU to issue an encouraging statement about our future access to their financial markets.' Turn to **518**

⇒ 'Best to do nothing. Sure and steady makes you look like you're in charge.' Turn to **857**

332

Look at your Brexit Memo Pad. If you have the keyword REGENT *and* EU Trade Talks are not marked as complete, turn to **831.**

Otherwise turn to **385**.

333

You were told that it might be possible to secure continued access to the single market once the question of security and defence was resolved.

If Goodwill is still 16% or greater, you have the option to reopen those discussions: turn to **548**.

If Goodwill is 15% or less, or if you decide not to bother with staying in the single market, turn to **666**.

334

The question of Britain's outstanding financial obligations to the EU has been referred to the International Court.

The risk is that the ruling may award more to the EU than you might have been able to negotiate across the table in Brussels. On the other hand, whatever the ruling you can sell it to the voters as a case of dastardly foreigners conspiring against Britain.

'Prepare some minutes from the exit fee talks, Terri,' you tell your press secretary.

'They're all typed up, Prime Minister.'

'Well retype them. And leave a space for the sum the EU were asking for. Whatever the court's decision, the minutes should quote a figure £10 billion higher. Then we can leak that to the press after the ruling.'

'Falsify the minutes?' She looks perturbed. Perhaps she doesn't have the backbone for this job.

'We'll leave it a few days, let the story simmer, then we'll deny it and present the real minutes. The EU can't accuse us of lying, but the public will be sure to believe the dirtier version.'

Turn to **666**.

335

Look at your Brexit Memo Pad.

If you have the keyword QUORUM, turn to **389**.

If not, turn to **197**.

336

You've agreed to restrict EU immigrant numbers for five years and then take another look at the situation.

The Brexiters aren't happy. They hate and fear any kind of transitional deal. The Leave vote came, not from areas with a high proportion of immigrants, but from those that had experienced a rapid increase in the immigrant population. Given time those people might get used to living alongside EU immigrants. They might change their minds about the EU. So your proposals don't go nearly far enough to satisfy that extreme right wing.

And the EU aren't overjoyed about it either. To them, EU citizens living and working in each others' country isn't migration, it's one of the great social and economic boons of the European project. Putting more red tape in the way damages both sides' economies and discourages workers from wanting to relocate as they feel they're unwelcome.

Record on your Brexit Memo Pad:

- ❖ -5% Goodwill – the EU aren't too happy, but it could be a lot worse.
- ❖ +5% Popularity – voters are mostly content with the message that immigration is being tackled.
- ❖ Mark Immigration as complete.

Then turn to **150.**

337

You decide the best approach is to pursue a package of small-scale trade agreements. They'll be individually worthless but it'll make for a drip-feed of positive news stories over the next few months.

The Chancellor drops a copy of the *Tomahawk* on your desk and glumly points to a photo of the International Trade Minister shaking hands with President Pandillero of the Philippines.

'Why the long face, Alan – or is it the shape of your head? I know it's below the fold, but this is just what we want. Front page coverage of Britain taking its new place in the world.'

'He's talking about "shared values",' says Stollard. 'This with a populist leader who encourages his own people to murder criminals.'

'Haven't you seen the polls? Most Leave voters not only want capital punishment brought back, they'd be happy to see criminals hanging from the lampposts.'

'Leaving the brave new world to one side, it seems a lot of fuss to go to for such paltry rewards. Do you know that only 0.1% of our exports go to the Philippines? We'll need a hundred deals like that to make up what we're going to lose in trade with the EU.'

'Barkwell will be racking up a lot of air miles, then,' you say with a laugh. But after the Chancellor has gone you start to think that he's right. Penny-ante deals like the one with the Philippines aren't going to impress the media for long.

⇒ Switch your attention to a deal the EU are already working on – with somewhere like the US, for instance. Turn to **254**

⇒ Ratify a trade agreement that Britain is already signed up as an EU member. Turn to **234**

⇒ Stick to your guns. An all-new trade agreement will

demonstrate that Britain has what it takes to make a success of Brexit. Turn to **694**

338

'That's right,' says Barkwell, sitting back with the satisfied air of a well-fed cat. 'The stick instead of the carrot. You watch them all line up to kowtow us then. Sixth biggest economy. Sixth biggest!'

'We could raise tariffs,' agrees the Chancellor, 'but WTO rules oblige us to raise them to all countries equally. So the EU will continue to import our goods at an average tariff of 2%, while the £300 million's worth of goods we import from them every year would be charged at – how big a stick were you thinking of?'

'We'll iron all these details out,' says Dent. 'I'm not a bit worried. The rest of the world isn't going to miss out on the juicy deals to be made.'

'I'm sure there's unbridled excitement over there in Turkmenistan,' says Stollard. 'But in fact you've touched on another issue. The moment we try to change any tariffs, we're open to the WTO's dispute resolution procedure. We'll probably run up against that sooner, in fact, when we divvy up tariff-rate quotas with the EU. Any WTO member can object on the grounds of being unfairly treated. In any case, tariffs aren't the big headache.'

⇒ 'Then what is?' Turn to **781**

⇒ 'All this talk about trade disputes. I need an example.' Turn to **741**

⇒ 'Britain has the sixth biggest economy in the world. Surely that counts for something?' Turn to **443**

⇒ 'The advantage of WTO rules is that they give us access to international markets.' Turn to **590**

339

Going into the next round of voting, the candidates standing against you are the Brexit Secretary, the Home Secretary, and the Chancellor.

'All the heavyweights,' you muse. 'This is what civil war would look like on Mount Olympus.'

Ron Beardsley has his polling projections ready. 'With the hard Brexit wing split, next round's casualty could be you or Dennis Dent.'

'What about the soft Brexit wing? They're split too.'

'Of course. But we don't care about them, do we? If you stand against either Stollard or Rufus when it comes to the membership, they're bound to choose you. So Dent is the one to beat.'

Check your Brexit Memo Pad.

If you have the keyword LEAF and your Authority is greater than 50%, turn to **561**.

If not but you have Authority greater than 57% and Goodwill *less* than 41%, turn to **381**.

Otherwise turn to **377**.

340

'It'll give us the most accurate snapshot of public opinion,' says Tode. 'Suppose on the first ballot we have just hard Brexit, soft Brexit, or no Brexit– '

'No Brexit?' shouts Barkwell. 'Brexit is the will of the British people. Only a traitor would suggest having an option to cancel Brexit.'

'Steady on, old chap,' says Dent. 'I'm as sick of the bloody EU as you are, but we're not going to get away with leaving the option off the paper, are we?'

'Those three options, then,' says Tode with his usual robotic patience. 'And then after one round no-Brexit has come third, so that's knocked out. In the runoff it's now a choice between hard and soft Brexit.'

'All the no-Brexit lot will just vote for soft,' protests Barkwell. 'That might even win.'

Tode shrugs. 'We don't know. Really, it would be better to provide more choices. Highest priority immigration, the economy, sovereignty, whatever. But to look at the French example, Macron and LePen were almost neck and neck in the first round. If that had been the only vote, Macron would have pipped her at the post but France would look a badly divided nation. By going to a second round, it turned out two thirds of voters preferred Macron. So you not only find out voters' real priorities, you get a result that's unarguably legitimate.'

'We already have a legitimate result,' huffs Barkwell. 'Out of Europe, drawbridge up, that's it for these spongers.'

Everyone else is waiting for your decision.

⇒ 'The runoff sounds like a good system. We'll do it that way.' Turn to **44**

⇒ 'Let's have a look at the plain yes or no option.' Turn to **600**

⇒ 'A range of options on one ballot paper might be simpler.' Turn to **698**

⇒ 'On second thoughts, forget the whole thing. Another referendum would be madness.' Turn to **79**

341

'The first rule, in life as in politics, is to keep your seat at the table. If we don't stay on course to deliver the kind of Brexit that the party wants – and I do mean the party, not the country – we'll be replaced with a team who will do it. So there's no point in seeing all this as some kind of academic exercise where we only have to look for rational economic outcomes. Man is not a rational animal, gentlemen, but a political one. That's the reality; don't lose sight of it. Good day.'

On your Brexit Memo Pad:
- ❖ Tick the keyword UNCTION

Turn to **125.**

342

In your dream – if it is a dream – you're standing in the foyer of a crowded hospital. The place looks like a sketch by Hogarth redesigned for a steampunk movie. The place is filled with walking wounded, faces sour yellow in the dim lighting. From time to time everybody looks up as an airship looms against the upper windows and docks to unload one of the more privileged patients.

'Up there's where the good meds are,' mutters a woman slouched in a plastic chair. 'Been here eighteen hours, me, waiting to see a trainee assistant intern. I'll be lucky to get fobbed off with penicillin. About as much use as M&Ms, these days.'

A device like an old-fashioned television rolls to a halt in front of you. 'Greetings,' it says. 'Welcome to Merrick Metrodyne Inc hospital. Medical solutions for your every need. You are at…' It pauses: 'King's Cross! Your credit card has been scanned and found…' again a pause, then it adds chirpily: 'acceptable! Please select a service.'

On its front is a touch sensitive screen that now lights up with four options:

⇒ Geriatric unit — Turn to **413**

⇒ Miracle cure facility — Turn to **133**

⇒ The Innovative Medicines Initiative — Turn to **273**

⇒ Casualty — Turn to **57**

343

'It has to be a unanimous decision. So that'd be the Council of the European Union, I suppose. Or is it the European Council? See, by the time they've figured out who to ask it's already too late. On top of which, no country is ever obliged to deploy its national troops as part of a mission.'

'Of course. Because Europe isn't a federal state. Each country retains its sovereignty.'

'Does it, Prime Minister?' He squints at you, worried. 'Only Mr Tode and Mr Strewel in the referendum, they kept on about us having handed our sovereignty away, didn't they.'

Oops. 'Well, of course, they were right. We must get our sovereignty back. That's what this is all about.'

⇒ Ask him what kinds of mission EU forces undertake. — Turn to **632**

⇒ Ask about something else. — Turn to **432**

344

You have the distinct impression the EU negotiators are relieved that you still want Britain to be part of the single market.

'It's best for all concerned,' President Terlaman assures you. 'What kind of single market membership are you looking for?'

⇒ The so-called Norway model: a very close relationship

within the European Economic Area, giving comprehensive access to trade in goods and services.

Turn to **510**

⇒ The Swiss model: an arrangement outside the EEA with only partial access to trade in goods and services, but with more opt-outs and no contributions to the EU budget.

Turn to **277**

345

'The Prime Minister's exact words to me were, "I hope we can bury this Brexit madness and get on with the process of ever-closer union."'

You put down the newspaper. 'That's not right. I never said that.'

Terri Trough, your press secretary, glances again at the interview with Chloe Stoat, the Business minister. 'What do you mean, Prime Minister?'

'I mean it's not true!'

'I don't think factuality is the way we want to go with this. Maybe leak the news that she was going to be out in the next Cabinet reshuffle? Disgruntled also-ran cooks up story for revenge. That's easier to sell than the truth any day.'

'Didn't she spend a weekend at a health resort recently?' says Ron Beardsley. 'One of the tame papers can hint that she went there to dry out. She's certainly highly-strung enough to be a pill popper.'

Will the public buy your version of the story, or Chloe Stoat's? If you have the keyword GAZELLE, turn to **732**.

If not but you have Popularity of 62% or more, turn to **158**.

Otherwise turn to **653**.

346

EFTA is the European Free Trade Association. Britain was once a member, but left to join the EU proper. Currently EFTA comprises Iceland, Norway, Switzerland and Liechtenstein. They did a deal with the EU to create the European Economic Area. It gives EFTA access to the single market without being members of the EU. Except for Switzerland. They're in EFTA but not the EEA. They have their own separate deal with the EU to get access to the single market.

The whole thing is a big bag of tangled-up strings, including more bags of string, with bags of string inside them. You've got to get the bag labelled 'UK' out of the EU and unknot its contents. And that's got some bags inside it too, marked Scotland, Wales, and Northern Ireland...

Anyway, doing a Switzerland or a Norway is a possible way out for the UK after Brexit. Certainly for a transitional phase, anyway, always assuming you can convince the hardcore Brexiters to go along with it. Hmm, maybe you should call it an 'implementation period' rather than a transitional phase. Punchier, that. It sounds committed enough to allay the gimlet-eyed suspicions of the most short-fused Brexiters.

A plaintive meow interrupts your thoughts. The Number 10 cat, Roanoke. Has he got under the bed again?

'Here, Roanoke, here puss!'

But then you realize the sound is coming from your laptop. It's moved on to the next video after the meerkat. This one has a cat on a skateboard rolling down somebody's street. Hah, look at that. And they're calling it Brexit Moggy as the skateboard is painted with the British flag, and its collar is red, white and blue. Most amusing.

There's a screeching caterwaul as the skateboard cracks into a paving stone jutting up from the ground. It sends Brexit Moggy sprawling with an expression of outrage that only cats and dogmatic politicians can ever achieve. The cat's owner is giggling so much he can hardly hold the camera steady. Eight lives left.

Still, best move on. The Brexit clock is ticking.

What do you want to find out about next, if you haven't already?

- ⇒ Free movement? Turn to **414**
- ⇒ EU regulations and standards. Turn to **655**
- ⇒ You've had enough, and it's time for bed. Turn to **441**

347

Party members' whims can change faster than the weather. To find out how they feel on the day of the vote, toss two coins.

If both come up tails, turn to **782**. Otherwise turn to **519**.

348

Your hope is that a private chat with just the Chancellor might shed some light on the murkier issues. At the very least, the atmosphere in the room is less prickly once the Three Brexiteers have left.

On your Brexit Memo Pad:

- ❖ -1% Authority – the Chancellor is known as a Remain sympathizer, and the others distrust what you are going to talk about with him.

'In the War of Independence, American commanders had political officers assigned to watch them for signs of ideological wavering. Same thing in the Russian Revolution.'

Stollard is an old friend. You catch his drift. 'We need to be able to look at all this with a clear eye,' you assure him. 'Can't rule anything out. It's a big ship in a big storm, and here we are on the bridge. You've seen *The Caine Mutiny*.'

'Wasn't the lesson of that movie that moral courage is in short supply?'

'Just us and the four walls, Alan. Let's leave ideology out of it. I need honest answers.'

'All right. Ask away.'

⇒ 'What do you think about the long-term consequences of Brexit?' Turn to **233**

⇒ 'Is there any way for Britain to stay in the single market?' Turn to **520**

⇒ 'What should we be prioritizing in the negotiations?' Turn to **98**

⇒ 'What are the risks if we go it alone?' Turn to **588**

349

Fungale is knocked out. You've never felt better than as you look at his frog-like face trying to summon up a brave smile while his eyes show the desolation within. You don't even stay for his concession speech, though it would have been fun to heckle him.

'And that's the end of Colin Fungale,' says Ron Beardsley when you get back to Number 10.

'No. He's like the clap in an Old West prospecting town, there's no wiping him out. But he'll scurry off to President Windrip for a year or two, and when he tries to come skulking back we'll be ready to crush him.'

'Not to be a wet blanket,' says Ron, 'but the fight isn't over yet. You now have to face Tiffany Rufus in a ballot of the party members.'

'If I can't beat a closet Remainer like her then I deserve to go on the scrapheap alongside Fungale.'

Fighting talk, or famous last words? Look at your Brexit Memo Pad. If your Economy and Popularity scores are *both* less than 43%, turn to **782**. Otherwise turn to **519**.

350 ☐

If the box above is already ticked, turn immediately to **152**. Otherwise read on.

Maybe you feel like taking a break from running the country, in which case this would be a good point to cut out for a rest – if so, just make a note that you're on the third phase of talks at section **350** so you can find your place again. But if you're still raring to go, read on.

Time is limited, so you cannot personally oversee everything. A real pity, that, seeing as most of the people you have to delegate to are either bumblers or outright fanatics.

You only have time to take care of one issue yourself. Choose from any action points listed below that are *not* already marked as complete on your Brexit Memo Pad:

⇒ Deal with the Exit Fee (only if you have the keyword APRICITY and this issue is not already marked as complete) tick the box above and then turn to **720**

⇒ Deal with EU Trade Talks (if not already marked as complete) tick the box above and then turn to **688**

⇒ Try to call a General Election (if not already complete) tick the box above and then turn to **416**

⇒ Agree the Residency Rights of UK and EU citizens (if not already complete) tick the box above and then turn to **638**

⇒ Handle the question of UK/EU Security and Defence cooperation (if not already complete) tick the box above and then turn to **420**

⇒ Start preliminary talks on International Trade Deals (if not already complete) tick the box above and then turn to **335**

When you've dealt with one of these issues, or if all the negotiations are marked on your Brexit Memo Pad as complete, turn to **152**.

351

And finally, what do the British people think of you personally? Heaven-sent saviour, or prophet without honour?

If your Popularity score is 39% or less, turn to **823**.

If Popularity is 40% to 60%, turn to **462**.

If Popularity is 61% or more, turn to **292**.

352

'The people are telling us to bring down immigration, Chloe.'

'Was that the question on the referendum paper? I didn't see that.'

'It's one of the main issues. Look at the response to Colin Fungale's refugee posters.'

'He's a smug Nazi mollusk in a business suit. Most of the regions that voted for Brexit don't have high levels of immigration anyway.'

'But you must admit that voters are aggrieved that we seem to have no control over who comes here from the EU.'

'But we do have control, don't we? Immigrants can be sent packing after three months if they don't get a job, for example. So if those rules aren't being upheld we shouldn't look at the European Union, we should blame the Home Office.'

She gives you a pointed look, all angry twitches and darting eyes. You can see Wilkins hovering in the doorway.

⇒ Tell her you've got a meeting. Turn to **240**

⇒ Point out that some sort of customs union hasn't been ruled out. Turn to **248**

⇒ Explain the benefits of Britain being able to do independent trade deals. Turn to **786**

⇒ Tell her that privately you're hoping to reverse Brexit and stay part of the EU. Turn to **37**

353

The important thing is to knock Colin Fungale out of the running. You can win against Tiffany Rufus once the vote goes to party members, but that's exactly where Fungale's fish-and-chips fascism would play well.

If you have the keyword UNCTION *and* your Authority is greater than 60%, turn to **523**.

Otherwise turn to **93**.

354

You're given to understand that if Britain concludes a defence and counter-terrorism agreement with the EU, that would open the way to a trade deal that grants continued access to the single market.

If you agree to that, turn to **160**.

If not, you have the option to pursue a customs union like Turkey's arrangement (turn to **674**) or else a bespoke free trade agreement (turn to **294**).

355

You put a hand to your chin in thought. Sausages from Lincolnshire, it says on the menu. One of the most strongly Leave counties in the country. And the Cumbrian bacon… Cumbria was even more Europhobic than Lincolnshire. Is this some kind of breakfast themed omen?

Today's the day you have a conference call with Jean-Jacques Terlamen, President of the EU Commission. You've promised to outline the UK's position on the possibility of some kind of Norwegian model of Brexit that they have suggested we look at.

Joining the European Economic Area would almost certainly not go down well in Cumbria or Lincolnshire. On the other hand, we really need access to the EU markets in some shape or form, and the Scots would be on board, as would the City. But those Lincolnshire sausages... How can you sell a Brexit where nothing changes much except that we have even less say in the way things are run than we did before? Maybe it's time to bring home the bacon to Cumbria, even it the economy does take a hit.

Turn to **747.**

356

'I was going to point out the flaw in giving voters two outcomes to choose between before you actually find a way to implement them. They can say yes, we want X – but supposing X can't be delivered? Isn't it Indiana where they voted to make pi a rational number?'

'*Nearly* voted. It didn't pass.'

'But if it had, you'd have a democratic mandate whose only result is buildings would fall down and satellites would drop out of the sky. Canute pointed out the limits of political power a thousand years ago. Give them a referendum on changing the time of high tide. It's the only way they'll get the message.'

'You seem rather dismissive of democracy. Not to say unpatriotic.' He gets the full force of your prime ministerial stare. 'Are you, by any chance, an enemy of the people?'

'As to that – '

⇒ 'I was being rhetorical.' Turn to **668**

⇒ 'All right, justify yourself if you can.' Turn to **195**

357

Allowing UK ex-pats to remain in Europe following Brexit is pretty much a cost-free gesture for the EU, seeing as there are far fewer UK nationals living abroad than EU nationals living in Britain. The rest of the world won't trouble to drill down into the details, however, so the only effect is to make you look like the villain of the piece.

On your Brexit Memo Pad:

- -5% Economy – you'll be losing the tax revenue from three million EU nationals.
- Tick the keyword KOALA
- Mark Residency Rights as complete.

Now turn to **385.**

358

'No – although all of the things you've just been sneering at are signs of a diverse culture that we should be proud of. But I'm talking about on a purely practical level. Having citizens come here from other EU countries enriches our economy, because face-to-face contact promotes commerce. Don't curl your lip, Colin, it makes you look like a dyspeptic Bagpuss. You want proof? Look at Germany. The regions of East and West Germany that had the closest ties before reunification have been the quickest to benefit from the opportunities for growth after the Wall came down. You don't hear them complaining about lost jobs, do you? And why? Because they believe in "stronger together". Reunification has made everyone in Germany better off.'

'We've got off the point, haven't we,' says Tode. 'This isn't about forging close links with trading partners. We'll still be doing that after Brexit.'

'But I'm saying that when people are actually living and working here – '

Hopeless. She's trying to sell a utopian dream to a nation of suspicious shopkeepers. It's all you can do not to burst out laughing. Your job is so easy.

⇒ Mugglemore is throwing it back to the questioner. Turn to **135**

⇒ Find another question. Turn to **405**

⇒ Give up and get a good night's sleep. Turn to **125**

359

You discuss the matter with the EU chief negotiator, Armand Alprèves. He accepts it all quite sanguinely. It's standard EU stuff after all, hammering out the give and take of a deal.

'I'll have to consult with all twenty-seven member states,' he reminds you. 'But everybody wants a win-win.'

You'd like to think that's true, but you're not sure about Spain. They have the most British ex-pats, and they have political goals of their own that could muddy the waters.

Look at your Brexit Memo Pad.

If Goodwill is 50% or more, turn to **521.**

If Goodwill is 49% or less, turn to **656.**

360

Franjeboom is not convinced it will be possible to secure agreement on this, but he agrees to consult with the European Commission.

Check your Brexit Memo Pad. If your Goodwill score is 66% or more, turn to **214**. Otherwise turn to **280**.

361

Growth is less than you might have hoped for, and inflation is inching up, but so far the more extreme predictions of the Remain camp have not come to pass. Of course, that's mainly because Britain hasn't left the EU yet.

Your chief of staff has the latest metrics. 'The polls suggest most people are resigned to Brexit now but would favour staying in the single market.'

'Or having access to the single market.'

'Is that any different?'

'It sounds different, Ron. That's all that matters.'

Look at the Goodwill score on your Brexit Memo Pad. This gives a sense of how amicably the EU27 are behaving towards Britain at the moment.

If Goodwill is at 47% or higher, turn to **683.**

If Goodwill is 46% or lower, turn to **463.**

362

Where did several million British voters go to find out about the EU? Google, of course. Admittedly they typed in their search terms the day *after* the referendum, which smacks a little of stable doors and bolting horses, but the idea is sound.

Which is why, late one evening, you find yourself sitting in front of your laptop. You need to find out about the single market. There's barely two years to go until Brexit and you're still feeling shaky on some of the fundamentals. Of course, you could ask your chief of staff or one of those pinkly scrubbed graduates who assist your special advisors, but then you'd have to tolerate their ineptly veiled looks of contempt. Why put yourself through that, when the Internet knows all?

Your browser comes up with the last page you were looking at – wine tasting weeks. You've got a holiday coming up, but where to go? A wine tasting weekend or tour would be just the ticket. A good earthy red and a slice of cheese will restore your vigour for the fray. But where to go? Bordeaux or Burgundy? Or the Loire Valley? Or what about some Spanish wines? There's nothing like a good Rioja. Or maybe Italian, or...

Ah, but wait. It might not go down too well if you swan off across Europe drinking foreign wine in the middle of Brexit negotiations. What would the *Klaxon* or the *Daily Outrage* make of it? Some headlines leap to mind:

'PM's HOLIDAY LEAVES A NASTY TASTE'

'HARD WORKING ENGLISH VINEYARDS SNUBBED BY PM'

'WHAT'S WRONG WITH GOOD OLD BRITISH WINE?'

Actually, what *is* wrong with British wine? There are some vineyards in the Home Counties that have had decent write-ups. Except... we Brits are good on fizz and maybe a white or two, but frankly home-grown reds aren't so hot. And a wine tasting tour of the vineyards of Haywards Heath and Maidstone doesn't have quite the same appeal to it as the sun-kissed slopes of the Loire Valley.

Something to think about. For now, you start researching the single market.

Turn to **116.**

363

Alprèves ducks his head over the thick pad of paper in front of him. He pretends to be making notes, but you suspect he's hiding a smirk of triumph. It hasn't completely faded from his face as he looks up. 'It's good. The task before us is Herculean. By agreeing this now we lessen the workload by just so much.' He takes a sugar cube from the bowl in the middle of the table. 'It is not much, yet that's how Confucius said we can move mountains.'

- ⇒ Now to haggle over the amount. Turn to **631**
- ⇒ Agree the outlines of the deal, but stall over the final settlement. Turn to **704**

364

You were advised that if you granted residency rights to EU nationals already living in the UK, there was a chance of securing access to the single market.

Look at your Brexit Memo Pad. If you have the keyword TIGHTROPE *and* Goodwill is 24% or more, turn to **344.**

Otherwise turn to **666.**

365

A miracle. The court rules that the final settlement should not exceed €20 billion.

> On your Brexit Memo Pad:
> - ❖ +6% Authority – suddenly it looks as if you had a plan all along.
> - ❖ -3% Economy – some small financial pain, but for you it's a price worth paying.
> - ❖ -2% Goodwill – more sour grapes from the EU27 was inevitable.
> - ❖ Mark the Exit Fee as complete.

Then turn to **400**.

366

Colin Fungale wins the membership vote by a landslide. Incredible as it seems, given his very un-British penchant for apocalyptic pronouncements and threats of civil disobedience, he is to be the seventy-seventh Prime Minister of the United Kingdom.

'God save us all,' says Ron Beardsley.

'It seems like a good time to mention I have an Irish grandma,' says Terri Trough.

Turn to **782**.

367

'Like the Turks, eh?' says Strewel. 'Little chance of those fellows ever joining the EU. More likely they'd join the Russian Federation, ho ho. By the way, I hope nobody bears a grudge about those Leave posters. Seventy-six million Turks coming our way and all that. Just a wheeze, you know. All's fair in love and whatnot.'

'It seems the bigger risk now is that President Kulübe will put up posters warning of an influx of Brits into Turkey,' says Stollard.

Barkwell emits a snort like a kettle boiling over. 'We don't need the Turks' agreement to be in a European customs union. It simply allows tariff-free movement of goods. Nice and straightforward.'

'And any third party trade deals would be ironed out by the EU on our behalf.'

'That's right.' Barkwell looks puzzled. 'What? It's a good thing, isn't it? They've got a crack negotiating team.'

You sigh. 'What's your department called, Leslie?'

'Eh? International Trade... Oh. Oh, I see. Right. We can make our own deals, never mind those Brussels blaggers.'

⇒ 'Would somebody like to summarize the advantages of a customs union with the EU?' Turn to **681**

⇒ 'What are the drawbacks?' Turn to **799**

⇒ 'Let's move on to consider other options.' Turn to **703**

368

You sit up in bed with a sob. For a moment the sharp reek of antiseptic and sweet decay lingers, until you realize it's all in your imagination. From outside comes a patter of rain. A car's headlights wash across the curtains. No cause for alarm there. Number 10's windows could survive a bomb blast.

You're cuddling one of your pillows like it was a teddy bear. Casting it aside, you turn over and try to get back to sleep. It's only as you're starting to drift off that you remember what happened to Abednego. You operated on him with one of your mother's kitchen knives and his head came off.

Turn to **425**.

369

The EU aren't overjoyed about your decision. To them, EU citizens living and working in each others' country isn't migration, it's one of the great social and economic boons of the European project. Putting more red tape in the way damages both sides' economies and makes workers feel unwelcome, which discourages them from wanting to relocate.

> Record on your Brexit Memo Pad:
> - -5% Goodwill – the EU aren't too happy, but it could be a lot worse.
> - +5% Popularity – voters are mostly content with the message that immigration is being tackled.
> - Mark Immigration as complete.

Then turn to **150.**

370

Your aides spend an afternoon briefing you on the upcoming referendum campaign, but there's something they aren't saying. You let them tiptoe around it for a while, enjoying their discomfort, but finally it's time to grab the bull by the horns. Or the elephant by the trunk.

'We're wondering, Prime Minister,' says your chief of staff, 'whether you'll be taking part in the campaign yourself.'

⇒ 'Of course not. I intend to keep well out of it.'
Turn to **618**

⇒ 'Of course, I shall be leading the fight to Remain.'
Turn to **235**

⇒ 'I intend to campaign for a hard Brexit.'
Turn to **145**

⇒ 'A soft Brexit is best for the country, and that's what I'll be telling voters.' Turn to **538**

371

You can at least match Strewel's hard-Brexit credentials, if not his extravagant flights of Ciceronian rhetoric.

Turn to **528**.

372

'What's the modern equivalent of the spirit of the staircase, Wilkins?' you ask on returning to Number 10.

He hangs up your coat. 'I take it you refer to your reply to Mr Mugglemore's question, Prime Minister?'

'Ten minutes after leaving the studio I had the perfect answer.'

'It's one straw in the hurricane,' is Wilkins's consoling thought. 'I'll run your bath.'

On the night of the referendum you turn on the television and pace the room as the votes come in.

Toss two coins. If both come up heads, turn to **313**. Otherwise, turn to **403**.

373

The trade deal goes ahead and you get your photo-op with President Windrip on the White House lawn. It's a pity about the NHS. Already the corporations are circling it like buzzards. But it's just one casualty on the long road to building a new Britain for the Brexit age. And you'll be bee-keeping in Sussex years before the repercussions of the decision come into full focus.

Mark the NHS as complete on your Brexit Memo Pad and then turn to **450**.

374

An assistant is hovering in the doorway. The others have arrived. Your meeting is due to start, but you can spare a few minutes to ask Ron Beardsley to clarify any other points that are bothering you:

⇒ 'The budgetary overspend – what's that?' Turn to **6**

⇒ 'Tell me about funding for ongoing projects.' Turn to **316**

⇒ 'Pensions sound like a problem that won't go away soon.' Turn to **795**

⇒ 'Let's go over the risks.' Turn to **610**

⇒ 'There must be some factors in our favour.' Turn to **132**

⇒ 'What do we know about the chief negotiator?' Turn to **119**

⇒ 'All right, I think we've covered enough for now. Let's get down to business.' Turn to **507**

375

Only six months now remain of the two-year countdown to Brexit that began when you invoked Article 50.

Turn to **666** and tick one of the boxes there before doing anything else.

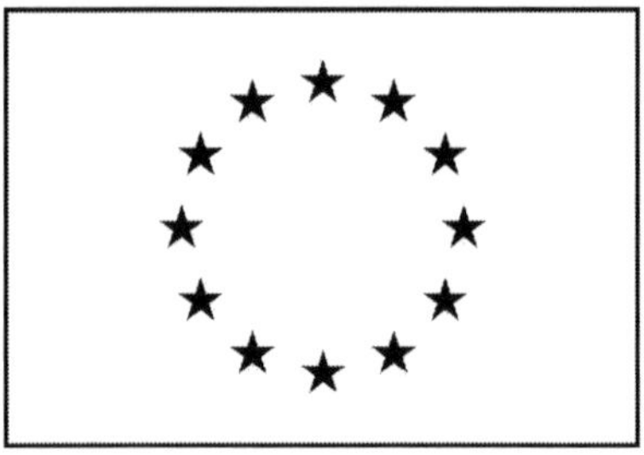

376

Talking to your dentist, of all people, at least gives you a chance to get out of the echo chamber of Number 10 for a while. Stifling the inner voice that protests it likes echo chambers, you fix him with a drilling stare.

⇒ 'The first referendum tells us the will of the people. Why should I try to overturn it?' Turn to **249**

⇒ 'If, like Burke, you object to direct democracy, why make an exception for a second EU referendum?' Turn to **571**

⇒ 'What's wrong with referendums anyway?' Turn to **68**

377

The leadership results are in. You sit gazing out of the window in a state of shock.

'What's that feeling?' you ask Wilkins. 'Like *déjà vu* only you get it before something happens, and you suddenly know what's coming next?'

'I couldn't say, Prime Minister.' He sets a cup of tea in front of you.

'I could tell before they announced the result of the leadership contest. That was it. I was out. All of this – gone, just like that. The rug, Wilkins, has been pulled from under me.'

'Distressing, indeed. I'm sure we shall miss you, and in that I include all of the Number 10 staff.'

You turn and look at him properly for perhaps the first time. 'I've appreciated your loyal service, Wilkins.'

He allows the trace of a smile to flash across his face. 'I would not use the term loyalty, Prime Minister. In my calling we answer to a higher demand than personal ties. It is a question of duty.'

And with that he goes to pack your things and make ready for the new Prime Minister.

THE END

378

So the Swiss model is a patchwork of ad hoc agreements that somehow holds together whichever way it's pulled. Not unlike their country, come to think of it.

⇒ 'Do the Swiss get anything out of their membership of EFTA?' Turn to **231**

⇒ 'How are treaties agreed between Switzerland and the EU?' Turn to **576**

⇒ 'Why did Switzerland opt out of the European Economic Area?' Turn to **754**

⇒ 'Do they make a contribution to the EU budget?' Turn to **691**

⇒ 'Let's take another look at the big picture. I want to be sure we've considered all our options.' Turn to **703**

379

'Yes,' says Barkwell, nodding vigorously. 'My thinking too. Maximum freedom for us to do our deals elsewhere around the world while keeping the best of what the old Common Market used to offer.'

'I'm glad I have your approval, Leslie. Now run along.'

Turn to **666.**

380

Peter Strewel had ten years as a newspaper columnist making up ever more outrageous stories about the EU. As the principal Brexit jeerleader, his bona fides are rock solid. You're not going to convince anybody that you're a more committed Europhobe than he is.

Turn to **727**.

381

No one could accuse you of currying favour among the EU27, and your grip on the party machinery is stronger than ever. So, even though Dent has been railing against the EU for most of his political career, you're seen as the one who can deliver the outcome the diehard Brexiters want.

With Dent knocked out, it's now between you, Rufus and Stollard. Two of you will go forward to the membership vote, but first there's one more round in the Parliamentary contest.

If you have the keyword YELLOW, turn to **791**.

If not, turn to **501**.

382

'Always assuming we get the chance,' says Stollard. 'Staying in the single market would be marvellous, but even so much as whisper it and in pretty short order there'd be three different people sitting round this table.'

'Speak for yourself.'

'All right, Dennis – two other people,' says Stollard laughing. 'But even you must admit there are some swivel-eyed nutcases on the right of the party who'd slap the Inquisition on us if they sense we're straying anywhere near rational negotiation.'

Dent frowns, perhaps unsure where his loyalties really lie. 'I've a bit more confidence in the British electorate than you, Alan. They're not stupid. If the country's best interests are at stake they can take that on board. They just don't want us toadying to the Brussels bullies.'

'All right,' you say, summing up. 'We won't be the first government that's had to do a bit of spin doctoring. The key thing is don't burn any bridges. Britain and the EU both want an outcome in which each side prospers. We'll be firm, we'll find areas of common ground, we'll accept the deals that we need to, and we'll find ways to explain those deals to the voters as and when. Good day, gentlemen.'

Turn to **125.**

383

'Ah, now hang on. I know this. Saw it on *News Talk* the other night. The thing is, you'd imagine the big thing in trade is tariffs, right? Sell us a crate of curry powder and we slap 5% on that. But it turns out that's a bit old hat. Guess the average import tariff on goods into the EU. Go on, guess.'

'One percent,' says Stollard.

'It is one percent. It is. Of course, you're the Chancellor, so no cigar for knowing that. Thing is, the much bigger drag on trade comes from these non-tariff issues. How straight is your banana – well, I made that one up, actually. But regulations about how much alcohol is in your *cassis*, whether your kiddie's toy is going to poison him or your car battery is going to blow up, all those things. And most important of all for Blighty, what about qualifications and standards for services? Although that's not so relevant when we're talking about the WTO.'

'Why not? Services are more than three-quarters of our economy.'

'We're out of luck, then. The WTO is more focussed on goods. They've made a little progress with services, but the vanilla WTO deal wouldn't really work for us. If we want to keep selling our services to Europe, we need to conform to EU regs.'

⇒ 'And what about quotas and schedules?'

Turn to **61**

⇒ 'What's this about most favoured nations?'

Turn to **38**

⇒ 'Those are all details we can cover in due course.'

Turn to **454**

384

One of the wonks at Campaign HQ has prepared a video presentation of the key points. You can't put off watching it any longer. TED Talks it's not.

'Three quarters of Leave voters favour a hard Brexit,' a hired-in marketing strategist is saying. 'We can expect that to entrench as nobody likes to be proved wrong, so the optimum strategy is to polarize Leave versus Remain so that pro-soft Brexit blocs can't get traction. The majority of Conservative and UKIP voters want a hard Brexit, of course. That's even more the case if we only look at paid-up members of the parties. Our recommendation is this: forget about the centre, tack to the right and pursue a hard Brexit. Few of your voters will even consider Labour at the moment. Even its own voters are giving up on it having any clear stance on Brexit. So hoover up UKIP's vote with promises of grammar schools and a return to the 1960s.'

You hit pause and fiddle with the remote, trying to get the figures on the whiteboard behind him into focus. In the foreground, his frozen trust-me smile and studio tan threaten to pixellate into a blur of light.

It's not the TV screen, it's you. Seventeen hours without a break. Even lunch was on the hoof, a sandwich wolfed down in the back of the car before you were whisked around a wind farm in Rutland. Or somewhere.

It's gone midnight. Maybe you should get a cocoa and a book to take to bed. You punch off the briefing video – time enough to watch that over breakfast – and head through to the kitchen.

The cleaner is in there talking to one of your security people who's filling himself up with coffee for the night shift. You wave them both away. 'I can make my own cocoa.' It annoys you when people fuss.

Waiting for the milk to heat up, you realize you're almost asleep on your feet. The cleaner's half-whispered conversation seems almost surreal:

'My son and his friends, they get together for their game, right, that's their gaming evening. Online I mean, but before they start playing they Facetime or Skype or whatever it is. And they have a vote to decide what they're going to play, which game I mean. I don't know the latest ones. Not *Donkey Kong* anymore, is it? Huh. Anyway, he's voting and I hear him say this game, and he turns to me with a sour look, like this. Look, like this.'

The security man looks up wearily as she turns to gurn at him. 'Is that right?' he says in a voice freighted with boredom.

'It's not a game he liked, you see.' She clears away his mug and puts it in the sink. 'But there was another one he didn't want to play either, and he knew that one was going to get plenty of votes, and the first one wasn't, so he voted for that to stop them both getting into the second round. Then he'd got more chance of the game he wanted to play getting picked, you see? He's a clever lad, our Melvin. Could end up going to university one day.'

The security officer is going to need a lot more caffeine, by the looks of it. You're listening so intently that you end up putting salt in your cocoa. Still, it's reminded you of an important truth. Sometimes you have to seem to be going after something you don't want in order to get what you do want.

Turn to **500**.

385

Oh, for more hours in the day so that you could personally oversee all aspects of the Brexit negotiations. Unfortunately you've had to delegate a number of topics to your ministers – in particular the Secretary of State for Exiting the EU. Now to see how much harm he and his cronies have done…

If you have not marked the NHS as complete on your Brexit Memo Pad, turn to **682**

Otherwise, if you have not marked Second EU Referendum as complete on your Brexit Memo Pad, turn to **165**

Otherwise, if you have not yet marked EU Exit Fee as complete on your Brexit Memo Pad, turn to **560**

Otherwise, if you have not yet marked Residency Rights as complete, turn to **812**

Otherwise, if you have not yet marked EU Trade Talks as complete, turn to **662**

Otherwise, if you have not yet marked Security & Defence as complete, turn to **765**

Otherwise, if you have not yet marked International Trade Deals as complete, turn to **297**

Otherwise, if you have not already marked General Election as complete, turn to **181**

When you have completed all the issues listed above, turn to **424**.

386

And after three years with you as Prime Minister, what's the outlook for Britain's economy? Let's find out.

If your Economy score is 37% or less, turn to **108**.

If Economy is 38% to 55%, turn to **46**.

If Economy is 56% or more, turn to **328**.

387

'Not frightened of Alprèves and his mob, are you?'

Armand Alprèves is the negotiator on behalf of the EU Commission.

'Not at all. It's a negotiation, not a punch-up. Hopefully we'll find a solution that both sides can live with.'

'I'll be frank with you, Prime Minister. After the referendum result I expected a little more enthusiasm, a little more zip. You're not arguing over an insurance claim, you're steering the country out of the entangling coils of a bureaucratic octopus.'

⇒ 'Of course, you're quite right, Sir Harvey.'

Turn to **567**

⇒ 'It's what we're steering into that worries me.'

Turn to **270**

388

So far the polls suggest the Remain side is in the lead. But it's early days.

'Voters are led by their pay packets,' your grandfather used to say. There's a lot of truth in that. Your ability to steer the economy through the rocky shoals leading to Brexit will make a big difference.

Look at your Brexit Memo Pad. If your Economy score is 51% or higher, turn to **649**. If it's 50% or lower, turn to **128**.

389

'We need to announce a range of exciting new free trade deals,' you tell the Cabinet. 'Let's show those doubters and nay-sayers that Britain has its arms open to the world.'

You look around at the downcast faces. Several ministers shuffle papers. Somebody coughs.

'What?'

'Prime Minister,' says Leslie Barkwell, 'we've agreed to remain in the customs union.'

'Yes. So? You're the International Trade Minister. Get out there and close some sweet deals.'

'That's just it. I can't. The agreement with the EU is that we share tariffs with them.'

'It's what a customs union means,' says the Chancellor.

'There are sectors that aren't covered, surely? What about agricultural goods?'

They look at each other. Nobody wants to meet your eye.

'A bit of a nightmare, that,' says the Foreign Secretary at last. 'Hellaciously complex, those sector by sector deals. Turkey had a stab at it but have pretty much given it up as a bad job.'

'Services, then. That's nearly 90% of our economy. Get to work on services deals.'

The Chancellor sucks his teeth. 'Not really worth it. The Trade in Services Agreement is already being negotiated by over twenty members of the World Trade Organization, including the EU. Those countries account for over two-thirds of international trade in services, so we might as well wait and implement those terms.'

You cast a dark scowl around the table. 'This is hardly the triumphant repatriation of sovereignty that the public were promised.'

The Chancellor shrugs. 'Few political promises survive contact with reality.'

Mark International Trade Deals as complete on your Brexit Memo Pad, then turn to **666**.

390

Bill Appleby deploys all his usual rhetorical thumbscrews, but you were careful to rehearse a number of nebulous platitudes beforehand and he can't pin you down. As you leave the studio you're still shaking from the encounter, but you think you got away with it. For now.

If you have the keyword NYLON, turn to **193**. If not, turn to **726**.

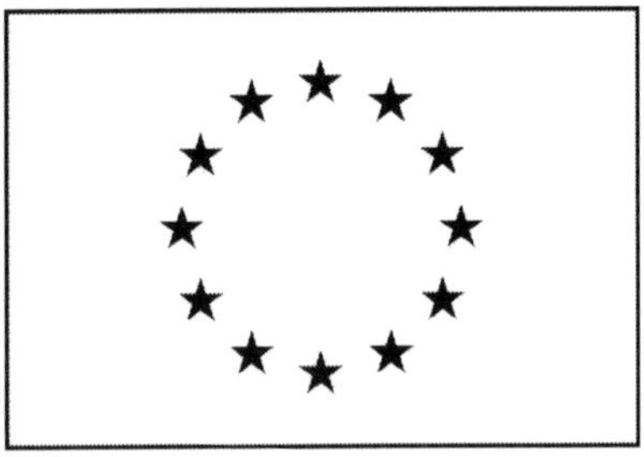

391

It's a weak response. A mistake to focus on whether there is even a viable chance of a Norway-type solution – the very idea that the other EFTA members would refuse admittance strikes at the national pride. You hear the shuffling of a discontented audience, but it's too late to take the words back. That's the trouble with live debates.

Still, it's one moment in a raging sea of discussion. Who knows if reason even plays a part in the decision making process now. People were asked if they wanted to jump off a cliff, and now they're confused because nobody mentioned the possibility of a painful landing.

On the night of the referendum you turn on the television and pace the room as the votes come in.

Toss two coins. If both come up heads, turn to **173**. If both come up tails, turn to **313**. Otherwise, turn to **403.**

392

'Glitzy new trade deals, for starters. There'll be some countries that prefer to deal with us than with the EU. Maybe we'll be more successful at closing deals with the USA. Then there's the opportunity of freeing up some of our tariff quotas – on oranges, for instance.

⇒ 'Oranges, eh?' Turn to **29**

⇒ 'What are our trading prospects with the US?' Turn to **260**

⇒ 'Go back a step. I want to hear about the bad as well as the good.' Turn to **700**

393

It's a good answer. Confident. Reassuring. Just enough clarity not to confuse, but empty enough to defy analysis.

Perhaps you have swayed enough voters to push the result in your favour, you muse as you drive back to Downing Street after the debate. You'll soon know.

On the night of the referendum you turn on the television and pace the room as the votes come in.

Toss two coins. If both come up heads, turn to **173**. If both come up tails, turn to **403**. Otherwise, turn to **127.**

394

'No access, really,' admits Dent sheepishly. 'Swiss financial institutions don't have financial passports to trade in the single market. Hence all the Swiss financial institutions based in the City.

⇒ 'Are they working on that? And other service industries?'
Turn to **673**

⇒ 'Let's review other aspects of the Swiss arrangement. Maybe something similar is right for us.'
Turn to **378**

395

It is an ignominious end to the brief, blazing glory of your career. You stepped into the breech to uphold the will of the people, only to find that it was a passing whim rather than a stern patriotic mandate.

Now the voters have come to regard their previous decision as a mistake, and in the way of human nature they must have scapegoats to blame. The helm passes to another and you must take your leave of Number 10, with only the prospect of lucrative book deals and highly-paid after-dinner speeches to console you.

THE END

396

'So it's a case of the only way is Norway,' says the Chancellor when you discuss the outline of the deal in Cabinet.

'It's a damnable compromise,' fumes Barkwell. 'Our courts will be obliged to track standards laid down by European courts, we'll have hardly any influence over regulations, and – worst of all – the fangs of the EU will still be sucking money out of us year on year.'

'Parasites,' chimes in a little voice from the far end of the room, reminding you that Thomas Tode is here.

'But compromise is the very soul of politics,' you point out.

At that Peter Strewel produces a meaty laugh. 'Yesterday's politics, that! We're on the other side of history now. People have lost patience with negotiation and compromise. They're demanding simple answers.'

'Politics is complex,' says the Chancellor. 'There are no easy answers.'

'Really?' chortles Strewel. 'Religion has been riding the high hog on the promise of simple answers since Man first wondered if it was all right to brain his neighbour and steal his wife.'

You look at the febrile light in the eyes of Barkwell and Dent and the other hardline Brexiters and you know he is right. This isn't politics any more; it's blind faith.

On your Brexit Memo Pad:

- ❖ -5% Authority – many of the hardcore Brexiters in the party are furious that you're keeping such close links with the EU.
- ❖ -3% Economy – even with EEA-level access to the single market, there will be some degree of disruption to trade in services on which the UK depends.
- ❖ +5% Goodwill – the EU27 may be hoping that in time Britain will return to the fold.
- ❖ -10% Popularity – after all the *sturm und drang* of negotiation, the voters resent such an undramatic conclusion.
- ❖ Tick the keyword CLARION
- ❖ Mark EU Trade Talks as complete.

Then turn to **385.**

397

'CSI stands for Comprehensive Sickness Insurance. Since anyone who isn't working or paying taxes over here can't get free healthcare, the idea is that you have to take out your own insurance. This applies to students and self-sufficient applicants.'

'Seems reasonable. So what happens if they haven't got this CSI?'

'Any years spent living in the UK without CSI don't get counted towards the five years you have to have lived here to be eligible for permanent residence.'

'From what I can gather, this is a bone of contention.'

'To put it mildly. It wasn't in any of the official guidance on the government website, and people have been complaining that it's suddenly been sprung on them in the application process. They feel it's a bit unfair to find out that their time doesn't count because they haven't had any health insurance that they weren't told they had to have.'

'Why haven't we been telling them about it?'

'Some would say it's deliberate. A tangle of Kafkaesque red-tape to reduce the number of residency applications.'

'Others might say it's just a bureaucratic oversight.'

'I couldn't possibly comment, Prime Minister. Either way, you may need to sort that out if your intention is to give most of our current EU citizens some kind of residency rights before it all blows up.'

⇒ 'What will happen to EU citizens in Britain if we leave without a deal regarding residency rights?'
Turn to **465**

⇒ 'What's the application process for permanent residence?'
Turn to **438**

⇒ 'What do you suggest is the best way to grant residency rights to EU citizens, should we choose to do so?'
Turn to **858**

⇒ 'That's all for now, thanks.' Turn to **666**

398

You join in a heated television debate in which you argue the case for remaining in the single market along the lines of Norway or Switzerland.

The ubiquitous Martin Mugglemore is chairing the debate. 'Come on, Prime Minister. We had a vote on this already. Just over half the country said they want out of the EU. Why not accept the result?'

⇒ 'If people have a right to make a decision, don't they have the right to change it? Democracy should never mean shutting down the debate.' Turn to **602**

⇒ 'Because the first referendum was badly thought out. We asked people if they want to leave the EU, but not what they want in its place. Now they have a chance to tell us they want a new deal that restores Britain's sovereignty without wrecking our prosperity.' Turn to **298**

399

As Britain has already broken off negotiations with the EU over the so-called exit fee, there's no chance of remaining within the single market. The very best you can hope for is to enter a customs union with the EU as Turkey has (turn to **674**) or else to create a new free trade agreement from scratch (turn to **294**).

400

If you have the keyword BLEAK, and this box ☐ is not ticked, tick it now and turn to **575**. Otherwise read on.

If you have the keyword NYLON, and this box ☐ is not ticked, tick it now and turn to **604**. Otherwise read on.

If you have the keyword VERTIGO, and this box ☐ is not ticked, tick it now and turn to **514**. Otherwise read on.

If you have the keyword HEMLOCK, and this box ☐ is not ticked, tick it now and turn to **331**. Otherwise read on.

To be briefed on the issues you're facing, turn to **425**.

Who has time for briefings? As the going gets tough, the tough get going! Turn to **450.**

401

Labour not only hang onto the seat, they actually increase their share of the vote. You can't see why that should reflect badly on you. What government is ever popular in the middle of a second term, especially when having to juggle the dozen razor-edged plates of Brexit?

Still, you get some glowering looks from your own back benches next time you walk into the Commons – and, worse, a derisory cheer from a few Labour wags. Oh, very funny.

> On your Brexit Memo Pad:
> ❖ -1% Authority – it's going to take you a while to live this down.

Turn to **350**.

402

You talk for a few minutes about making him Chancellor or Foreign Secretary, but somehow the conversation trails off without you managing to get a firm promise of support.

Later, while talking to the chief whip, you have a moment of epiphany. 'I'm not sure Thomas Tode even cares about being made Chancellor.'

The chief whip laughs. 'Of course not. In his own mind he's the secret leader of the party. He makes a few phone calls to cronies, they fob him off, and he thinks he's pulling the strings. So there's nothing you can offer him, you see.'

Turn to **727**.

403

The voters have spoken – again – and this time they're saying they want a soft Brexit. Out of the EU, but not out of the single market.

Look at your Brexit Memo Pad. If you have the keyword FOG or GAZELLE, turn to **484**. If you have the keyword SANCTION, turn to **91.**

If you have none of those keywords, turn to **10**.

404

If you have the keyword QUORUM, turn to **272**.

If not, turn to **390**.

405

You're watching the *Feeding Time* special on immigration. Struggling to stay awake, you look at the list of questions your press secretary has provided and decide which to fast-forward to next.

⇒ 'Do immigrants steal jobs?' Turn to **830**

⇒ 'Does immigration lower wages?' Turn to **530**

⇒ 'What are the actual EU rules on immigration?' Turn to **605**

⇒ 'Why do they have to come here?' Turn to **566**

⇒ 'Isn't it time we had a points system?' Turn to **208**

⇒ 'Why is immigration out of control?' Turn to **762**

⇒ Or you could switch off and get some sleep. Turn to **125**

406

With a sensation like a spider crawling up your back, you realize that your greatest threat is not Dent but Colin Fungale, newly installed in the Conservative Party after years as on-off leader of

UKIP. And indeed he shortly announces his intention to run.

'Aren't you worried that people will say you're just an opportunist?' asks an interviewer. 'After all, you've spent most of your political career in a different party?'

Fungale gives his trademark guffaw. You could fit a whole pint glass in that smirking mouth. 'Only because we Conservatives forgot the kind of party we were supposed to be. At times it was hard to tell us from New Labour. But let me tell you, Brexit has woken us up, and we know the direction we're headed now.'

'All the we and us stuff is a nice touch,' says Ron, muting the sound.

'Perfect for a audience of goldfish,' you snort. 'Who else has come out of the woodwork?'

'Tiffany Rufus and Amelia Dimple.'

'Dimple is a halfwit with the same grasp of political reality as you'd find in most care home patients. So obviously she'd appeal to party members, but I think the MPs will ditch her fast. The Home Secretary, though, she's a serious contender. Too soft on Brexit, of course.'

'It's dangerous to underestimate any of them,' says Ron. 'But that raises a good question. How are you going to pitch your approach to Brexit? Imagine you're on the *Now Then* programme and Bill Appleby wants to know where you stand. What do you tell him?'

⇒ 'There must be no attempts to remain in the EU. No attempts to rejoin it by the back door. The people have spoken. An overwhelming majority demand that we recover our sovereign position in the world. It is the will of the people. Take back control!' Turn to **671**

⇒ 'The duty of the government is to make a success of Brexit. I intend to negotiate our exit from the European Union while ensuring whatever arrangements are necessary to secure Britain's security and prosperity as an independent power.' Turn to **592**

⇒ 'If we're being honest, and I think we must be in these unprecedented and uncertain times, it's possible that the 2016 referendum was misjudged, the potential benefits mis-sold, and the result misguided. We should at least be open to the option of remaining in the EU if no better deal can be achieved.' Turn to **317**

407

You apply the whip, but to your frustration and fury a sizeable number of your own backbenchers defy it. You make a mental note of the rebels' faces. Their days in the party are numbered if you have anything to say about it.

Look at your Brexit Memo Pad. If your Popularity is 70% or more, turn to **695**. Otherwise turn to **58**.

408

'I'm not sure if I can make that promise, Prime Minister,' she says.

'Bargaining for a promotion? That won't – '

'It's not that. I must represent my constituents, you see.'

'And they voted for Brexit, didn't they?'

'Yes, but my job isn't just to rubber-stamp their opinions. It's to use my judgement in their best interests. And I don't think they want Britain to bolt so far out of the EU that we haven't even got the kind of relationship that Switzerland does.'

Privately you understand her point. 'I'm just advising you to tone it down,' you tell her. 'You can achieve more on your constituents' behalf as a junior minister than you will if I kick you to the back benches.'

Now turn to **275.**

409

After telling your staff that you'll need a briefing on immigration you decide to get an early night for once. These days that means getting to bed before one in the morning. You're looking forward to watching something mindless on TV before you drop off, but there's a blue folder on your pillow with a note from the Downing Street press secretary telling you she's recorded tonight's *Feeding Time*. 'A special on immigration,' reads the note. 'Highly recommend you watch.'

You flop back spread-eagled on the bed as if you'd fallen from a plane. So much for a stolen hour of leisure. Now you'll have to sit through the head-on collision of simplistic sound-bites and tedious spreadsheet recitals that passes for televised debate.

⇒ Might as well take a look. Turn to **746**

⇒ Never mind *Feeding Time*, there's a late night action movie on Sky. Turn to **467**

410

It seems like every time you speak, you push away more voters than you convince. 'People don't really want to engage with politics,' muses Ron Beardsley, your chief of staff. 'They want to walk down to the polling station every few years. After they've marked their cross, all they want politicians for is to blame when things don't go smoothly. We're the Judas goats of the modern secular world.'

'I'm a politician, Ron. You're a fixer. So fix this.'

He shrugs. 'It's gone too far. Every time we ask the electorate to vote again on Brexit, they're picking up on what a Gordian spaghetti tangle it is. Now they'll start to punish us for failing to make it all go off smoothly.'

'Again: *me*. They'll punish me. Not us.'

On voting day the exit polls indicate only that the public remain conflicted on the issue. You sit up watching the results come in and wondering how you can turn the final outcome to your advantage.

Toss two coins. If both come up heads, turn to **127**. If both come up tails, turn to **403**. Otherwise, turn to **173.**

411 ☐

If the box above is empty, put a tick in it and turn to **774.**

If the box was already ticked, turn to **699.**

412

If you have the keyword LEAF *and* your Goodwill score is 33% or less, turn to **85**.

Otherwise turn to **594**.

413

You follow the signs to a area that seems unnaturally chilly. There's a mechanical hum and an etherish scent in the air.

'Welcome to the Costa del Cryo,' says an intern.

'I thought this was Geriatrics?'

She gestures at the coffin-sized pods lining the ward. 'They're all here. We call them the grandpopsicles.'

You wipe the condensation off the thick glass plate in the nearest pod. A gaunt, wrinkled face looks sightlessly back, blue with cold, sparkling with frost.

'Are these people alive?'

'The official answer? Of course they are. They're resting while they wait for medical science to come up with a cure for whatever ails them. In the meantime we spray the essence of fish and chips in their nostrils and pipe Ravel and old episodes of *Fawlty Towers* over the pod speakers. It's just like being in Spain. Probably.'

'What's the unofficial answer?'

'Eh?'

'You said that was the official answer. But unofficially..?'

'Unofficially we'll know if they're alive when we try waking them up. OK, your friend here is good to go under.'

You don't remember handing Abednego over, but there he is in his own cryo pod. The intern is attaching the refrigeration pipes. As you rush over, Abednego stares out at you through the glass with an accusing look. 'Is this the fate of unwanted toys?' he seems to be asking.

'You *are* wanted!' you tell him. But he cannot hear you. The patterns of frost spread across the glass until his face is entirely hidden.

Turn to **368**.

414

Freedom of movement means anyone can move anywhere they like within the EU. Citizens can study, live, shop, work and retire in any member state. It isn't just about the free movement of people though. It includes capital, goods and services. Goods can be moved and sold anywhere within the single market without tariffs, custom barriers, or taxes of any kind. The same goes for capital. Banks, companies, investment funds, ordinary consumers, can all simply move money around Europe with the click of a mouse button, with no fear of extra taxes or capital controls.

This is also true for services, but not entirely. Services include things like financial services (from hedge funds to accountancy), insurance, banking, and so on. Services as a whole haven't been entirely harmonised across the EU, it's still an ongoing process. And the City of London dominates financial services across the EU. Well, for now, anyway. You need to make sure that remains the case after Brexit if you want that cushy, 70 grand, one day a week non-exec job with a global finance company.

What do you want to find out about next, if you haven't already?

⇒ EFTA? Turn to **346**

⇒ Regulations and standards? Turn to **655**

⇒ You've had enough, and it's time for bed. Turn to **441**

415

Strewel falls back on his favourite Europhobe tactics, thumping the tub for Britain's simple commonsense against, as he puts it, 'this empire of fussy pen-pushers that wants to extend an insidious octopoid grip around every aspect of our lives, banning bananas if they're not straight enough, insisting on one size for condoms, and telling us we can't buy a packet of prawn cocktail crisps.'

Interviewed shortly afterwards, you're asked to comment on his claims.

⇒ 'Some of Mr Strewel's examples are rather fanciful, but his underlying point is quite right. The EU has become an inflexible bureaucracy.' Turn to **496**

⇒ 'All these things he's claiming are completely untrue. They're just lies he made up to fill a newspaper column.' Turn to **687**

416

The first step is to sound out Barry Scraggle, the Labour leader. You set up a lunchtime meeting in your office at the Commons, but the hour ticks by with no sign of him. As you cross the lobby you spy him tucking into a sandwich.

'Mr Scraggle, could you not make our meeting? I could have laid on some nibbles if you were hungry.'

'Meeting?' He talks with his mouth full. Of course.

'I'd like to sound you out about something confidential.'

He snorts, giving you a whiff of canned tuna. Or perhaps it's Co-op fish paste. 'Deals in smoke-filled rooms, is that it?'

'Neither of us smokes, do we? Now look – ' you cast a glance around to check there are no reporters nearby – 'you know that we're in the same boat. I wasn't elected to this position.'

'I was elected,' he says, taking another bite of the sandwich. 'A landslide.'

'Yes, yes. But that was your own paid-up members. It's like *Flash Gordon* fans voting for Brian Blessed. I'm talking about the country as a whole.'

'As a whole? Riven by Tory policies. Divided by austerity.'

'To hear you tell it they ought to be outside with tumbrils and a guillotine.'

'So they should.'

This seems to be going better than you could have hoped. He actually seems to think he can win.

⇒ Broach the possibility of a snap election. Turn to **525**

⇒ You've learned enough. No need to let him in on it just yet. Turn to **13**

417

'Better than leaping off a cliff with an anvil,' says the Chancellor when you tell him the outline of the deal. 'We'll have minimal influence over the regulations we have to abide by, of course.'

'The crucial distinction, Alan, is that we don't *have* to abide by them. British law will track the rulings of the European Court, but with the option to go its own way.'

'If we ever do opt out, that could cut off our remaining access to the single market.'

'The point is we can sell it to the voters as sovereignty regained. Better to rule in an EFTA limbo than get booted out of office by voters who would never be happy with either the financial hell of a hard Brexit or the docile compromise involved in the Norway model.'

On your Brexit Memo Pad:

- -5% Economy – Britain's service industries will find it harder to trade with Europe.
- -2% Goodwill – the EU are already sick of the complexity of dealing with the Swiss under similar terms.
- -5% Popularity – the voters are dimly resentful that all the fireworks of Brexit has ended in the damp squib of thoughtful diplomacy.
- Tick the keyword CLARION
- Mark EU Trade Talks as complete.

Then turn to **666.**

418

'The EEA agreement – ' begins Strewel, peering at his phone. 'I'm reading this off their website, by the way. The agreement guarantees the freedom to provide services anywhere in the European Economic Area. Hang on, that's the EEA, what about the EU?'

'The EU is also within the EEA,' clarifies the Chancellor with elaborate patience.

'You sounded just like my old Latin master then. "People called Romanes they go the house", eh? Ho ho.'

Dent jumps in. 'The important point for our purposes is that all EEA service providers have to comply with EU law even if they don't trade with the EU. Which might be all right for the likes of Liechtenstein, but we can't have Britain playing second fiddle to Brussels. Not anymore.'

Turn to **66.**

419

The one advantage of trading on WTO rules is that there's no trade agreement that one of the twenty-seven EU states could veto.

'We dodged a bullet there,' you tell the Chancellor.

'Yes, but only by taking poison instead.'

Britain will slowly create a new web of trade agreements around the world, but with less leverage than you enjoyed as part of the EU. The irony is that, in the decades those agreements will take to finalize, most of the Leave voters will die off and you could be left with an electorate that wants to rejoin the EU.

But after all this, would the others ever want Britain back?

Turn to **865.**

420

Negotiations start off simply with a discussion of the European Arrest Warrant. This is a fast-track extradition treaty allowing EU countries to extradite criminals even if they are their own nationals.

'Even if we are able to continue opting into the EAW,' points out the Home Secretary, 'that's pretty much foregoing our own legal sovereignty. Imagine if a native Brit has to be shipped off to France because he robbed a bank there.'

She has a point.

⇒ Opt out of the European Arrest Warrant.
Turn to **286**

⇒ Request that the UK remains a party to it.
Turn to **65**

421

'I'm sure you're familiar with the Vienna Convention on the law of treaties, Monsieur Alprèves. Specifically clause 70, which releases the parties terminating a treaty from "any obligation further to perform the treaty". After Britain leaves the European Union, we don't owe another cent.'

'It's a point of view. And yet the same clause goes on to say that the party in question remains bound by its obligations under the treaty. Like so many points of law, it appears solid until you reach to seize it, and then it slips through the fingers.' He takes off his reading glasses and gives you a frank look. 'Do you really want to take the case to the Hague? Blow up the talks, walk away, lose everything – and after all that the court will still insist you pay.'

You could just forget the talks. 'No deal is better than a bad deal,' is how you could sell that to the voters. But the economic fallout would be bruising, and in fact it's not your only option. By calling in a lot of favours you might get a majority of the other member states to go along with Britain's payments ending after 2019. You just need them to see that €60 billion is not worth scuppering the whole negotiation over.

⇒ Try to keep the talks going while insisting Britain owes nothing. Turn to **444**

⇒ Accept that'll put paid to any trade negotiations with the EU. Turn to **540**

⇒ Back down and agree to pay. Turn to **363**

422

You make a brief announcement: 'With regard to the status of citizens of the European Union currently resident in Britain, I can confirm that following Brexit they will be regarded as foreign nationals and subject to the same immigration requirements as nationals of any other country.'

The next day the *Daily Outrage* has turned this into: ON YOUR BIKES and the *Klaxon* leads with: SLING EU'RE HOOK. Despite your announcement, the EU decides to let UK ex-pats stay in Europe anyway. Easy for them to say – it's less than half as many people spread over a total population ten times bigger than Britain's.

'Now we're the bad guys again,' you mutter indignantly as international reactions flood in.

'I suppose that's why Hollywood loves a villain with an English accent, Prime Minister,' says Wilkins as he brings you a cup of tea.

> On your Brexit Memo Pad:
>
> - -5% Economy – you'll be losing the taxes those three million EU nationals were paying.
> - -2% Goodwill – the other EU states had low expectations to begin with.
> - Tick the keyword KOALA
> - Mark Residency Rights as complete.

Now turn to **666.**

423

'Everything I hear convinces me I'm right,' says Tode, oddly giving a little sigh as if carrying the weight of the world on his slight shoulders.

'Think about what we discussed,' you call after him as he walks away.

Apparently he does, because a few hours later he declares his support for Peter Strewel. And this the man who he previously said was constitutionally incapable of leading the country!

Tode's endorsement of your rival is going to make it very hard for you to win now. Turn to **727**.

424

If you have either the keyword MAPLE or the keyword CLARION, or both, turn to **49**.

If you have neither of those keywords, turn to **306**.

425

The clock is counting down. Soon Britain will have left the European Union. There's still so much to do, but fortunately you have people to brief you on the key issues. What do you want to find out about?

To review possible models for Britain's future trading relationship with the EU, turn to **651.**

To search your soul as to the wisdom of calling a general election, turn to **69.**

To look into possible international trade agreements after Brexit, turn to **291.**

For a briefing about Britain's exit payments, turn to **112.**

To discuss the pros and cons of holding a second referendum, turn to **660.**

To mull over the prospects for the NHS, turn to **835.**

To look into the status of EU citizens already living here in Britain, turn to **612.**

To consider security and defence issues, turn to **628.**

When you've had enough of experts, turn to **450**.

426

If you have the keyword LEAF *or* if your Authority score is 76% or greater, turn to **710**.

Otherwise turn to **102**.

427

The EU will agree to a reciprocal rights deal, but the Spanish are insisting that all UK citizens in Spain take out health insurance to replace of the old system whereby the NHS would cover their healthcare bills. On top of that, the insurance has to be with healthcare insurance providers approved by the Spanish government, and the plans are quite expensive.

Accepting the deal would be a blow for the British pensioners who were looking forward to an easy retirement in Spain. Some of them are bank robbers, of course, but the rest will struggle to afford these insurance plans. Alternatively you could refuse point blank and try to bluff it out.

⇒ Agree Turn to **129**

⇒ Refuse Turn to **215**

428

Scraggle and Fobber, the Labour and LibDem leaders, call for you to face them in a televised debate. Predictably the Scottish First Minister, Pike, soon adds her strident voice.

'I haven't even refused to go on television yet,' you remark to Wilkins – or, more accurately, you remark rhetorically while Wilkins happens to be in the room.

He gives you a quizzical look but says nothing.

'There's nothing to be gained,' you go on. 'The voters I need aren't the sort to be swayed by the tedious hair-splitting of a debating society. All I need is a memorable slogan.'

'Get your country back?' suggests Wilkins.

'Something more muscular. "Tough and tenacious" – something like that. I'll work on it.'

The next few weeks are entirely taken up with campaigning. At each appearance you repeat your slogan and insist that a larger majority in the Commons will give you more negotiating leverage with the other EU states.

Finally the fateful day arrives. From the way the loyal press announce it, you could think it was D-Day.

Look at your Brexit Memo Pad.

If your Popularity is 66% or more, turn to **697**.

If your Popularity score is from 51% and 65%, turn to **568**.

If your Popularity is in the range 41% to 50%, turn to **593**.

If your Popularity is 40% or less, turn to **825**.

429

An unexciting campaign culminates in a slim but definite majority for Leave, thanks largely to a confused message from Labour, most of whose pro-Remain MPs lacked the gumption to stand up to their Europhobic leader Barry Scraggle and his coterie of Trots. The result was disenchantment among younger voters, whose turnout is low.

Scraggle is ambushed on his doorstep by Sky reporters who ask if he will continue to hold the government to account.

'Our concern is what it has always been,' he says, clutching an empty milk bottle in front of millions of viewers. 'The security of British jobs and the interests of the working man or woman.'

'Does that mean quitting the single market?' presses the reporter.

'It means, uh, that outside the single market, with full access to the single market, is where the interests of working people lie.'

Rolling over in delighted laughter, you sit on the remote and turn the TV off. Whatever happens now, it's a relief to know that Labour will continue to mill about aimlessly in your wake. But the important question is how you are going to respond to the public.

Look at your Brexit Memo Pad. If you have the keyword EIGER, turn to **506**. If not, turn to **446**.

430

Salmon… That makes you think of Kirstin Pike, the First Minister of Scotland. Not to mention the previous bloke, what's his name. Another fishy character.

Your brow furrows. Today's the day you have a conference call with Jean-Jacques Terlamen, President of the EU Commission. You've promised to outline the UK's position on the possibility of some kind of Norwegian model of Brexit that his people suggested taking a look at.

Staying in the European Economic Area would almost certainly stave off another Scottish independence referendum. Even if not, it would pretty much guarantee they'd vote to stay again. But what if it all goes wrong? Will Scotland walk away from the Union after all these years? And what will the rest of the UK think if we follow the Norway model? Nothing would really change, except we'd have no influence on the laws and regulations of the single market. On the other hand, we really need trade access to the EU in some shape or form, and the EEA model gives us that in full.

Turn to **747.**

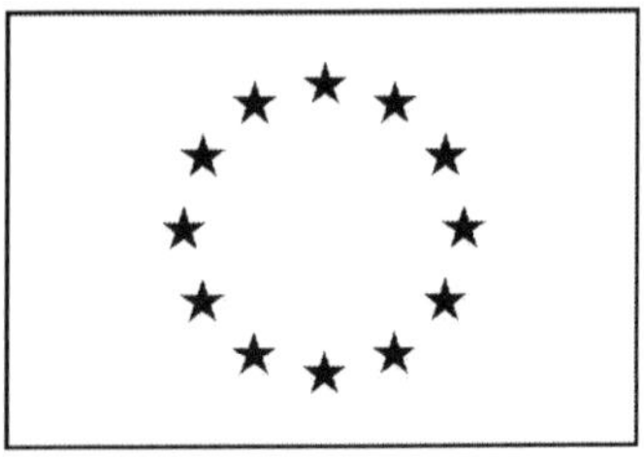

431

The cost of your free trade agreement with President Windrip is starting to make itself felt. US pharmaceutical firms are already lobbying for you to reduce the authority of the National Institute for Care and Health Excellence.

'Well, that's nice,' says the Health Secretary at the next Cabinet meeting.

'It's just politics,' says the International Trade Minister.

'No, that's what it's called. NICE. It's the body that evaluates the cost and effectiveness of drugs and sets clinical guidelines.'

'So why do the drug companies object?' asks Barkwell.

'They want to sell expensive medicines that aren't as effective.' The Health Secretary pauses, surprised to find everybody looking at him. 'What? What did I say?'

'You make it sound as if freedom of choice is a bad thing,' says Barkwell.

'Take a look at Australia,' says the Health Secretary. 'They had to relax the rules for public drugs purchasing in order to close a free trade deal with the US back in 2004. Because of that, companies are finding it easier to patent drugs, which has the effect of stifling development of alternative generic drugs for the less affluent. Supermarket painkillers versus the brand name variety, for example. And so the cost of treatment in Australia is going up.'

'What worries me,' says the Home Secretary, 'is that the US proposals would allow pharmaceutical firms to take direct legal action against the British government to challenge the NHS's monopoly.'

'It doesn't look good,' you have to admit.

⇒ Sweep it under the carpet. The US trade deal is more important than the NHS, which was going to collapse eventually anyway. Turn to **373**

⇒ Bite the bullet. You're going to have to cancel the US deal for the sake of the NHS. Turn to **586**

432

Your protection officer spent ten years in the Army before joining the Met's special operations division. Some would say he only has boots on the ground experience, but to your way of thinking where's the 'only'? You've had your fill of being briefed by bespectacled experts with graphs who wouldn't recognize an SA80 if they found it in their golf bag.

What will you ask him?

⇒ 'What do you see as the military issues around Brexit?'
Turn to **168**

⇒ 'How about the implications for policing and counter-terrorism?' Turn to **314**

⇒ 'What's with all the acronyms the security services use?'
Turn to **503**

433

Look at your Brexit Memo Pad.

If Goodwill is 41% or more, turn to **36**.

If Goodwill is 40% or less, turn to **821**.

434

'Painful to be on the losing side,' says Peter Strewel at the next Cabinet meeting. 'That's the trouble with integrity. Comes back to bite you.'

You look along the table. The ministers all gaze back with a new, brittle, eager light in their eyes. Like relatives crowding around the deathbed of a rich great-uncle.

'On with the job,' you tell them.

> On your Brexit Memo Pad:
> - -10% Popularity
> - Mark Second EU Referendum as complete.

Then turn to **450**.

435

They are aghast. 'So you start by threatening the security of Europe?' says Alprèves, clearly shocked.

'No, that's not – '

'A tit for tat.' Franjeboom's mouth turns down, and for a horrible moment you think he might burst into tears. 'Mighty Britain will continue to extend the umbrella of her military force, and in return we should reward you with plum trade terms?'

'I think you're both – '

'It's good that we know where we stand,' says Alprèves. 'But that's enough horse trading for today.'

> Record on your Brexit Memo Pad:
> - ❖ +3% Authority – the hardline Brexiters in your party enjoy any tactic that the EU disapprove of
> - ❖ -5% Goodwill – overnight the other EU states have less confidence in talks having a positive outcome
> - ❖ +3% Popularity – on balance the voters feel you're gaining the upper hand, but there's an undercurrent of trepidation
> - ❖ Mark Negotiation Strategy as complete.

Turn to **150.**

436

He nods so vigorously that you're reminded of the toy dogs that used to be seen in car rear windows. With herculean effort you manage to keep from laughing out loud as he says, 'If you don't mind me saying, Prime Minister, you're one of the few people who appreciates the real significance of Brexit. Times will be hard, but this is our opportunity to create a new Britain. It's like Nero having to burn the old Rome down to make a better city.'

And you reply:

- ⇒ 'Of course. That's it exactly.' Turn to **633**
- ⇒ 'Nero didn't actually do that, it's just Hollywood nonsense.' Turn to **308**

437

'The Netherlands had a referendum and nearly shot it down,' says Dent. 'More than 60% of them voted against the deal even though none of them actually understood it.'

'The scary thing is it only takes one country that doesn't trade much with us, or that stands to gain at our expense,' says Strewel. 'And God forbid that they put it to a referendum where the foreign *hoi polloi* can give vent to their seething Anglophobic neuroses.'

'Luckily in the case of the Ukraine trade agreement, the Dutch referendum was only advisory,' says Dent. 'So that was the loophole that allowed them to press on with it regardless.'

'I seem to remember another advisory referendum not so long ago,' says Stollard, stroking his chin.

⇒ 'What sort of provision can we make for financial services in a new free trade agreement?' Turn to **220**

⇒ 'If we can't get a deal with the EU, what can we expect if we revert to World Trade Organization rules?' Turn to **826**

⇒ 'That's enough mind-numbing detail for one day, gentlemen.' Turn to **81**

438

'After Brexit, EU citizens will be covered by the same terms as any non-British national. That means to stay here they have to be working, studying, or be self sufficient.'

'Self-sufficient in what way?'

'It could just mean personally well-off. Or they might be retired with a good pension. That's how most of the British folk sunning it up on the Costa del Sol will hope to stay on. Or they could be the wife or husband of an EU national who is supporting them while they're at home looking after the kids or whatever. And they have to have been here for five years or more.'

'That's it?'

'There's also the minimum income requirement for immigrants outside the EU. To qualify for permanent residence you've go to earn at least thirty-five thousand a year. But not if you've been here ten years already, or if you're on the job exemptions list. That's for nurses, care workers, people like that.'

'Thirty-five grand, eh?'

' I believe you brought that in, Prime Minister, when you were Home Secretary.'

'Did I? Well, it's all part of getting the immigration numbers down, and I'm sure it's been a great success.'

'No doubt it has, Prime Minister. What else can I help you with?'

⇒ 'What will happen to EU citizens in Britain if we leave without a deal regarding residency rights?'
Turn to **465**

⇒ 'I keep hearing about CSI. What is that, and why is it relevant?' Turn to **397**

⇒ 'What do you suggest is the best way to grant residency rights to EU citizens, should we choose to do so?'
Turn to **858**

⇒ 'That's all for now, thanks.' Turn to **666**

439

That conversation you had with your police protection officer in Kent... What was his name? McKay? He provided you with some insights you could never have got from a civil service briefing. Not that you often listen to civil servants. After all, they're paid to be independent.

Turn to **432.**

440

President Terlamen warms to his theme. 'It would be possible for the UK to set up a mirror of EU treaty regulations in British law. So you would recover the sovereignty that your voters prize – '

'Insofar as sovereignty is even meaningful in a world of interlocking relationships and compromises,' puts in the prime minister of Finland.

Terlamen nods. 'You would be able to apply a free movement emulator, so to speak, allowing the same terms and restrictions as currently apply. But it would be a matter of British law in sync with a new EU treaty. Then there would be no obstacle to you having full access to the single market.'

What he's proposing is the softly softly of Brexits – undoubtedly the best deal if you want Britain to continue trading with its nearest, biggest and most sympathetic market. The problem is how you'd sell it to the hardcore Brexiters in your own party.

You consider the suggestion over the next day, drilling down into details. What's your decision?

⇒ 'All right, we'll establish a UK legal framework that mimics current EU free movement regulations. Turn to **59**

⇒ 'It's still not enough. We need to get immigration numbers right down. Britain will issue work and study permits to eligible EU citizens.' Turn to **779**

441

That was positively brain numbing. Still, you reckon you've got your head around the single market. You turn off your laptop and pull up the duvet cover, thoughts of the single market whirling around inside your brain. If you let yourself agonize over that you'll be awake all night. You need to think about something else – holidays for instance. Ah yes, much more soothing. You start to doze off, thoughts of wine and roses in your head.

What's it to be? Wine tasting in France? Or wine tasting in Sussex and Kent?

Make up your mind, and then turn to **619.**

442

Look at your Brexit Memo Pad. If you have the keyword UNCTION, turn to **833**.

If not, turn to **634**.

443

Stollard scoops some fruit out of the bowl in the middle of the table. 'Let's say this grapefruit is the EU. The other grapefruit is the US, roughly the same size economy. China is the orange. Japan is about a quarter as big as the EU economy, so it's this apple. A nice juicy plum will do for Germany – I love these mirabelles; they're prohibited by US import laws, you know. And then Russia, Brazil and Britain are half a tangerine each.'

'Ooh, I'll have that other half tangerine if it's going spare.'

'That was France,' says the Chancellor as Strewel pops it into his mouth.

'So you're making out we're just half a tangerine, alongside a grapefruit!' protests Dent. 'That's a pretty unpatriotic picture to paint.'

No doubt the sight of the fruit bowl has put him in mind of a Cézanne still life. You all sit looking at it in contemplative silence for a few moments while Stollard pulls up a chart on his iPad. 'The EU's economy is about $18 trillion. Ours, given the pound now, is here – a pip or two over $2 trillion, just ahead of France before Peter scoffed it.'

'If only we had a melon,' says Barkwell. You turn to look at him. 'I mean… the sky's the limit now we don't have the EU holding us back, eh? We don't have to settle for a grapefruit, we can have the whole bowl.'

Turn to **454.**

444

You manage to get the Commission to accept a stopgap solution. Britain will pay its membership fees up until the point of Brexit, along with ongoing payments for British EU officials' pensions and limited contributions to the EU budget for investments that will benefit the UK. Those comprise the bare minimum you'd have to pay anyway while still an EU member, with none of the threatened exit fee payments. On the principle of a bird in the hand, the general mood of the 27 is to go along with it for now and get to the meat of negotiations.

That's the part of the deal you let the press get excited about. A couple of weeks later the news leaks out that Britain will also continue to pay into the EU budget to secure a transitional arrangement after 2019. Some of the more extreme Europhobes get in a fury about that, but their fulminations are drowned out by the general euphoria of having apparently stuck it to the EU.

Record on your Brexit Memo Pad:

- +10% Authority – nobody is going to challenge your leadership of the party for a while now.
- -15% Goodwill – your confrontational approach has lost friends among the other EU states.
- +5% Popularity – the voters perceive this as a strong move.
- Tick the keyword BLEAK

'We might end up having to pay the full bill anyway,' your chief of staff points out back at Downing Street. 'They'll take the exit fee as far as the International Court, which is hardly likely to decide that a country can break commitments willy-nilly.'

'Oh, Ron, try to see the glass half-full for once. If the court does rule against us, we can argue that the transitional payments should be counted as down payments against the full fee. And that will all come home to roost after the next election, when I should have a pretty unassailable majority as long as Labour don't wake up.'

He sticks his unlit pipe in his mouth and chews the stem fretfully. 'Maybe. But we'll need to ride out the reduced value of Britain's word internationally, along with a probable drop in credit rating. The storm's not rattling the teacups at home just yet, but out there it's raising Cain.'

Turn to **150.**

445

You throw yourself into a heated TV debate in which you argue the case for a soft Brexit.

The ubiquitous Martin Mugglemore is chairing the debate. 'So, Prime Minister,' he asks, 'you're saying we can have our cake and eat it.'

'Only if you think that Norway is, or Switzerland. Look, Martin, no club can have a one-size-fits-all. Britain's circumstances are different from Lithuania's or Poland's. We have one foot on the world stage, one foot in Europe. It makes sense for all concerned to find a deal that helps us to remain close to the EU while being free to pursue our global interests too.'

'But staying in the single market, that means remaining subservient to the rulings of the European Court of Justice, doesn't it? What's the point of leaving at all if we're still having to sacrifice our sovereignty?'

- ⇒ 'Every market has to have laws. When a trader wheels his barrow into the town square and stacks up his loaves of bread, he's agreeing to abide by the laws of the street market. It doesn't mean he isn't in charge of his own business.' Turn to **689**
- ⇒ 'There's no loss of sovereignty if we *voluntarily* accept the European Court's rulings.' Turn to **723**

446

Look at your Brexit Memo Pad. If you have the keyword FOG, turn to **91**.

If you have the keyword GAZELLE, turn to **434**.

If you have neither of those keywords, turn to **10**.

447

Time to give him a lesson in the new politics of Britain. You wave a dismissive hand at the chamber behind you. 'What do you think happens if they reject the deal we have?'

'I suppose we have to go back and ask the EU for an extension. Hammer out a new deal?'

'Not a bit of it. We're quitting the EU on 29 March. Nothing can stop that. They already voted to trigger Article 50, bless their cotton socks, and that date is on the front page of the bill. So the only power they have now is to say no to the trade arrangement we've negotiated, in which case that blows up and we crash out to WTO rules instead.'

'And that means…'

'No deal is worse than the worst negotiated deal, as any fule kno. So this vote they're going to get, it's just rubber-stamping the inevitable.'

You're right. The Commons votes almost unanimously for the deal you have struck with the EU, and although there is some criticism in the Lords you can safely ignore that.

Turn to **806**.

448

If you have the keyword CLARION, turn to **794**.

If not, turn to **321**.

449

Check your Brexit Memo Pad. If you have either the keyword BLEAK *or* the keyword HEMLOCK, then your track record speaks for you: turn to **645**.

If you have neither of those, turn to **778**.

450 ☐

If the box above is already ticked, turn to **385**. Otherwise read on.

Perhaps you need a break? Pressure of the job starting to take its toll? If so, make a note that you're on the final phase of talks at section **450**, that way you can find your place later.

On the other hand, if you have the energy to make that final push towards a successful Brexit, just read on.

Time is running out, and you can't be everywhere at once. Still, don't they say that a good leader learns to delegate? With only a few months left before Brexit, you can see to just a single major issue in person. Choose from any below that are not already marked as complete on your Brexit Memo Pad:

⇒ Deal with the NHS (if not already marked as complete)
tick the box above, then turn to **803**

⇒ Decide whether to hold a Second Referendum on Britain's membership of the EU (if not already complete)
tick the box and then turn to **192**

⇒ Tackle the issue of Residency Rights of UK and EU citizens (if not already complete)
tick the box and then turn to **638**

⇒ Deal with the question of UK/EU Security and Defence cooperation (if not already complete)
tick the box and then turn to **420**

⇒ Attempt to call a General Election (if not already complete)
tick the box and then turn to **416**

⇒ Agree the Exit Fee (only if you have the keyword APRICITY and the issue is not marked as complete)
tick the box and then turn to **611**

⇒ Deal with EU Trade Talks (if not already complete)
tick the box and then turn to **688**

⇒ Start preliminary talks on International Trade Deals (if not already complete) tick the box and then turn to **335**

When you have dealt with one of these issues, or if all issues are already marked as complete, turn to **385**.

451

'There's been enough bickering. What we need to do now, what the people are telling us to do, what I've always been very keen to do – is get on with the job.'

On your Brexit Memo Pad:

- ❖ +2% Authority – your rivals get the message.

If you have ticked the keyword YELLOW on your Brexit Memo Pad, turn to **670**. If not, turn to **163**.

452

You throw yourself into a heated TV debate in which you argue the case for a soft Brexit.

The ubiquitous Martin Mugglemore is chairing the debate. 'So, Prime Minister,' he asks, 'you're saying we can have our cake and eat it.'

'Only if you think that Norway is, or Switzerland. Look, Martin, no club can have a one-size-fits-all. Britain's circumstances are different from Lithuania's or Poland's. We have one foot on the world stage, one foot in Europe. It makes sense for all concerned to find a deal that helps us to remain close to the EU while being free to pursue our global interests too.'

'But staying in the single market, that means remaining subservient to the rulings of the European Court of Justice, doesn't it? What's the point of leaving at all if we're still having to sacrifice our sovereignty?'

⇒ 'Every market has to have laws. When a trader wheels his barrow into the town square and stacks up his loaves of bread, he's agreeing to abide by the laws of the street market. It doesn't mean he isn't in charge of his own business.' Turn to **614**

⇒ 'There's no loss of sovereignty if we *choose* to accept the European Court's rulings.' Turn to **757**

453

After some more exchanges, many of them heated, the President of the Council asks you what you would propose.

'One option is to invoke the emergency brake. Article 112 of the European Economic Area agreement allows for restrictions to be placed on freedom of movement. If Britain were to apply that same principle, we could get our immigration under control while still remaining eligible for access to the single market.'

'I have the relevant article from the EEA agreement here,' says the President of the Commission. 'I will read it for the benefit of the ministers. "If serious economic, societal or environmental difficulties of a sectorial or regional nature liable to persist are arising, a contracting nation may unilaterally take appropriate measures."'

'I don't understand,' says the French President. 'Those EU citizens aren't a drain on your social services. In fact, they create wealth for Britain. And you have fewer EU citizens living in Britain than we do, or Germany, or Spain.'

'We have a million Britons living in our country,' puts in the Spanish prime minister. 'Should I call a state of emergency?'

'The British don't call their own people immigrants,' the Greek prime minister tells him. 'When they're living in your country they're ex-pats.'

'There you have it,' says the French President. 'How can you justify using the emergency brake? In what way is this an emergency?'

⇒ 'It's a social emergency.' Turn to **147**

⇒ 'Well then, what do you suggest?' Turn to **223**

⇒ 'If we can't use the brake then it'll have to be a visa system.' Turn to **839**

454

Apparently World Trade Organization rules aren't the smooth, regulation-free trading nirvana you'd been led to expect. Better drill down and find out where the snares are.

⇒ 'What kind of trade disputes might we need to watch out for?' Turn to **741**

⇒ 'Britain has the fifth or sixth biggest economy in the world. Surely that gives us some leverage?' Turn to **443**

⇒ 'Presumably the big advantage of WTO rules is that they are truly international.' Turn to **590**

⇒ 'If we fall back on WTO rules, what are the benefits and disadvantages of that?' Turn to **813**

⇒ 'Let's look at the alternatives.' Turn to **56**

455

For reasons of their own, Labour go along with the motion. Perhaps it's true that Scraggle's faction actively welcomes the decimation of the party as a means to rebuild it in a more Marxist form. Who cares? Now that their support has granted you the snap election you sought, they will never be in power again.

Turn to **428**.

456

Fungale leans back in his chair. 'I just wanted to point out that Bob is answering a completely different question.'

That gets a big laugh. Fungale milks it by looking around with a smirk. Bob Owlbear blinks behind his glasses, baffled as a panda that's been poked awake with a stick.

'Does immigration have an effect on wages?' Mugglemore reminds him. 'I think that was the question. Was it? Yes.'

'All right,' says Owlbear. 'Well the simple answer is that in skilled professions immigration doesn't make any difference to wages. There's a shortage of people to do those jobs anyway. In lower-skilled areas, all right, the projections I've seen are that shutting off immigration altogether might raise wages, but only by a tiny amount. Just half a percent. Negligible compared to the economic benefits to the country.'

'That's what the experts say, is it?' says Fungale. 'I wonder if any of them ever carried a hod full of bricks on a freezing cold day.'

'Unskilled workers aren't coming here,' puts in Lucy Tooth. 'They go to countries where there's lots of unskilled work. Duh.'

'Stupid woman!' you yell at the screen. 'You could have scored a point there if you'd asked Fungale the last time he worked on a building site.'

⇒ Listen to what else she has to say. Turn to **771**

⇒ Find another question. Turn to **405**

⇒ Give up and get a good night's sleep. Turn to **125**

457

'Free movement is one of the bits of the agreement that keeps threatening to push everything else over,' says the Chancellor. 'Switzerland has a free movement treaty with the EU, but their referendums keep sticking a spoke in the bicycle wheels. A few years ago they voted to give employment priority to Swiss citizens. The Swiss government watered it down, but not enough for the EU's liking. Now there's a ninety-day limit on Swiss nationals offering services in the EU, and Swiss universities lost out on £1.5 billion in scientific research funding they had been due to receive from the EU.'

'It's outrageous, really, and another clear case of EU bullying,' snorts Barkwell. 'Immigration to Switzerland is out of control. It's twice what it is here in Britain. They try to apply some sanity and the EU start shaking the stick.'

Strewel is nodding vehemently. 'Some EU chimp named Popocatapetowski or something had the cheek to tell the Swiss they needed to rethink their logic. He more or less told them to hold another referendum and get it right this time.'

⇒ 'What about financial services?' Turn to **394**

⇒ 'I think the takeaway here is the Swiss do have sovereignty. They can stand up against EU laws if they want to.' Turn to **509**

458

As you've agreed to a modified form of free movement, the issue of EU and UK nationals living in each other's countries is now superfluous. You announce a mutual agreement permitting those citizens to keep their residency status following Brexit.

On your Brexit Memo Pad:

- ❖ +5% Economy – that's three million taxpayers you don't have to say goodbye to.
- ❖ +10% Goodwill – your reasonable approach is making you friends in Europe.
- ❖ +5% Popularity – to your surprise, the decision is welcomed at home too.
- ❖ Mark Residency Rights as complete.

Then turn to **200**.

459

'I'm not sure if that will quite wash, Prime Minister. Not so long ago you were campaigning for us to stay in the EU. Do you deny it?'

'Yes. Well, no, but… Um. There were different… er… The circumstances, Bill. That was then, and now is – well, now.'

The rest of the interview goes like a dream. A fever dream. The sort of dream where your toys leer at you from rough pillow canyons and your own limbs feel like beached whales. When you come out of the studio, Terri Trough greets you with a face like her cat just died.

'Apart from that one tricky question, how did the rest of it sound?' you ask her.

She looks at you with shell-shocked eyes. 'The rest of it? That's all they'll remember.'

Turn to **377**.

460

Strong conviction is so often the cause of bad governance. Who in their right mind would choose to be led by a Robespierre or a Franco? And yet it's the pragmatists of history who get a bad press. Machiavelli, Talleyrand – 'shit in silk stockings,' Napoleon called him. Why? Because he wasn't dogmatic enough to get half a million men killed in a pointless invasion of Russia?

'It's not fair!'

Everyone's looking at you. Sir Harvey Doggerbank still has the results of the last round of Parliamentary voting in his hand.

'Did I say that out loud? Sorry.'

You lost. And so Noysom-Reek and Stollard go through to the membership vote. Whichever of them is picked, surely Labour will be the eventual winners. But that's no longer your problem.

'Where do you think you will go, Prime Minister?' asks Wilkins later as he packs your things.

You gaze out of the windows of Number 10 at the driving rain, the sullen streetlight, the grey streets, the huddled umbrellas.

'Anywhere but Britain, Wilkins.'

THE END

461

An audacious move. Will it pay off?

If your Economy score is 60% or more and your Popularity is 64% or more, turn to **615**.

Otherwise turn to **287**.

462

Lord Elmstead is going over the results you commissioned from his polling company. 'Given the circumstances, Prime Minister, your poll ratings aren't that bad.'

'That's faint praise, I must say.'

'It could be a lot worse,' he points out. 'You've managed to steer a course that didn't alienate either of the two great tribes of modern politics. At least, those who are against you are no more alienated than they were three years ago. That's probably thanks to them having low to zero expectations in the first place.'

Depending on how things pan out with the EU and how that affects the UK economy, you have a pretty solid base of support on which to build your next election campaign. And if it all does fall apart – well, it was what the people asked for. They can't blame you.

THE END

463

All indications of the national mood suggest that a soft Brexit is on the cards.

'It's both the best and the worst of all possible worlds,' is the opinion of one political pundit. 'At least Britain would be spared the economic calamity of leaving the single market, but while bound to Europe's standards products and services we'd no longer have much influence over them.'

If you have the keyword FOG, turn to **587.**

If you have the keyword GAZELLE, turn to **531.**

If you have the keyword SANCTION, turn to **398.**

If you have none of those, turn to **820.**

464

You took some flak from the hardliners in your party at what they perceived as giving in to the EU over Britain's financial obligations. Blinkered by their ideology, they failed to see the advantages of giving a little ground then to win some friends on the other side of the negotiating table.

Of course, none of those hardliners wanted the soft Brexit deal you're about to close. They're the kind who want to burn it all down. But dealing with them is tomorrow's challenge. For now you must think of the future prosperity of the country.

Turn to **82.**

465

'We'd be in a real legal pea-souper then. At the stroke of a pen they'd all be working over here illegally and could all be deported. Best guess, they'd all revert to three-month tourist visas. Businesses would be liable for fines for employing illegal immigrants. Presumably this scenario is entirely hypothetical?'

'Everything since June 2016 has been entirely hypothetical. I'd just like a sense of what the worst-case would involve.'

'In short, a traffic jam of residency applications, requiring more civil servants, more lawyers, more paperwork. Then there'll be the question of what happens to non-EU spouses and families of EU nationals. You know *Little Dorrit*? The bureaucratic snarl up this would unleash would make the Circumlocution Office look as efficient as a German car factory.'

⇒ 'OK, I've heard enough.' Turn to **666**

⇒ 'Tell me how permanent residence works.'
Turn to **438**

⇒ 'What is this CSI I keep hearing about?' Turn to **397**

⇒ 'What's your advice on guaranteeing the residency rights of EU citizens, should we choose to do so?'
Turn to **858**

466

'The first is that Britain will no longer have a say over EU financial rules, not officially anyway. And that's bad for everyone, because to be brutally honest they would be in a terrible mess if not for our input over the years. The reform of the securities market over the last decade has been entirely due to Britain's initiative. We helped temper some of the more immoderate Continental responses to the credit crisis, too.'

'They're not going to throw that expertise out with the dirty bathwater, are they?' says Strewel.

'It will be an exercise in soft power,' concedes the Chancellor. 'Hopefully we'll still have some influence over EU financial regulations. The other problem is harder to overcome, because it directly relates to the whole question of sovereignty. Within the EU, financial legislation automatically gets copied into the law of each member state. But Norway has to ratify any change in legislation and enact it into domestic law. And then the EU has to confirm that's been done in compliance with the original legislation.'

'Just rubber-stamping,' scoffs Dent. 'If there's one thing the EU are good at it's bureaucracy like that.'

'It's more glue than rubber,' says Stollard. 'A lot of EU financial regulation introduced in response to the 2008 crisis wasn't in place in Norwegian law five years later. Even if we can get the lag down to one year, it means our financial services will be going into the ring with one arm tied.'

Turn to **66.**

467

The movie is *Ways of Warcry*, a computer-generated whale of a blockbuster based on a children's comic. Perfect bubblegum for the mind. But as you settle back to watch, the voice of your conscience pipes up. Would President Windrip sit and veg out on two hours of mindless pap? You think he almost certainly would – which is a very strong argument against you doing the same.

⇒ Turn back to *FeedingTime*. Turn to **746**

⇒ No, damn it, even the Prime Minister is entitled to some time off now and again. Turn to **599**

468

Those decisions have already been taken. It remains to be seen whether they make Britain and her allies safer or play into the hands of terrorists, criminals and enemies.

The main thing, after all, is how the public perceive the danger. After the USSR collapsed, politicians were quick to talk up the 'peace dividend', even though overnight the world had become a lot less safe. But as long as a voter sleeps sound in their bed, and gives you the credit for it, that's all that really matters. Perception is the new reality.

Turn to **666**.

469 ☐

If the box above was already ticked, turn immediately to **350**.

If the box is empty, put a tick in it and then turn to **677**.

470

Most of Strewel's friends become enemies eventually. Just knowing him long enough has that effect. So who should you talk to?

⇒ A contact from his old journalism days.
Turn to **547**

⇒ One of people who campaigned alongside him in the Leave campaign. Turn to **103**

471

Your earlier willingness to reach a deal over the rights of EU citizens in Britain now stands you in good stead. Those countries with nationals living here will help to influence the Commission towards an amicable agreement.

Turn to **417**.

472

'What about the Heathrow expansion for a start? A few years back weren't you all, like, never never never, not in my back yard? And now you've spun right around and it's all about the marvellous economic windfall of stuffing another runway into an already congested and noise-polluted corner of London.'

'We must keep the UK open for business, you see. Before I was just thinking of my constituents, whereas now – '

'Whereas now you're thinking about your career.' She laughs. 'But it's not just one strip of tarmac. What about the Welsh politician who was bleating about how opening up the market to New Zealand lamb could destroy the Welsh farming industry? He's right, but to get trade deals we're going to have to do things like that. Scrapping the Hilton beef quota, for example. Devastating to farms, that. What are you going to do with all the abandoned fields? I suppose you could turn them into fracking sites.'

'Not necessarily. We could turn them over to solar panels and wind farms.'

'Right. 'Cause your Brexit voters are going to just love that.'

Turn to **700.**

473

'Another fine mess, Ron,' you say as your chief of staff comes in. 'What questions are we going to put on the ballot paper in the next round?'

He tugs his beard thoughtfully. 'We didn't think we'd have to. None of the focus groups pointed to a Remain victory.'

'Better decide now, then, hadn't we?'

'I suppose the obvious question is do voters want more concessions from the EU – a bigger rebate, something like that – or do they want closer links, EU army, and so on?'

It'll have to do.

Toss two coins. If both come up heads, turn to **620**. If both come up tails, turn to **578**. Otherwise, turn to **676.**

474

'Never going to work really, is it?' reckons McKay. 'First off we've already got NATO, though admittedly with Windrip in the White House nobody knows whether America would come in on our side or Putin's. But even so an EU army would really be British and French forces with German money. And now it won't even include us.'

'Have any steps been taken towards a more cohesive EU military strategy, though?'

He gives a short rattle of laughter like double-tap gunfire. 'Committees, lots of committees. Enough reports to rebuild the Berlin Wall out of paper. And the Commission set up EDA battlegroups in 2004. They're rapid response forces made up from a rotating roster of national troops that are meant to be capable of deploying at ten days' notice.'

'And can they?'

He gives a slab-shouldered shrug. 'On paper. Because of budgetary reasons, politics, and organizational issues they've never actually been tested.'

⇒ 'Who pays for the EDA? Turn to **113**

⇒ 'Let me ask you something else.' Turn to **432**

475

Gervais Noysom-Reek made the right ideological noises, but the MPs are still rational enough to prefer a leader with some experience and political skill. He is knocked out of the running, leaving you and Tiffany Rufus to go through to the final selection by the Party members.

If your Popularity is 30% or less, turn to **782**.

Otherwise turn to **519**.

476

'We can't get the agreement of all the states,' Chief Negotiator Franjeboom informs you sadly.

'That's madness. Don't they want to be able to get rid of British criminals and get back their own nationals?'

'Of course they do. But you see, it's a matter of sovereignty. The European Union is not the federal super-state your Brexit campaigners claimed. We can't make individual countries agree to relinquish their nationals to a foreign power.'

A foreign power? What does he mean? This is Britain!

Turn to **286**.

477

'In many services industries,' explains the Chancellor, 'setting up subsidiaries in other countries is just as important these days as the passporting that allows services to operate across borders. And if we don't have freedom of movement, it becomes quite hard to staff those overseas offices.'

'I don't see that at all,' says Barkwell. 'You just have to hire locals.'

'Companies can do that. They'll probably have to. But it does rather negate the point of Britain having such a high standard and large number of well-trained and qualified service sector workers.'

'Can't be helped,' insists Barkwell. 'If we don't get control of our borders, the green hills of home will soon be swamped by hordes of foreigners.'

⇒ 'What factors will help us in striking a good deal?' Turn to **495**

⇒ 'What are the pitfalls to watch out for?' Turn to **616**

478

Sterling is down, sending the costs of the weekly shop spiralling, while inflation is rising far too quickly.

'It'll only get worse after Brexit,' warn the Remain campaigners, and the public seem to take heed. More and more polls show that a large proportion of people who voted for Leave last time have either changed their minds or forgotten having voted at all.

'If it was just down the economy then we'd be looking at a full reversal of Brexit,' reckons your chief of staff.

'But?'

He holds up a copy of the *Daily Heil*. BRITAIN STANDS UP TO THE BRUSSELS BULLIES, thunders the headline. 'A lot depends on the English sense of grievance.'

Look at the Goodwill score on your Brexit Memo Pad. This gives a sense of how amicably the EU27 are behaving towards Britain at the moment.

If Goodwill is at 41% or higher, turn to **683.**

If Goodwill is 40% or lower, turn to **463.**

479

'We can say it's too early to set a figure as these investment projects must respond to need, changes in the economy, and so on.'

'Not changes in the economy. That'll just remind everybody that we're drowning in debt and sterling is about to do a bungee jump without a rope. But having to wait and see what the most deserving cases are, that sounds fiscally responsible, as the Chancellor would say.'

'There were plans for a spaceport at Newquay. You might get asked about that.'

'Perfect. What a completely ridiculous use of money.'

'Well, it was part of investment in some key aerospace projects.'

'Not the way I'll describe it. "The EU wanted to build a launch pad for space tourists, but Cornish men and women have their feet on the ground, and what they want are real jobs."'

'Are we promising jobs?'

'Are we buggery. We're just dissing the Mos Eisley scenario. Now give me some more ammunition against EU funds.'

Turn to **258.**

480

You rack your brains for an excuse, but you've already wriggled out of this meeting once. Now you're going to have to bite the bullet. Your footsteps rattle like gunfire across the tiled floor of the

Westminster lobby as you head towards the Pugin Room. Heads turn. Seeing the grim set to your features, they no doubt imagine you're on your way to do something decisive. Whereas the truth is that you're going to spend the next few hours fighting mind-shredding boredom.

Turn to **259**.

481

Time will tell what the return of border posts will do to the peace process, but the immediate effect is going to be on businesses and tourism.

> Record on your Brexit Memo Pad:
> - -1% Economy – queues and holdups take their small but significant toll on cross-border trade.
> - -1% Popularity – nobody is going to welcome more bureaucracy.

Turn to **49**.

482

Over breakfast you discuss the best negotiating strategies with your chief of staff Ron Beardsley. He looks sourly at your bowl of muesli, no doubt thinking of when he'll get a chance to pop out into the garden for a smoke.

'I've been thinking about the EU's stance, Ron,' you tell him. 'They say Britain's deal mustn't be better after Brexit than the deal we had as a member.'

'Logically that's rather an odd assertion.' He twirls his unlit pipe thoughtfully. 'If a better deal than membership is achievable, why shouldn't everyone have it? What they should be saying, if they thought it through, is that Britain's deal must not make things worse for any of the remaining 27 states.'

'Quite. Well it's things like that we need to think about. How do we frame the topics that are being negotiated? Look at it one way, it sounds like vindictiveness, setting out to punish Britain for no reason. If they see it the other way, then there's room for us to do well and for the other countries' interests to be served too.'

'A good point,' admits Ron. 'If there's a deal that is even slightly beneficial to the other states, they shouldn't refuse it simply because it is good for Britain. Except, of course, *pour encourager les autres.*'

'Well, that's a damp squib, Ron.' You put down your coffee mug with a sharp crack that makes him sit up. 'Any more *bon mots* before I gird myself for the fray?'

'Um... Only that obviously trade talks are the matter of paramount importance, but the EU negotiators are unlikely to get into those until we've settled at least one of the top line issues.'

'Those being?'

'The exit fee, obviously. Residency of EU and UK citizens in each others' territory. And the thorny issue of how we'll liaise on policing and defence.'

Turn to **125**.

483

'We should be nimbler than the EU at making deals, for one thing. They have to factor in so many individual interests. What do the Spanish fruit growers think, what does Polish industry have to say about it. Tie that into EU bureaucracy and no wonder it takes them ten years to agree a tariff quota on sugar cane.'

'That's good. You're like your father only more personable, photogenic and articulate.'

She blows a huge pink bubble that splatters across her lips with a sucky plop. 'Yeah, thanks. Anyway, there's also the option for us to loosen up regulations. We can adopt lower environmental standards, buy in genetically modified crops from the US, get a bit lax about financial controls.'

'Let's say "liberalize" rather than "get lax".'

'Oh, okay. I didn't realize I was getting marked on this, seeing as it's free advice. But that last one is the kicker, of course, because service markets are what we're most interested in.'

⇒ 'Services, yes. That's a strength.' Turn to **219**

⇒ 'What about our weaknesses?' Turn to **326**

⇒ 'Let's list the opportunities.' Turn to **392**

⇒ 'We'd better go over the threats.' Turn to **11**

⇒ 'I'm going to let you get back to your homework.' Turn to **666**

484

The big question now is whether you can hang on. The electorate want a soft Brexit, but perhaps you can spin your own campaign stance as a thing of the past.

'The people have spoken. Britain is a democracy. We have a job to do...' mutters your press secretary in your ear as you head off to the Commons.

> On your Brexit Memo Pad:
> - -5% Popularity – your misjudgement in the campaign will take some living down.

Turn to **490.**

485

Look at your Brexit Memo Pad. If the Exit Fee is marked as complete, turn to **722**. If not, turn to **659.**

486

It's a close call, but you scrape to victory against Gervais Noysom-Reek, the darling of the grassroots members.

'Experience and hard work still count for something,' says Ron Beardsley.

You laugh. 'That – or luck and base cunning.'

Turn to **519.**

487

'Thomas Tode,' says the host. 'Are immigrants flooding in? Is it all out of control?'

'It is, Martin. I've talked to immigration officials, the men on the front line. And women. And they all say the same thing. We're at breaking point, and the public sensed that, which is why they voted to leave the EU. Now at last we'll have our borders back under control.'

'To do what?' says Tooth, incredulous. 'We can't bring immigration down to the tens of thousands the PM's been talking about. For heaven's sake, just students alone account for thirty thousand EU immigrants a year.'

'Oh, and we certainly don't have enough students, now do we?' Chortling at his own comment, Fungale looks as pleased with himself as a baby who's just done an enormous poo.

Bob Owlbear wades back in. 'With university fees, which Labour are committed to restructuring more fairly, foreign students provide a nice little earner. But even so, those students are the doctors, scientists and office workers of tomorrow. A third of British doctors are foreign-born, for example. These aren't people pouring into the country with begging bowls. They're honest, talented, hard-working people. They're your neighbours.'

'Good luck selling your house, then,' says Fungale. His eyes crinkle shut in a grin, but this time his comment just draws a mutter of disapproval.

⇒ It's time you got some sleep. Turn to **125**

⇒ Watch a little more. Turn to **405**

488

Even Colin Fungale, whom many regard as the godfather of Brexit, is unable to mobilize enough support against your hard Brexit line.

'It's a matter of trust,' one crusty old backbencher confides to you over late-night drinks in the Strangers' bar. 'Obviously old Colin wants the job, and nobody doubts his credentials. Fellow positively despises Eurocrats. But can he deliver? His only experience is dog in the manger stuff, isn't it? What do they call it now? Disruption. I don't actually think he'd have the first idea how to go about it. I'm not the only one, either. Oh, well maybe one for the road if you're twisting my arm, Prime Minister.'

And so it turns out. Fungale is eliminated in the next round of voting. So that leaves you, Dennis Dent and Tiffany Rufus.

'Are you feeling confident, Prime Minister?' your chief of staff asks as you start planning for the final round before it goes to a members' ballot.

'Unassailable, Ron. Nothing can stop me now.'

We'll see. If you have the keyword OPAL and you do *not* have the keyword LEAF, turn to **853**.

Otherwise turn to **169**.

489

You're now seen as the candidate who is softest on Brexit. In the early, heady days just after the referendum that would be like spitting on Princess Diana's grave, but a lot of MPs have had a chance to take a considered view of Brexit over the last couple of years, and others who supported Remain from the start have recovered their backbone.

It's enough for you to knock Tiffany Rufus out of the running, at least. Serves her right for being neither fish nor fowl. But now the choice goes to the membership, and you can't expect them to weigh the issues up as rationally as the Parliamentary party.

If you have the keyword NYLON, turn to **80**. If not, turn to **843**.

490

You face your first challenge as soon as you arrive at the House. The chairman of the 1922 Committee wants to discuss your position. You'll need the support of the backbenchers if you're to stay in power.

Look at your Brexit Memo Pad. If Authority is 60% or more, you convince the MPs to back you: turn to **10**.

If your Authority is 59% or less, they insist you resign: turn to **232**.

491

Given the concessions you're willing to make, it's easy to sketch out some stellar terms for a future UK-Thailand trade agreement. The damage to British poultry farming won't be felt until you're safely through the general election. A couple of the broadsheets bring it up, but typically they make the explanation so confusing that the average reader has as much chance of understanding it as a headless chicken. The main thing is that right now this deal makes you look like you're firmly in control.

> On your Brexit Memo Pad:
> - +5% Authority – you've shown you're willing and able to make bold new deals.
> - -5% Goodwill – you've queered the pitch for the EU's own hopes of an FTA with Thailand.
> - +5% Popularity – voters eat up the promise of cheaper takeaways in the years to come.
> - Mark International Trade Deals as complete.

Then turn to **666**.

492

Stollard clicks his pen in a brisk gesture that seems to indicate you're getting somewhere. 'Norway is outside the customs union but in the European Economic Area, so it has the ability to negotiate its own trade deals and set its own external tariffs while enjoying tariff-free trade with the EU. In many ways the best of all possible worlds.'

'Except it has to pay dearly for the privilege,' insists Barkwell. 'And it gets no say in how the EU is run.'

'Not quite true,' says Stollard. 'Norway has indirect ways of influencing EU policy quite significantly. Perhaps we'll get into that.'

'Would they even want us muscling in?' wonders Dent. 'The EEA is their baby. We'd rather queer the pitch for them, wouldn't we?'

⇒ 'That's a good point. Would Norway block our membership?' Turn to **42**

⇒ 'What about the free movement problem?' Turn to **237**

⇒ 'Norway still has to pay a lot of money to the EU every year.' Turn to **601**

⇒ 'Would we have any influence in EFTA if we did join?' Turn to **330**

⇒ 'What would EFTA membership mean for the UK services market?' Turn to **579**

493

Machiavelli's advice is familiar but it's useful to be reminded of it. You should use proxies wherever possible to avoid trading off your own reserves of goodwill. For example, Ireland is heavily dependent on the UK economy, so you can count on them to argue for a good post-Brexit trade deal. Similarly you should be able to count on Germany. Britain takes over £60 billion in imports from them every year, including a fifth of all their new cars.

The Florentine also reminds you not to be distracted by appearances, but to look to the true pattern of power. Many decisions about Britain's future relationship will be taken by a vote among the EU27. Every state carries equal weight, so you mustn't focus all your efforts on France and Germany. Find something that every state wants. If you can't give it to them, find another state that can and get them on side.

Most of all, arrange matters so that others do your work for you. Congruent interests can create a web of interdependence in which nobody can afford to see Britain fail.

You close the book. From Machiavelli's portrait on the cover, you could almost fancy a family resemblance. Flattered by the thought, you put out the light and drift off into a contented sleep.

Turn to **482.**

494

Check your Brexit Memo Pad.

If you have ticked the keyword MAPLE, turn to **281**.

If not, turn to **623.**

495

'Currently none of the individual member states has direct control over relations with Britain. Everything is handled at the EU level. Why that's good for the UK is we'd just be negotiating with a single party, the EU Commission. This or that country can't suddenly throw a spanner in the works by claiming that our new free trade agreement needs the nod from them.'

'That would be a real madhouse,' says Dent.

The Chancellor holds up one finger. 'But there's a catch. It's nice and simple when we're just discussing tariffs on goods, which is what matters most to places on the far side of the world, but as soon as any new trade deal includes services it usually gets treated as a "mixed agreement", meaning that it's no longer just up to the Commission. Then every separate state in the EU gets a veto.'

'Access to the EU services market is what matters most.'

'Precisely, Prime Minister. So we might have to break out the straitjackets after all.'

- ⇒ 'What's a mixed agreement?' Turn to **122**
- ⇒ 'But surely every state only gets a veto when the EU is dealing with foreign countries, not an existing member like us?' Turn to **550**
- ⇒ 'What problems might we face in getting access to the services market?' Turn to **616**

496

As long as you're just matching Strewel's tactics, you can't pull ahead. It's like competing in a yacht race. Copying whatever the front runner does will only ever ensure you come in second. And in this contest there's no prize for second place.

Convening a council of war, you ask your chief of staff and press secretary what they suggest.

'What about talking to one of his old colleagues?' suggests Ron. 'They might suggest an angle.'

'Everybody has some dark secrets,' says Terri.

'In Peter Strewel's case it's an embarrassment of riches,' you say. 'Let's pick one and leak it to the press.'

If you take Ron's advice and talk to one of Strewel's former cronies, turn to **470**. If you dish the dirt on him instead, turn to **71**.

497

'That is not acceptable,' protests the French President. 'On such a basis all the member states could decide to apply quotas.'

'Is free movement so unpopular that it has to be enforced by legislation, then?'

'No. Only Britain has this big problem with it.'

'I don't think it's only Britain, monsieur. But instead of busting my *boules* you could work with me to find a solution that doesn't scupper us all. You remember what happened to the last British prime minister whom the EU sent packing with half a deal.'

'We want a deal,' puts in the German Chancellor. 'But you must see our position too. Let us find a meeting point halfway.'

It sounds like she might approve the emergency brake built into EU law. And why dig your heels in? Most of the immigrants that Leave voters are so bothered about aren't coming from EU countries anyway. On the other hand, every concession you make is another stiletto in the hands of your enemies. Knives, that is, not shoes.

⇒ Compromise: you'll apply quotas under the emergency brake for five years and then review the situation.

Turn to **336**

⇒ No, you have to reject freedom of movement even if it means losing access to the single market.

Turn to **216**

498

You've led by example, steering away from the polarized zero-sum politics of the populists towards a kinder and more inclusive kind of democracy. Or, at least, so it appears to your supporters and critics alike. And if there is one force in politics that can beat all the angry invective of the last few years, it's the promise of a brighter and more united future.

Turn to **519**.

499

Addressing a meeting of hand-picked loyalists on the eve of the voting, you paint them a word-picture of the sunny uplands of Brexit. From the glow in their eyes you can see they're dazzled by the thought of lucrative new trade deals and the heady freedom that will come after Britain is unshackled from European bureaucracy. Probably a few of them also imagine it will mean fewer black and brown faces on the streets, but best not to dwell on that faction.

The message, they like. But are they convinced by the messenger? As they file out of the hall, you try to judge whether or not they've bought your latest *volte-face*. A lot will depend on whether other respected voices in the Party are speaking out on your behalf.

If you have either the keyword UNCTION or the keyword YELLOW, turn to **533**.

Otherwise, if you have either BLEAK, FOG, HEMLOCK or KOALA, turn to **801**.

If you have none of those keywords, turn to **50**.

500

The cleaner's story about her son has set you thinking about negotiation strategy. It's the metagame that underpins the talks, after all. Not that politics is a game, obviously, but it couldn't hurt to bone up on game theory.

You pause at the bookcase by the foot of the stairs. You need something to take up with you. A little light bedtime reading…

- ⇒ *Getting To Yes: Negotiating an Agreement Without Giving In*, by Fisher & Ury — Turn to **591**
- ⇒ *The Art of Sticking It to the Other Guy*, by Dumpster P Windrip — Turn to **176**
- ⇒ *The Prince*, by Niccolò Machiavelli — Turn to **493**
- ⇒ *Death on the Throne*, by Martin RR George — Turn to **564**

501

'It's turning into a circus. Just when we thought it was nearly over, now Pooh Bear has joined in.'

Your press secretary is referring to the fact that Peter Strewel, following the Home Secretary's lead, has chosen this moment to throw his hat into the ring.

It is a worrying development. Although widely regarded as an unprincipled clown, Strewel's combination of over-simplification, facetiousness and posh bonhomie make him a favourite of the grassroots supporters. If you and he were to go through to the final vote by the membership, you wouldn't stand a chance.

Turn to **105**.

502

'Don't say: "the pound in your pocket will not be devalued",' is all the advice you get from the Chancellor.

> On your Brexit Memo Pad:
> - ❖ -5% Popularity – your policies are getting the blame for the decline of choice in the shops.

Then turn to **200.**

503

'It's quicker, isn't it?' says McKay. 'By the time you've chewed your way through some of these department names, the red button's pushed and we're all on top of a mushroom cloud.'

'Run me through some of them.'

'Well, there's CSDP. That's the Common Security and Defence Policy of the EU. On the basis of that you've got SDIP, which is the Security and Defence Implementation Plan that's being developed to decide how the EDA – European Defence Agency, obviously – should operate. They'd like there to be an OHQ, Operational Headquarters that is, to coordinate EU military missions, but we've always opposed that, and Poland, Lithuania and Latvia aren't too keen on it either.'

'Why?'

'Well, just doing what NATO already does, isn't it? Assuming President Windrip doesn't put up a wall across the Atlantic too. On the policing side you've got SIS II – the Schengen Information System, second gen – that handles data about terrorist suspects, international criminals and so forth. The European Arrest Warrant – EAW to any man who types with one finger – is the protocol that allows quick extradition between member states.'

He pauses and looks off into the dazzling haze out to sea.

'What is it, McKay?'

'Just wondering if 5 Eyes counts as an acronym. No, I suppose not. Still, there's enough there to keep those Brussels bureaucrats bending over the photocopier for years to come.'

⇒ 'What's your view of the military implications of Brexit?' Turn to **168**

⇒ 'How do you think it might impact policing and counter-terrorism?' Turn to **314**

⇒ 'Let's get back to London. This photoshoot's a washout.' Turn to **666**

504

'Well, you know my dad went off to Indonesia a few months back to tell them the UK was opening for business. Fanfare, tickertape, his suitcase full of samples. Very Willy Loman. And do you know what the head of their investment board said? He was talking about the trade deal that Indonesia is thrashing out with the EU, and he said they could copy and paste it to do a similar deal with Britain.'

'Well, there you go. Perfect.'

'Not the *same* deal. See, what he then went on to say was: "Of course, the UK's going to be in a much weaker bargaining position once it leaves the European Union, so Indonesia will expect much more favourable terms of trade with the UK compared to the EU."'

Turn to **700.**

505

The Party must feel you're a better person to deliver a strong but not utterly crazed Brexit, as Dent is knocked out in the next round of voting.

If you have the keyword NYLON, turn to **193**. If not, turn to **726**.

506

A majority for Leave leads to the obvious question for the second heat: do the British people want to quit the single market in a hard Brexit, or are they in favour of something more like the so-called Norway model?

'Given that the previous referendum came out 48% for Remain and 52% for Leave, I think we could have spared ourselves all this bother,' says the Chancellor. 'It's pretty obvious that the overall public mood will be for a soft Brexit.'

'It's politics, Alan. Nothing's obvious till long after it's happened.'

Toss two coins. If both come up tails, turn to **637.** Otherwise, turn to **157.**

507

The others sweep in. First is the Chancellor, Alan Stollard. The threat of the Treasury having to find an extra €60 billion has had him pacing his bedroom all night. You know because you heard him through the wall.

Behind him is the compact, strutting figure of Dennis Dent, the Secretary of State for Exiting the EU, beaming like a two hundred watt bulb. Dear God, how can he be so perky this early in the morning? The answer is pretty obvious, though. Ever since the referendum he feels like he's had a letter from Hogwarts.

A gaggle of assistants sweep in behind the two ministers like a bridal train styled by Moss Bros. You could swear one of them is actually speaking into his watch – until he catches your hooded stare and taps it off. If only these junior civil servants would spend a little more on clothing and less on their ubiquitous gadgetry.

'Sixty billion, they're asking. That's – ' The Chancellor glances at an iPad hastily held out in front of him by a lackey. 'That's a quarter as much as trade with the EU is worth to us in a year. Half as much again as our defence budget.'

'Outrageous,' splutters Dent. 'Sheer extortion. It's the sort of punishment beating the Foreign Secretary was talking about. Where do they think we'll find it, down the back of the sofa?'

'It's a tidy sum,' concedes the Chancellor. 'Especially with spending already cut to the bone.'

⇒ 'I already know the problems. Tell me some solutions.' Turn to **750**

⇒ 'Let's go over the options.' Turn to **151**

508

Your backbenchers make it clear in no uncertain terms that they are not going to let you blackball Fungale.

'We need him,' says Sir Harvey Doggerbank, chairman of the 1922 Committee. 'All of this is happening because of him. He's the architect of Brexit, and his flavour of politics is what a lot of people want.'

'Oh, I know what you're driving at. Honest bloke, likes a pint, always guffawing away like the kind of unrepentant rapscallion who knows he'll get a pass from an indulgent granny. Not a remote, middle-aged, over-educated career dinosaur like me, eh? I suppose you'd like to hand him the keys to Number 10 while you're at it?'

You mean it as a bitter joke, but what's most disturbing is the look of wild surmise that flashes across Doggerbank's face. You've given him an idea.

> On your Brexit Memo Pad:
> - Get the keyword NYLON.

Then turn to **375**.

509

'We can sell it that way, certainly,' says Dent. 'Broadly speaking, the Swiss have opted into the single market through a framework of their own – well, a framework that's been mutually agreed with EU, but still they can break it at any time.'

'Which means that for once the boot isn't on the EU foot,' adds Barkwell. 'They have to deal with the Swiss as a sovereign nation. How they must hate that.'

'Might be a bit of a snag, actually,' says Strewel. 'After all, if the Swiss deal is such a headache for all concerned, we might find it's put the EU right off doing any new bespoke deals.'

Turn to **378.**

510

'So it's a case of the only way is Norway,' says the Chancellor when you discuss the outline of the deal in Cabinet.

'It's a damnable compromise,' fumes Barkwell. 'Our courts will be obliged to track standards laid down by European courts, we'll have hardly any influence over regulations, and – worst of all – the fangs of the EU will still be sucking money out of us year on year.'

'Parasites,' chimes in a little voice from the far end of the room, reminding you that Thomas Tode is here.

'But compromise is the very soul of politics,' you point out.

At that Peter Strewel produces a meaty laugh. 'Yesterday's politics, that! We're on the other side of history now. People have lost patience with negotiation and compromise. They're demanding simple answers.'

'Politics is complex,' says the Chancellor. 'There are no easy answers.'

'Really?' chortles Strewel. 'Religion has been riding the high hog on exactly that promise for four thousand years.'

You look at the febrile light in the eyes of Barkwell and Dent and the other hardline Brexiters and you know he is right. This isn't politics any more; it's blind faith.

On your Brexit Memo Pad:

- ❖ -5% Authority – many of the hardcore Brexiters in the party are furious that you're keeping such close links with the EU.
- ❖ -3% Economy – even with EEA-level access to the single market, there will be some degree of disruption to trade in services on which the UK depends.
- ❖ +5% Goodwill – the EU27 may be hoping that in time Britain will return to the fold.
- ❖ -10% Popularity – after the high drama of negotiation, the voters resent such an unexciting conclusion.
- ❖ Tick the keyword CLARION
- ❖ Mark EU Trade Talks as complete.

Then turn to **666.**

511

'We could announce special visas for doctors and nurses. Tie it to an amped-up points scale to measure the level of training. That way we sell it as inviting the brightest and best physicians to come to Britain.'

'It's still risky, assuming what you're most concerned about is getting immigration down. Some demented old biddy is going to pop up on a phone-in grumbling that her GP has a Jamaican accent or took a few days off over Ramadan.'

⇒ 'All right. Let's do nothing. It's not like the staffing levels will collapse overnight.' Turn to **854**

⇒ 'We'll issue special medical visas. A few hardcore xenophobes might grumble about it, but getting waiting lists down wins more votes.' Turn to **824**

512

As your strategy so far has pointed towards a hard Brexit, you can hardly switch around now. Nor is there any chance to avoid campaigning without opening yourself up to charges of hypocrisy.

> On your Brexit Memo Pad:
> ❖ Tick the keyword FOG.

Then turn to **302.**

513

Tiffany Rufus is knocked out in the final Parliamentary round of voting. Now it's just you and Peter Strewel.

Turn to **67**.

514

If EU Trade Talks are *not* marked as complete, turn to **364**.

If EU Trade Talks are already complete, turn to **666**.

515

While the majority of Tory MPs are behind you, there remain pockets of dissent. The naysayers, the cavillers, the mutineers who refuse to sacrifice their self-indulgent scruples to the common good. You can picture them huddled around in their clubs or back-slapping in their locker rooms, scheming and plotting and sharpening the knives. And when your back is turned…

But now that you've steered Brexit in for a landing, you can focus your attention on taking care of those traitors. The tumbrils will be coming for them soon enough.

Turn to **386**.

516

The media aren't buying the spin this time. They mock your steady-as-she-goes strategy with caricatures of you as captain of a foundering ship, a toddler trying to build a sandcastle as the tide comes in, and – worst of all – a scruffy weirdo making crappy models out of matchsticks.

On your Brexit Memo Pad:

- ❖ -5% Authority – even backbenchers are smirking at you from behind their newspapers.
- ❖ -5% Goodwill – the EU disapprove of the UK talking up trade deals while still a member, even when those deals are going nowhere.
- ❖ -5% Popularity – voters are starting to see you as out of your depth.
- ❖ Mark International Trade Deals as complete.

Then turn to **666**.

517

When you get the chance to look at the staffing figures for NHS trusts throughout the UK, you're even more convinced that you made the right decision. The regions with the highest concentration of EU doctors and nurses are London, the South-East, and urban areas up through the country.

'It's almost exactly a map of Remain voting,' you say to your chief of staff. 'I don't give two hoots if they suffer from a drop-off of NHS staff. They didn't think Brexit was a good idea in the first place.'

'Traitors,' says Ron, morosely sucking on his unlit pipe. 'Now they'll get their just deserts.'

Record on your Brexit Memo Pad:

- ❖ -2% Popularity – a few of the more disloyal media say you're allowing the NHS to die, but not enough to worry you.

If you have ticked the keyword DODO, turn to **431**. Otherwise, mark the NHS as complete on your Brexit Memo Pad and then turn to **450**.

518

You put a Skype call through to the President of the European Commission.

'Are you going to tell me it was all an April fish?' he says.

'What?'

'You know. "Surprise! We never meant to leave. When I declared Article 50 I had my fingers crossed." That sort of thing.'

'No. Look, Jean-Jacques, what I'm hoping is the EU could grant

Britain equivalence status under – what's it called? MILF?'

He looks puzzled for a moment. 'Oh, you mean the directive on Markets in Financial Instruments. Hardly something we can decide overnight.'

'But you could say that Britain is being fast-tracked for equivalence. If we can announce that now, it might stop some of the overseas investment banks from pulling up sticks.'

Look at your Brexit Memo Pad. If Goodwill is 25% or more, turn to **583**. If it is 24% or less, turn to **246**.

519

Your staff at Number 10 give three rousing cheers as the votes are announced. Your own inner rush of triumph shows only as a slight upward curl of the lip.

Shortly after, standing in front of the cameras in Downing Street, you're asked how victory feels.

⇒ 'Everyone watching knows that already, because this is the people's victory.' Turn to **148**

⇒ 'It's not about victory, it's about the party making a clear and decisive choice of who should lead us into Brexit.' Turn to **451**

⇒ 'The important thing is we've put an end to uncertainty.' Turn to **47**

520

'No doubt that's what Margaret Thatcher would prefer, if she's looking down on us now. The single market is her legacy, after all.'

'I don't suppose she anticipated it turning into a federal state, though. In her day it was just supposed to be what it said on the tin. A market. But now we've got people flooding over our borders. Foreign legislation dictating to British courts.'

'The freedom of movement issue seems like a red line, I admit. I'm not quite sure how it got so blown out of proportion, mind you, but that's a discussion for another time. The fact is that all commerce involves an inevitable give-and-take over sovereignty. Unless we pull the shutters down like the Tokugawas in the 17th century, somebody has to decide on the size of washers, the purity of steel to be used in girders, that sort of thing. And those specifications need to be standard across a market.'

'But it has to be up to British courts whether to accept them.'

'That's a cake or death sort of choice if you ask me. Like saying that a shopkeeper has the right to chain up all his stock so you can't buy it.'

'And he should have that right.'

'The irony is that more and more these days the trading standards are being set at a level above the EU regulatory bodies, by the International Standards Organization and, for vehicle regs, by the UN Economic Commission for Europe. We could take a tip from Norway there. They go straight to the ISO and influence regulatory law at the global level, much of which is then adopted by the EU.'

'How much?'

'Take out the ISO regs and less than 10% of the legislation Norway has to accept as part of EFTA originates in the EU itself.'

⇒ 'What do you think our highest priority should be in negotiation?' Turn to **98**

⇒ 'What are the biggest risks of dropping out to WTO rules?' Turn to **588**

⇒ 'Sorry, Alan, I've got another meeting.' Turn to **666**

521

Despite some rumblings from the Spanish, who have the most UK residents, the EU have agreed to a quid pro quo deal. They will affirm the right of all UK citizens currently living in the EU to remain as long as you do the same for EU citizens residing in Britain.

You've got some good news to announce to the press for once.

> On your Brexit Memo Pad:
> - ❖ +5% Economy – the UK economy needs those EU nationals, and it helps not to be handed back a million pensioners from Spain.
> - ❖ Mark Residency Rights as complete.

Then turn to **666**.

522

It's come down to the wire. As you wait to hear the results of the next round of voting, how do you feel?

⇒ Quietly confident. Turn to **597**

⇒ A bag of nerves – but no one can tell. Turn to **377**

523

You're well known for ruthlessly gaming the system – exactly the quality that many MPs look for in a leader. Traditionally the Tory party has been suspicious of ideologues, and Fungale is an out-and-out evangelist. To beat him, you have to make him look dangerously unstable. Which shouldn't be too difficult.

Turn to **708**.

524

A couple of issues have been sitting in your in-tray for a while. Now that you have a little time, decide which you want to deal with:

⇒ A visa deal with Turkey — Turn to **629**

⇒ Trouble brewing with Spain over Gibraltar — Turn to **598**

525

Consult your Brexit Memo Pad.

If your Popularity is 67% or greater, turn to **222.**

Otherwise, turn to **253.**

526

Britain's influence in Brussels, once second only to Germany's, is now greatly diminished, but you still have some sway. Working through the countries most friendly to the UK, you're able to get some amendments to the draft agreement.

> On your Brexit Memo Pad:
> ❖ +3% Economy – every small concession helps.

Now turn to **865.**

527

Whether you have made the right decisions, only time will tell. In any case, there's no way to turn the clock back now on trade talks. And you have other matters urgently demanding your attention.

Turn to **666**.

528

Party members' whims can change faster than the weather. To find out how they feel as they cast their votes, toss a coin.

If you get tails, turn to **519**. If you get heads, turn to **782**.

529

As the EU is not itself a sovereign state, it cannot bring a case against the UK in the international courts. The individual twenty-seven member countries can, however, and many of them will personally feel the pinch now that Britain is refusing to pay the full sum agreed under the treaty.

And come to that, what is the full sum? As usual for anything involving EU finance, it's a bureaucratic spaghetti of treaties and addenda that not even Stephen Hawking could untangle. Which is not to say the court won't have a stab at it.

How are you feeling about the International Court's ruling?

⇒ Time will tell. Turn to **365**

⇒ Lap of the gods. Turn to **104**

⇒ *Que sera, sera.* Turn to **146**

530

Owlbear eagerly jumps on that one. 'On average EU immigrants contribute far more in taxes than they take out. For every £1 an EU immigrant working here costs the state, he or she puts back £1.34.'

Brilliant. He's already getting bogged down in statistics. Labour frontbenchers can't grasp how this stuff just glides off the mind of the listener. You can see Fungale next to him grinning away like his face is about to fall in two. He knows. Could be dangerous, that one, for all that he seems like a throwback to 1970s sitcoms, ill-fitting pinstripe suit and all.

Owlbear drones on. 'EU migrants arriving in Britain over the last five years contributed £3 billion more in taxes than they received from public services. The treasury estimates they're helping to grow the economy by over half a percent every year.'

'I see Colin Fungale might want to come in there,' says Martin Mugglemore.

⇒ See what he has to say. Turn to **456**

⇒ Fast-forward to Lucy Tooth for the Lib Dem view. Turn to **771**

⇒ Find another question. Turn to **405**

⇒ Give up and get a good night's sleep. Turn to **125**

531

You join in a heated television debate in which you argue the case for remaining in the EU.

The ubiquitous Martin Mugglemore is chairing the debate. 'People are saying they like the Norway model. Stay in the single market but with the possibility of opting out of the EU's "ever-closer" policy. And it costs us less per head than remaining a full member. What's so bad about that?'

⇒ 'There's all this talk of a Norway model, but where would we fit in? As part of the European Free Trade Association? We don't know if they'd have us. It would be a minnow swallowing a whale. And it's not that much cheaper, either. Norwegians pay about three-quarters per head of the full EU membership fees Britain pays.'
Turn to **391**

⇒ 'Quite simply, Martin, Norway has very little leverage with the EU. If we are going to be subject to EU decisions – as we would in the European Economic Area – it's better if we keep a seat at the table.' Turn to **539**

532

'Look at the trade deals I've been lining up for after Brexit. Is that the hallmark of somebody who can't make up their mind? I have my hand firmly on the tiller, I can assure you.'

You leave the studio with a slight swagger to your step, feeling more confident than you have at any time in the last two years.

Whether that confidence is justified remains to be seen. If you have the keyword NYLON, turn to **193**. If not, turn to **726**.

533

You call in every favour, draw on every case where you've shown pragmatic leadership. The only thing that could count against you is if you're on record as having made a strong stand against Brexit. In the eyes of the members, that's the one unforgivable sin. That and not showing enough emotion in public.

If you have any of the keywords CLARION, GAZELLE, or SANCTION, turn to **50**.

If you don't have any of those, turn to **519**.

534

Strewel backs out of the race with a surprisingly moving speech. When he admits that he has reluctantly decided he is not the man to unify party and country, you hear echoes of Edward VIII's abdication crossed with the death of Little Nell. You even shed a tear – of laughter, admittedly.

Now it's a vote of the party membership to decide between you and Tiffany Rufus. In a prepared announcement outside the door of Number 10, you say, 'I will ensure that Parliament delivers on the views of the British people and respects the democratic decision that they've taken.'

'What does that mean, Prime Minister?' calls out a journalist. 'Hard or soft Brexit?'

You sense a moment of destiny. What you say now has the potential to decide everything. Remember that while your words will be heard by everyone in Britain, the only voters who count now are the Tory party members.

⇒ 'Full tilt for a strong Brexit, that's the overwhelming mandate of the people.' Turn to **519**

⇒ 'The vast majority of British voters would now prefer a close relationship with the EU, rather like Norway has.' Turn to **782**

⇒ 'Frankly, there has to be an end to divisive politics or we risk tearing the country down the middle.' Turn to **672**

535

'As far as the NHS is concerned, funding isn't even the primary issue anyway. Staffing is the big problem.' You see him disappear from the screen as he reaches across his desk, reappearing a moment later with a report that he leafs through. 'One in nine of our doctors is from an EU country. And one in twenty of our nurses.'

'One in twenty? As few as that, eh.'

'It's more pressing than it sounds. Nurses are getting older – '

'Funny. Doctors always seem to get younger.'

'I mean it's an ageing workforce. One third of nurses are due to retire in the next ten years. And when they retire they're going to need nurses and doctors to look after them. Where do we recruit all the medical staff we need?'

If you have ticked the keyword HEMLOCK, turn to **323**. If not, turn to **511**.

536

Your tone doesn't go down well.

'Do we really have to bring this tub-thumping rhetoric into the negotiating room?' asks Franjeboom, wincing in disappointment. 'I had hoped that here, without the cameras to play to, we could talk as adults.'

> Record on your Brexit Memo Pad:
> - +3% Authority – laying down the law helps quell any thoughts of rebellion from your unruly backbenchers
> - +5% Popularity – whatever the EU27 think, your strong stance goes down well with voters at home
> - Mark Negotiation Strategy as complete.

Turn to **150.**

537

The Chancellor consults his iPad. 'Here's a statement that was made during the referendum campaign, and I quote: "It is absolutely crazy that the EU is telling us how powerful our vacuum cleaners have got to be, what shape our bananas have got to be, and all that kind of thing."'

There's a moment of silence. All eyes turn to Strewel, who looks shifty for a moment, then gives a big, belly-shaking peal of laughter. 'Might be one of mine. Still, what of it?'

'It's not true. The EU directive didn't specify how powerful vacuum cleaners had to be, it was a ban on inefficient designs. Because of that directive, vacuum cleaners and other appliances like freezers use about a third less energy than they did five years ago.'

'You've got to admit the bananas rule was… bananas.'

'A good story spoiled by the facts. The EU rule simply places bananas into different classes according to size and shape. No bananas were banned in the making of this directive. And, crucially, neither that or the vacuum cleaner rule were just conjured out of the blue by bored bureaucrats. They were implemented to bring EU specifications into line with international standards set at the World Trade Organization.'

⇒ 'Still, it all smacks of the nanny state at work.'
Turn to **596**

⇒ 'So you're saying we could we exert influence at the international level?' Turn to **684**

⇒ 'Rewind a few steps. I don't want to lose the big picture.'
Turn to **17**

538

You're throwing your weight behind the campaign for a soft Brexit.

> On your Brexit Memo Pad:
> ❖ Tick the keyword SANCTION.

Then turn to **302.**

539

You feel that your arguments have helped swing the result, but nothing is certain till the votes are counted. You settle down in front of the television with a glass of milk and a plate of sandwiches and wait to see which way it will go.

Toss two coins. If both come up heads, turn to **403**. Otherwise, turn to **313.**

540

The International Trade Minister is beside himself with joy. 'This is the opportunity I was waiting for. Wait till the EU see the juicy new deals I'm going to be doing under World Trade Organization rules. There'll be more countries jumping off the sinking ship, you mark my words.'

> Record on your Brexit Memo Pad:
> - +6% Authority – MPs are scared and look to you to fix the mess.
> - -20% Goodwill – you've left the EU in no doubt of the little regard you have for them.
> - +7% Popularity – rightly or wrongly, the voters see this as a strong move.
> - Tick the keywords BLEAK and ZEBRA

Now turn to **150.**

541

Jan sees you don't understand. 'You have to be working here for five years to get permanent residence, but because my wife is at home looking after kids – not working in the eyes of the law – she has to have CSI for her years to count. Comprehensive Sickness Insurance. Yet nobody told us this. Nobody tells anyone this. It is not even mentioned on government website. You didn't know about it?'

'What? Oh yes, of course. Sickness insurance, yes,' you say, lying with the practised ease of a hustings-hardened politician. 'But don't worry, it's in both sides' interests to guarantee the rights of our EU citizens here and the UK citizens in Europe. Everything will be fine.'

Heading back to Downing Street, you wonder if you ought to get a legal opinion on the question of residency rights.

⇒ It can't hurt to do some research. Turn to **686**

⇒ Less facts, more action – that's your motto. Turn to **666**

542

You announce the snap election and that Barry Scraggle is in agreement. Your own party can hardly oppose it, but they aren't happy that the Labour leader got to hear about it first.

> Record on your Brexit Memo Pad:
> - -2% Authority – some of your rivals in the party are stirring up discontent.

Turn to **428.**

543

You apply the whip. Other than a couple of old Tory grandees, who give speeches invoking 'principle' and other archaisms before lumbering through the Lobby like grizzled elephants defying the herd, your MPs do as they're told. So too, for reasons of their own, do Labour. The vote is carried.

Outside you face the press with a triumphant cry of, 'To the ballot boxes!' Turn to **428**.

544

If you have the keyword LEAF and your Goodwill score is 30% or less, turn to **787**. Otherwise turn to **664**.

545

If you have either the keyword DODO or the keyword JEWEL, or both, turn to **532**.

If not but you have the keyword IRIS, turn to **32**.

If you have none of those keywords, turn to **729**.

546

There's no mistaking the fruity mock-bonhomie on the other end of the line. 'Hello, Peter.'

'Look here,' says Strewel. 'Tide in the affairs of men and all that.'

'Have you called a plumber?'

'Ho ho. Plum job, more like. Yours for the plucking. I'm talking about Number 11.'

'I'm comfortable where I am, thanks. Why would I want to move next door?'

'Better than moving back to your constituency, isn't it?'

⇒ 'You're asking me to withdraw from the race. Are you mad?' Turn to **642**

⇒ 'It's a deal. Let's talk turkey.' Turn to **77**

⇒ 'Why don't *you* take Number 11? It's less work than PM, you know.' Turn to **20**

547

'It was a hoot talking to Peter about his columns from Brussels,' recalls Strewel's old newspaper editor, who is Skyping you from the poolside of his villa in Spain. 'He'd grin like a naughty kid and he used to almost sort of hug himself. Gleeful as a monkey on a banana mountain, he was. I remember him saying how it used to seem – '

'The Prime Minister is going to need a quote,' interjects Ron Beardsley, leaning across in front of you.

'All right. He said, "Filing this gallimaufry of EU nonsense every week is like tossing bones over a fence and listening to the dogs bark. The whole Tory party is absolutely hanging on my every word. It's really the most marvellous great gulp of power."'

'That sounds like him.'

What do you want to do with what he's told you? If you release the quote to a friendly journalist in the hope that it will undermine Strewel's image, turn to **563**. If you decide it's not worth it, turn to **528**.

548

You have the distinct impression the EU negotiators are relieved that you still want Britain to be part of the single market.

'It's best for all concerned,' President Terlaman assures you. 'What kind of single market membership are you looking for?'

⇒ The so-called Norway model: a very close relationship within the European Economic Area, giving comprehensive access to trade in goods and services.
Turn to **84**

⇒ The Swiss model: an arrangement outside the EEA with only partial access to trade in goods and services, but with more opt-outs and no contributions to the EU budget.
Turn to **654**

549

A junior minister breaks ranks, giving a speech in which she warns of the dangers of a hard Brexit.

'You have to make an example of her,' says your chief of staff, Ron Beardsley.

'You mean..?'

'Sack her.'

He has a point. If you don't, people will start to suspect you're a secret Remainer. But having recently seen a documentary about the Killing Fields of Cambodia, the whole idea of doctrinal purity and political histrionics rather sticks in your craw.

⇒ Overcome your misgivings and dismiss her. Turn to **166**

⇒ Speak to her privately in the hope she'll moderate her remarks in future. Turn to **408**

550

'True, Britain's case is different because we're already part of the EU. So possibly the Commission would have to decide whether to hand jurisdiction to the national governments.'

'Possibly?'

Stollard shrugs. 'It could go to the courts to decide. Or the Commission might bow to political pressure. We're talking about twenty-seven different national interests, and they aren't all going to be feeling in the mood to throw Britain a bone.'

'If the Commission have any backbone they can claim jurisdiction on the basis of the centre-of-gravity doctrine,' puts in Dent. He turns to you: 'That's a legal principle that says when an agreement covers multiple objectives, the law that takes precedence should be in line with the agreement's main purpose. In trade agreements, the EU has exclusive competence, so it wouldn't need to defer to the national governments.'

'Unless it chooses to,' says Stollard.

'Unless it does,' Dent reluctantly agrees.

'So really there's no telling which way it will go,' says Strewel. 'Typical bloody EU, like organizing an escape tunnel in a chicken run. We'll just have to suck it and see.'

⇒ 'What can we learn from similar agreements the EU has done in the past?' Turn to **22**

⇒ 'What advantages have we got in these negotiations?' Turn to **495**

⇒ 'In a worst case there's always the World Trade Organization, right?' Turn to **826**

551

The shooting range is located in an underground room below the Palace of Westminster. These days it's all kept on the QT. The story put out to the press is that it closed a few years ago. Rather like the underground polo arena, it painted too elitist a picture of the nation's leaders. And indeed it reeked of testosterone-fuelled elitism in the days when all the posh Bollinger Club boys used to hang out there with their hunting rifles. But you prefer a handgun. Oh yes, there's a new sheriff in town.

Your protection officers have cleared the range. It wouldn't do to have other MPs taking potshots within yards of the Prime Minister. Some of them are Monday Club members, for heaven's sake. You order your own customized targets hung up – pictures of political rivals whose careers you've left bleeding in the gutter on your way to the top – and spend a happy few hours peppering them with bullets.

> Record on your Brexit Memo Pad:
> - +1% Authority – you've established who's the boss.

Turn to **666.**

552

Look at your Brexit Memo Pad. If you have the keyword OPAL *and* an Authority score less than 61%, turn to **209.**

Otherwise turn to **412.**

553

'I know, I get it from my dad over breakfast. "We're not giving up the benefits of membership, we're just opening up to the rest of the world as well." But the EU is the most like us culturally.'

'I don't know. What about India?'

'Oh, you think they look back fondly on the Raj? Just 'cause you order a takeaway curry once a fortnight doesn't give you any insight into the Indian psyche. They don't want us to push them to liberalize their financial services, in fact they're not inclined to listen to us much after British banks pulled down the shutters on their branches in India after the financial crisis.'

'Were you even born then?'

'Internet, duh. Truth is, our closeness to India is like the "special relationship" with America – it's all from one end. Those guys don't feel any great attachment to us. Like, did you know Germany is India's sixth biggest trading partner in the world? We're at number eighteen. We do as much trade with India as Iran does. We only receive two or three percent of India's exports.'

'Room for improvement, then.'

Nobody can curl their lip like a teenage girl. 'You politicians really have your brains wired up differently, don't you? Look at the figures sometime. We have a £2 billion trade deficit with India. Other EU states are way ahead in the queue to do deals there.'

Turn to **700.**

554

You make a brief announcement: 'With regard to the status of citizens of the European Union currently resident in Britain, I can confirm that following Brexit they will be regarded as foreign nationals and subject to the same immigration requirements as nationals of any other country.'

The next day the *Daily Outrage* has turned this into: SEND THEM PACKING. Oh well.

> On your Brexit Memo Pad:
> - -5% Economy – you're losing the taxes those three million EU nationals were paying.
> - Tick the keyword KOALA

Now turn to **150.**

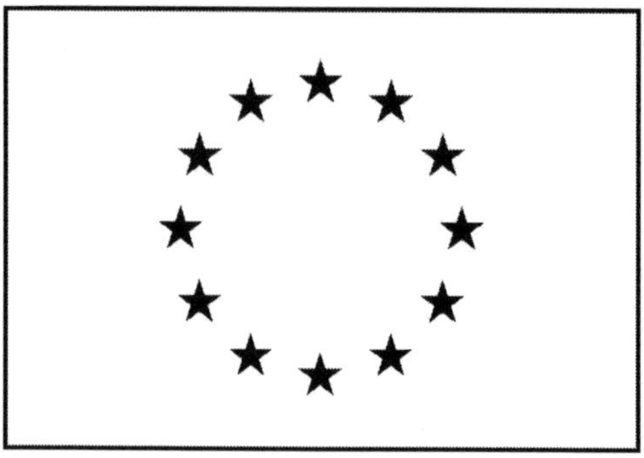

555

Ironic that one of the main claims of the Leave campaign was that Turkey was about to join the European Union, opening Britain up to a threatened influx of 76 million people. And instead those Turkish workers will be a lifeline for Brexit Britain.

> On your Brexit Memo Pad:
> - ❖ +1% Economy – a tiny boost, but you're going to need every bit of good news you can get.
> - ❖ Tick the keyword JEWEL.

Then turn to **175.**

556 ☐

If the box above is empty, put a tick in it and turn to **639.**

If the box was already ticked, turn to **5.**

557

'Depends on the Brexit deal, doesn't it? If we dive into World Trade Organization rules, the minute we try negotiating any deal we're going to have somebody somewhere insisting we should drop protection on oranges.'

'I don't see why you think that's a problem.'

'OK, say we had no tariff on oranges. And this is just one example, mind you, there are loads of other goods just like oranges. So we're buying in all these South African ones. What if we go to sell some of those cheap oranges to the EU? Spain's going to kick up a fuss. Not only that, but a UK with no import duties on African oranges is going to impact the Spanish economy. We take 10% of Spain's oranges at the moment. About three hundred thousand tonnes a year – the weight of two New York skyscrapers. If Spain looks set to lose that revenue, you think they won't find some way to put thumbscrews on us in the trade talks?'

Two skyscrapers indeed. Real know-it-alls, these modern school kids. Turn to **700.**

558

The EU Commission's chief negotiator, Armand Alprèves, is pleased by your suggestion that some rules and guidelines should be established at this early stage.

'Ever since the days of Hammurabi, it has always been better to be governed by principles than by whims,' he agrees.

Willy Franjeboom, the EU Parliament's negotiator, is not so quick to acquiesce. 'It depends, of course, on what those principles are.'

What will you suggest?

⇒ 'Let's try to find solutions that benefit all sides. It won't always be possible but it can be our first goal in all talks.'
Turn to **87**

⇒ 'Britain hopes for a win-win, but if you try to punish us we'll break off talks. No deal is better than a bad deal.'
Turn to **536**

⇒ 'Britain's armed forces are vital to the security of Europe, and in return we want a good trade deal. Let's get that out of the way upfront and we can stay friends.'
Turn to **435**

559

'They hate it, naturally. It's a messy jerry-built fudge to a system that they think works fine as is. And the Swiss deal isn't as simple as the Bilateral Agreements make it sound.'

'It doesn't sound remotely simple!' laughs Strewel.

'Exactly,' says the Chancellor. 'There are actually over a hundred individual agreements covering all sorts of different bespoke versions of standard single market rules. The EU won't be in a hurry to do another deal like that.'

You massage your temples, sure that you have a migraine coming on. It feels like you've listened to all this many times before.

Turn to **378.**

560

'I thought I had your personal assurance that the financial settlement would be handled long before this,' says the President of the European Commission on your weekly call.

'To be fair, Jean-Jacques, I've had a couple of hundred other things on my mind.'

'Britain's promises used to count for something.'

'Don't try that line. We're still an international power with – '

'A nuclear button? Here's another one. The settlement will be €40 billion.'

'With no discussion? Just, "here's your bill, don't forget to tip"?'

'We had two full years for discussion. And please don't think this comes from me. We have twenty-seven heads of state who are all at the end of their tether. If you don't agree to pay, there are some who are determined to veto every possible agreement Britain proposes from now on. You'll be stonewalled at every turn.'

You give him a piece of your mind and then hang up, but you know you have no choice. Time is running out and the cliff edge draws ever nearer.

On your Brexit Memo Pad:

- -4% Authority – there's no way to spin this that makes it look as if you had a choice.
- -7% Economy – the payments must be made somehow.
- -5% Popularity – the media are saying that there could have been a better deal if you hadn't left it so late.
- Mark the Exit Fee as complete.

Then turn to **385**.

561

The ruthlessness with which you dealt with a junior minister who proposed going soft on Brexit is already a legend in the party. Even though Dent has been railing against the EU for most of his political career, you're seen as the one who can deliver the outcome the diehard Brexiters want.

With Dent knocked out, it's now between you, Rufus and Stollard. Two of you will go forward to the membership vote, but first there's one more round in the Parliamentary contest.

If you have the keyword YELLOW, turn to **791**.

If not, turn to **501**.

562

'A weak pound would discourage British holidaymakers from going aboard, and it'll encourage foreign tourists as they'll have more to spend.'

'I can't imagine the average New Yorker wants to spend two weeks in a Cornish B&B, but I suppose to somebody from up north it'll seem like a tropical paradise.'

You gaze out of the window. A few fat raindrops spit out of a gunmetal sky. A mournful huddle of seafront houses appear in a watery haze.

'We're here,' says the aide, gathering your things.

Turn to **203.**

563

'Well, that backfired spectacularly,' says Terri Trough despondently as she flips through a cacophony of tweets. '"Good old Pete…" "Toss us another bone, you beauty…" "He's the kind of man we need…" If anything they like him even more now.'

'Nobody cares about facts,' says Ron Beardsley. 'Politics is a branch of mass entertainment. And Strewel is stealing our ratings.'

It's going to be hard to claw back a lead – if indeed you ever had one. If your Popularity score is 66% or more, turn to **528**. If it's 65% or less, turn to **727**.

564

What you thought was a biography of Elvis turns out to be the first volume of an ongoing fantasy series. It describes a world of cutthroat double-dealing where the only certainty is brutal betrayal.

After a few chapters you let the book drop with a thud on the floor beside you. On second thoughts, you could trip over it in the night. You kick it under the bed. Your only takeaway is that you should prepare for treachery, both from your own party and from the EU. Also, it seems that money is main force to wield against skulduggery. Well, you knew that. You have to get business on your side. Financial interests will be the lever with which you can shift the immovable objects around the Council table.

As you drop off to sleep, your thoughts are of dragons. If only you could hatch a few of those you could sweep the armies of Europos into the ocean. Dragons shaped like fighter planes. Dragons shaped like German cars. Dragons with the heads of Thatcher and DeGaulle.

You do not enjoy a restful night.

Turn to **482.**

565

Tiffany Rufus and Peter Strewel both concentrate their fire on you. 'They must have made a deal!' you rage at your advisors.

Ro Beardsley nods. 'The trouble is, between them they sew up most of the Parliamentary party. Barring a miracle, this is the end of the line.'

Turn to **377**.

566

'We're just a small overcrowded island,' is the questioner's point, 'so I don't see why these people have to come over here. They must think our roads are paved with gold or something. That's for Bob Owlbear.'

'We're lucky they do want to come here,' Owlbear says. 'They work hard. They're a vital part of our economy. And culturally they're in tune with our British values. If you take away the EU citizens working here, you're just going to have to replace them with foreign workers from elsewhere, some of whom may not find it so easy to fit in.'

Well now. The ungainly lump can occasionally show off a bit of deft footwork. He's almost managed to sound both pro- and anti-immigration. It's a balancing act Labour will have to perfect if they don't want their white working-class vote slipping off to join the 'Kippers.

⇒ How does the Lib Dem representative respond to that? Turn to **595**

⇒ What about the UKIP view? Turn to **650**

⇒ See what your own man says – if you can call Tode your man. Turn to **487**

⇒ Skip to another question. Turn to **405**

567

'I think we're going to get on very well, Prime Minister,' he says, offering his hand. 'I won't keep you from your meeting. Just wanted to say I'm looking forward to working with you.'

As he leaves, you catch Wilkins' eye and nod for him to show the Chancellor in.

Turn to **507**.

568

You are returned to power with an increased majority, but not the landslide you'd hoped for.

'A low turnout owing to bad weather? Election fatigue? Tactical voting on the part of the resistance – I mean the opposition?'

You chew over the possible causes late into the night, but there is no definite explanation. It is a victory, and you know you should be celebrating, but without the crushing success you'd expected there is a taste of ashes too.

> Record on your Brexit Memo Pad:
> - ❖ +5% Authority – your enemies can hardly claim now that you have no mandate to rule.
> - ❖ Mark General Election as complete.

Then turn to **666**.

569

The new referendum gives you an opportunity to pull the country back from the brink. If you can make the case for a soft Brexit, you may not only succeed in delivering Britain from the calamitous fate of being cast adrift outside the single market, thus protecting her vital industries, but you might also be able to heal the rancorous divisions within society. Perhaps there is a form of compromise Brexit that will satisfy the majority on both sides.

Or you could push it even further, advocating that Article 50 should be rescinded and Britain should stay in the EU.

⇒ Campaign for a soft Brexit. Turn to **538**

⇒ Make the case for Remain. Turn to **235**

⇒ Safer to avoid campaigning altogether. Turn to **618**

570

You throw yourself into a heated debate in which you argue the case for a hard Brexit. Although, as you repeatedly have to remind the other participants, the preferred term is 'strong Brexit'.

The ubiquitous Martin Mugglemore is chairing the debate. 'So, Prime Minister,' he asks you, 'how do you justify the course your government has chosen to steer since the first referendum?'

'We have been carrying out the will of the people, Martin. You're not against democracy, are you?'

'I'm all for it. But a referendum is not the same as a first-past-the-post election, is it? I'd say that a 52 to 48 vote is a snapshot of a country with very mixed feelings. It certainly didn't suggest that the majority wanted a more distant relationship with Europe than even Turkey or Switzerland have. So why did you take it to mean hard Brexit? I'm sorry, *strong* Brexit.'

⇒ 'In a divorce you have to make a decision. There's no "I'm leaving but I'll still pop back for Sunday dinner". It's the rough with the smooth. The public voted for Brexit, and so I had to decide the form of Brexit that would be best for Britain.' Turn to **731**

⇒ 'Remember that the referendum was only advisory. I took the result into account but I know I'm on the right course, and I'm going to stick to that course.' Turn to **410**

571

'Because the referendum result was pretty close. If I put 52 loose teeth in this dish and 48 in that one, you wouldn't be able to tell them apart. But the vote has been interpreted as an overwhelming mandate for a very specific and extreme form of Brexit.'

'The people have spoken. It's all about immigration.'

'Really? Because if it was just that, you could have got immigration down years ago. Half our immigrants come from outside Europe. But more to the point, that wasn't the question we were asked. The Leave politicians kept telling us we were in thrall to EU laws, that it wasn't democratic, that it cost too much. So we said, okay, on balance, the country leans toward leaving, just by a smidgen.'

'I hardly think a 52% majority is a smidgen. That's over a million people.'

'I could yank the tooth or leave it. What if I told you I was leaning 52% toward extraction?'

'But will it rot if you leave it in? You're going to fill it? Or crown it?'

'I didn't tell you enough to let you make an informed decision, did I? But that's as much as we were told about Brexit. Stay or go? It'll be fine, they said. Now we can see that they never had any idea about what would happen next.'

'So you're not going to pull the tooth?'

'What I'm saying is, whatever flavour of Brexit people were voting for, it's now set in stone. Circumstances can change – a narcissistic bully becoming President of the United States, for instance – and normal policy could adapt. But a referendum result… Few politicians have the guts to challenge that. It's like holy writ. So the only way to fix it is a second referendum.'

'If it needs fixing.'

Turn to **668.**

572

Your answer is well received, and you press your advantage with talk of the unelected bureaucrats of the EU, the threat of Turkish immigrants, and all the old bugbears that whipped up voters for the first referendum.

'But have I done enough?' you ask yourself as you settle down on the night of the vote to watch the results come in.

'More than enough, Prime Minister.'

'Don't creep about, Wilkins! You nearly gave me a heart attack. Go and get me a G&T.'

Toss two coins. If both come up heads, turn to **403**. Otherwise, turn to **173.**

573

'It's like how the Germans have had to build up the former GDR. Funding improves infrastructure, so that means increased prosperity, ergo more wealth created by trade. It helps businesses to become more competitive. It encourages further investment, and that in turn stimulates employment.'

She had been looking out of the window, conjuring vistas of shining new enterprise across the shabby Cornish landscape.

Turning, she sees your glare and falls silent.

'Don't stop now, that was positively Keir Hardie. Are you thinking of applying for a job with the other lot?'

'No, Prime Minister.'

⇒ 'Forget places like Poland or East Germany. How do the funds specifically get spent in Cornwall?' Turn to **86**

⇒ 'Britain could hardly have been getting much money compared to the really poor regions of the EU.' Turn to **228**

⇒ 'There's got to be some flab in all this spending. Give me something outrageous I can have a go at.' Turn to **236**

574

You can't possibly watch the whole programme. You'd go hoarse from shouting at the screen. Terri, your press secretary, has helpfully provided you with a list of the questions and where they come in the playback. So you can fast-forward through the important bits without sending your blood pressure into orbit.

⇒ 'Do immigrants steal jobs?' Turn to **830**

⇒ 'Does immigration lower wages?' Turn to **530**

⇒ 'What are the actual EU rules on immigration?' Turn to **605**

⇒ 'Why do they have to come here?' Turn to **566**

⇒ 'Isn't it time we had a points system?' Turn to **208**

⇒ 'Why is immigration out of control?' Turn to **762**

⇒ Or switch off and get some sleep. Turn to **125**

575

Look at your Brexit Memo Pad. If the Exit Fee is already marked as complete, turn to **400**.

If the Exit Fee is not yet complete, turn to **529**.

576

'Everything's dealt with on a case by case basis,' says Strewel. 'So if you think of the EU as having printed out a road map before setting out, what the Swiss do is pile in the car and then say, oh, better turn left here, then cut across here, and if we take the second left I think I know a short cut. Gets to the same place in the end, just by a more roundabout route.'

'Both sides end up wasting a lot of time hammering out the details,' adds the Chancellor. 'And nobody wants to go back to the table every time one small detail changes. So there's some attempt now to simplify the process with what's called dynamic clauses.'

'The problem as I see it,' snaps Barkwell, 'is that it gives free rein to the EU. They just lay down the law and the poor old Swiss have to go along with it.'

⇒ 'If Britain wanted to strike a similar deal, how long could it take?' Turn to **780**

⇒ 'What are dynamic clauses?' Turn to **120**

⇒ 'Britain's a lot bigger than Switzerland, so we won't get pushed around..' Turn to **776**

577

Rufus is knocked out in the next round. That leaves you and Alan Stollard, the Chancellor. If he becomes Prime Minister, Brexit will be watered down or even called off. What you're counting on is that the so-called ultras will unite to stop that, even if they're not entirely sure which way your own sympathies lie.

The winner will be picked by the Party membership. And so a hundred and fifty thousand people get to decide the future of Great Britain.

If your Popularity score is 39% or less, turn to **782**.

Otherwise turn to **519**.

578

The second round of voting reaches more or less a dead heat between those who want to pitch in to the EU's goal of ever-closer union and those who think that Britain should remain on sufferance but ought to be granted some concessions by the EU27.

Armand Alprèves, the EU's chief Brexit negotiator, can't help himself. 'Like many a dog that chases its own tail,' he tells the press, 'after much noise and scuffle Britain has decided to continue as usual.'

'If I ever propose another referendum,' you tell Wilkins as he serves your tea, 'I want you to pour that over my head.'

'With milk, Prime Minister, or lemon?'

Turn to **714**.

579

'Admittedly that's not so well developed,' says Dent.

'Not within EFTA itself,' says Stollard. 'The focus there has been on goods. Obviously services are more important to us, being four fifths of our economy, but we'd have to push through a new agreement from scratch.'

'Hang on,' says Barkwell, riffling through a thick wad of documents. 'Didn't I see something about Norway having passporting rights?'

'By dint of belonging to the European Economic Area,' says the Chancellor, nodding. 'That's not in the raw EFTA arrangement, it's something that's been bolted on. If we're considering the Norway model then yes, we could retain financial service passports, but even so it's not as good as what we enjoy under full EU membership.'

⇒ 'In what way isn't it as good?' Turn to **72**

⇒ 'Surely the EU will bend over backwards to retain British financial services?' Turn to **327**

⇒ 'Remind me about passporting.' Turn to **318**

⇒ 'Aren't financial services really just a London issue?' Turn to **807**

⇒ 'That's finance. Let's not forget about other service industries.' Turn to **418**

580

While you have been attending to the areas of negotiation you consider most important, you've had to delegate other topics to your ministers. Now it's time to see how they've done.

⇒ If you have not marked Negotiation Strategy as complete on your Brexit Memo Pad, turn to **26**

⇒ Otherwise, if you have not marked Immigration as complete on your Brexit Memo Pad, turn to **227**

⇒ Otherwise, if you have not completed the Exit Fee and do *not* have the keywords APRICITY or BLEAK, turn to **797**

⇒ Once you have completed all the issues listed above, turn to **524**.

581

The media construct a stark us-and-them narrative which is only reinforced by the rather superior attitude struck by the EU negotiators.

'Apparently the President of the European Commission is on record as saying he likes doing deals in dark back rooms,' says your chief of staff.

You remember that very meeting. 'He said something like, "If we talk about currency openly it has a catastrophic effect on the markets, so you could say I'm in favour of secret talks in dark rooms." A sort of joke.'

'Fortunately for the Leave camp, humour is very often lost in translation. The *Heil* is painting him as a supercilious Anglophobe bully.'

If you have the keyword FOG, turn to **570.**

If you have the keyword GAZELLE, turn to **60.**

If you have the keyword SANCTION, turn to **452.**

If you have none of those, turn to **83.**

582

If anything, releasing the story to the media backfires on you. All it really shows is that Noysom-Reek can be slapdash in his judgement. Although it's likely that Noysom-Reek personally is just as appalled as you are at the far-right organization's views, they actually chime with a small but significant percentage of the Party members. Thinking he's racist makes them keener to cast their votes for him.

Turn to **782**.

583

'You still have a few friends in the EU,' says Terlamen. 'I'll see what I can do.'

Over the next few weeks, Treasury officials work with the Commission to draft a statement. The thrust of it is to create a ratification process for equivalence status under the MFI directive. In effect, financial institutions currently based in Britain will go to the head of the queue.

> On your Brexit Memo Pad:
>
> ❖ +1% Economy – a tiny uptick, but in these troubled times you'll take what you can get.

- ❖ +2% Popularity – the voters don't understand what you've achieved, but they dimly recognize it as a good thing.

Now turn to **400.**

584

'We won't be held over a barrel.'

'Excuse me?' says Alprèves. 'A barrel?'

'As diplomatically as possible, I'd like you tell the Spanish to go and play with their castanets. I'm not giving in to blackmail – not where blameless pensioners are concerned. No way, José.'

He can see you have a strong case, or at least so it will seem to the media. A day or so later he comes back with new terms. It turns out the Spanish have backed down and agreed to the deal.

On your Brexit Memo Pad:

- ❖ +2% Authority – you've shown you can drive a hard bargain.
- ❖ +5% Economy – the UK economy needs those EU nationals, and it helps not to be handed back a million pensioners from Spain.
- ❖ Mark Residency Rights as complete.

Now turn to **666.**

585

Curse the luck – it was a safe Conservative seat, where the deceased had been the MP for over twenty-five years. Will his constituents show the same loyalty to a new candidate parachuted in by Central Office? Or rather 'Campaign HQ' as you must, absurdly, refer to it these days.

Look at your Brexit Memo Pad. If your Popularity score is 53% or more, turn to **196**. Otherwise turn to **304**.

586

Calling off the US trade deal gives you an almost physical pain.

'I'm not sure how we're going to spin this,' says your press secretary.

Good grief, why should you do her job for her? 'Brief some journalists off the record. Imply that the deal might still go ahead once a few unspecified wrinkles have been ironed out. We couldn't have signed it anyway until 2019.'

But even with the media mostly on-side, you still take a devastating hit from having to backtrack.

> On your Brexit Memo Pad:
> - ❖ -1% Authority – your own MPs can see you've been forced into this decision, making you look weak.
> - ❖ -15% Popularity – voters aren't good with facts, but they can smell indecision and prevarication.
> - ❖ Mark the NHS as complete.

Now turn to **450**.

587

You join in a heated television debate in which you argue the case for a hard Brexit – although, as you repeatedly have to remind the other participants, the preferred term is 'strong' Brexit.

The ubiquitous Martin Mugglemore is chairing the debate. 'So, Prime Minister,' he asks you, 'how do you justify the course your government has chosen to steer since the first referendum?'

'We have been carrying out the will of the people, Martin. You're not against democracy, are you?'

'I'm all for it. But a referendum is not the same as a first-past-the-post election, is it? The first referendum result was a snapshot of opinion in 2016. Why can't we change our minds?'

- ⇒ 'When you pick a course, Martin, you stick to it. That's the British way.' Turn to **372**
- ⇒ 'People are nervous, of course. They see the collapse in the pound and all the scare stories. But we never said this wouldn't be a rocky road. As a country we can see this through if we keep our nerve.' Turn to **393**

588

'The most immediate effect of coming out of the European Economic Area would be our external tariffs at the World Trade Organization. To start off we'd keep the same tariffs as the EU, of course.'

'But we can drop them any time we like?'

'As long as we drop them for everybody. That's the "most favoured nation" rule – which really ought to be called the "no favoured nation" rule, but never mind. Where I was going with that was what about areas we'd like to protect but that aren't currently covered by the EU rules? Those are cases where we'd like to raise tariffs. On certain vegetables, say.'

'We might need to do that to placate the farmers when they learn they aren't going to be getting EU subsidies any more.'

'Ah, but see, we can't. Raising tariffs is not nearly so simple as lowering them. If you raise tariffs on, I don't know, artichokes, then under WTO rules you have to lower them for something else.'

'Fine, we'll lower them for oranges.'

'A good solution, with only one drawback. Any of the hundred and sixty WTO members might raise an objection. Now repeat that for every single product we might want to protect. It'll keep Barkwell's department working weekends into the middle of the century.'

'Perhaps he should have been careful what he wished for. Well, thanks, Alan. If I haven't got my head around this yet then I'm never going to.'

Turn to **666.**

589

You make your announcement the next day: 'EU nationals currently living in Britain will be permitted to stay.'

The press go wild. No change there, then. The *Hypsterion* editorial calls it 'doing the right thing' while also putting pressure on the EU to reciprocate.

The *Daily Heil* headline? They're not happy, naturally. 'SOLD FOR A SONG!' blares the headline. The *Klaxon*? 'IT'S BRUSSELS HOLD 'EM AND THE PRIME MINISTER FOLDS!'

And so on. Encouragingly, the *Tomahawk* thinks it's risky but might work. 'THE HIGH ROAD' they call it.

Your bold move leaves the EU little room to manoeuvre. They shortly reciprocate by announcing that UK nationals living in Europe will be allowed to remain after Brexit.

On your Brexit Memo Pad:

- ❖ +2% Authority – you're showing who calls the shots in these talks.
- ❖ +5% Economy – those three million EU nationals are a considerable net benefit to UK finances.
- ❖ +5% Goodwill – the announcement sets a collegiate tone for future talks.
- ❖ Tick the keyword TIGHTROPE
- ❖ Mark Residency Rights as complete.

Now turn to **666.**

590

'We already enjoy international trade by way of the EU,' points out Stollard.

'We all know you're a Remainer at heart, Alan,' grumbles Barkwell. 'Give it a rest, eh?'

'I'm a realist, and we're here to thrash out the hard facts. So you can leave your soapbox at the door, Leslie. The point is that the WTO rules require us, in the absence of a free trade agreement, to apply the same tariffs worldwide. But our largest market by far is the EU itself. It has a similar economy to the UK and is hungry for services, in which we excel. Even more importantly, it's right on our doorstep, and trade has been shown to drop off inversely with distance.'

'Like Newton's laws,' says Strewel. 'By the way, I'll have that apple if nobody else wants it.'

'But as I always say, what we lose in trade with Europe we'll make up with the rest of the world,' Dent puts in.

'Not on default WTO rules. Europe is right there, and it's half our import and export market. Unless you can pick up the British Isles and plonk them down in the South China Sea – oh, and incidentally convert our economy to heavy industry while you're at it – then the WTO is not going to be our glorious new dawn.'

⇒ 'Will somebody please give me the executive summary version of what the WTO actually allows.'

Turn to **678**

⇒ 'Let's step back and look at the bigger picture.'

Turn to **454**

591

Despite your resolution to get an early night, you soon get caught up in the book and you end up reading it from cover to cover.

The central premise is not to negotiate from a fixed position, but to agree principles that both sides refer back to. A bit like how your cleaner's son and his friends must have established voting rules for which videogame to play, rather than each of them shouting for his own favourite.

You let the book fall to the duvet as you consider how to apply it to the upcoming Brexit talks. The authors make frequent use of divorce as an example of their method, which is strangely appropriate to your own situation.

An example might be the so-called Brexit bill. Rather than setting a figure, which is something your teams might haggle over for months only to end in a rancorous split, you could agree the underlying principles. So that part of the bill that relates to the EU's seven-year budget might, for instance, include payments made back into Britain during a transitional period. If talks reach an impasse, both sides have the pre-agreed rules to fall back on.

The authors also emphasize that you should always be mindful of your best alternative to a negotiated agreement. Is no deal better than a bad deal? That's something you need to have worked out before you get up and walk away from the table.

Tired as you are, you drift off to sleep with a feeling of renewed confidence for the task that lies ahead. Perhaps there's a win-win in all this somewhere.

Turn to **482.**

592

Dimple is knocked out in the first round of voting. At her concession speech she has her usual expression, that of an elderly relative woken in the middle of an afternoon nap. 'I will offer my services whenever and wherever the country needs them,' she is saying.

You laugh out loud, snapping off the television with a hatchet-like gesture of the remote. The ridiculous woman. You wouldn't trust her to arrange a bowl of flowers, much less run the country.

It's good to have the distraction out of the way. Amelia Dimple was the taste of meat you needed to get your blood up for the fight. And now you need a plan to deal with the serious opposition.

And that's when the phone rings.

Look at your Brexit Memo Pad. If your Authority is greater than 55% and your Goodwill is *less* than 41%, turn to **759**.

Otherwise turn to **546**.

593

You win, but without increasing your slender majority in the House of Commons.

'Will they paint it as a defeat?' wonders the Chancellor.

'Hardly, Alan. Before today I could only claim to have taken the reins of power from my predecessor. Now I have the personal support of tens of millions of voters.'

He nods sombrely, turning to gaze out of the window at the assembled press standing in the rain. You always knew he was weak. Perhaps now you should consider getting rid of him. If only you could absorb all Cabinet posts into your own office.

Well, perhaps in another five years. The Queen will have stepped down by then, and it would be so much easier to run the country with an executive presidency.

> Record on your Brexit Memo Pad:
> - ❖ -2% Authority – you gambled and came very close to losing.
> - ❖ Mark General Election as complete.

Then turn to **666**.

594

The moment of truth. What will the next round of voting bring? Sitting up late into the night on the eve of the vote, you ponder what you'll call this chapter in your memoirs.

- ⇒ 'The Moving Finger Writes.' Turn to **349**
- ⇒ 'Buffets and Rewards.' Turn to **814**
- ⇒ 'A Tide in the Affairs of Men.' Turn to **377**

595

'I agree with Bob,' says Lucy Tooth. 'Immigrants add value. The simple fact is that free movement isn't a dumb loophole in EU regulations. It's not some kind of penalty they're trying to foist on everybody. It's not a bug, it's a feature. We need them because we have an ageing population. Britain has a higher proportion of dependent old people than even France.'

Mugglemore tries to steer her back to the point. 'So we need these people as nurses?'

'It goes much further than that,' says Owlbear, his mental gears starting to whir up to speed at last. 'An ageing population is driving up the cost of health care, it's putting a strain on pensions. And when elderly people are no longer able to retire to Spain because the falling pound makes it too expensive, we're going to need those younger immigrants here to support the economy.'

Tooth is glaring at him. So she doesn't like being interrupted. A bit of temper behind the middle-class curtains, there.

'Of course,' she adds, 'with the NHS in terminal decline and foreign doctors finding it harder to come here, our ageing population won't be a problem for long. The harsh fact is that because of Brexit people will die off sooner.'

⇒ What does Fungale have to say? Turn to **650**

⇒ What about Tode? Will he toe the party line? Turn to **487**

⇒ Skip to another question. Turn to **405**

596

'Societies have rules to protect their members,' says Stollard with a shrug. 'You can get out of that by living on a raft in international waters. Otherwise I'm afraid we'll just have to put up with health care, sanitation, education, public safety, and all the other things foisted on us by the state.'

Strewel rummages in his briefcase. 'I've left my copy of *Das Kapital* at home, I'm afraid, or I could tell you which chapter that's from.'

Turn to **17.**

597

The MPs aren't fools. They've got enough experience of Peter Strewel's antics over the years to know that he can't be trusted to keep his word on anything. Any man who deliberately musses his own hair so as to come across as a loveable scamp has a swag bag full of secrets and falsehoods. He's knocked out in the next round, leaving you facing Rufus and Stollard in the final parliamentary vote.

Turn to **791**.

598

Never mind the rain in Spain, the thunder and lighting all seem to be concentrated on Gibraltar these days. Britain's ownership of the Rock has been a sore point for years and now the combative Spanish prime minister has just lobbed the ball into your court by proposing a co-sovereignty deal.

'He doesn't seriously expect us to take him up on it,' is the opinion of your press secretary Terri Trough. 'He's just playing to his own voters.'

'But what will ours think? And then there's Gibraltar's own population. They voted almost unanimously to stay in the EU.'

'They're worried about what loss of freedom of movement would do to the local economy,' says Terri. 'Ten thousand Spanish workers commute to Gibraltar every day. Turn that tap off and they'll have to survive on selling tat to tourists.'

If you decide to ignore the Spanish prime minister's comments, turn to **175**. If you respond with a declaration that as a British dominion Gibraltar will be pulling out of the EU come what may, turn to **266**.

599

The plot concerns a bunch of soulful tusked monsters who are driven from their homeland and end up teaming up with the knights who used to persecute them to fight an evil dictator in a black cloak. It's probably a metaphor but you absolutely refuse to let your brain get in the way of dumb pleasure. You just sit back on the pillows and let the digital explosions and spells flood past. It's like a firework display, only without the rigorous intellectual content or coherent narrative.

A bit like Tolkien, mutters your analytical mind, refusing to sit quietly. The Fellowship of the Ring... now there was a union of disparate interests coming together for the common good. So the Fellowship are the EU and orcs are immigrants..? Seems a bit iffy, that. Almost racist. Anyway, the hobbits have got to be Britain. So does that mean Aragorn and his lot are the French? Who's America? Dwarves. Wait, that leaves out the Germans. They can't be Mordor, that must be Syria or somewhere. And immigrants – are they the ents..?

A snore comes from the bed as the movie plays on and you drift deeper into dreams of Brexit.

Turn to **125**.

600

'Nothing wrong with the old yes-no,' is Strewel's opinion. 'Clear to everybody and his uncle, isn't it? Here's the carrot, here's the stick. Nice and simple.'

'Simple, anyway,' says Stollard wryly.

'What were the reasons for a binary choice last time?' you ask Tode. 'You must have discussed it with my predecessor.'

'To be quite honest, Prime Minister, we've already spent longer discussing a second referendum than we did the first one.'

⇒ 'Okay. If it was good enough then, it's good enough now.' Turn to **274**

⇒ 'Offering range of options on one ballot might be the perfect compromise.' Turn to **698**

⇒ 'I'm still leaning towards the runoff idea. That sounds modern.' Turn to **340**

⇒ 'Actually, let's not bother. We can't fit in another referendum along with everything else.' Turn to **79**

601

'Norway does have to pay a significant fee towards the EU budget every year,' says the Chancellor. 'It amounts to about 80% of Britain's per capita contribution as a full member. Some of that it gets back in participation of research projects – not to the same extent that Britain has benefited, mind you. And then there are the indirect costs, such as having to satisfy rules of origin requirements.'

⇒ 'How much would we have to contribute to the EU budget if we followed the Norway model?' Turn to **767**

⇒ 'Rules of origin? What are they?' Turn to **718**

⇒ 'We won't drill down into details just now.' Turn to **17**

602

It's a good answer. You're selling people the idea of a solution that will let them moderate the earlier referendum result and keep the best features of the EU without losing face. It doesn't hurt that the public mood was already trending in that direction.

Still, that's one debate in a maelstrom of lies, wild claims, ill-tempered rejoinders and outright hysteria. Reason is a tiny voice at the bottom of Pandora's box.

On the night of the referendum you turn on the television and pace the room as the votes come in.

Toss two coins. If both come up heads, turn to **313.** If both come up tails, turn to **173**. Otherwise, turn to **403.**

603

'Does the Prime Minister agree that the principle of Parliamentary sovereignty has been established since the Civil War and that therefore the final decision on Britain's future relationship with the European Union should be ratified by a vote in this chamber?'

Oh, how you enjoy Prime Minister's Questions. They always help you work up an appetite. In this case, the point so windily made by the honourable member for who-cares-where would be as easy for you to shoot down as a child's balloon with a 12-bore shotgun. But you decide to indulge them all.

'Of course there will be a vote on the deal.'

There's a murmur of contented harrumphing, like hens settling down for the night. As you leave the chamber, your private secretary falls into step beside you. You notice the fretful way he's chewing his lip. 'You're surprised?'

'Well… the majority of the House are against a hard Brexit, Prime Minister.'

If you have the keyword CLARION, turn to **226**.

If not but you have the keyword QUORUM, turn to **25.**

If not but you have the keyword ZEBRA, turn to **745.**

Otherwise turn to **447**.

604

'He's only gone and done it,' says your chief of staff, flinging down the paper in disgust.

'SHEEP WATCH OUT! FUNGALE BACK IN THE FOLD,' reads the headline. So he made it. Colin Fungale will be taking his seat as a Conservative MP.

'I only hope his attendance record in the Commons is better than it was in the European Parliament.'

You may try to make light of it, but this feels like storm clouds gathering.

Now turn to **400**.

605

'To move to Britain,' explains Bob Owlbear, 'an EU citizen must be either coming to take up a job, studying here, or they must demonstrate that they're financially self-sufficient. That's how come all those British pensioners can soak up the sun in Alicante.'

⇒ Find another question.	Turn to **405**
⇒ You've seen enough.	Turn to **125**

606

Amazingly you are seen as even more dogmatic than Colin Fungale, who once said, 'If we don't get the Brexit the people asked for, I'm willing to grab a shotgun and man the barricades.'

'How do you feel, Prime Minister?' asks your press secretary as the votes come in.

'As if Stalin had strolled in and said I was a bit too brutal for him.'

Turn to **519**.

607

With Peter Strewel's faction backing you, you're able to present yourself as the strongest candidate for Brexit who isn't actually mad. That enables you to knock out Dennis Dent in the next round.

You take the trouble to find him after the result is announced and shake his hand. 'Sorry, Dennis. I suppose the contest only has room for one candidate who isn't either a clown or a stealth Remainer.'

'Oh, I don't mind too much. I'm not getting any younger, and two years spent confronting the realities of Brexit has made me a lot keener on gardening and golf, I can tell you.'

> On your Brexit Memo Pad:
> ❖ Tick the keyword YELLOW.

Then, if you have the keyword NYLON, turn to **261**.
If not, turn to **310**.

608

'It depends whether we want to benefit from European development programs,' Stollard explains. 'Ukraine for instance is opting to make a contribution to the EU budget in order to get access to the Erasmus student exchange scheme, regional development, things like that.'

'The public aren't going to like us sending good British money to Brussels,' says Barkwell. 'The referendum was a clear mandate to stop all that malarkey.'

'I agree,' says Dent. 'It smacks of them trying to reel us back in. Anyway, we've got too many students, and if they want to see the world there's always hop-picking in Kent.'

Strewel goes misty eyed. 'Reminds me of a little bit I met in my gap year,' he mutters. 'Tight tee-shirt and the shortest shorts you ever saw. Welsh, she was, so quite well padded, but it's nice to have something to hold onto. Sorry, am I talking out loud? Thought I was day-dreaming. Don't mind me.'

⇒ 'All right, what are the biggest obstacles to us getting a good deal from the EU? Turn to **616**

⇒ 'What are our trump cards?' Turn to **495**

609

'It's true that a lot of the business, tech and education investment primarily benefits demographics that are likely to skew for Remain.'

'Turn down the marketing hyperbabble.'

She nods. 'I'm saying you could dismiss all that funding as irrelevant to ordinary people's lives. What about the fishermen, the farmers, the... are there still clay miners?'

'I think it's gone the way of tin. But yes, they're not going to be learning IT skills at a chrome and glass innovation centre, are they? "EU funds have left Leave voters behind." I like it.'

'And Brexit could be a real boost for tourism.'

⇒ 'In what way?' Turn to **562**

⇒ 'Remind me how EU funds were getting spent in Cornwall.' Turn to **86**

610

'Here's where it gets complex,' says Ron – as if it wasn't already. 'Money buys us negotiating leverage. The EU-27 will all be concerned about these payments, either because they'll have to foot the bill if we fall short or because there are payments that are meant to be coming their way. But of course, any payments we do agree to will enrage the Eurosceptics.'

'So we can have goodwill in the negotiations or good press at home, but not both.'

'The other states can agree to reduce the bill – that just requires a majority vote, and we know that many of them thought the Commission's opening figure was a bit on the audacious side. But now they'll all be thinking how nice it would be if we did just roll over to the €60 billion. Our best allies in getting the estimate bumped down are the poorer countries, because they'll be expecting the EU to honour its cohesion funding commitments either way. But the likes of France and Germany will be mightily pissed off.'

'What if we just walk away? Say to them: here's our membership fee up to the day we leave, and after that it's a farewell to alms.'

Ron twirls his pipe thoughtfully. He's not allowed to smoke it in here, of course, but there's still a reek of stale tobacco strong enough to knock flies out of the air.

'It's pretty iffy. Nobody likes to see a country failing to stick to its promises, so we'd need to take the case to the Hague. Now, the court might very well say we don't owe anything but our membership fee through to 2019. But as soon as you open that door, it's the end of all negotiations. Europe would be united against us in hostility, we'd be looking at WTO rules, sterling would be in freefall without a parachute...' He throws up his hands. 'I'm struggling to see an upside.'

'Political, Ron. The press would carry us shoulder high. We'd bask in a warm glow of Eurosceptic approval.'

'Except that the International Court might eventually rule for the EU, at which point you've got to pay the bill in full having scuppered negotiations for nothing. Better line up some lucrative non-exec positions and a lecture tour if that happens.'

Turn to **374.**

611

You cannot keep putting off the outstanding financial settlement to the EU – not least because the world is watching to see if Britain is still as good as her word.

The final sum agreed is just over €30 billion, and with some massaging you're able to sell that as a triumph, having more than halved the original highest estimates of the bill. The pro-Brexit press are annoyed that you agreed to any payment at all, but in general it's about as good an outcome as you could have hoped for.

'If only the rest of the talks go that well,' the Chancellor remarks to you back at Downing Street. He shows you the morning papers. 'The *Heil* led with "Daylight Robbery", but the broadsheets generally took a measured view. "Britain Shows Strength in Early Talks," as the *Mimeograph* put it.'

On your Brexit Memo Pad:

- -5% Economy – the payments must be made somehow.
- -5% Goodwill – the EU are annoyed that you dragged out the agreement till the eleventh hour.
- Mark the Exit Fee as complete.

Then turn to **450**.

612

Look at your Brexit Memo Pad.

If Residency Rights are marked as complete, turn to **265**.

If Residency Rights have not been completed, turn to **556.**

613

You took some flak from the hardliners in your party at what they perceived as giving in to the EU over Britain's financial obligations. Blinkered by their ideology, they failed to see the advantages of giving a little ground then to win some friends on the other side of the negotiating table.

Of course, none of those hardliners wanted the soft Brexit deal you're about to close. They're the kind who want to burn it all down. But dealing with them is tomorrow's challenge. Right now you must focus on the future prosperity of the country.

Turn to **417**.

614

Your answer argues vigorously for the common sense of finding a middle way. With the electorate by now so fatigued by the whole issue, there's no way of telling if they will heed you. The country has the feeling of an animal caught in a trap that is now almost as likely to give up as to try and escape.

Toss two coins. If both come up heads, turn to **127**. If both come up tails, turn to **403**. Otherwise, turn to **173.**

615

It's come down to a coin toss. Sometimes life really is that random.

If you get heads, turn to **475**. If tails, turn to **377**.

616

Stollard explains. 'Trade agreements over services fall outside the Commission's sole competence. They're what's called "mixed agreements", meaning they're a mix of things the EU can sign off on and things that the individual member states get a say in. Those have to be ratified by all the twenty-seven countries.'

'And that could stick a spoke in our wheels,' says Dent. 'Because there's obviously an incentive for some of the other states to hamper our access to the EU services market so as to get more of a share for themselves.'

'The conniving sneaks,' says Barkwell. 'They know that services are Britain's lifeline, and they want to choke us off.'

'In fact there's still a lot of work to do there for the EU as a whole,' says Stollard. 'The single market isn't fully integrated yet.'

⇒ 'How so?' Turn to **179**

⇒ 'Explain to me about mixed agreements.' Turn to **122**

⇒ 'What about financial services?' Turn to **220**

⇒ 'Wasn't there a hitch in the Ukraine trade agreement caused by individual member states having a say in it?' Turn to **437**

617

He must go straight to Tiffany Rufus and offer her the same deal, because within hours they are double-teaming to attack you.

'Let's face it,' says Strewel in a speech, 'putting this Prime Minister in charge of Brexit is like asking Mother Theresa to run the Bank of England.'

Rufus's speech is almost a carbon copy. 'The Prime Minister's heart has never been in Brexit. And if you don't agree with something, don't believe in something, and don't care passionately about something, you will never be able to do that thing.'

They're slinging plenty of mud. How much of it will stick? It depends on your record to date.

If you have the keyword GAZELLE or SANCTION, turn to **377**.

If not but you have either FOG or LEAF, turn to **513**.

If you have none of those keywords, turn to **172**.

618

You announce that you will not be taking part in the campaign. 'The role of Prime Minister is in some ways similar to the monarch's,' you tell the interviewer on *News Talk*. 'We must both be above day-to-day politics.'

'Masterful,' says Ron Beardsley as you watch the programme later at Number 10. 'He would have caught you on that one, but they were out of time.'

The following morning, Peter Strewel calls a press conference. 'The Prime Minister may be out of the politics business,' he chortles, 'but the rest of us have to muck in all the same. So I'm throwing my hat in the ring. I shall be out on the road banging the drum for Britain staying in the single market. A nice, soft, comfortable Brexit is what we all need now.'

'Clever bastard,' you spit at the TV.

'Does he even believe in soft Brexit?' wonders Ron.

'Does it matter?'

Turn to **302.**

619 ☐

If the box above is empty, put a tick in it and turn to **230.**

If the box was already ticked, you have an untroubled sleep and wake refreshed: turn to **125.**

620

The public vote in favour, not only of staying in the EU, but of forging stronger political links.

'Ever-closer union, eh?' says the Chancellor, dropping in with the morning papers. "HERE COMES THE FEDERAL SUPERSTATE!" That's the *Bilabong*'s headline. "EU WANTS TO ABOLISH QUEEN." That's the *Klaxon*.'

'They've never been the same anyway since Freddie Mercury popped off.'

'So what do we do? I don't think the referendum quite made it clear to the public that not every decision regarding the EU is the exclusive prerogative of Her Majesty's Government. There are twenty-seven other countries in this marriage and they all want a say.'

'Whatever happens will happen at its own rate. We've got to learn to be fatalists, Alan. In this brave new world of referendum rule, there's no point in getting attached to any given policy.'

Turn to **714.**

621

The Chancellor sighs at the very thought of explaining it. 'I'm not sure if you want to know.'

⇒ 'You're right. Forget it.' Turn to **378**

⇒ 'Tell me anyway.' Turn to **832**

622

Along with the other EU heads of state, you attend a summit of the European Council in Rome. The hope is you can hammer out preliminary terms for a deal on free movement. On the way to the first meeting you're still going over the options with your press secretary.

'Lizzie, you know, I'm wondering – if even Denis Dent now admits we will need to keep EU labour coming into Britain for "years and years", why don't we trade that off against a transitional acceptance of free movement. That way we can do a Norway-type deal rather than leaving the single market outright.'

'The trouble is, Prime Minister, that the steaming mad Brexit contingent would see any interim plan like that as a threat to actually going ahead and leaving. In fact, Fungale said exactly that yesterday in a speech. We can't lift that rock even a crack or there's no telling what will come out from under it.'

You gaze out of the car window at the shattered façade of the Colosseum. 'Is it possible that human beings can produce such a sound?'

'Pardon me, Prime Minister?'

'Nero. In the Peter Ustinov film. It didn't end well for him or the empire.'

At the meeting you're greeted first by Chancellor Käsen of Germany. 'So, free movement.'

What is she, a sphinx? 'Yes, free movement,' you echo back.

'You will need it too. Yours is a service economy, and that often means workers must live abroad, not true?'

'That's what we're here to discuss.'

The other ministers take their places and wait for you to state your case. After some preamble you get to the point. 'The British people have voted largely on the basis of immigration.'

'And why does Britain need special treatment?' asks the Austrian chancellor. 'You don't have so many more EU citizens relocating compared to others.'

'We're a rich country, so people want to live in Britain. But we're an island nation, so our culture is precious to us and it's hard to integrate people from the continent.'

'Even so, are the British people so insular, then?'

⇒ You won't stand for that kind of talk! Turn to **712**

⇒ Count to ten. Be conciliatory. Turn to **15**

623

Before presenting your proposals to the EU negotiator, you hold a final consultation with the Home Secretary, Tiffany Rufus, and the Secretary of State for Exiting the European Union, Dennis Dent.

'As I see it I have three options,' you begin. 'The first is to unilaterally guarantee the rights of EU citizens to remain here, irrespective of the EU's stance to our own ex-pats.'

'That'll earn us some goodwill,' says Dent, with as much enthusiasm as he might show for the benefits of chemotherapy. 'We'd expect the EU to do the same for our citizens in return, of course.'

'Which is not a foregone conclusion,' says Rufus. 'The Spanish might kick up a stink, for one. The Gibraltar question, I mean.'

You wave her point aside. 'That's a risk in any case. Another option is to simply fail to guarantee residency rights. I don't mean we should come out and say we're going to repatriate them. We just say nothing. Kick the can down the road a bit. Hold out for some concessions.'

'The risk there is we end up with no deal,' says Rufus.

Dent shakes his head. 'They'll give in. They've got more to lose than us. Loads more EU citizens over here than we've got over there.'

'The problem is that many EU citizens over here hold vital jobs in the NHS, care homes, agriculture and so on,' points out Rufus. 'The Spanish aren't quite so dependent on all the British pensioners pushing Zimmer frames up and down their seafront.'

'The third option is to simply start negotiations right away. I could call Alprèves, tell him we want to thrash out a deal giving reciprocal rights to our citizens on both sides.'

'There's a fourth option,' says Dent.

'Which is?'

'Boot them out. So what if the EU retaliate by sending ours home? We get to announce that three million immigrants are being sent home.'

'There'll be champagne toasts in every chip shop and bingo hall throughout the land,' says Rufus drily.

Decision time. What's it going to be?

⇒ Unilaterally guarantee EU citizens' right to remain in Britain. Turn to **139**

⇒ Start negotiating with the EU to agree reciprocal rights for UK and EU nationals currently residing aboard. Turn to **319**

⇒ Announce that EU citizens in the UK will be told to leave after Brexit. Turn to **554**

⇒ Ignore it and see what the EU Commission decides to do. Turn to **150**

624

With your chief of staff and some other Downing Street staff, you settle down to watch the votes come in. Exit polls hint that the public mood is for moderating or even reversing Brexit altogether. At least, having kept out of the fray, you should escape any fallout whatever the result may be.

Toss two coins. If both come up heads, turn to **173**. If both come up tails, turn to **403**. Otherwise, turn to **313.**

625

That's music to Barkwell's ears. He visibly puffs up with thoughts of soaring patriotism. 'That's the ticket. Make them squirm. They need us more than we need them, after all.'

'Maybe,' says the Chancellor drily. 'You've seen *Blazing Saddles,* haven't you? "The next man that makes a move..."? Hopefully the EU27 will fall for it.'

Turn to **666.**

626

Luckily Labour doesn't know where to turn. Its young, educated, metropolitan voters are for Remain, but to avoid losing the dependable old working class vote the party has had to get behind Brexit. As long as Labour let you take the lead there, surely they're going to keep dropping in the polls faster than Icarus on a sunny day. Or perhaps you should say Lucifer after his rebellion.

The Almighty puts a thought in your head. Scraggle will try to turn the debate to issues where Labour is on stronger ground. The NHS, schools, public services, and other Trotskyite notions. No chance – the next election will be about one thing only. Brexit.

'Citizens of nowhere!' you cry aloud. 'Bring me my chariot of fire.'

Wilkins looks around the door. 'Prime Minister?'

'Get out. Can't you see I'm praying?'

Wilkins tiptoes out and quietly pulls the door to, in much the same way as you foresee Barry Scraggle departing after the next election. Gone without a trace. Not even a ripple on the political consciousness. Or perhaps that's unfair. You will remember him kindly for one thing, at least – consigning his party to a couple of decades in limbo. And you have that assurance on the very highest authority.

⇒ But what about the Liberal Democrats?
Turn to **784**

⇒ What's the procedure for calling an early election?
Turn to **35**

⇒ Presumably you'd pick up no seats north of the border.
Turn to **3**

⇒ Say amen and get on with the business of government.
Turn to **666**

627

Your backbenchers are reluctant to blackball a man with the grassroots support of Colin Fungale. But Sir Harvey Doggerbank, the head of the 1922 Committee, has been your staunch ally since you impressed him at that meeting in your office shortly after triggering Article 50. Over drinks in the Commons bar and golf games out in Berkshire he drums up support for your view, and Fungale's application is duly rejected.

Turn to **375**.

628

Look at your Brexit Memo Pad.

If Security & Defence is marked as complete, turn to **468**.

If Security & Defence has not been completed, turn to **705**.

629

'We're going to have a shortage of labour after Brexit,' the Chancellor reminds you.

'Doctors, nurses... Yes, I suppose we'll have to step up immigration from India and the Caribbean, even though the Brexit voters are going to hate that.'

'Actually I was thinking of unskilled and semi-skilled workers. The sort of menial job that no coddled British school-leaver would dream of doing.'

'Alan, I've told you before about this. Don't bring me problems, bring me – '

'I have the solution right here, Prime Minister. A special visa deal with Turkey. President Yalayip Kulübe will go along with anything that makes it look as if his country is getting more acceptance by the West.'

'If only to cock a snook at the EU.'

Will you agree to the deal making it easier for Turkish workers to get a visa to the UK? If so, turn to **555**. If not, turn to **175**.

630

'Might as well get this show on the road, eh?' says Strewel.

The hush of an angel passing. No one seems in a particular hurry to get the ball rolling.

'Prime Minister, why don't you start by telling us your thinking?' asks Barkwell after a few moments. Dent and Stollard look at you expectantly. What will you say?

- ⇒ 'Clearly our highest priority should be remain within the single market.' Turn to **247**
- ⇒ 'Our interests are best served by forging a new bespoke trade arrangement.' Turn to **836**
- ⇒ 'While we obviously cannot accept the terms the EU would impose for staying in the single market, we could opt for membership of the European Customs Union.' Turn to **367**

631

'But not so much, monsieur.' He looks across the table, his smile now more quizzical than amused. You hold up your fingers, just as far apart as a sugar cube, then narrow them to half that. 'In Britain we have an expression: "What's the discount for cash?"'

'Prime Minister, really, we are not horse trading now.'

'Come. You asked for this to be resolved quickly. We're accommodating you. But you can't expect us to simply agree to the sum you stuck a pin in. Where's the goodwill?'

'I don't see how you can dispute the fairness of the calculation.'

It would be a good line if he didn't immediately start pulling out spreadsheets. You've got him on the defensive. And *that's* how you move a mountain.

Negotiation of the next few days is hard, but it is in everyone's interest to reach an amicable solution. You manage to restrict Britain's payments to the seven-year budget, not the extra three years that Alprèves started out by demanding. You manage to get contingent liabilities excluded – that is, payments for which EU members are liable in the event of unexpected circumstances like Greece defaulting on its loans. Then there are deductions that reflect Britain's share of EU assets such as the European Investment Bank. Best of all, you succeed in getting Britain's 2018 rebate factored against the total.

The final sum is just over €30 billion, and with some massaging you're able to sell that as having halved the bill. The more extreme right-wing press are annoyed that you agreed to any payment at all, but in general it's about as good an outcome as you could have hoped for.

'If only the rest of the talks go that well,' the Chancellor remarks to you back at Downing Street. He shows you the morning papers. 'The *Heil* led with "DAYLIGHT ROBBERY", but the broadsheets generally took a measured view. "BRITAIN SHOWS STRENGTH IN EARLY TALKS," as the *Mimeograph* put it.'

On your Brexit Memo Pad:

- -5% Economy – the payments must be made somehow.
- +5% Goodwill – the EU are encouraged by your cooperative approach.
- -5% Popularity – the right-wing press are not happy that any concessions are being made.
- Mark the Exit Fee as complete.

Then turn to **150**.

632

'You've got the humanitarian stuff. Making sure medical supplies get through, sorting out clean water, and so on. Trouble starts with shooting and moves on to the other horsemen, you know. Then there's peacekeeping, like Operation Artemis in the Congo where the job was to de-escalate a sticky situation. That one was the first EU mission without NATO involvement. France was what they call the "framework" force there. Another one of those is monitoring the ceasefire in Georgia. And thirdly you've got your military advice and assistance, e.g. –' he actually says that – 'to a lawful government that's facing rebels, or buffing up border patrols in Ukraine to watch out for smugglers and Russian troublemakers.'

'You mentioned France taking part in these operations, but I imagine Britain plays her part?'

He sucks his teeth. 'We're ranked fifth in terms of our commitment to joint military operations. As far as civilian-type missions – well, you wouldn't expect us to get so involved there, would you? Don't put an attack dog at the garden gate, do you? So there we're seventh.'

You both stand contemplating how to spin this. Naturally it comes to you first: 'But we're constantly pulling our weight in NATO, aren't we? So overall we're doing far more than all the others.'

⇒ Ask him how such EU missions are authorized. Turn to **343**

⇒ Talk about something else. Turn to **432**

633

Tode agrees to throw his support behind you. It's not that he commands a large following in the party so much as that a stiletto in his hand, slid between Strewel's amply gristle-padded ribs, carries extra poison.

Strewel's campaign is duly scuppered. He struggles on, but he's a dead man walking. Turn to **519**.

634

It's going to be hard to pull off a switch to the soft-Brexit side of Tiffany Rufus. Do you have the credentials to back up your strategy?

Look at your Brexit Memo Pad. If you have the keyword OPAL, turn to **74**.

If not but you have the keyword CLARION, turn to **652**.

If not but you have the keyword SANCTION *and* your Popularity is 54% or more, turn to **489**.

Otherwise turn to **19**.

635

Dent backs out of the contest in return for your promise to appoint him to the Treasury. With his open support, you are seen as the most statesmanlike candidate between the extremes of lashed-to-the-mast nationalism on one hand and the backroom deals and backsliding of a diluted Brexit on the other.

If you have the keyword UNCTION *and* your Popularity score is 46% or more, turn to **728**.

Otherwise turn to **818**.

636

Chancellor Käsen just doesn't get it. Even though five years might be long enough for the Remain vote to overtake Leave, the Europhobic mindset is firmly entrenched in British political thought. Having once ruled three-quarters of the globe, we can never sit among the rest as mere equals. Throughout the UK's four decades as part of the European Union we were never able to commit to membership, never willing to participate in the shared project, and that's why this day was always inevitable.

⇒ Maybe it's not too late to propose a form of associate membership, with reduced involvement by Britain in EU funding and government in return for a partial opt-out of freedom of movement. Turn to **842**

⇒ The simplest solution is just to introduce visas. EU citizens will be able to apply to move to Britain and, if eligible, will be granted a work permit. Turn to **839**

637

The second and final heat results in a solid majority in favour of hard Brexit.

'We've been down this road before, haven't we?' says the Chancellor.

'But it wasn't clear then, was it? Did the public want a mere tweak to the status quo, or did they want us to crash them through to a whole new reality? Now we know.'

He frowns. 'I wonder if they would have voted for hard Brexit if it had been an option in the original referendum? Probably not. The last two years have moved the goalposts.'

'Get used to the new normal.'

Turn to **446.**

638

Before presenting your proposals to the EU negotiator, you hold a final consultation with the Home Secretary, Tiffany Rufus, and the Secretary of State for Exiting the European Union, Dennis Dent.

'As I see it I have two options,' you begin. 'The first is to unilaterally guarantee the rights of EU citizens to remain here, irrespective of the EU's stance to our own ex-pats.'

'That'll earn us some goodwill,' says Dent, with as much enthusiasm as he might show for the benefits of chemotherapy. 'We'd expect the EU to do the same for our citizens in return, of course.'

'Hardly a foregone conclusion,' says Rufus. 'The Spanish for one might kick up a stink. The Gibraltar question, I mean.'

You wave her point aside. 'That's a risk in any case. The other option is for us to throw the EU nationals out. Following Brexit they'll just be regarded like any other foreigners applying to live here.'

'The EU won't like that,' says Dent. 'It'll go down a storm in the Conservative heartlands, of course, which should put paid to what's left of UKIP.'

'But what if the EU respond by allowing our citizens to stay over there?' says Tiffany Rufus. 'We'll look like the nasty party.'

'There's another option,' says Dent.

'Which is?'

'Do nothing. Let Europe take the lead.'

Decision time. What's it going to be?

⇒ Unilaterally guarantee EU citizens' right to remain in Britain. Turn to **589**

⇒ Announce that EU citizens in the UK will be told to leave after Brexit. Turn to **422**

⇒ See if you can negotiate a joint announcement by Britain and the EU. Turn to **359**

⇒ Ignore it and see what the EU Commission decides to do. Turn to **666**

Before you can get around to arranging a formal briefing on EU citizens living in Britain, you get an unexpectedly personal insight into their concerns.

'We're here, Prime Minister.'

You look up from the pile of papers strewn across the back seat in time to see the quaint gateposts and beautifully trimmed hedge of your new holiday home. Beyond you catch a tantalizing glimpse of the sea.

'It's a shame the place in the Algarve had to go, Wilkins. But this doesn't look too bad.'

The house itself is an 18th century stone rectory, currently half-hidden by scaffolding. The limousine crunches to a halt on the gravel drive and as you get out the sounds of hammering, sawing and multilingual swearing can be heard from inside.

'Prime Minister!' cries a booming voice. 'Come see your new home. No, wait there. You need hard hat.'

A burly man in scuffed overalls comes out to greet you. This is Jan Dobrinski, the Polish owner of the building firm. He shows you around, introducing you to his team of about fifteen, several of whom are British.

A little later you're having a cup of tea on the lawn with Jan and his foreman, a wiry Yorkshireman called Bob, as you look over the architects' plans together. You mention future improvements you'd like to see. Perhaps a guest chalet. 'Not for this year, of course.'

'I hope I can do all this for you,' says Jan.

'Why shouldn't you?'

'I don't yet know what will happen to me and my company after Brexit.' Jan dunks a digestive into his tea like a true Brit. 'I mean my remain right.'

'I'm sorry about your vote, but democracy is democracy. The other side won.'

You glance at your watch. A few more minutes and you can claim pressing matters of state and get back to London.

'No, no – I didn't get a vote,' Jan reminds you, 'though I would have voted Remain, of course. But I mean my right to remain in the UK, along with all the other EU people.'

As Jan says this, you're looking at Bob. His eyes flick shiftily to one side. He voted Leave, then. Interesting. Maybe he wants get his boss out of the way so he can take over the business. A lot of the

Cabinet probably feel the same way about you.

'There is a way to stay here,' you say, turning back to Jan. 'How long have you been in Britain?'

'Seven years now, with my wife and kids. They're at the local primary.'

'Then why not apply for permanent residence?

'Yes, I can do that after five years working, here, but actually it's my wife.'

'What about her?'

'It's her CSI.'

⇒ CSI? Does he mean the cop show? Turn to **541**

⇒ You won't learn anything talking to builders. You need to find an expert. Turn to **686**

640

'It's typical of the sort of glitz EU funds are spent on. There have been three major innovation centres set up in Cornwall in the last decade catering to business and tech research, providing support to both established companies and start-ups.'

⇒ 'Toys for the elite, then?' Turn to **609**

⇒ 'Apart from innovation centres, what else?' Turn to **86**

641

You tell them your intentions at the next Cabinet meeting. It's worth it just to see the expressions around the table: shock, puzzlement, resentment, delight, and a few instances of downright incomprehension.

From the far end of the table there's the sound of someone clearing their throat. 'Prime Minister…'

'Could you lean forward, please? I can't see who's talking.'

The others all sit back as if they'd just been told the table is radioactive. You're looking at the frowning face of Baroness Pulborough, the Leader of the House of Lords.

'Lady Pulborough, you were saying?'

'I'm inviting you to consider the purpose of the Cabinet, Prime Minister. We are not yet in the position of the United States or Turkey in having a single executive leader. I remind you that this is, so to speak, the board of directors and you, as managing director, simply *prima inter pares*. In short, we should be consulted before such decisions are taken, not informed after the event.'

'I'm consulting with you now.'

'What if we say no?'

The others are all looking out of the window or pretending to study their notes. 'No one is saying no, Lady Pulborough. The press conference is in half an hour.'

Later, after announcing the election to the media, you consider what to do about Baroness Pulborough.

⇒ Fire her from the Cabinet. You can't allow challenges to your authority. Turn to **849**

⇒ Let it pass. You'll look stronger by allowing a little controlled criticism. Turn to **542**

642

Peter Strewel's next call must be to Dennis Dent, as only a few hours later he's publicly throwing his ample weight behind the Brexit Secretary's campaign. That figures. Strewel is too lazy to want to slog through the leadership contest when he can get a starring role while somebody else does the work.

So there are two more rounds of MP voting before the membership get to decide. And with Tiffany Rufus the only candidate favouring a soft Brexit, the rest are a tight pack. Somehow you have to pull ahead.

If you have the keyword LEAF *and* your Popularity score is 51% or more, turn to **505**.

Otherwise turn to **647**.

643

'Structural funds are what matter here, Prime Minister. Cohesion funding is targeted on building transport links and renewable energy. That goes to member states whose GDP is below 90% of the European average.'

'All right, so the structural funds?'

'Mostly for businesses, especially small- to medium-sized local enterprises. Also digital connection, research and development, energy efficiency – '

'No, no, no. That won't do. All far too positive. We need to hear about bureaucracy and waste. Millions spent on white elephants. Come at this like a Fleet Street hack on a deadline.'

'There's the social fund. It's about £10 billion a year on lifetime learning, social inclusion, combating poverty – '

'More like it. Liberal twaddle and handouts for spongers. Add that to the speech, how we're cutting the EU fat and so on.'

The aide frowns. Annoyingly she's so young that barely a wrinkle shows on her face. 'The social fund does also go towards education, employment, and improving the efficiency of administration.'

'Leave that bit out. Can't cover everything if I want to get back to London tonight.'

She makes a note. 'We'll be in Penzance shortly, Prime Minister. Anything else you wanted to cover?'

⇒ 'What's the EU's aim with all these funds?' Turn to **573**

⇒ 'Give me more detail on how the money actually gets spent in Cornwall.' Turn to **86**

⇒ 'No, that's all for now.' Turn to **203**

644

There's been a lot of talk about a second referendum on EU membership. Surprising, that, considering how much trouble the first one caused. You cast your mind over the arguments for and against.

Turn to **376**.

645

You're too seasoned a player to be wrong-footed by little road-bump. Before long you have your entire team spinning like industrial centrifuges to discredit Chloe Stoat's account of your meeting and throw up enough distractions to keep her interview out of the public eye.

'It looks like you'll hang on by the skin of your teeth,' says the Chief Whip.

'What on earth possessed you to say such a thing to Chloe Stoat, of all people?' asks Ron Beardsley.

'I probably forgot she was in the room. Some of these identikit politicians, it's like talking to yourself.'

Turn to **169**.

646

'Well, it's sort of a dating agency, isn't it?' says Strewel.

Silence in the room. You all turn to look at him. The Chancellor scrawls a note and tilts the paper so that you can read it: 'This should be good.'

Strewel sits forward, warming to his subject. 'You go through a divorce. All the arguments about money and who gets the house. Divvy up the LPs. Somebody has to take the kids. It's just like leaving the EU when you think of it. But now you're back on the market. You've gone through all the females in your little black book. The available ones know what you're like, or they're talking to your ex. Oh-er. So you can hang around singles bars – '

'Making trade deals, if I'm following you,' says Stollard.

'Right. Negotiate on a one to one. Lot of bother, though. Or you can go to this sort of club that already has all the rules and what-have-you in place. They've got the list of all these totties ready to deal. The preliminary negotiations are done. The agency does the legwork so you can get your leg over.'

Stollard gives you a big bland smile and you know what he's thinking. *You made this man foreign secretary.*

⇒ 'What are the pros and cons of falling back on WTO rules?' Turn to **813**

⇒ 'Trading internationally through the WTO has got to open up more opportunities than we have within the EU.' Turn to **590**

647

You and Dennis Dent are probably the most experienced and realistic candidates at this point, but for that very reason one of you is about to fall at the next fence.

It's a tight contest and it could go either way. What do you think tomorrow's headlines will say?

⇒ 'A CLOSE SHAVE.' Turn to **505**

⇒ 'A NARROW SQUEAK.' Turn to **377**

648

'The ballot will present voters with three choices,' your chief of staff explains with the aid of an expensive-looking AV deck.

'Three options, Ron. Not three choices. The choice is to pick one of the options.' He turns, blinking above the great bush of his beard like a cyclist caught urinating in a hedge. 'Never mind, go on.'

'Choice... er, option one: stay in the European Union by reversing our declaration of Article 50. Like cutting the wire on the bomb before it goes off.'

'I must make sure to do it with only seconds to spare. And option two?'

'Remain within the single market but no longer as an EU member. Something like Norway's or Switzerland's deals, details to be decided, et cetera. And option three, of course, is to exit the EU, customs union, single market, the whole shebang. Brexit to the max.'

If you have the keyword CLARION, turn to **569.**

If you have the keyword HEMLOCK, turn to **512.**

Otherwise turn to **370.**

649

Every few days comes a new poll, but none of them is conclusive. There's almost no difference between support for Brexit and support for staying in the EU.

'Not another close call,' you say to God in your evening prayers. 'Whatever the result is, let it be clear cut.'

The answer comes to you by divine revelation. There *are* no close calls. Whichever side wins, you should declare it a landslide and a mandate for your government's policy.

Look at your Brexit Memo Pad. If your Goodwill score is 52% or higher, turn to **204**. If it's 40% or lower, turn to **864**. If it's between the two, turn to **245**.

650

Colin Fungale chooses to ignore what the rest of the panel are saying and address the audience directly. 'We're not the only nation in Europe that's had it up to the back teeth with this, are we? You go down the high street these days, you can't tell what half the shops are selling. And when you get inside they don't speak English. We're getting crowded out of our own country by people who can't even do us the courtesy of learning our language.'

There's a smattering of raucous approval from somewhere in the room, but his rhetoric goes just a little too far for most of them.

Fungale is such a natural populist that he'd be a real threat if not for the fact that he reflects his supporters' views rather too overtly. Lots of people are racists, but they don't like admitting to that out loud.

'Actually,' says Lucy Tooth, 'the groundswell of feeling that Colin is describing is mostly in his own fevered imagination. Four in every five Europeans support free movement within the EU. Two-thirds of Brits support it. You'd like to think you're surfing a wave, Colin, but in fact you're splashing about in a tiny little stagnant pond of xenophobia.'

Oh, a rare burst of effective rhetoric there. Fungale responds with his trademark smirk, but he's visibly nettled by the cheer that goes up from the audience.

⇒ See what Tode has to say. Turn to **487**

⇒ Skip to another question. Turn to **405**

651

Look at your Brexit Memo Pad.

If EU Trade Talks are marked as complete, turn to **527**.

If EU Trade Talks have not been completed, turn to **411.**

652

Your soft-Brexit credentials are pretty solid. You did after all opt to keep Britain in the single market, but it isn't long before Tiffany Rufus is claiming the credit for that. She makes out that you weren't sure about it and only made the decision after a long talk with her.

'Ridiculous. I wouldn't take her advice on a used car. The longest talk I've ever had with her is when I gave her the job.'

'I'm sure that's true, Prime Minister,' says Wilkins, bringing you a plate of biscuits for elevenses. 'But I suppose what matters is what the honourable members believe.'

He's right. It comes down to which of you has the greater credibility. If your Popularity is 50% or more, turn to **489**. Otherwise turn to **377**.

653

You can't shake off the story, and it does no good to try and spin it as evidence of your rationality and pragmatism. People don't feel that a politician who changes their mind is being sensible, just shifty. The final round of Parliamentary voting knocks you out of the contest.

So that means the members will now have to choose between Rufus and Stollard. It's extraordinary. Though Rufus has done her best to sound hawkish about Brexit of late, the truth is they're both Remainers at heart. And now one of them will lead the Party.

'Politics is a funny old game,' muses your chief of staff.

'It's not a game, Ron. A game is something you can control. Politics is just a lottery.'

THE END

654

'It's not the worst deal we might have struck,' says the Chancellor when you tell him the outline of the deal. 'We'll have minimal influence over the regulations we have to abide by, of course.'

'The crucial distinction, Alan, is that we don't *have* to abide by them. British law will track the rulings of the European Court, but with the option to go its own way.'

'If we ever do opt out, that could cut off our remaining access to the single market.'

'The point is we can sell it to the voters as sovereignty regained. Better to rule in an EFTA limbo than get booted out of office by voters who would never be happy with either the economic inferno of a hard Brexit or the bovine compromise involved in the Norway model.'

On your Brexit Memo Pad:

- -5% Economy – Britain's service industries will find it harder to trade with Europe.
- -2% Goodwill – the EU are already sick of the complexity of dealing with the Swiss under similar terms.
- -5% Popularity – the voters are dimly resentful that all the fireworks of Brexit has ended in the damp squib of thoughtful diplomacy.
- Tick the keyword CLARION
- Mark EU Trade Talks as complete.

Then turn to **666.**

655

The ultimate purpose of all the EU rules is to make the single market a level playing field. And to do that there have to be regulations and standards, otherwise, one country could, for instance, subsidise its toilet seat manufacturing industry, or pass laws on the working week allowing its companies to employ a smaller workforce working longer hours than its competitors, and thus undercut everyone else's toilet seats. And so on.

That's not to say there aren't differences in wages paid across the EU, but the goal is to move over time to closer economic convergence. If you've got the harmonisation of standards and regulations, what's the point of having the same veterinary qualifications recognized across the EU if all vets can't travel where they like to practice their profession? You need the same rules on standards, safety, packaging, and so forth. And these rules need to cover everything from the text on product packaging to the power of vacuum cleaners. Having to follow the same rules and regulations means handing a bunch of legislative powers over to Brussels. And that's why you get the bendy banana rule, along with stuff like the working time directive. And health and safety. And the rules on mobile phone roaming charges. And... well, there's just loads of it.

Mind you, it's not like we didn't have our own regulations on fruit and veg (and everything else of course) before we joined the EU. We did – they were just a lot simpler. Though, to be fair, those rules only had to apply to one country, the UK, not twenty-eight different countries all vigorously trading with each other. Everyone can be sovereign if they just bolt the garden gate and live off what they grow on the allotment.

What do you want to take a look at now, if you haven't already?

⇒ More about regulatory bodies — Turn to **123**

⇒ EFTA — Turn to **346**

⇒ Free movement — Turn to **414**

⇒ That's enough research for now — Turn to **441**

656

The EU will agree to a reciprocal rights deal, but the Spanish are insisting that all UK citizens in Spain take out health insurance to replace of the old system whereby the NHS would cover their healthcare bills. On top of that, the insurance has to be with healthcare insurance providers approved by the Spanish government, and the plans are quite expensive.

Accepting the deal would be a blow for the British pensioners who were looking forward to an easy retirement in Spain. Some of them are bank robbers, of course, but the rest will struggle to afford these insurance plans. Alternatively you could refuse point blank and try to bluff it out.

⇒ Agree — Turn to **740**

⇒ Refuse — Turn to **584**

657

Alan Stollard is isolated on the soft wing of the party as Tiffany Rufus tacks towards a firmer stance. Remainer MPs desert him in droves, no doubt counting on Rufus to deliver a tempered version of Brexit if she should win.

Stollard drops out after the next round leaving you, Rufus and Strewel to go through to the final parliamentary ballot.

Will you focus on knocking out Rufus next (turn to **679**) or is Strewel the bigger threat (turn to **802**)?

658 ☐

If the box above is empty, put a tick in it and turn to **551.**

If the box was already ticked, turn to **480.**

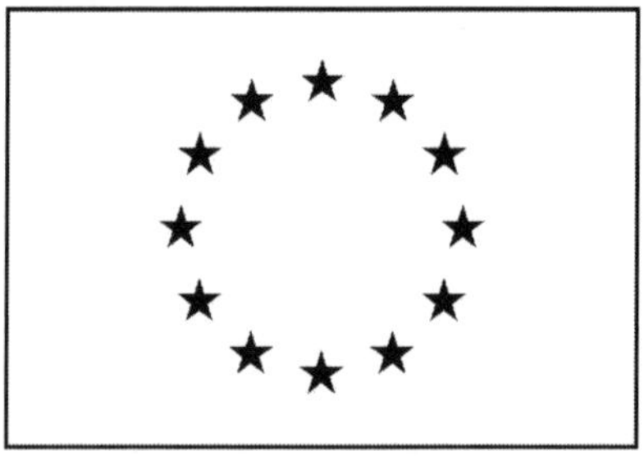

659

The sword of Damocles hangs over you in the form of Britain's financial settlement with the EU. You managed to sweep the matter under the carpet for a while, but the time is coming when you'll have to deal with it.

The problem is that the public don't understand this is an obligation that Britain undertook as a member state. They perceive the settlement as a fine. If you pay up, the newspapers will screech about you giving in to blackmail. But if you don't pay, that will not only damage Britain's standing in the world, it will be an impediment to all future dealings with our largest trading partner.

'What became of Damocles?' you ask Peter Strewel the next time you see him. The tow-headed buffoon may have the morals of Frank Sinatra's tomcat, but he does know his Classics.

'Gave up the seat of power, didn't he? Got too hot for him.'

A salutary lesson. Turn to **666**.

660 ☐

You get some advice on referendums from an expert, but not the kind of expert you might have expected.

If the box above is empty, put a tick in it and turn to **54.**

If the box was already ticked, turn to **644.**

661

Your earlier willingness to reach a deal over the rights of EU citizens in Britain now stands you in good stead. Those countries with nationals living here will help to influence the Commission towards an amicable agreement.

Turn to **82**.

662

You would have liked to get more personally involved in negotiating Britain's future trading relationship with the EU, but too many other matters demanded your attention.

'We're hammering out the details of a free trade agreement,' says the Secretary of State for Exiting the EU as he briefs the Cabinet on the latest round of talks.

'With respect, Dennis, you've been doing that for the past year. How long is it going to take?'

'I'm sure we can settle the bulk of it within the – um, implementation period.'

The Chancellor gives a yelp of uncharacteristic laughter. 'I can't see it getting signed in less than a decade. Look at Canada.'

'Nobody had any incentive to push the Canadian deal through,' protests Dent. 'In our case there are several states who want a settlement as much as we do. Ireland, Belgium, the Netherlands…'

'Because their economies will suffer from Brexit almost as badly as ours,' agrees the Chancellor. 'But that's four or five countries out of twenty-seven. France and Germany, and even Poland, don't stand to take nearly as much of a hit. They're going to have other priorities.'

Dent folds his hands thoughtfully and for a moment you think he's going to reveal a masterstroke. But then he says, 'The EU needs this deal more than we do,' and you realize the only thing left to fall back on is dogma.

> On your Brexit Memo Pad:
> - ❖ -10% Economy – a bespoke FTA will take years, and even then it's a case of damage limitation.
> - ❖ -5% Goodwill – two years of facing your ministers across the conference table has soured many EU officials' opinion of Britain.
> - ❖ Mark EU Trade Talks as complete.

Then turn to **385**.

663

There's a political cost to restoring the border in any form, and naturally you get some screaming and shouting from the civil liberties snowflakes, but on the whole it seems like the least damaging solution.

> Record on your Brexit Memo Pad:
> - ❖ -1% Authority – you take some of the blame for making the Northern Ireland situation more strained.
> - ❖ -1% Popularity – the left-wing press try to make out this is the first step in building a police state.

Turn to **49**.

664

The leadership contest is touch and go. What about it? Are you feeling lucky?

⇒ You make your own luck. Turn to **189**

⇒ It's all just a roll of the dice. Turn to **377**

665

You've led by example, steering away from the polarized zero-sum politics of the populists towards a kinder and more inclusive kind of democracy. Or, at least, so it appears to your supporters and critics alike. And if there is one force in politics that can beat all the invective of the last few years, it's the promise of a brighter and more united future.

Turn to **486**.

666 ☐ ☐ ☐

This is different from any other section in the book. Do *not* put a tick in one of the boxes above *unless* you were specifically told to do so in the section you've just turned from.

If none of the boxes is ticked, turn to **100**.

If one box is ticked turn to **200**.

If two boxes are ticked turn to **300**.

If all three boxes are ticked turn to **400**.

By the way, if you need a rest from running the country – well, it's a stressful job and nobody could blame you. This is a good place to take a break. Just be sure to note down this section number (**666**) so you can find your place later.

667

'They verify that a product really is from the free trade area. If so then it gets in duty-free, but that's not the case for goods that simply passed through the country on their way to the EU.'

'Sounds simple enough.'

'It's a little bit of additional red tape, but I don't think it needs to worry us too much.'

⇒ 'So what can we expect from a free trade deal? The pros and cons.' Turn to **303**

⇒ 'Do these deals take a long time?' Turn to **276**

⇒ 'Maybe it would be simpler just to revert to World Trade Organization rules.' Turn to **826**

668

Listening to somebody else's opinions often puts you in a foul mood. But at least it's taken your mind off the toothache.

⇒ 'What's wrong with referendums anyway?' Turn to **68**

⇒ 'The first referendum result was an overwhelming majority for hard Brexit. Why hold another?' Turn to **249**

⇒ 'If you object so strongly to referendums, why make an exception for another EU one?' Turn to **571**

⇒ 'I don't have time for this. I have a country to run.' Turn to **425**

669

You reach for the tea. 'Bring me up to speed, Wilkins. Any early appointments?'

'Three, Prime Minister. Mrs Stoat, Mr Beardsley, and Sir Harvey. Whom should I schedule for the breakfast meeting?'

Chloe Stoat is Secretary of State for Business, Energy and Industrial Strategy. She's a jittery, brittle type with a habit of shooting her mouth off to the press if she feels she's being left out of the loop. Nonetheless, talking to her would help you get a picture of Brexit's economic impact.

As the Downing Street chief of staff, Ron Beardsley is your policy advisor. If there is any philosophical agenda underpinning your political strategy, it comes from him, and he's prepared a brief on the exit payment the EU wants from Britain. Ron is a little intense, though, and hard to take first thing in the morning. As is his pipe.

Sir Harvey Doggerbank is the chair of the 1922 committee. A hardcore right-winger whose wide-eyed glare always make you think of Yeats's 'Second Coming'. But maintaining your authority means keeping him close.

You remember that the Chancellor is arriving for a meeting about the EU exit fee at 8:30, so there'll only be time to see one of them now and the others will have to wait.

⇒ 'I'd better see the minister.' Turn to **800**

⇒ 'I have some things to talk over with Mr Beardsley.' Turn to **263**

⇒ 'Let's get Sir Harvey out of the way first.' Turn to **737**

670

Much as you'd like to, there's no squirming out of the deal. Who knows if you even needed Peter Strewel's support to get this far, but he has too many friends in the Commons and is too popular with the voters for you to stitch him up. You're going to have to appoint him to the Treasury.

'At least he's off the international stage,' says Ron Beardsley. 'He might muck up the domestic economy but we'll no longer be a laughing stock around the world.'

> On your Brexit Memo Pad:
> - ❖ +5% Authority – with Strewel's faction joined to yours, your position as leader is stronger than ever.
> - ❖ -3% Economy – the markets recoil from the news like a slug from salt.

Then turn to **603**.

671

Look at your Brexit Memo Pad.

If Authority is 61% or *more* and Goodwill is 30% or *less*, turn to **40**.

Otherwise turn to **792**.

672

'That's a bold move,' says your chief of staff as soon as you step back inside.

'Say what you mean, Ron. You think it's a mistake.'

'Not if you can get people to believe you mean what you say.'

Look at your Brexit Memo Pad.

If you have the keywords APRICITY or TIGHTROPE, turn to **498**.

If not but you have Popularity of 56% or more, turn to **519**.

Otherwise turn to **180**.

673

'Switzerland has limited access to the EU services market, and that only in some sectors,' explains Stollard. 'In theory they have been moving towards greater integration, more along the lines of the EFTA states inside the European Economic Area, but in practice that ship keeps foundering on the rocks of free movement.'

'I say, I might use that nautical jibber-jabber in a speech,' says Strewel. 'I'll try and give it a funnier punchline obviously, maybe make it one of those inflatable dinghies stuffed with Libyan rapists, but it's a nice vivid image.'

Turn to **378.**

674

'This makes my whole department irrelevant!' screams Leslie Barkwell when he hears the news. 'What's the point of being minister for international trade when I'm not allowed to do any trade deals?'

'Calm down, Leslie, you look like a faulty pressure cooker.'

'I don't like it either,' says Alan Stollard.

Now that is surprising. They don't normally land on the same side of any issue. 'And what's your objection?'

'A customs union doesn't make any provision for trade in services. Our exports to the EU in services alone amount to £4290 million a week. That's a dozen of your red buses, by the way, Peter.'

Strewel gives a hearty chuckle. 'It's doing sums in your head that got you the Treasury job, Alan. Personally I have more faith in abracadabra than in the abacus.'

Stollard throws his arms wide. 'Do please wave a magic wand and transform the UK economy. We'd all like to go to the ball.'

'I'm sure it'll be fine,' says Strewel. 'A lot of these service industry johnnies could do proper jobs if they put their mind to it. How many baristas does one country need, anyway?'

And so, far too late, you realize that your own Foreign Secretary has absolutely no grasp of how big and mean a genie he's let out of the bottle.

On your Brexit Memo Pad:

- -7% Economy – your own experts calculate the hit for leaving the single market to be at least two percent of GDP.
- -5% Popularity – the people were promised fabulous new trade deals around the world, none of which are possible now.
- Tick the keyword QUORUM
- Mark EU Trade Talks as complete.

Then turn to **666.**

675

He just laughs in your face. 'Britain's economy amounts to about ten percent of the EU total and just over two percent of the global GDP. Don't you think the big behemoths like the US, China and the EU are more likely to concentrate on trade with each other, Prime Minister? Or is this an Ealing comedy where the plucky little guy wins the day?'

You're forced to fall back on platitudes about Britain's continued greatness and the supposed benefits of going it alone. Appleby continually interrupts you, undermining you even further. When you walk out of the studio, your press secretary can't even look you in the eye.

The vote rolls inexorably closer like one of those wheeled idols in an Indian saturnalia. Turn to **377**.

676

The final heat of the referendum concludes with the resounding decision by the British people that they are willing to stay in the EU but they want more concessions.

'Your predecessor tried that,' points out the Chancellor. 'And where's he now?'

'Sunning himself on some oil tycoon's yacht, no doubt. We can find some concessions, can't we? Immigration, for instance. We can tighten that up using existing EU laws and package it up for the voters as a victory.'

'If we do stay, the EU27 will be in a good mood. So I suppose there are a few minor concessions we might be able to deliver.'

'The rebate?'

'Money.' He sucks his teeth. 'Probably not.'

Turn to **714**.

677

An MP is walking through the lobby when he clutches his chest, gives a groan, and slumps to the floor. You suspect a ruse to avoid the rolling juggernaut of horror that is Brexit. But no, it turns out to be a *bona fide* heart attack, and a fatal one at that. An immediate by-election is triggered.

What are your thoughts?

⇒ It's a setback, but you'll turn it to your advantage.
Turn to **585**

⇒ It's a silver lining with a possible cloud attached.
Turn to **329**

678

'I suppose that falls to me as International Trade minister,' says Barkwell. He shuffles some papers around like a nervous father giving a speech at a wedding. 'Um.. based in Geneva, not Brussels. Almost every country in the world is a member. Even Turkmenistan.' He peers at the sheet of paper. 'No, they're not a member. One of the unhappy few.'

Dent reaches across and puts his hand down on Barkwell's notes as if closing the lid on something embarrassing. 'The World Trade Organization establishes default tariffs between nations not covered by a free trade agreement or customs union,' he explains. 'So the moment we're out of the EU we'll be falling back on WTO rules. Are we a member in our own right? Yes we are. The WTO's director general is on record: "The United Kingdom is a member of the WTO today, it will continue to be a member tomorrow. There will be no discontinuity. Trade will not stop." That's one in the eye for the naysayers, hmm?'

For some reason his gaze comes to rest on the Chancellor, who takes it as a cue to pick up the thread. 'On leaving the EU, the most likely scenario is that we'll do a cut-n-paste: apply the same tariffs to other countries as we previously did as an EU member. Our tariffs in respect of the EU itself would be WTO boilerplate.'

⇒ 'Can't we change those tariffs?' Turn to **52**

⇒ 'What other WTO rules do we need to be aware of?' Turn to **454**

679

Peter Strewel comes to you with an offer. 'It's like the Hunger Games, this, eh?'

'You don't look as if you've been going short of food, Peter.'

'Just getting my appetite if you want the truth. I'm going to bite this off and run with it. You know you can't beat me. So what about joining up? You throw your weight behind my campaign and I'll give you the Treasury. I'll be in Number 10, you'll be in Number 11. Just like a BBC sitcom.'

⇒ Take the deal. Turn to **77**

⇒ Tell him no thanks. Turn to **617**

680

Fungale wastes no time in announcing his intention to stand as a Parliamentary candidate if the Conservatives will have him. He's picked a clapped-out East Anglian seaside town where the current incumbent is a forlorn hope of the Remain wing of the party.

The local constituency are fawning over him already, so it seems to be a done deal. Probably just as well that you didn't try to block his membership. These days you need to pick your battles carefully.

> On your Brexit Memo Pad:
> ❖ Get the keyword NYLON.

Turn to **375**.

681

'As I understand it,' says Dent, 'it means no tariffs on trade with the EU. But we would have to abide by EU tariff arrangements with goods from outside the ECU. And we'd get the benefit of the EU's negotiating team when it comes to hammering out new deals – but as we've discussed, that might not be a benefit at all. After all, we sold Brexit on the basis of the cornucopia of economic opportunities once Britain could go it alone. I for one don't want to see us having to hide under the table and scoff the scraps the EU tosses to us.'

'Oh, hang on,' says Strewel. He leans down and rescues a fried mushroom that had fallen off his plate. 'Not sure if I should eat that. Oh, hang it, five-second rule, eh?'

⇒ 'Peter's breakfast aside, what are the drawbacks of a customs union?' Turn to **799**

⇒ 'What about other possible trade models?' Turn to **703**

682

You distance yourself from all the decisions on the grounds of being too busy with Brexit. Let your Health Secretary and Chancellor take the flak. Any bad news regarding the NHS is far too toxic for you to allow it to taint you.

The end result is that the NHS receives its usual drip-feed of inadequate funding. Barry Scraggle gets up in the Commons to criticize it but ends up getting sidetracked by free walking frames for pensioners. You thank God for giving you such a leader of the opposition.

> On your Brexit Memo Pad:
> - ❖ -2% Popularity – the voters get the message that the NHS is in trouble, and they're not happy.
> - ❖ Mark the NHS as complete.

Now turn to **385**.

683

With the polls suggesting a swing towards Remain, it comes down to the final television debates. Not for the first time, it could all be decided by weather and whim.

If you have the keyword FOG, turn to **837.**

If you have the keyword GAZELLE, turn to **788.**

If you have the keyword SANCTION, turn to **445.**

If you have none of those, turn to **624.**

684

'That's Norway's usual tactic,' says Stollard. 'Although they have no direct say in EU regulations, most of those regulations must conform to international standards – of course, because the EU trades throughout the world. So Norway can lobby at the WTO, the United Nations, and so on, and directives agreed there are taken up by the EU. It's the global arena that counts. We could remain within the European Economic Area, reduce our fiscal transfer, keep our current arrangements for services and tariff-free goods, and still have a say in EU directives. We just have to be smart about it.'

'Free movement is always going to be the spanner in the works,' says Strewel. 'The Spaniard in the works, I should say. Ho ho.'

'Agreed,' says Dent. 'The public voted by an overwhelming majority to end free movement and turn off the gushing tap of immigration.'

'Overwhelming,' agrees Barkwell. 'An irresistible mandate. We can only do as the public demands – and that means no to the EEA.'

Turn to **17**.

685

The Department for International Trade. Ugh. It's not the name itself that irks you. At least it's more succinct than its predecessor, the Department for Business Innovation and Skills, which always used to put you in mind of a made-up ministry from *The Thick of It*. But the building looks like the concourse at a Docklands railway station. All the more so at this time in the evening, with strip lights casting a merciless zombie light over rows of empty desks.

You glance at your watch. Only nine thirty. A bit early for them all to have knocked off. Imagine if Churchill had run the War Rooms like that: 'You'd better all go home or your dinners will get cold. Jerry can wait till morning.'

You glance into the minister's office. No sign of him either, but at least his coat and briefcase are here. Unless he picked up that trick from the merchant bankers of leaving a spare coat behind to fool people. Still, you don't need to talk to him. You just need to find a copy of the international trade report that ought to be lurking around here somewhere.

Five minutes later you're surrounded by piles of papers but there's no sign of the report. You're on the point of calling up your protection officers to look for it. Let them earn their hundred grand a year for once.

'Can I help you, Prime Minister?'

You turn. The girl looks about twelve years old. But then, so do most doctors and policemen these days.

'Are you a civil servant?'

She shakes her head. Twelve-year-olds wouldn't have a green streak in their hair, would they? And is she chewing gum?

'A special adviser?'

'No, I sometimes do my homework here while I'm waiting for my dad. He's gone to dinner at his club.'

The penny drops. 'You're Mr Barkwell's daughter.'

She looks past you at the scattered files. 'Looking for something?'

'The report your father's been working on, actually. But never mind.'

'Yeah, I've read it. What do you want to know?'

Turn to **700.**

686

Back at Number 10 you lose no time. 'Wilkins, get me an expert on UK residency rights.'

'Right now, Prime Minister? It's the weekend.'

'The Government Legal Service employs over two thousand barristers and solicitors. You can surely rustle one up on a Saturday.'

A few minutes later you're on the phone to a QC who can give you the t-shirt version of EU citizens' residency rights.

'Essentially,' he says, 'anyone can be one of three types of UK resident. Resident, permanent resident or citizen. If you've been resident here for at least five years then you can apply for permanent residency. And if you're a permanent resident, you can apply after another year for citizenship. So it takes a minimum of six years for an immigrant to become a British citizen.'

⇒ 'So, how does that work for EU citizens?'

Turn to **284**

⇒ 'Can an EU national apply for UK residency?'

Turn to **295**

687

'Like any market, the EU classifies goods according to things like size and shape, whether they've been squashed in transit, and so on. You want to know that before you hand over money for something.

There was never a rule banning straight bananas or different sizes of condom. And as for the prawn cocktail crisps – '

You notice the blank looks. Seeing you pause, several reporters put their hands up. Nobody will report on what you said. In this post-facts world, an item is newsworthy if it entertains people, with bonus points if it's short enough to tweet. If you want to beat a freewheeling populist Peter Strewel, you aren't going to do it by countering his wild assertions with reasoned argument.

Turn to **34**.

688

This is it. The big one. The whole future trading relationship between Britain and our nearest, largest and most natural market will depend on the next round of talks. This is far too important for you to leave to those bunglers and blowhards in the Cabinet. You're taking care of this in person.

Flanked by a small army of well-prepped negotiators, you face Alprèves and his team across a no-man's-land of glass tabletop. As usual they look sleekly confident, but you've been assured by your Brexit ministers that the EU needs this deal more than Britain does. What was it Peter Strewel said as you were about to get on the plane? 'We've got all the cards in this game, PM. Just be sure to deal from the bottom.'

Over the next few days, your aim is to hammer out the terms under which the EU and the UK will trade after March 2019. You have three existing models of trade relationships that you can choose between as templates.

The Norway model, much touted by the Brexit campaigners during the referendum but since disowned by fundamentalists, keeps Britain within the European Economic Area. As something close to associate membership, it requires some payments into R&D ventures but gives maximum benefit.

The Swiss model, outside the EEA but still in the single market, gives a little more freedom, at least in the form of being nominally able to opt out of free movement and EU standards legislation. In practice, of course, opting out would mean losing access to the market, but at least the choice is there.

Turkey is outside the single market but has a customs union with the EU. That means no tariffs on goods sold between the two, and gives Turkey the benefit of all trade deals negotiated by the EU – which naturally has far more clout than any individual country.

The downside of Turkey's arrangement is that it only covers goods, while the vast majority of the UK's trade is in services. Some have suggested rewinding the clock and getting Britain's shipyards and foundries back to work like in the great days of Isambard Kingdom Brunel. But you don't think the stovepipe hats and teenage prostitution would catch on, so on balance it would be preferable to draft a completely new free trade agreement with the EU. The fly in the ointment being that you had that and much more with full membership. What would a bespoke deal offer?

⇒ Aim for something like the Norway model. Turn to **111**

⇒ Use Switzerland and the European Free Trade Association as your benchmarks. Turn to **167**

⇒ Propose a customs union along the lines of Turkey's agreement with the EU. Turn to **674**

⇒ Set out guidelines for a completely new free trade agreement. Turn to **294**

689

It's a good answer. You're selling people the idea of a course that lets them keep the best features of the EU without losing their pride. You can almost feel the audience at the debate relaxing into the model you're describing.

Still, that's one debate in a maelstrom of lies, wild claims, ill-tempered rejoinders and outright hysteria. Reason is a tiny voice at the bottom of Pandora's box.

On the night of the referendum you turn on the television and pace the room as the votes come in.

Toss two coins. If both come up tails, turn to **313**. Otherwise, turn to **403.**

690

'Yes. Those cover non-trade issues. Tourism, cooperation on security, the environment, political asylum, cultural affairs, things like that. All agreements that nudge Switzerland closer to being an associate member of the European Union in the least efficient way possible.'

'And they took ages to agree,' adds Strewel. 'I heard that Bilateral Agreements II alone took over two years to thrash out, and that's just the actual negotiations. Each part of the deal then went through a mutual approvals phase, averaging three years apiece. Aspirins all round. Almost faster to do it by yodelling.'

'Why didn't they include service industries?'

'Originally that was the main thing Bilateral Agreements II was supposed to achieve. They ended up with the chips and the salad, but no steak.'

⇒ 'How come?' Turn to **457**

⇒ 'Any other points I should know about?' Turn to **378**

691

'It's roughly 40% of what Britain pays as a full member, per head,' Stollard tells you.

'What do they get in return?'

'Ah, well that's interesting. It can't be sold as membership dues, obviously. The SVP – that's the Swiss UKIP, only not so shambolic – would jump on anything like that. So it goes to cover regional development and funding for research programmes.

⇒ 'And in return they get access to the single market in services as well as goods?' Turn to **673**

⇒ 'And what about freedom of movement?' Turn to **457**

692

So what if you campaigned for a soft Brexit and instead the public want to stay in the EU? You can spin it as a clever strategy to bring the hardcore Leave voters round. 'I wanted us in the single market and so we shall remain,' you'll tell them. No need to resign.

'What now?' call the reporters waiting for you in Downing Street.

You turn to face the barrage of popping flashlights. You have never felt more certainly the wind of destiny in your sails.

'Now,' you tell them, 'I get on with the job.'

> On your Brexit Memo Pad:
> - ❖ -5% Popularity – your misjudgement in the campaign will take some living down.
> - ❖ Mark Second EU Referendum as complete.

Then turn to **450**.

693

Playing for time might be the best course, but Alprèves doesn't like it. From his perspective, any uncertainty over Britain paying its way in the current funding period would mean a yawning chasm in the EU budget.

'I feel as though the term "exit fee" is clouding British sentiment on this issue,' he says a little petulantly. 'This is not a bill that the rest of the European Union is throwing down before you. Nor is it, as some of your newspapers would portray it, a duellist's glove slapped across the face. It is Britain's share of legitimate expenses incurred while a full member.'

'Nobody is disputing that. The United Kingdom takes its responsibilities very seriously.'

'There was a time that was true, yet if we look at your international credit rating, for example – '

'Still on a par with the EU average, I think you'll find.'

'But severely damaged by your referendum, and with a negative outlook since you have decided to amputate yourselves from the other twenty-seven states.'

⇒ Amputate? That's inflammatory talk! Show him you won't have it. Turn to **421**

⇒ Steady as you go. The waters ahead will get a lot choppier than this. Turn to **288**

694

Inspiration comes to you a few days later when you have your driver pull over to pick up a Thai takeaway. Munching at a carton of noodles in the back of the car, you call up the Chancellor.

'I've got two words, Alan. Thai chicken.'

'Oh, pick me up some tod mun pla while you're at it, then. I've been working on these spreadsheets and I missed dinner.'

'Too late, I already ordered. Stick a pizza in the microwave if you're peckish. My point is, we buy an awful lot of chicken from Thailand, don't we?'

'More than 100,000 tonnes a year. Britain accounts for about half the chicken Thailand exports to the EU. But why are you...?' There's a sound like static on the line. Although usually static doesn't swear.

'Yes, Alan, you got it. I want to increase our chicken quota, negotiate a preferential tariff, loosen up food safety standards – whatever it takes to get a big grinning "sawasdee" out of Thailand.'

'The downside is that the UK poultry industry will end up looking like a fox got in.'

He has a point.

⇒ Go ahead in any case. Turn to **491**

⇒ Forget about one big deal and just concentrate on building up a slew of smaller ones. Turn to **242**

695

The very success of your leadership counts against you. Labour, terrified of the certain decimation they would suffer in a general election, vote against the motion. It fails to go through.

For a few hours you consider the option of ordering one of your tame backbenchers to propose a vote of no confidence. If that passed with a simple majority it would give you the excuse you need to call an election.

'But it would make me look weak!' you cry. You look around but the Chapel of St Mary is empty, your security officers outside the door. Only the Lord is here to witness your impotent rage.

On your Brexit Memo Pad:

❖ Mark General Election as complete.

Then turn to **666**.

696

'You'd have to talk to Mr Tode and Mr Strewel about that,' you say when the question comes up. 'I don't know which of them wielded the brush, but he can come round and paint my garden shed anytime.'

It gets a laugh, but as Peter Strewel is in your Cabinet it doesn't play so well with the backbenchers.

> On your Brexit Memo Pad:
> - ❖ -1% Authority – there are rumblings of discontent from some factions of the party.
> - ❖ +1% Popularity – the voters see you as a firm hand on the tiller.

Then turn to **125**.

697

A glorious day. You are returned to power by a landslide.

'A great victory for the Party,' says the Chancellor as you set off to Buckingham Palace.

'For the Party? No, Alan. The victory is mine.'

> Record on your Brexit Memo Pad:
> - ❖ +15% Authority – nothing can stop you now.
> - ❖ +5% Economy – the icing on the cake; the markets are reassured by the promise of strong and stable government.
> - ❖ Mark General Election as complete.

Then turn to **666**.

698

'A menu, sort of thing,' says Strewel. 'Brexit à la carte.'

'It's a recipe for disaster, if you ask me,' says the Chancellor. 'Just suppose we had 30% in favour of a Norway-type deal, 30% saying they want to stay in the EU, and 40% wanting out of the whole shebang, no single market, no customs union, and so forth?'

'Then Leaves wins,' says Barkwell. 'That's how democracy works in my book. The majority view carries the day.'

'It's just an example, Leslie. These aren't the actual figures. But there you can see that 60% of the voters did not want a hard Brexit but they'd be getting one anyway. It could just end up causing more bitter divisions in a country that's already on the ropes.'

'Oh yes, oh yes. That's the sort of defeatist talk that's at the root of all our problems. The country is not divided. The will of the people is for a hard Brexit under strong and stable Conservative leadership.'

There's a moment of silence as everyone contemplates Barkwell's rant. He reaches out and discreetly wipes a fleck of spittle from the polished surface of the table. All eyes turn to you.

⇒ 'I like this à la carte idea. Let's make it so.' Turn to **648**

⇒ 'I'm not sure what's wrong with the tried and tested yes/no option.' Turn to **600**

⇒ 'What about the runoff idea? If the French can figure it out, surely we can.' Turn to **340**

⇒ 'I'm going off the whole idea. We've had too many referendums lately anyway.' Turn to **79**

699

To reflect on your earlier discussions about trade inside the single market, turn to **774**.

For a briefing on Britain's options outside the single market, turn to **322**.

700

Miss Barkwell seems to have a thorough grasp of the trade report and enough sassy self-confidence to power an Academy Award ceremony. 'I've got to get back to my Economics prep,' she says, 'but I can give you a quick SWOT analysis.'

⇒ 'OK, what are Britain's strengths?' Turn to **483**

⇒ 'Our weaknesses?' Turn to **326**

⇒ 'Tell me about the opportunities.' Turn to **392**

⇒ 'We'd better go over the threats.' Turn to **11**

⇒ 'Never mind, you get back to your homework.' Turn to **666**

701

'It's good,' says Franjeboom with the sleek contentment of a cream-fed cat. 'Your forces and our forces should continue to work together hand-in-glove for the sake of… the future.' He looks at your scowl. 'That's not the correct expression? Hand-in-glove?'

'I'd like to know what you meant by it being good for the future.'

'In case, you know, your country comes to its senses. Then the whole family can come together again.'

> Record on your Brexit Memo Pad:
> - -3% Authority – the EU has forced you to back down; you fear it won't be the last time
> - -3% Popularity – the voters are waking up to Britain's reduced importance in the world, and they blame you.
> - Mark Security & Defence as complete.

Turn to **269.**

702

When you reflect on Britain's place in global politics these days, it's hard not to picture the opening sequence of *Dad's Army* – even if it's not clear anymore which side of the Channel has more Nazis.

The UK and the EU now face each other angrily across an unbridgeable gulf. From now on any agreements with the other twenty-seven states are going to be an uphill struggle on harsh terms. Trade will be fraught with difficulties and the economy and the country as a whole will suffer because of it.

But surely there must be some good to come out of all the acrimony. If only you could see it.

As you're gathering up your papers after a Cabinet meeting, you're surprised to hear a discreet cough from a chair at the end of the room. It was half-hidden behind a pillar, so it's only when you walk over that you're reminded that Thomas Tode is back in Cabinet these days.

'Great days,' he says, with the perky little smile that always makes you want to slap him.

'Right. Because who needs friends and allies?'

'That's it exactly. Cutting off all our options with the EU makes life so much simpler. Now that Britain is out of Europe, we're insulated from all those confusing foreign ideas. The people will turn back to British values and British leaders.'

So there's the good news. By reason of a sort of diplomatic Stockholm syndrome, the British people will become isolated and impoverished, but at the same time more unified. No wonder you kept thinking about *Dad's Army*.

Turn to **351**.

703

What do you want to discuss next?

- ⇒ Britain's prospects outside the single market. Turn to **836**
- ⇒ Possible arrangements that keep Britain in the single market. Turn to **247**
- ⇒ Joining the European Customs Union. Turn to **367**
- ⇒ That's enough for today. Turn to **810**

704

'Of course, Confucius didn't say the mountain would get moved overnight.'

He looks at you, eyebrows raised. 'Excuse me?'

'We're willing to settle this budgetary matter first, but you can't expect us to simply take the bill and pay it. There has to be some drill down into those figures.'

'Then we are just back to negotiating this alongside everything else. I don't think you appreciate the strain that puts – '

You hold up your hand. 'Of course I do. And I'm not backtracking. I'm suggesting that we begin by agreeing the principles that will govern the calculation. We can hammer out those criteria quite quickly. What's Britain's share of contributions, for example – twelve percent, fifteen percent, or somewhere between the two? And our share of assets has to be considered too. Let's lay out the ground rules, then the actual sum can be assessed without rancour. I'm sure you don't need me to tell you that is the fairest and most objective approach.'

He makes a show of reluctance, but finally agrees. With luck you can drag out any announcement of the final exit fee until after Brexit. Not a great victory, but at times like these you are content just to avoid a clear defeat.

On your Brexit Memo Pad:

- ❖ Mark the Exit Fee as complete.

Then turn to **150**.

705 ☐

Your briefing on post-Brexit security and defence issues comes from an unorthodox but highly qualified source.

If the box above is empty, put a tick in it and turn to **155.**

If the box was already ticked, turn to **439**.

706

You're not convincing anyone. More likely the reverse. Even the other campaigners for Remain no longer mention you in their speeches.

'I feel like a veritable Jonah, Wilkins,' you say as you watch the results announced on the night of the vote.

'I don't know that one, Prime Minister,' he says, leafing through the book of cocktail recipes.

Toss two coins. If both come up heads, turn to **313**. If both come up tails, turn to **173**. Otherwise, turn to **403.**

707

'Well yes, they do,' says Stollard, 'but not through EFTA. In order to replicate that part of single market access they have a bunch of sectoral deals, including agriculture. It's a bespoke deal just for Switzerland.'

⇒ 'So they are in the single market?' Turn to **809**

⇒ 'What are those sectoral deals?' Turn to **621**

708

Ron Beardsley brings you the news. 'Fungale is calling you an EU lapdog. He says you've been paving the way for us to re-enter the EU by stealth.'

'Who knows what will happen in a few years. A lot of the Leave voters will have had their life support switched off by then, especially as the NHS collapses.'

'We won't say that out loud, though, will we?' says Ron, suddenly looking worried. 'You should make a statement.'

⇒ 'I intend to ignore him.' Turn to **777**

⇒ 'I'll say that while Fungale has been sulking his way through the few EU Parliament sessions he's bothered to attend, I've been thrashing out the hundreds of details needed to secure an orderly Brexit.' Turn to **238**

⇒ 'I'll say that the Brexit decision, like everything else in a democracy, can be upheld, altered or reversed by the public will. It's my job not to burn any bridges in the meantime.' Turn to **141**

709

'Quite,' says Barkwell. 'No point in taking that deal, no point at all.'

Stollard disagrees. 'It's the best option we have post-Brexit. Just because it's less attractive than full EU membership is no reason to seek an even worse deal. It's like if somebody said don't cut off your foot, you won't like it, and we said, okay, in that case we'll cut off the whole leg.'

Turn to **17.**

710

Bill Appleby has been known to reduce the iron men of politics to quivering lumps of jelly, but you know you've got what it takes and he sees it too. You stare him down, even when he says, 'You seem confident, Prime Minister, but I suppose we'll only know when the votes are counted.'

It's like training a dog, that's all. And you know your rivals will have seen the interview, and they won't sleep easy tonight.

If you have the keyword NYLON, turn to **193**. If not, turn to **726.**

711

The NHS is perhaps the most beloved of British institutions – which is surprising in a nation of zero-sum thinking and dreams of lottery millions. Brexit will almost certainly be the kidney punch that cripples the health service. Yet it would be a brave politician who thought of dismembering it and selling the pieces to the highest bidder without a ready group of scapegoats to blame.

You cast your mind over everything you've learned. Turn to **342.**

712

'It's a bit different for you, isn't it? An Austrian can go into Germany and people hardly notice he's foreign. He might even get himself elected Chancellor.'

Did you say that out loud? The frowns and shocked stares suggest that you did. Oops.

> Record on your Brexit Memo Pad:
> - ❖ -1% Goodwill – you might as well have mentioned the War.
> - ❖ +1% Popularity – the papers will love you blaming the Austrians for Hitler.

Turn to **453.**

713

You try turning on a dime, playing on your adversarial relationship with the EU. 'Mr Fungale only knows how to cock a snook at them,' you tell the reporters outside Number 10. 'I'm the one who actually goes out there and reads them the riot act.'

Is it enough? Toss two coins. If both are heads, turn to **606**. Otherwise turn to **366**.

714

Look at your Brexit Memo Pad. If you have the keyword FOG, turn to **805**. If you have the keyword GAZELLE, turn to **775**.

If you have neither keyword, turn to **206**.

715

The matter of Britain's financial obligations to the EU is just too politically sensitive to resolve now. These may indeed be payments that you agreed to as a member, and hence legally and morally binding, but that isn't how the press at home would spin them.

Maybe there's something else you could offer instead to free up the negotiating log-jam?

Look at your Brexit Memo Pad. If Residency Rights is not complete, turn to **53**.

Otherwise, if Security & Defence is not complete, turn to **354**.

Failing those, there is no outstanding issue you can use as a bargaining chip right now; turn to **855**.

716

'Well, of course,' blusters Barkwell, trying to save face. 'That's where I was going with that. Just meant that when you're ready to reveal your thinking, should you want to discuss... as it might have an effect on my brief, so to speak...'

You give him a withering look. 'Class dismissed.'

> On your Brexit Memo Pad:
> ❖ +2% Authority – now they know who's boss.

Then turn to **666.**

717

Addressing a meeting of hand-picked Party loyalists on the eve of the voting, you say, 'I have no problem with Mr Noysom-Reek's beliefs, but just having the right ideas isn't enough. Plenty of people go on *Dragon's Den* with great business ideas, but how many of them have the skill, the attitude and the determination to win? So I'm not going to stand here tonight and say my opponent is wrong. I won't say he's misguided or that his heart's not in the right place. But I will say that the difference between us is that he just wishes things were better for Britain, whereas I can actually deliver.'

Stirring words. Your audience gives you a standing ovation, at any rate. But that's only a couple of hundred people in a membership of a hundred and fifty thousand. The acid test will be whether your track record backs up your claims.

If you have *two* of the keywords BLEAK, HEMLOCK, JEWEL, KOALA or LEAF, turn to **519**.

If you have only one of those keywords, turn to **801**.

If you have none, turn to **50**.

718

'Rules of origin are used to check whether a product is really from the free trade area. If it is then it gets in duty-free, which doesn't apply to goods that simply passed through the country on their way to the EU.' The Chancellor looks around for a way to illustrate his point. 'Take this breakfast... Suppose the croissant is from France, the jam from Britain, the butter from New Zealand. Overall that's all right if our hypothetical agreement allows one third of components from outside the free trade area. But what about the plate itself? Is that British china or perhaps Chinese? Don't turn it over to look, Strewel, you're getting HP everywhere.'

'Villeroy and Boch, by Jove,' chortles Strewel, obvious of the brown sauce dripping onto the table. 'That's naughty. The Queen has Wedgewood, you know.'

'What about goods that are brought in from outside to be reprocessed?' you ask Stollard. 'Steel that gets used in making a car chassis, for example.'

'The free trade agreement has to have rules for that, usually in the form of a minimum added value from processing within the UK. We can't just stick a label on it and ship it out again. Using Chinese steel in the manufacture of British cars should be fine because most of the value is added right here. Turn the same steel into girders, though – not so clear cut, that; depends on the precise terms.'

'Sounds like a kettle of fish,' mutters Barkwell. 'All that red tape.'

'It is. That's what will be keeping your department busy until the middle of the century, old man.'

⇒ 'If we did take up the Norway model, how much would we be paying into the EU budget?' Turn to **767**

⇒ 'We won't drill down into details just now.' Turn to **17**

719

Check your Brexit Memo Pad. If you have the keyword GAZELLE or the keyword SANCTION then your attempt to undermine Chloe Stoat's account is belied by your own record: turn to **778**.

If you have neither of those keywords, turn to **645**.

720

You cannot keep putting off the outstanding financial settlement to the EU – not least because the world is watching to see if Britain is still as good as her word.

The final sum agreed is just over €30 billion, and with some massaging you're able to sell that as triumph, having more than halved the original highest estimates of bill. The pro-Brexit press are annoyed that you agreed to any payment at all, but in general it's about as good an outcome as you could have hoped for.

'If only the rest of the talks go that well,' the Chancellor remarks to you back at Downing Street. He shows you the morning papers. 'The *Heil* led with "DAYLIGHT ROBBERY", but the broadsheets generally took a measured view. "BRITAIN SHOWS STRENGTH IN EARLY TALKS," as the *Mimeograph* put it.'

> On your Brexit Memo Pad:
> - ❖ -5% Economy – the payments must be made somehow.
> - ❖ Mark the Exit Fee as complete.

Then turn to **666**.

721

'We can assure them not a penny will be lost from funding through to 2020.'

'Which is when the current funding program runs till anyhow.'

'Exactly, Prime Minister. The EU already expect that investment to be covered by the exit fee, so it's no skin off the Treasury's nose.'

⇒ 'And after that?' Turn to **479**

⇒ 'I need an angle here. What's the upside of losing EU funding?' Turn to **258**

722

All divorces come at a painful cost. At least for you personally it didn't end in Shakespeare's "long divorce of steel" – or its equivalent in modern times, the long divorce of the P45. Not yet, anyway.

Turn to **666**.

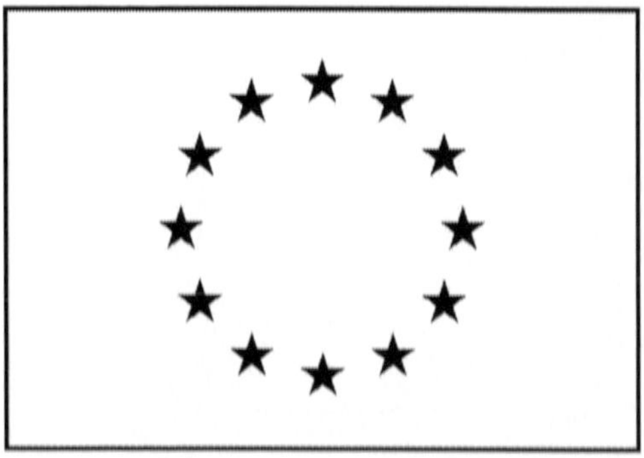

723

It's a weak response. You see the satisfied gleam of a blow well struck in Mugglemore's eyes, hear the shuffling of a discontented audience, but it's too late to take the words back. That's the trouble with live debates.

Still, it's one moment in a raging sea of discussion. Who knows if reason even plays a part in the decision making process now. The people are angry that the entire question of Brexit hasn't been solved as simply as they were promised the first time. They could vote to punish the government, or as a protest against ongoing austerity, or simply because they don't like seeing foreign faces in the supermarket.

On the night of the referendum you turn on the television and pace the room as the votes come in.

Toss two coins. If both come up heads, turn to **173**. If both come up tails, turn to **403**. Otherwise, turn to **313.**

724

As you face the stern and measured expressions on the other side of the table, it's never been clearer that Britain's internal squabbling over Brexit has cost you friends who could have helped now. These men and women have been called 'the enemy', likened to school bullies and concentration camp guards, accused of corruption and hatred of freedom, and excoriated in the UK press with cartoonish glee.

'There are few simple truths in politics,' says Armand Alprèves. 'The people have little patience to hear this, but we at this table know that the kinds of win-win deal that benefit all parties – the very deals on which the EU was built – are complex and hard to come by. Such deals must be supported by many strands.'

You wave your hand impatiently. 'You're going to say we haven't done enough to move onto the question of the future trading relationship.'

'Before we can discuss access to the single market,' puts in Willy Franjeboom, 'Britain should address the issue of her financial obligations.'

So it's that. Of course. Doesn't every problem come down to money?

⇒ Agree to their terms. Turn to **324**

⇒ Offer a trade-off in lieu of the exit fee. Turn to **715**

⇒ Drop this line of negotiation and go for a free trade agreement instead. Turn to **294**

⇒ You sense that a few of the EU27 are sympathetic to Britain. You could try back-channelling with them. Turn to **433**

725

The answer blazes in front of your tightly closed eyes. Authority. At the moment you govern by a thread, with a working majority barely in double figures. That puts you in thrall to special interest groups within the party – in particular to the certifiable fringe of hard-right Europhobes who would rather see Britain go back to the days of privateering and gunship diplomacy than do any kind of deal with the EU.

But what if you could rout Labour? Win a hundred new seats? And all of those new MPs would need to be from a shortlist provided by Central Office to the local party associations, giving them no time to drum up extremists and fruitcakes. You'd have a phalanx of malleable new MPs loyal only to you.

'Nothing could stop me then!' you blurt out, before hastily asking God to forgive your moment of hubris.

⇒ 'Is there any threat from Labour?' Turn to **626**

⇒ 'What about the Liberal Democrats?' Turn to **784**

⇒ 'How would I call an election anyway?' Turn to **35**

⇒ 'We can forget about Scotland.' Turn to **3**

⇒ 'Amen and goodnight, Lord. Your humble servant thanks You.' Turn to **666**

726

The contenders have been whittled down to just you, Tiffany Rufus, and Gervais Noysom-Reek.

'Surely I can't lose to that risible dope?'

Your chief of staff looks fretful. 'The party members lap up everything he says.'

'Of course they do, Ron. Half of them think *Dad's Army* is an accurate reflection of our relationship with Europe.'

'He's pushing for the kind of Brexit they want. No deal, no immigrants, tell the scurvy foreigners to get lost.'

'Luckily, before it reaches the membership, we have one more round of Parliamentary voting. Tiffany Rufus will probably scoop up all the moderate votes. I just have to come across as more likely to deliver a strong Brexit than Noysom-Reek.'

If you have the keyword OPAL *and* your Authority is down to 45% or less, turn to **107**.

Otherwise turn to **615**.

727

Party members' whims can change faster than the weather. To find out how they feel on the day of the ballot, toss two coins.

If both come up tails, turn to **519**. Otherwise turn to **782**.

728

You agree to appear on the BBC, but you're barely a minute into the interview when you start to regret it. Being grilled by Bill Appleby on the *Now Then* programme is like being waterboarded at Guantanamo Bay, only without a good cop offering to make it all stop.

'You're on record as admitting you'll just say whatever the public want to hear.'

'I don't think I ever said that on the record, Bill.'

'So you did say it.'

'I can't recall the exact – '

'Stress playing tricks with your memory? The job getting too much for you? Or is it the old tangled web? Which, Prime Minister?'

You dab a bead of sweat from your cheek as you consider your reply.

⇒ 'I've said and done whatever has been necessary to keep the country on an even keel.' Turn to **426**

⇒ 'This is more fake news cooked up by the saboteurs. I'm happy to be judged by actions, not words.' Turn to **545**

729

'All right, let's dig a little deeper there,' says Bill Appleby, and you know he's at his most dangerous when he takes that reasonable tone. 'What have you achieved? What trade deals have you done, for example?'

⇒ 'We can't do deals until after Brexit, Bill. You ought to know that.' Turn to **404**

⇒ 'Deals will come to us. We'll be fighting them off. The rest of the world needs Britain more than we need them.' Turn to **844**

730

No stars are visible in the dull yellow static of the sky. Only stadium-sized screens, helium-filled, luminous with cascading pixels, that slide between the grime-smeared skyscrapers advertising sunlit beaches and impossibly glamorous pleasures. To the bowed and shuffling masses such promises are beyond even the reach of hope.

The man behind you in the queue sniffs at the air and smacks his lips. 'Iodine. That'll be the early evening casualties. Fights at the food banks, that sort of thing. Bit of an MRSA tang too, don't you agree? The forecast said there's a chance of suppurations.'

'I don't…'

You don't know what you're doing here. You're in overlarge pajamas and there's a teddy bear under your arm. Why, it's Abednego. You haven't seen him in years.

A nurse comes along the queue accompanied by two burly guards with electric prods. 'Is it you or the bear?' he asks, stylus poised over the battered tablet in his hand.

Abednego has a bandage across one eye. You hadn't noticed it before. A red blotch that you must have made with a marker pen adds to his woebegone look.

'Come on,' says the nurse. 'Nearly at the door, aren't you?'

He's right. The people just ahead of you are shuffling under a fluttering neon light into the hospital. A taped-up piece of card covers one broken window. You hold up Abednego. 'It's for him.'

The nurse writes something down and moves onto the next patient. 'Have your credit card ready,' he says over his shoulder.

Turn to **342**.

731

To the delight of the right-wing press, you whip up anti-EU feelings to fever pitch. Front page images depict you as a woad-painted chief of the Iceni, a bulldog with its teeth in Europe's plump leg, and a plucky Tommy guarding the White Cliffs against a Hun invasion.

Once you might have decried such an important decision being made on the basis of cartoons instead of reasoned debate. But it is a new world now in which logic is scorned, and you may as well adapt to it.

On voting day the exit polls point to overwhelming support for a hard Brexit, but even so you sit up nervously as the results start to come in.

Toss two coins. If both come up heads, turn to **173**. Otherwise, turn to **127.**

732

Having quite recently campaigned to remain in the EU, your attempt to pass yourself off as pro-Brexit fails to convince anybody.

Turn to **653**.

733

'Here's a can of worms, then,' you say to your chief of staff. 'No, don't sit down, Ron. No time for that. You've got to tell me what questions are going on the ballot paper in the next round.'

'Tricky. None of the focus groups pointed to a Remain victory. We never thought it would come to it.'

'I can't very well go out and say that, can I? "Give us a minute, we didn't expect this." Just-in-time government wouldn't go down too well, would it?'

Ron stands wringing his pipe. The moment the meeting is over, he'll be out in the garden puffing up a bonfire of noxious tobacco. 'All we can ask – do they want more concessions from the EU, or do they want closer links?'

It'll have to do.

Toss two coins. If both come up heads, turn to **620**. If both come up tails, turn to **676**. Otherwise, turn to **578.**

Over the course of the next few days, your opponents reveal themselves.

Tiffany Rufus, the Home Secretary, was a Remain campaigner and now seeks to reposition herself as the voice of a moderate and rational Brexit.

Amelia Dimple, who looks like the mad aunt who starts talking nonsense after a single sherry, throws her hat into the ring as a candidate with no clear policies other than the conviction that moderate and rational are dirty words.

And from the back benches comes a dark horse in the form of Gervais Noysom-Reek, the sort of upper-class twit whose reactionary views would be rejected by a BBC script editor as too clichéd to be credible. Naturally the party faithful love him.

And of course there's Dennis Dent, the minister for Exiting the EU.

'Three flavours of Brexit you could break a tooth on,' says your press secretary, Terri Trough. 'And then there's Ms Rufus, who would obviously prefer to remain in the EU but is certainly not going to come out and say that.'

'Which raises the question of where you stand, Prime Minister,' says Ron Beardsley. 'Excuse me, I mean where you're going to say you stand. Somehow you've got to differentiate yourself from the pack.'

'Surely that's easy. Rufus is a closet Remainer and the rest are certifiably insane.'

'Think of it as a reality TV show,' says Terri. 'People don't vote for the nice one. They want the one who's unpredictable and theatrical, because they're more interesting.'

'Yeah. No. I don't really do theatrical.'

'Then it comes down to your take on Brexit,' says Ron. 'You have to get through to the final two by appealing to the majority of the Parliamentary party, then the party members get to choose between those two candidates.'

'That's tricky, seeing as quite a few MPs see hard Brexit as a running jump, whereas the membership think it's going to take us soaring into the sky.'

'You have to decide,' insists Terri. 'Imagine you're doing the breakfast show and one of those dreadful yappy DJs asks you, "So, what do you think, Prime Minister? Are we heading for burnt toast or a delicious Full English?" What'll you tell him?'

⇒ 'The only risk is if we lose our nerve. There are those – enemies of the people – who would try to water down Brexit. We must be vigilant. I see myself as the champion of pure Brexit, elected by the people to weed out those traitors and backsliders.' Turn to **671**

⇒ 'Britain is leaving the European Union. That's not in doubt. But what sort of relationship do we want with Europe and the rest of the world in future? I stand for a firm, clean Brexit opening up the possibility of a bright future.' Turn to **592**

⇒ 'Edmund Burke said that a politician betrays the public trust if they only do what voters demand rather than considering the voters' best interests. Is Brexit the right course? As long as I'm leader, it's my job to decide that – and if the people disagree they can vote me out.'
Turn to **317**

735

A few days later, the press reacts to your holiday choice. You sigh resignedly as you pick up the *Daily Crusade*.

The lead editorial lambasts you for holidaying in France, spending good British money on those tractor-blocking, tyre-burning French farmers who'd like nothing better than to 'put hard working English farmers out of business'.

Even papers like the *Hypsterion* are having a go at you for being rich enough to have a nice holiday in France while making it more expensive for everyone else because of the Brexit pound crash. They point out that if border and visa controls come in, everyone will have to pay more to go to Europe.

Still, it's really slow news day stuff and it will be soon forgotten.

Record on your Brexit Memo Pad:
- -1% Popularity – your foreign holiday doesn't look so good to the typical Leave voter on the street.

Now turn to **125.**

736

You've survived the two-year run-up to Brexit, but what kind of condition are you and the country in? It's time to take stock of how you've done and what the future might hold.

First, your grip on power. If your Authority score is 39% or less, turn to **850**.

If Authority is 40% to 75%, turn to **515**.

If Authority is 76% or more, turn to **804**.

737

An hour later, invigorated by a shower, you're sipping strong black coffee in the main conference room when Sir Harvey Doggerbank is shown in.

'Sir Harvey. I'm sorry I only have a few minutes before my meeting with the Chancellor.'

'Appreciate you're busy, Prime Minister. Exciting times, these. Opportunity knocks for Britain, eh?'

⇒ 'Well, that all depends on the Brexit negotiations.'
Turn to **387**

⇒ 'Let's hope it's a matter of opportunity not calamity.'
Turn to **153**

⇒ 'Quite. A glorious new future awaits us.'
Turn to **567**

⇒ 'To be honest, the task now is damage limitation.'
Turn to **270**

738

Fighting talk, but have you got the record to back it up?

Look at your Brexit Memo Pad. If you have any of the keywords BLEAK, HEMLOCK, KOALA or LEAF, turn to **371**.

If you have none of those keywords, turn to **380**.

739

The problem doesn't go away, and in the long run it's going to inflict real harm on the peace process, but in the short term the hit is mainly political.

> Record on your Brexit Memo Pad:
> - -2% Popularity – you are in effect leaving Northern Ireland to operate as if it's still part of the EU, to the ire of the Brexiteers.

Turn to **49**.

740

The deal is done. But it's not going to look good back home.

> On your Brexit Memo Pad:
> - -2% Authority – your critics are calling you a weak negotiator.
> - +5% Economy – the UK economy needs those EU nationals, and it helps not to be handed back a million pensioners from Spain.
> - Mark Residency Rights as complete.

Then turn to **666**.

741

'Chinese steel, for instance,' says Stollard. 'Currently that's covered by EU anti-dumping measures, which of course cover the British steel industry too. But once we move over to WTO rules, if we try to maintain the same level of anti-dumping protection, China can raise an objection just as any WTO member could. They'll insist we carry out a new investigation to demonstrate that the existing anti-dumping levels are not an unfair restraint of trade.'

'But the EU has already established those levels.'

'That's between the EU and China. As soon as we're out in the WTO it's a new ball game – one in which we have only a tenth as much influence. We'll need to build up our own departments for investigating trade remedies, and recruit dispute settlement lawyers, and even then it could drag on for years.'

'There's a simple enough remedy,' scoffs Barkwell. 'We'll just accept China's steel while we progress the investigation.'

Stollard pinches the bridge of his nose. You know how he feels.

You could use an aspirin yourself. 'First of all, it's not just China. We'll be hit by dozens of these cases, if for no other reason than our competitors will see we're not able to respond to all these disputes at once. And secondly, imagine what happens to the domestic steel industry if we get deluged by twenty million tonnes of cheap Chinese steel.'

'Not sure I'd say deluged,' puts in Strewel. '"Iron-undated", perhaps. A test of our mettle. Ho ho.'

Turn to **454.**

742

Trade and immigration fuelled most of the media's reporting of the Brexit discussions, but foremost in many people's minds was how Britain would continue to cooperate with the rest of Europe on issues of counter-terrorism, policing and military missions.

'You made some useful friends by settling those questions early on,' remarks Jean-Jacques Terlamen, the European Commission President, over an informal dinner.

'Really? I thought some of them were disappointed by the outcome.'

'Far from disappointed. Heartened. It's in all our minds that one day you will lead the British people out of the jungle and back to the city on the hill.'

'So now the Brexit hardliners are the Khmer Rouge?'

'I hope not. But when an insane project starts to go wrong, that rarely turns down the level of insanity. Pol Pot didn't start out having experts beaten to death, you know.'

Perhaps it's just as well EU is receptive to whatever deal you want to propose. A softer Brexit will please more of the voters and minimize the danger of Britain sliding into doctrinal authoritarianism. Will you ask for a EEA-like relationship such as Norway has (turn to **82**) or a slightly more distant Swiss-style model (turn to **417**)?

743

Another election? That would be madness. And nowadays there's already quite enough madness churning up the political waters without you adding to it.

Turn to **666**.

744

Rufus cannily shifts her position towards a firm but not extreme Brexit while Stollard remains on the soft Brexit wing. That pits you directly against Strewel for the ultra-hard Brexit vote.

'It's quite smart,' says Ron Beardsley grudgingly. 'I wouldn't be surprised if Stollard and Rufus colluded to arrange it this way.'

'What does it mean?'

'I rather think either you or Peter Strewel will go out in the next round, Prime Minister.'

'Which of us?'

'Whoever is less convincing about their commitment to Brexit.'

If you have either the keyword GAZELLE or the keyword SANCTION, turn to **377**.

If not but you have *two* of the keywords BLEAK, HEMLOCK and KOALA, turn to **597**.

Otherwise turn to **522**.

745

'What do you think happens if MPs reject the deal?'

He looks like a schoolboy who hasn't done his homework. 'Er… we go back to the negotiating table?'

'No. The date of leaving the EU is on the front page of the Brexit bill, and the sheep have already been counted for that one. In a few weeks we'll be out. The choice I'm going to be giving that lot is no deal or no deal. So guess which way they'll jump.'

On the day there's a long and acrimonious debate as MPs grasp that they no longer have any say over events. Whichever way the vote goes, Britain will be quitting the EU and future trade will be on WTO rules for the decade or two that new free trade agreements will take to iron out.

Turn to **419**.

746

As usual the debate is hosted by ageless TV icon Martin Mugglemore and is being broadcast from some regional hellhole. The audience have the sour look of a crowd of Romans who haven't been given their bread. You fast-forward to the point where Mugglemore introduces the panel. That'll tell you whether it's going to be a heavyweight championship or a pillow fight.

First up is Colin Fungale. Is he leader of UKIP at the moment or not? You can never remember. There's the mouth like the lid of an old handbag. Eyes like two big marbles, giving him the look of a smug trout. He's always good value, at least, in a chuck-a-brick-at-the-screen kind of way.

Next up is Bob Owlbear, the deputy leader of the opposition. Well, the deputy leader of the Labour Party, anyway, if you can count them as the opposition; sometimes it feels as though your own ministers are a far more effective pack of enemies than Labour could ever be. As usual, Owlbear is sitting there blinking behind his heavy glasses looking like a slightly slimmer Billy Bunter on powerful medication.

For the Lib Dems there's the show's token woman. Lucy Tooth, you think Mugglemore called her. In fact you have a feeling you've seen her around the House of Commons. Given that the Lib Dems only have about five MPs you'd think they'd be easier to remember. You could rewind and check, but that would mean all the effort of reaching for the remote. Who cares, anyway? She seems educated, articulate, reasonable, and she smiles a lot. So obviously the hoi polloi will hate her.

'So who's representing us?' you demand of the screen. Oh good grief, no. It's that pustule Thomas Tode, failed relic of the Leave campaign. There he is, grinning in the studio lights like an albino tadpole that's been stranded on a rock to dry out. And he's in an open-necked shirt, too. Trying to look like a man of the people, the little weasel.

⇒ Fast-forward through the questions. Turn to **574**

⇒ Watch the late-night movie instead. Turn to **467**

747

There's a knock on the door and Wilkins ushers in three of your senior ministers. Alan Stollard strolls in looking more like a Labour leader from the seventies than the Chancellor of the Exchequer. He's holding a leather briefcase that's virtually bursting at the seams with documents and files.

He nods at you. 'Morning, Prime Minister,'

He sits and meticulously lays out neat piles of documents across the table in front of him before reaching for the breakfast menu.

Behind him comes the International Trade Minister, Leslie

Barkwell. He's looking dapper and well-coiffeured, with a finely tailored suit and a bright blue tie with small polka dots. His tie actually reminds you of the EU flag, which is odd, given that Barkwell is a die-hard Brexiter.

He smiles at you politely, and with his usual facetious over-courtesy asks permission to sit. You nod. He sits, rather primly, straight backed, hands folded neatly in front of him, eyes focused on you. He looks like a burglar whose brief has made him put on a suit to appear before the judge.

After him comes Denis Dent, the Secretary of State of the newly created Ministry of Exiting the EU. Blue suit, red tie, grinning the whole time. His hair white as snow and neatly cut. Red tie, blue suit, white hair – a walking Union Jack. He strides to his chair and sits purposefully.

'Morning, gentlemen,' you say, glancing at your watch. 'Just need another minute or two.'

'Peter running late again, eh?' says Barkwell.

You nod ruefully. Stollard raises his eyes. Dent chuckles.

The door bursts open and in stumbles Peter Strewel, the Foreign Secretary.

'Cripes, chums, sorry I'm late!' he says loudly, as he straggles his way to his seat, a wallet folder under one arm. His suit's a dishevelled mess and his hair resembles a wig made from the hair of an albino orang-utan, although you know it's real. He bundles into his chair, looking like some kind of bloated cloth-headed doll.

One of the Downing Street staffers comes forward. 'I'll have the continental,' says Stollard, handing her his menu.

'Nothing for me, thank you,' says Barkwell. 'I've eaten already.'

Dent grins up at the waitress. 'Scrambled eggs, no salmon for me, thank you.' He turns to Strewel.

'English breakfast, by golly!' says Strewel, slamming his fist down on the table and rattling the plates and cutlery.

You sigh and reach for the coffee. This could be a long morning.

Turn to **630.**

748

Over the next few days, Tiffany Rufus tips her stance more strongly towards Brexit. You suspect she's done the deal with Dennis Dent that you refused, as he's backed out of the race.

In an appearance on the *Now Then* programme, you're asked about Rufus's strategy by Bill Appleby. 'She says she's in favour of a clean break with the EU but without burning any bridges. Is that possible? The sort of divorce where you still get together for family holidays?'

⇒ 'To be honest, Bill, who can keep up with what Tiffany Rufus believes this week?' Turn to **171**

⇒ 'Whatever words may come out of Tiffany Rufus's mouth, the fact is she's a Remainer at heart.' Turn to **241**

⇒ 'We need the best Brexit for Britain. Never mind terms like hard or soft, what I want is a common-sense Brexit.' Turn to **442**

749

Despite some rumblings from the Spanish, who have the most UK residents, the EU have agreed to a quid pro quo deal. They will affirm the right of all UK citizens currently living in the EU to remain as long as you do the same for EU citizens residing in Britain.

You've got some good news to announce to the press for once.

On your Brexit Memo Pad:

- +5% Economy – the UK economy needs those EU nationals, and it helps not to be handed back a million pensioners from Spain.
- Mark Residency Rights as complete.

Then turn to **200**.

750

'The EU would like the financial question settled quickly,' says the Chancellor. 'That would give us some leeway in arguing the price down. Also, we might be able to lump the exit fee in with our ongoing payments for a transitional period after 2019. Makes it a sweeter pill for the Leave press to swallow.'

Dent stares at him, always on the alert for any signs of ideological impurity. 'The patriotic press, you mean. The loyal press.'

'Ich bin ein Brexiter,' retorts Stollard, with a paper-thin smile at Dent's obvious confusion. 'Well, then there's the option to reject the bill. It might be possible to parcel up an appeal to the International Court as the optimum policy for all concerned. "In view of our

limited time for Article 50 talks... Complex matter... Contractual issues... Best decided by the law..." Et cetera. With a bit of back channelling via the smaller states we might sell that to the EU and not have to face a press lynching. Also, it puts off the problem till another day.'

Even Dent is pleased by that. 'Good, good. It makes us look defiant, and whatever the court decides nobody can say it's our fault. That's much better than whipping the bloody chequebook out as soon as we sit down.'

'A win-win, you might say,' murmurs Stollard, 'if not for the fact that we still have to find the money. As in so many of these issues, the question is not how to find a solution, but which problem are we trying to solve? The best economic outcome, or the best political one?'

⇒ 'Both, obviously.' Turn to **305**

⇒ 'We must do what's best for the country.' Turn to **382**

⇒ 'Seeing as we're politicians....' Turn to **341**

751

You're pretty sure Rufus would keep Britain in the EU if she had the chance, but you wouldn't know it to hear her recent speeches. She's all about taking back control and doing the people's will, leaving herself just enough leeway to tack back to a softer position later.

In the meantime, she's pitching her stall on your side of the street. You deliberately make it a head to head between the two of you, and the next round of the contest will come down to which of you has more Brexit credibility.

If you have either the keyword GAZELLE or the keyword SANCTION, turn to **377**.

If not but you have either FOG or LEAF, turn to **39**.

Otherwise turn to **290**.

Inspiration comes not from the bookshelf but from a movie about Nelson Mandela. He's addressing his people and he says, 'As long as I am your leader, I'm going to give you leadership. As long as I am your leader, I'm going to tell you always when you are wrong.'

You sit up. 'Did you hear that, Wilkins? That's what's called being presidential.'

'The word is somewhat devalued since President Windrip's election, Prime Minister, but I see what you mean. Mr Mandela was benign but very firm in his principles. Of course, in this case he's being played by an actor and I suspect those words are the scriptwriter's.'

'All that matters is that it's the cure for what's poisoning British politics.'

A couple of days later, a piece by you appears in the paper headed TOGETHER FOR A BETTER BRITAIN. You read it to your press secretary, who is fidgeting only because she probably wishes she'd seen it before publication.

'What are the values of our country?' you say. 'Patience. Fairness. Justice. Throughout the world these are things Britain is known for. And we're known also for the Mother of Parliaments, a beacon to democracies and those who yearn for democracy throughout the world.

'Democracy is built on a platform of consideration for others. It breaks down if it turns into a winner-takes-all battle. To survive, democracy must go hand in hand with compromise. On every issue a consensus must be reached. Because even if your side wins today, there may be something else to vote on tomorrow. You won't get everything. You can't. You must be willing to meet those with different views halfway.

'In the referendum, 52% of us voted to Leave the EU, and 48% voted to stay. That is not a crushing mandate for hard Brexit. It is a vote that says we will leave, yes – but only just. To reflect the true will of *all* the people, we need to find a new relationship with the European Union that keeps us close friends and allies. That is the only honest form of Brexit that we, your representatives, should be working for. To characterize the vote in any other way is divisive and only serves political goals at the expense of this country's unity.

'For the sake of all of us, I urge all of you to reach out and take your neighbour's hand in a spirit of patriotism. True British patriotism. Not jingoism, not contempt for others' wishes, but magnanimity and brotherhood.'

It's easy to assert there's a better way than the partisan us-or-them politics of Strewel and his ilk. But *are* you better? Your own record is the yardstick by which people will judge the sincerity of what you're saying.

If you have any of the keywords APRICITY, SANCTION or TIGHTROPE, *or* if your Economy score is 53% or more, turn to **9**.

If not but you have either the keyword FOG or the keyword GAZELLE, turn to **727**.

If none of the above but you have Popularity of 66% or more, turn to **347**.

Otherwise turn to **528**.

753

Despite the near-unanimous support of your own party, Labour and the rest vote against and so you fail to muster the two-thirds majority required to pass the motion.

'Why two thirds?' you bark at Wilkins when he brings you a consoling cup of tea later.

'I believe two thirds is the usual margin taken to indicate sufficient support for any sweeping change to established rules, Prime Minister.'

'A good job we didn't insist on that for the EU referendum, or I'd still be stuck working for that public school pig-sticker, eh?'

'As you say, Prime Minister. There is the other option, of course. A vote of no confidence in the government. That only requires a simple majority.'

'I'd look foolish doing that now. Worse, I'd look weak. No, Wilkins, the Lord has determined the cross I must bear.'

> On your Brexit Memo Pad:
> - Mark General Election as complete.

Now turn to **666**.

754

'They had a referendum. The SVP – that's the Swiss People's Party – railed against loss of sovereignty, foreigners pouring in, rampant bureaucracy. Does any of this sound familiar? The referendum result was even tighter than in our case, in fact – a 50.3% majority not to join the EEA.'

'What nonsense,' grumbles Barkwell. 'Our referendum wasn't tight. It was an overwhelming mandate for Brexit.'

'I forgot. Doubleplus good, obviously.'

⇒ 'How did the Swiss deal with the question of free movement?' Turn to **457**

⇒ 'But they do at least retain sovereignty.' Turn to **509**

755

'For too long Britain has paid a hefty share of EU funds with no say as to where and how it's spent. Now we're bringing control back to the taxpayers.'

The alternative fact about not having a say is only challenged in a few papers, and your message of set-jawed defiance goes down well with voters. Unfortunately the implication of having to find billions to cover infrastructure investment at a time of increasing austerity sends a flutter of alarm through the markets.

On your Brexit Memo Pad:

- ❖ -1% Economy – the financial sector is alarmed at you issuing too many promissory notes.
- ❖ +1% Popularity – the voters see you as a firm hand on the tiller.

Then turn to **125**.

756

Barkwell pauses as he's gathering up his papers. 'It would be quite helpful to know what you're planning, Prime Minister. Free trade deal or what?'

The others were on their way to the door, but now they're all turning to see how you respond.

- ⇒ 'If I wanted you to know that at this stage then I'd have told you.' Turn to **716**
- ⇒ 'Obviously we need to negotiate a free trade agreement.' Turn to **379**
- ⇒ 'If necessary we'll fall back on WTO rules and let the EU come begging.' Turn to **625**
- ⇒ 'The ideal outcome would be to remain in the single market.' Turn to **808**

757

Your own voice is drowned out by the shrill and increasingly vicious rhetoric of the two extremes. It is as if the country has gone mad. It almost doesn't matter what the result is. How can the two sides live together after this?

Toss two coins. If both come up heads, turn to **173**. Otherwise, turn to **127.**

758

Have you ticked the keyword PEDAL on your Brexit Memo Pad? If so, turn to **627**. If not, turn to **508**.

759

You've hardly got the phone to your ear before Dennis Dent starts his pitch. 'Prime Minister, you're in a very strong position.'

'Unassailable, I'd call it.'

'That's over-egging it. Nothing is certain in love and war, and politics covers both of those. But I can help you turn your current advantage into a commanding lead.'

'Is that for love, or…?'

'You can't mean to keep Alan Stollard at the Treasury.'

Ah, so that's it. What will you say?

⇒ 'Dennis, no offence, but I don't want you as a next-door neighbour.' Turn to **748**

⇒ 'It's a deal. Back me and you get to be the Chancellor.' Turn to **635**

760

'Fortunately staffing isn't a problem. A high proportion of Britain's doctors and nurses come from Europe, and thanks to our deal with the EU that will continue. But funding is still critical. Britain has an ageing population and we spend less per capita on health care than almost every other country in Western Europe.'

You wince. 'Let's make sure we don't say that out loud in public, eh. The average voter fondly imagines the NHS to be streets ahead of any foreign alternative.'

'It's not going to help that the European Medicines Agency is moving out of the UK either. That gave us a degree of control over the primary regulator.'

'We have our own agencies for that.'

'More bureaucracy means more training, more civil servants. And who has to find the cash for all this?'

⇒ 'We don't need to spend anything. Just let the NHS die a natural death and the private companies will take over.' Turn to **110**

⇒ 'We'd better announce token investment in new hospitals.' Turn to **213**

761

Check your Brexit Memo Pad.

If the Exit Fee is complete or if you have the keyword APRICITY, turn to **464**.

Otherwise turn to **834**.

762

The questioner is a middle-aged woman with skin the colour of a supermarket chicken.. 'I seen the poster,' she says. 'All them hordes of refugees. That's why I voted for us to leave Brexit.'

Lucy Tooth actually laughs out loud in astonishment. That'll lose her votes. Dumb people are touchy about mockery and they're spectacularly unforgiving.

'That poster was Photoshopped,' blurts Bob Owlbear, frowning at Colin Fungale. 'Frankly I'm surprised the Nazis didn't sue for copyright infringement.'

Useless. Most Brexit voters are still in the last century; they think Photoshop is where you go to get holiday snaps developed. No wonder Fungale's grin only grows wider.

'Did you have a question?' Martin Mugglemore asks the woman in the audience.

She looks confused, but searches around for something to ask. 'What I want to know is can we stop the illegals now? It's not just the EU ones. Some Pakis moved in up my street – '

'A question!' yelps Mugglemore.

'Awright. Are you going to stop handing out benefits to foreigners and make sure money goes to British people from now on? That's for the Conservative one, Mr Tode.'

You can see Tode's quandary. He'd love to score some tub-thumping points with the crowd, but simple principle gets the better of him.

'I'm not sure if you're actually talking about the EU… You mean refugees from places like Syria and Libya?'

You were definitely justified in banishing Tode to the political wilderness. Peter Strewel would have caught that and run with it as far and as fast as his fat legs could carry him. Nor would any whisper of conscience have given him pause.

⇒ See if he can recover some ground. Turn to **41**

⇒ Skip to a different question. Turn to **405**

763

Stamina, more than anything else, is what you need for this job. And you've got it in spades.

> On your Brexit Memo Pad:
> - ❖ Mark Second EU Referendum as complete.

Then turn to **450.**

764

The EU chief negotiator and his team get in touch. He's discussed your proposals with the other member states of the EU and can now give you their response.

Look at your Brexit Memo Pad.

If Goodwill is 50% or more, turn to **749.**

If Goodwill is 49% or less turn to **427.**

765

You've had no time to deal with this, among all the other issues demanding your personal attention. You can only hope that your ministers haven't made a mess of it.

They return with news that Britain will retain an associate role alongside Europe's armed forces, and in police matters will continue to liaise with Europol while detaching from data sharing and extradition agreements.

> Record on your Brexit Memo Pad:
> - ❖ -5% Goodwill – the EU resent the increased threat level caused by Britain's disengagement from full participation in counter-terrorism and military peacekeeping initiatives.
> - ❖ -5% Popularity – the voters are waking up to how Brexit is weakening the country's security, and they're blaming you.
> - ❖ Mark Security & Defence as complete.

Turn to **332.**

766

Early polls give Leave a narrow lead. But polls are a notoriously unreliable barometer of public opinion these days. A more telling factor is whether young people will bother to vote. The last referendum having, as they see it, set a bomb under their future, this time they might turn out in larger numbers.

'It drives to the deeper question of public apathy,' says your press secretary Terri Trough. 'People make the effort to vote when their dander's up. And that happens when they see their wages getting squeezed. That's why the youth vote doesn't matter. They don't have homes and school bills to pay.'

'I know. "It's the economy, stupid."'

She looks at you seriously. 'I would never call you stupid, Prime Minister.'

Look at your Brexit Memo Pad. If your Economy score is 51% or higher, turn to **23**. If it's 50% or lower, turn to **649**.

767

'We'd pay less than they do, certainly.'

'Hmm. Might cause resentment among the other EEA members.'

Stollard shakes his head. 'More like pity. Britain is poorer than Norway in terms of GDP per person, so we can demonstrate good grounds for a reduced fee. Also, we'd still get back a lot of the rebate as there are more opportunities for profitable investment by the EU in British science and so forth.'

'Bottom line?'

'Our full membership contribution is just under £100 per person annually. That's factoring in the rebate, money that's cycled back for investment in the UK, and foreign aid commitments that we currently pay via the EU. If where we land after Brexit is in the European Economic Area, that might be more like £75 a head.'

'How will that go down with the voters?' snorts Barkwell. 'We saved you the price of a takeaway!'

'Actually it would be a net gain,' points out Stollard. '£75 a year against about £750 per household that we'd lose outside the EEA.'

'Even if that were true, Alan,' says Dent, 'you don't get it. This is politics, not spreadsheets. The people voted to stop sending any money at all to Brussels.'

Turn to **17**.

768

As expected, the Commission's view on Britain's exit payment is that it should be agreed before any other talks.

'We have a lot to get through in the next two years,' you tell the EU's chief negotiator, Armand Alprèves. 'Surely we can run other negotiations in parallel with any discussion of our exit fee?'

'What is there to discuss? Is the calculation not clear? The United Kingdom is obligated to pay the sum of €60 billion.'

'That is one calculation. Many people think it was scribbled on the back of an envelope. I've seen more rigorous sums that put the figure at half that, or even less.'

His eyes crinkle in a smile. 'Half? Perhaps you need to turn over the page, prime minister. It is a long bill.'

'There's a strong case that says we owe nothing. Just our membership fee up until the point that we leave. If we took it to the courts – '

He looks up sharply. Better not go there. You try another tack: 'Many of the member states agree with us. At any rate, we aren't going to get into the rights and wrongs of that fee here today. Why don't we put that off to one side and progress it while we continue other talks?'

'This is a matter of, shall we say, trust. If Britain is unwilling to show that it keeps past promises, what value is there in any negotiation? Agreeing the exit payment now is a demonstration of good faith.'

That's the crux of the matter. But if you go home and announce a €60 billion settlement to the EU, there'll be removal vans outside Number 10 inside a month.

⇒ Stick to your guns – discussion of the fee must happen alongside other negotiations. Turn to **693**

⇒ Flat-out refuse to pay. Turn to **421**

⇒ Agree to a swift resolution, then look for wriggle room. Turn to **363**

769

Check your Brexit Memo Pad.

If the Exit Fee is complete or if you have the keyword APRICITY, turn to **613**.

Otherwise turn to **185**.

770

'You're not really committed, though, are you? Not to an ultra-hard Brexit that will sever all the old ties and get us out of the single market and the customs union and all the rest of it.'

What do you say to that?

⇒ 'I may not have your degree of conviction, but it's my duty to deliver hard Brexit and I intend to do so.' Turn to **859**

⇒ 'A softer Brexit is what the majority of the people want. We can still leave the EU without creating a divided nation.' Turn to **308**

771

'Bob is wrong in any case,' she says. 'It's not true that immigration lowers even unskilled wages. When America ended its Mexican seasonal workers program in the 1960s, that didn't have any effect on wages. And that's tomato pickers, jobs like that.'

Tode comes in now, stabbing his little finger at the air with all the charismatic emphasis of a wooden puppet. 'That's because back in the 1960s removing the cheap migrant labour didn't make companies hire local workers. Instead it drove them to automate.'

'And that's what we're going to do here,' says Fungale. 'Automate. Streamline. Become more efficient. Britain has a long tradition of technical innovation. We gave the world the steam engine, television, and the bouncing bomb. This is exactly the kind of challenge that British business thrives on.'

'How are we going to do that?' says Lucy Tooth. 'About a quarter of the scientists and technicians working in Britain today come from other EU countries. Those are the very people we need to build a prosperous future.'

A smattering of applause. Useful to be reminded that there is still a sizable minority who'd hold their hands up to "*Civis Europanus sum*." Not that you should ever say anything like that out loud. Too grammar school. You have to be more like Peter Strewel. He can translate the *Oresteia* off the cuff but to hear him talk you'd think all his learning came out of the pages of *Viz*.

⇒ See what the others say. Turn to **187**

⇒ Maybe it's time you got to sleep. Turn to **125**

⇒ Skip to another question. Turn to **405**

772

'Trade is good for the obvious reasons.'

'Brings in money.'

'Right. But it has secondary effects. Switching over to new channels means reduced productivity. Reduced trade lowers competition, so that impacts business efficiency.'

'But we'll have more competition.'

'Maybe. We'll be hustling and bustling to do deals, which may not amount to the same thing. Certainly we'll have less access to the superior intermediate goods from the EU, chemicals used in pharmaceuticals for example, and as a result innovation could suffer.'

⇒ 'People will have to rise to the challenge.'
Turn to **142**

⇒ 'You've started, so you might as well finish.'
Turn to **188**

⇒ 'That's enough doom and gloom for one day.'
Turn to **666**

773

'We've got the European Arrest Warrant,' says McKay. 'That makes it really simple to extradite suspects to the state where they committed a crime. In the old days, the French might have made a stink if a court in London wanted a Parisian felon shipped over, say. Under the EAW it's as straightforward as sending him up to Scotland.'

'And you don't think that can remain in place after Brexit?'

'I don't see how. It wouldn't even be constitutional for many countries. They can send their nationals to another EU state's court because that's all under one roof, so to speak. Once we're out the door we're another country in their eyes.' There's a dim flicker of memory in his eyes and he glances again at the ruined Victorian fort. 'Like the past.'

⇒ 'What about cooperation in tracking criminals and terrorists? Turn to **138**

⇒ 'How about international policing? Our cops and Europol, I mean.' Turn to **315**

⇒ 'Let me ask you something else.' Turn to **432**

774

You find yourself mulling over the shape of a trade deal with the EU as you sit down to another breakfast meeting. You seem to be having a lot of these early starts lately, and working into the small hours too. If only you could add another hour to the day. The thought makes you give a yelp of near-hysterical laughter, swiftly suppressed. An extra hour? Crazy, of course. Impossible. But then, so is negotiating a satisfactory Brexit in less than two years.

Wilkins glides in and puts a menu in front of you. 'What will you have, prime minister?'

⇒ Perhaps the Scottish smoked salmon and scrambled egg. Turn to **430**

⇒ Or the traditional English breakfast… Turn to **355**

⇒ On the other hand, the continental looks a lot healthier. Turn to **785**

⇒ You're always partial to maple syrup on pancakes. Turn to **282**

775

As usual, your astute political judgement has placed you on the side of history. The will of the people is the god of the age, and you are now able to style yourself as its undisputed prophet.

> On your Brexit Memo Pad:
> - ❖ +5% Authority – by backing the winning side you've cowed your rivals in the party
> - ❖ +10% Popularity – to the winner the spoils

Turn to **206.**

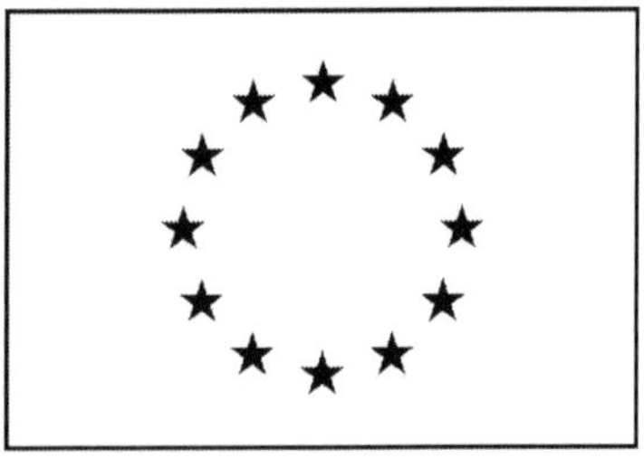

776

'I suppose,' says Strewel, trying to sound hopeful. 'Mind you, it's Switzerland we're talking about here, not Ruritania. Their economy is a quarter the size of ours. Be a lot bigger too if they had full access to EU service industries.'

'Poppycock,' says Barkwell. 'Far too much is made of services if you ask me. What is that? Topping up somebody's coffee? Giving them a haircut? Britain's future is in manufacturing.'

It's quite alarming to hear that from your International Trade Minister, but you assuage your concerns with the thought that maybe he's just being ironic.

Turn to **378.**

777

Look at your Brexit Memo Pad. If Goodwill is 46% or more and Popularity is 50% or *less*, turn to **141**.

Otherwise turn to **238**.

778

'*Parla, parla, ascoltando ti sto.*'

The chief whip gives you a stony look. No opera fan, he. Another alumnus of some horrid Midlands redbrick. 'I'm afraid the vote is against you, Prime Minister. Mr Dent and Ms Rufus will go forward to the membership ballot.'

It seems impossible. To have come so far, struggled with so many problems, prevailed in so many battles – only for it to end like this, because of a single careless remark to a faithless courtier.

'Wilkins!'

He comes in no great hurry, adding to your irritation.

'Were you hiding under the table like Leporello?'

'No, Prime Minister, I was packing your things. I believe, to put it in the vernacular, that the fat lady has sung. *La commedia è finita*.'

THE END

779

'I'm sure the ministers will need some sense of how many such permits would be issued each year,' says President Terlamen.

'Realistically, perhaps fifty thousand a year for the first five years. After that we'll review the numbers.'

'But currently you are admitting a quarter of a million EU citizens a year,' points out the Swedish prime minister.

'And that's the problem. It's too many. Communities can't cope with so many foreigners pouring in.'

'But to cut it to one-fifth…' Chancellor Käsen is shaking her head, making her look more than ever like a lugubrious pug. 'It's too drastic.'

'EU citizens want to move to Britain because you are a wealthy country,' puts in the prime minister of Spain. 'And they make you wealthier. If you want so badly to turn off the tap, just walk away from the single market. When you're as poor as we are, you'll see how few people are queuing up to immigrate.'

⇒ You won't be dictated to. Tell them your decision is to say no to free movement and institute a points system instead. Turn to **216**

⇒ You'll win more by giving ground. Agree to keep strictly to current free movement restrictions with the final say resting with UK courts. Turn to **183**

⇒ Be firm but fair. You'll apply a quota of fifty thousand EU immigrants a year. They can take it or leave it. Turn to **369**

780

'It's not going to be quick,' says Dent. 'The Swiss negotiations took five or six years just to get three-quarters access to the single market.'

'The EU would speed it up for us,' reckons Barkwell. 'They'd be like a hungry dog looking at a juicy bone.'

'While I agree it's in nobody's interests to keep Britain waiting for a deal,' says Stollard, 'we have to remember that the sort of bespoke agreement we'd be proposing needs to be a lot more extensive than the Swiss one. And we remain understaffed in the skills we need for complex negotiations of this sort. If I had to guess, I'd say it's going to take a minimum of five years.'

'If we go that route,' counters Dent. 'Maybe we're better off under World Trade Organization rules rather than EFTA.'

Turn to **378.**

781

'Non-tariff barriers to trade,' says the Chancellor. 'Think about it. Average international tariff on goods is just over 2%. The average on goods coming into the EU is half that, thanks to the EU's trade deals. But the bigger factors influencing trade these days are standards, qualifications, quotas – inevitable paperwork that guarantees the customer is getting a fair deal, made a lot smoother when an item being shipped or a service being offered across Europe doesn't have to be checked at a dozen borders. Going it alone is quite frankly going to be as big a pain as having to carry a passport to Pimlico.'

Turn to **454.**

782

When the moment of your defeat comes, you don't meet it with any of the violent emotions you expected. Anger, grief, regret, denial. All you feel is a vast numbness. Perhaps God felt this way when He beheld what He had created.

'What will you say to the new incumbent, Wilkins?' you ask as he oversees the removal men carrying your belongings.

'I shall say what I have always said. "Welcome, Prime Minister." But first…'

You wait. 'Yes?'

'Goodbye, Prime Minister.'

THE END

783

'You know sometimes I have to pinch myself,' chuckles Peter Strewel in an interview. 'Am I dreaming? Is the Prime Minister actually on our side in these talks? Because it seems to me there's a sight too much chumminess going on with the EU leaders. If I were a cynical fellow – ' a huge ate-all-the-pies wink at this point – 'I'd have to wonder if the PM feels more in common with the internationalist elite than the ordinary working man and woman of Britain.'

As you leave Number 10 later, the press pack is eager to get your comment. One shouts, 'Prime Minister, do you agree with Mr Strewel that you're too pally with Brussels?'

What will you reply?

⇒ 'No comment.' Turn to **528**

⇒ 'Good negotiation is about giving both sides some of what they want. It's not a zero-sum game.' Turn to **243**

⇒ 'If he sat in on the talks he'd know that I'm just as determined an opponent of the EU as he is.' Turn to **738**

784

God gives you a moment of quiet contemplation, allowing you to see that you have nothing to fear from the Lib Dems. Even at the height of their popularity, with nearly a quarter of the vote, they won less than sixty seats. Of course, at the time it was painful having to go into coalition with them, having them put the brakes on the Conservative austerity program and so on.

But it turned out well in the end. People still blame the Lib Dems more than they blame your own party, and they were forced to drop their highly capable and articulate former leader in favour of bumbling evangelist Bob Fobber.

That thought gives you a moment's pause. What if Fobber has his own conversations with the Almighty? But no – you're sure he'd be put on hold, content to listen to twenty minutes of celestial harmonics before finally getting a recorded message from an angel.

So what of the Lib Dems under Fobber's amateur-hour leadership? On current polling they might claw back a dozen seats, but not enough to be a serious threat. You can rest easy on that score.

⇒ 'What about Labour?' Turn to **626**

⇒ 'How would I go about calling an election?'
Turn to **35**

⇒ 'We'd be trounced in Scotland.' Turn to **3**

⇒ 'Amen and goodnight, Lord.' Turn to **666**

785

A continental breakfast is just what the doctor ordered. Croissants, coffee, Belgian ham, and fruit. Hold on, though, according to the menu it's actually Wiltshire ham, and croissants baked round the corner. Of course, how would it look if the Prime Minister tucked in to a foreign-sourced breakfast? The *Outrage* and the *Heil* have reporters sniffing around the bins behind Number 10 to catch you out on things like that.

You curl your lip in frustration. Outside the EU there are going to be a lot fewer choices on the menus of Britain. And, let's face it, the best outcome for the economy would almost certainly be to remain in the European Economic Area, like Norway. If we have to leave the EU, let's do it in such a way that we don't take any risks with the economy. And it'd be the easiest exit package to negotiate with the EU. Really, nothing much would change except we'd have less influence. And God knows, the rest of the EU would be happy with that. We could have it all done and dusted in the two years as well.

But how to sell that to the anti-Europe press, let alone your own party?

Turn to **747.**

786

She's not impressed. 'After forty years as part of the EU, frankly we lack the expertise to close international trade deals. And even if we had, it would take decades to set up agreements valuable enough to replace what we're losing. People certainly weren't voting to be worse off, which is what will happen if we're not careful.'

'Oh, come, I think you're being a bit negative. Britain is still a great nation, you know. Many countries will fall over themselves to come and do a deal with us.'

'It's still going to take years and in the meantime business takes a hit. Will you guarantee regional development grants? Investment in business? Research funds? Access to our universities for the cream of European students? Britain benefits from all these things by dint of EU membership and we simply can't afford to cut them off.'

Wilkins is signalling to you that the Chancellor and the others are ready to see you.

⇒ Wind up this meeting. Turn to **240**

⇒ Reassure her you'll reverse Brexit if you can. Turn to **37**

787

Your Brexit credentials are solid. Didn't you dismiss a junior minister for expressing heretical Remainer sympathies? Noysom-Reek questioning the sincerity of your determination to bring Britain out of the EU is like Cesare Borgia accusing Savonarola of being insufficiently devout.

Turn to **189**.

788

You throw yourself into a heated debate in which you argue the case for staying in the EU.

The ubiquitous Martin Mugglemore is chairing the debate. 'So, Prime Minister,' he asks, 'do you really think it's possible for us to turn back now?'

'I don't see why not, Martin. The other EU states have repeatedly said they're willing to welcome us back into the fold. And Article 50, which let us remember was only intended to be used in the event of a coup, can be legally rescinded right up until the two-year limit.'

'I don't mean that. I was thinking that the big problem that Britain has had with the EU is that we've always seen it as something we have no control over. Instead of working to change the things we didn't agree with, we just went into a characteristically British passive-aggressive sulk. It's like being shipwrecked. Somebody suggests banding together to build a shelter. But there's one person who gripes about where the shelter is, what it's made of, who does what. And when we don't get everything our own way we swan off in a huff.'

'Are you asking me a question?'

'Is there any point in Britain remaining in the EU if we're so unable to act as team players?'

⇒ 'We can be a team player. But not all members of a team are identical. The EU needs to recognize that Britain has unique skills to bring onto the field. Our military expertise, our financial sector skills, our international diplomatic reach. So this last two years will hopefully have taught both sides something.'

Turn to **109**

⇒ 'If your child makes a noise in class and pulls another child's pigtails, is that any reason to give up on them? I think the country has learned its lesson from the sharp shock of Brexit. We'll be better behaved in future.'

Turn to **706**

789

You remind the public of the Nazi-style posters that were put up during the referendum campaign. 'Mr Fungale's conduct falls far short of the standards we require of a Conservative politician,' you say in a hastily-arranged interview. 'Given his inflammatory brand of politics we feel he would do better to jump on a plane and offer his dubious talents to President Windrip.'

It leaves the right wing of the party fuming. Many of them saw nothing wrong with those posters and the xenophobic scare-mongering tactics Fungale employed to whip up the Leave vote. Very well, then – let them go off and join UKIP. But he's not getting in to the Tory Party on your watch.

Turn to **375**.

790

'Frankly we could do with at least ten years of continued EU membership, or at least associate membership,' says Stollard, 'while we hammer out the details of the new trade agreement.'

'This is tantamount to conspiracy!' thunders Barkwell.

'It's not called conspiracy when Cabinet ministers do it, Leslie,' says Stollard gently.

You know why Barkwell is worried. Ten years is plenty of time to hold a second referendum – and many of the staunchest supporters of Brexit will have died off in that time.

'For one thing, don't let's call it a transition phase,' you decide. 'It sounds mealy-mouthed. We'll refer to it as the implementation phase. We're implementing Brexit.'

'Just not as fast,' puts in Stollard. 'The transition – sorry, implementation phase is our parachute as we drift to a hopefully soft landing on the shores of a new free trade agreement.'

'And it can't take ten years. This has to happen in the term of the next Parliament. That way we can go into a general election saying, here, we're delivering Brexit. We win that and try to dot all the i's and cross all the t's by 2025 at the latest.'

'Just as long as the EU give us that breathing space,' says Dent. 'Some of them will probably hope we'll change our minds, so they won't oppose a transition period, but the jealous ones might want to boot us out sooner.'

Turn to **137.**

791

Rufus tacks towards a harder line on Brexit, citing her experience as Home Secretary as cementing her conviction that British sovereignty and borders need to be secured.

You respond by doubling down on your own Brexit rhetoric, determined that if it comes to a choice you will be seen as the stronger Brexit candidate.

'Let's hope there are no skeletons in the closet,' says Wilkins as he lays out your clothes on the morning of the next vote.

Do you have the keyword OPAL? If so, turn to **345**. If not, turn to **577**.

792

To nobody's surprise but her own, Amelia Dimple is knocked out in the first round of voting. At her concession speech she wears her usual expression, that of a lifetime stoner trying to comprehend quantum electrodynamics. 'I will offer my services whenever and wherever the country needs them,' she is saying.

You laugh out loud, snapping off the television with a hatchet-like gesture of the remote. The ridiculous woman. You wouldn't trust her to arrange a bowl of flowers, much less run the country.

It's good to have that distraction out of the way. Dimple was the taste of meat you needed to get your blood up for the fight. And now you need a plan to deal with the serious opposition.

If you have the keyword NYLON, turn to **27**. If not turn to **73.**

793

'Norway has plenty,' points out the Chancellor. 'And if Britain joined the European Free Trade Area, that's 65 million people adding our voice to EFTA's current 5 million. Our presence would triple the GDP of the whole bloc overnight.'

'Wait a moment,' you say. 'We're so much bigger but we only increase overall GDP by three times?'

'Remember that EFTA already includes Norway and Switzerland, Prime Minister, both very rich countries in per-capita terms when compared to the UK.'

Dent reddens at this, hating to hear any facts and figures that fail to portray Britain as the greatest nation in the northern hemisphere.

'The important thing is we'd be the catfish to their minnow,' puts in Strewel. 'Mind you, the EU is a bloody big pike. The European economy would still be five times as big as EFTA plus the UK combined.'

⇒ 'So the EU would push us around.' Turn to **131**

⇒ 'Is there any way to use our international standing to gain trade leverage?' Turn to **684**

794

Your good relationship with the other EU states, combined with your obvious willingness to remain a close ally and trading partner after Brexit, reassures them that it will be possible to keep the UK within the European Arrest Warrant.

'Who knows?' says Willy Franjeboom, the Chief EU Negotiator. 'We may hope that Britain's departure is only temporary.'

Record on your Brexit Memo Pad:

- ❖ +2% Authority – the media report it as a triumph of your negotiating skills.
- ❖ +2% Goodwill – the EU27 are starting to feel more certain of Britain's continued engagement.
- ❖ +3% Popularity – the voters feel secure.

Turn to **286**.

795

'Not ever,' says Ron drily. 'Well, not until all currently serving EU officials are dead, so effectively we can say there's no time limit on that one.'

'Surely we can just agree to cover the pensions of British citizens working for the EU. What's the percentage there?'

'Eight percent. But – '

'That's not too bad. I can sell that to the press more easily than footing the bill for a bunch of superannuated Eurocrats. Why the long face, Ron?'

'It's not just Britons, prime minister. The EU's position on this is that the nationality of an official is irrelevant. They'll expect us to cover our share of pension payments for all EU officials who began employment while we were still a member.'

'Is that more?'

'At least half as much again. But it's arguably a legal commitment. A company has to do the same for employees when it sells a business.'

'Yes, see, now that's not going to help sell it to the Europhobes. Picture the headlines. "SPONGERS." "EXTORTION." "THEY'RE BLEEDING US DRY."'

Under the heavy tweed jacket, his shoulders heave in a shrug. 'That's why it's called politics, prime minister.'

Turn to **374**.

796

Even the most ardent Brexiter on the Tory back benches is satisfied that you're driving a hard bargain with the EU. The only question is whether Labour will nod the motion through.

Look at your Brexit Memo Pad. If your Popularity is 69% or more, turn to **455**.

If your Popularity is 39% or less, turn to **149**.

Otherwise turn to **753**.

797

Your civil servants report that the minister tasked with negotiating the exit fee flew into a temper when the EU team contradicted him. He stormed out saying that he wouldn't stand for what he called punishment beatings. There's even a rumour that he likened the German delegation to concentration camp guards.

'It could have gone worse,' is your chief of staff's view. 'I made sure to have his hip flask filled with tonic water.'

'But what now? The EU27 will take it to the International Court. We may end up having to pay more.'

He nods. 'But not until after the next election, at least.'

Record on your Brexit Memo Pad:

- ❖ -5% Authority – nobody is sure if you have any control of your cabinet
- ❖ -15% Goodwill – the Foreign Secretary's antagonism has lost you friends among the other EU states.
- ❖ +5% Popularity – the voters perceive this as a strong move.
- ❖ Tick the keyword BLEAK

Now turn to **580**.

798

Just when it seemed everything was settled, you're hit with a host of amendments from multiple EU countries.

On your Brexit Memo Pad:

- ❖ -3% Economy – yet more red tape ties up Britain's exports.
- ❖ -2% Popularity – the voters doubt your ability to deliver on your promises.

Now turn to **865**.

799

'We couldn't conduct our own trade deals,' says Barkwell. 'I call that a pretty major drawback. And make no mistake, the people will see it as an admission of failure too.'

It's not the first time Barkwell has hinted at taking his grievances out of the Cabinet Room. You let your glare chill him down a few degrees, then turn to the others.

'We'd have to abide by European Court rulings,' ventures Dent. 'Technically UK courts would be independent, but there'd be a forest of compliance issues. How much cereal in a choccie biccy, that sort of thing. And the EU being bigger would mean their rulings would dominate.'

'Possibly we could sell the sovereignty sizzle to the press without biting down into the textured protein meat substitute.' Your glance passes over Strewel, still tucking into his full English with the gusto of an overgrown schoolboy. 'Alan, anything to add?'

Stollard nods. 'A customs union only gives a trade benefit in goods. That's fine for Turkey, but 80% of our economy is in the service sector. So we'd have to do a special deal on that anyway.'

⇒ 'Let's go over the advantages of the Turkey model.'
Turn to **681**

⇒ 'Other than a customs union, what options do we have?'
Turn to **703**

800

An hour later, invigorated by a shower, you're sipping strong black coffee in the main conference room when Chloe Stoat is shown in.

'I'm hoping you'll give me some good news,' she says the moment she enters the room. From her tone you'd think she was the one in charge.

'Perhaps it's all a dream.' You mime smacking your head. 'No, not a dream. We're stuck with it.'

A blank look. She's too young to remember *Fawlty Towers*.

'Nothing about the situation is funny, Prime Minister. Having come out of the referendum without a defined plan for Brexit, I'm concerned that it will be hijacked by right-wing ideological elements. The sort of people who play with fire without knowing that fire is hot.'

'Isn't that usually the left-wingers?'

She's built up too much furious energy to stop. 'Without freedom of movement we're going to lose valuable workers. And it will be harder for our businesses to trade with the continent.'

⇒ Remind her about the immigration problem.
Turn to **352**

⇒ Point out that some sort of customs union hasn't been ruled out. Turn to **248**

⇒ Tell her that privately you're hoping to reverse Brexit and stay part of the EU. Turn to **37**

801

'It's too close to call,' says Ron Beardsley, handing you an exit poll of comments made by Conservative Party members.

'I don't know what our members do to the enemy, Ron, but by God they terrify me.'

As you sit waiting to hear the results announced, what are you thinking?

⇒ The die is cast. Turn to **782**

⇒ Let the chips fall where they may. Turn to **486**

802

Tiffany Rufus phones you to propose a deal. 'Let's team up to get Peter Strewel out of the running.'

'And then what?'

'Then it's just you and me, and the membership gets to decide. But neither of us wants to be running against Peter when it's no longer the parliamentary party doing the voting, do we?'

⇒ 'All right, we'll both focus on undermining him.' Turn to **307**

⇒ 'I don't like backroom deals. Let's just see how it plays out.' Turn to **94**

803

'There isn't any money, that's the problem.'

'You're the Chancellor of the Exchequer, Alan. If you can't find a way for me to pay for the NHS, what's the point of you?'

You're Skyping, even though he's only next door. These days you both want to make a show of being busy, so he's typing away and occasionally taking quick calls while you deal with a succession of aides who are continually popping into your office.

'Oh, I can cook the books for you. You want more hospitals, I can cut defence spending, how about that? Or foreign aid.'

'That's a vote winner right there.'

'Not on the diplomatic stage, or even in our own long-term interests.'

'Five years is as far out as you need to be looking, Alan.'

If you've ticked the keyword MAPLE, turn to **760**. Otherwise turn to **535**.

804

Love. What does it mean? You had a puppy once that followed you everywhere until the milkman drove his float over it. But was that love? Or the simple anxiety felt by a helpless creature at the thought of being left alone?

And your teddy. He loved you, you think, but your relationship with him was always conflicted and bore the seeds of betrayal. Goldilocks must ever have been on her guard in case one morning porridge wasn't enough.

Now at last you know something better than love. Abject, toadying fear. You see it in the taut smiles and too-bright eyes around the Cabinet table, in the eager replies and fawning postures of the MPs you stop to speak to. They know your power is absolute. With a wave of the hand you could raise them to the inner circle or banish them to reselection.

It's only in the small hours, when you wake and see the streetlight on the bedroom wall, that you feel a tiny inner squirming of disquiet. For uneasy hangs the head that wears the crown.

Turn to **386**.

805

Can you hang on in the job after a setback like this? It will take iron resolve.

> On your Brexit Memo Pad:
> ❖ -10% Popularity – you pay the price for choosing the losing side

⇒ It's time to throw in the towel. Turn to **395**

⇒ You're not going anywhere. There's a job to be done. Turn to **206**

806

Armand Alprèves, the EU Commission chief negotiator, reminds you that there are a number of stages your deal must go through. 'The EU27 must reach a two-thirds majority on the terms of the new relationship. That's the minimum majority that should always be required in any democracy to enact a radical change.'

'Touché. And what else?'

'The trade deal can be vetoed by any member state.'

'Why would they do that?'

'Perhaps Poland doesn't want British potatoes. Perhaps Spain wants joint control of Gibraltar.'

'Bargaining chips,' you say with scorn. 'That's your vaunted EU democracy in action, is it?'

'You have never really understood that we are not a federal state. You are dealing with twenty-seven sovereign countries, each with its own interests.'

If your Goodwill score is 10% or less, turn to **798**.

If Goodwill is 70% or more, turn to **526**.

Otherwise turn to **88**.

807

'Not really,' says Stollard. 'Financial services and related professions account for one in fifteen British jobs. And two thirds of those are outside London.'

Turn to **66.**

808

Barkwell's eyes almost start out of his head, while Dent gives an angry cough.

'You gentlemen don't agree?'

'Remember that the people have given us an overwhelming mandate to get out of the single market,' snaps Barkwell. 'They have spoken. Who are we to betray their wishes?'

'We're the elected government of the United Kingdom, not high priests of Baal. We'll do what's in the people's interests.'

'And after all, two-fifths of those who voted Leave actually wanted us to adopt the Norway model,' says Stollard. 'So it's the preferred solution of 69% of the electorate.'

'Lies!' snorts Barkwell, storming out.

> On your Brexit Memo Pad:
> - -1% Authority – it's not wise to let your enemies in on your plans.

Then turn to **666.**

809

'Officially, yes.'

'It's a bit "sellotape and string", though, isn't it?' says Strewel.

'It is a pretty confusing set of fudges,' admits the Chancellor. 'If an EU regulation changes, the Swiss have to add a footnote to hundreds of pages of agreements that are intended to replicate the rules of the single market in domestic law.'

'And it's a work in progress,' says Dent.

Strewel gives a table-shaking guffaw. 'As in lots of work, little progress.'

Turn to **378.**

810

'Thank you, gentlemen. It's a long and rocky road ahead, but we've made a start.'

'Rocky road, yum,' says Strewel. 'If I wasn't on a diet I'd go and get a couple of scoops of that for elevenses.'

⇒ Ask the Chancellor to stay behind for a chat.
Turn to **348**

⇒ You have other urgent matters to attend to.
Turn to **666**

811

Remain have an overwhelming lead in the polls. On the day, a high turnout of younger voters makes it a dead cert. On television you see Peter Strewel leaving his house. He's grinning like Pooh Bear in a honey factory. No doubt he's relieved that, after the proverbial plate of pasta, he had the good sense not to campaign for Leave again.

Look at your Brexit Memo Pad. If you have the keyword EIGER, turn to **733**. If not, turn to **714**.

812

Willy Franjeboom, the EU's chief negotiator, phones you to say they have come to a decision about the fate of British nationals living in Europe. 'You'll be relieved to hear we're not deporting all those pensioners from the Spanish beaches,' he says with a laugh.

'Or the British financiers, lawyers, scientists and doctors. You wouldn't want to forgo collecting their taxes, eh?'

'Oh, it is not so much that. We just couldn't let those families become pawns in a political game.'

It's your turn to laugh. 'That would merit the world's smallest violin if you'd announced it a year ago. You've just been letting this slide in the hope that Britain would make a decision first.'

'And what is your decision?'

That's tricky. If you don't match the EU's gesture you're going to look petty. But there are three million EU nationals in Britain, and less than one and a half million UK nationals spread throughout the whole of Europe, so the situation is hardly equitable. What will you tell him?

⇒ 'EU nationals already living here can stay.' Turn to **182**

⇒ 'I'm giving notice that EU nationals have to pack their bags and be out once Britain leaves the EU.' Turn to **357**

813

'The upside is pretty clear,' says Dent. 'It's getting shot of EU courts dictating to us at every turn. Winning back our sovereignty. Though maybe we will have a few wrinkles to iron out on the trade dispute front, we won't have all those tedious regulations about labour law, product specifications and so forth.'

'Actually we already have the least regulated labour and product markets in the EU,' says Stollard.

Everybody turns to look at him, but this time he folds his hands and sits back. 'What if I say nothing? Would the rest of you really pretend that the WTO promises us plain sailing? Dennis, you've already admitted it doesn't. So why doesn't somebody else tell us about the possible stumbling blocks?'

'You mean quotas and schedules?' says Strewel through a chocolate éclair. 'Most favoured nation rules? Non-tariff barriers? Things like that?'

You all gawp at him in astonishment. He grins a chocolaty grin and pokes the remains of the éclair into his mouth as if stuffing scraps into a waste disposal pipe.

⇒ 'All right, Peter. Tell us about schedules and quotas.' Turn to **61**

⇒ 'What's a most favoured nation when it's at home?' Turn to **38**

⇒ 'Non-tariff barriers? Now it's getting scary.' Turn to **383**

⇒ 'Actually, never mind.' Turn to **454**

814

The leadership results are in. You sit gazing out of the window in a state of shock.

'It is a tale told by an idiot, Wilkins.'

He sets a cup of tea in front of you. 'Are you looking at President Windrip's tweets again, Prime Minister?'

'No, man. The damned leadership contest. The rug – pulled from under me.'

'Distressing, indeed. I'm sure we shall miss you, and in that I include all of the Number 10 staff.'

'Thank you, Wilkins.'

He turns at the door and regards you solemnly. 'If it is any consolation, I would say it is rare that one gets to let go of a tiger's tail without getting one's hand bitten off.'

And with that he goes to pack your things and make ready for the new Prime Minister.

THE END

815

True to his word, perhaps for the first time ever, Peter Strewel endorses your views.

'The Prime Minister is right,' he tells reporters. 'Can't have a democratic solution that rides roughshod over the wishes of nearly half the country, can we? Not a question of hard or soft, we're going to have a *better* Brexit. The kind of Brexit everyone can get behind. Then we can show the world a bit of that British pluck last seen in the War, eh? All pulling together to get to the promised land.'

Turn to **486**.

816

'I believe wholeheartedly in Brexit. The people have spoken, now we must cut our ties with Europe.'

If you have the keyword HEMLOCK, BLEAK or KOALA, turn to **28**.

If not but you have the keyword GAZELLE, turn to **459**.

Failing all the above, turn to **594**.

817

You'd forgotten Terri's nephew, who's here on sufferance because she and Ron thought a kid-to-work day would humanize you. He flicks a bored glance at you through a long fringe of gel-spiked hair before going back to his phone.

'It's a very big Death Star..?' says Terri uncertainly.

'Dunno what that is,' grunts the nephew. 'But it's mustard, blows up planets and shit.'

'And that helps us how?'

'Always a weak point, isn't there? Gerbil Whassis-Feet, he'll have something you can turn against him.'

There are a few minutes of silence, punctuated only by the muted *ping-ping-ping-BOOM* of the wretched child's phone game, as you all mull over that. Then everyone speaks at once.

'I could dig up some dirt on him,' suggests Terri.

'We need to play on his lack of experience,' says Ron.

'Beat him at his own game?' you say, thinking aloud. 'Show the members I can be even more ultra on Brexit?'

'Go judo,' says the nephew. 'He moves one way, you shift the other. Unexpected. Element of surmise or whatever. That's how you throw 'em.'

What's it to be?

⇒ Look for a scandal. Everybody's got something to hide.
Turn to **856**

⇒ Emphasize Noysom-Reek's lack of experience.
Turn to **717**

⇒ Beat him at his own game. Pivot back from soft to very hard Brexit. Turn to **499**

⇒ Be statesmanlike. Draw back from extreme positions and make the case for moderation. Turn to **121**

818

As you approach the final round of Parliamentary Party voting, it's time to take stock of your opponents.

If you have the keyword NYLON, turn to **193**. If not, turn to **726**.

819

A burgeoning economy gives the lie to all the Project Fear scare-mongering from the 2016 campaign. Retail spending is up – on credit, admittedly. And the hike in prices on imported goods hasn't hit the shops yet. The general mood of the country seems to be that Britain would fare very well outside the EU.

'If people just vote on the basis of their purses and wallets, it'll be a shoo-in for a hard Brexit,' reckons your chief of staff.

'It's never that simple. People care about their finances, but they care almost as much about their feelings.'

Look at the Goodwill score on your Brexit Memo Pad. This gives a sense of how amicably the EU27 are behaving towards Britain at the moment.

If Goodwill is at 52% or higher, turn to **463.**

If Goodwill is 51% or lower, turn to **581.**

820

As the country dissolves yet again into a cacophony of recrimination, regret and hatred, you're just glad you had the sense to keep out of it. When the smoke clears, each side will despise the other and you alone will remain untarnished by the vituperative debate.

Toss two coins. If both come up heads, turn to **173**. Otherwise, turn to **403.**

821

If you have marked Security & Defence as complete, turn to **742**.

If not, turn to **855**.

822

At least there's no need to discuss Britain's continued involvement with Europol. There's already a precedent for close cooperation between EU police forces and other countries. You quickly agree a relationship along the same lines that the US and Australia currently enjoy, with British liaison officers at Europol and EU officers based at key UK police departments.

You meet with Chief Negotiator Franjeboom. 'Now we have our ducks in a row,' he says, 'it is time to consider the drake.'

'That probably loses something in translation.'

His smile doesn't waver. 'I refer to military cooperation in the aftermath of Brexit.'

'My government has repeatedly assured the EU that we will continue to cooperate proactively. As Britain is the most significant military power in Europe, I'm sure that's in everyone's interests.'

'You have the largest military budget, at any rate,' he says. 'The way the pound is now, that doesn't go as far as it used to. In any case, you should be aware that Britain's departure removes one of the main obstacles to much greater integration of European armed forces. Will you be willing to engage with the "EU army" your Leave politicians fulminated over?'

⇒ 'I'm afraid Britain can't possibly subordinate her forces to missions over which we have little strategic or tactical control.' Turn to **301**

⇒ 'We're willing to pull our weight, but we must insist on a special arrangement that gives us equal influence over the planning of joint military ventures.' Turn to **279**

823

'You're the least popular Prime Minister since Eden bungled the Suez crisis.'

Lord Elmstead is going over the results you commissioned from his polling company. It doesn't make comforting reading.

'But sometimes the most unpopular leaders also get the highest scores in popularity,' you remind him. 'Think of President Windrip. The deplorables absolutely love him.'

'True, and there's the silver lining. As long as you have high approval ratings among your core supporters, and as long as the opposition is divided and your grip on the party is strong, overall unpopularity can't hurt you.'

The key is to continue the erosion of Parliamentary sovereignty that has been going on for at least a hundred years. Concentrate power in the executive, who are answerable to party members rather than the electorate as a whole, and you should be able to hang on.

And if not, and you're ousted before the next election, so what? You'll easily nab a few directorships. You'll coin it in with after-dinner speeches. And then there are the memoirs. If history looks back on you unkindly for your handling of Brexit – well, at least nobody's calling you a war criminal. And anyway, you only did what the people told you.

THE END

824

The Health Secretary goes on *News Talk* to discuss the visa initiative. 'The NHS is the envy of the world,' he says. 'And our message today is that we want the best doctors, the best nurses. Brexit isn't about pulling up the drawbridge, it's about deciding who gets to come here. No more floods of half-qualified quacks taking out the wrong kidney. From now on, our health care is on the gold standard.'

He's a blithering idiot, obviously. And his quip about the drawbridge will lose some of the madder hard Brexit voters. But all in all you can bask in the satisfaction of a job spun to look as if it's being done well.

> Record on your Brexit Memo Pad:
> - +1% Economy – any message of welcome sent out to qualified immigrants helps reassure the world that Britain hasn't entirely shut up shop.

If you have ticked the keyword DODO, turn to **431**. Otherwise, mark the NHS as complete on your Brexit Memo Pad and then turn to **450**.

825

As the results start coming in, you stare at the television in growing disbelief. By the small hours you can no longer escape the truth.

'We've lost…'

Your team, bone-weary and despondent, look at you with drawn faces. Finally one of the special advisers speaks up. 'Labour had a very strong manifesto, Prime Minister. Curbing the power of corporations, investing in the NHS, moderating Brexit. All popular policies.'

You shake your head. 'The explanation is very simple. The party failed me. In my hour of greatest need, I stood alone.'

Barry Scraggle will now be hustling to form a government, swallowing his principles to do deals with the Liberal Democrats and the SNP. Small wonder if the strain of the next five years doesn't kill him. You smile sourly as you unscrew one of the bolts in your office chair. That can be his welcoming present.

But for you, it is all over.

THE END

826

'I'm not going quite so far as to advocate boilerplate World Trade Organization rules,' says Dent, throwing Barkwell an apologetic glance. 'It's potentially more of a bureaucratic nightmare than the EU, if we're honest. Every WTO member – '

'How many are we talking about?'

'A hundred and sixty plus, prime minister. And every single one of them can trigger a trade dispute if they're unhappy with arrangements.'

'But they're not going to do that, are they? I mean, they'll want to trade with us.'

'I'm sure they will trade with us,' puts in Stollard. 'But in the short term some of our competitors will use the opportunity to reset trade relations. It could get nasty.'

⇒ 'Give me an example.' Turn to **741**

⇒ 'Surely they won't mess with us given the size of our economy?' Turn to **443**

⇒ 'What actually is the WTO?' Turn to **646**

827

It's the moment of truth. Have you done enough to see off the threat of Fungale? And, if so, did you do it without crossing a moral line that you can't come back from?

⇒ No use crying over spilt milk. Turn to **349**

⇒ The ends justify the means. Turn to **377**

828

Immigration was undoubtedly one of the major factors in the Leave vote. There was a very informative television debate about it that you remember watching. You cast your mind back…

Turn to **746.**

829

The *Outrage* and the *Daily Heil* dutifully run the story with just the spin you want, but the *Tomahawk* is a little more restrained. No great surprise there; many of its readers work in the financial sector.

> On your Brexit Memo Pad:
> - +1% Authority – seeing the media toeing your line serves as a warning to your opponents in the party.
> - -2% Economy – the haemorrhaging of financial services from the City is going to impact everyone's standard of living.
> - +1% Popularity – you've given the public their favourite villain: bankers.

Now turn to **400.**

830

Terri's summary is a lot politer than the actual question, which is more along the lines of: 'Why do we keep letting these people come over here taking jobs that could go to British workers?'

Mugglemore throws it to the Lib Dem woman. 'Immigrants don't subtract from our way of life,' she says. 'They add value, both in the taxes they pay and in terms of social value.' So she's both contradicting and avoiding the question. Double waffle points there: a rookie mistake.

Fungale is straight in like a rash on a hot day. 'What are you talking about, "social value"? National costume? Henna tattoos? Zither music? That isn't much consolation when an immigrant jumps the queue at the job centre, is it?'

⇒ See how she answers that. Turn to **358**

⇒ See if Bob Owlbear can string a non-soporific thought together for once. Turn to **135**

⇒ Find another question. Turn to **405**

⇒ Give up and get a good night's sleep. Turn to **125**

831

You were told that it might be possible to secure continued membership of the single market once the question of security and defence was resolved.

If Goodwill is still at 16% or greater, you have the option to reopen those discussions: turn to **257**.

If Goodwill is 15% or less, or if you decide not to bother with single market access after all, turn to **385**.

832

'OK. Back in 1999, Switzerland and the EU signed a bunch of sectoral deals known collectively as the Bilateral Agreements I. There are seven of them, covering agriculture, free movement, non-tariff barriers, public procurement, research, aviation, and transport. Those are all linked by a guillotine clause, meaning that if one agreement is broken, they all go. That's why the Swiss continue to tolerate free movement in spite of all the nationalist agitation about it.'

'So the Bilateral Agreements I are in effect a bolt-on emulator of the single market rules,' puts in Strewel helpfully. 'Sort of like that free Open Office program you used to be able to get that did the same as Microsoft Word.'

The Chancellor laughs. 'The difference being that Open Office was simpler than the original, whereas the Swiss agreements are much, much more complicated.'

⇒ 'And do they cover services?' Turn to **673**

⇒ 'Not to be masochistic, but I assume there's a Bilateral Agreements II?' Turn to **690**

⇒ 'What does the EU think of all this palaver?' Turn to **559**

833

'You're coming across as a little soft on Brexit,' says Ron Beardsley as you go over your campaign strategy. 'Also, the Party members regard you as having a reputation for Machiavellian scheming coupled with no moral compass whatsoever.'

'Oh dear. But – '

'No, that's a good thing. Perfect leadership material.'

If you have the keyword NYLON, turn to **193**. If not, turn to **726**.

834

Do you have the keywords TIGHTROPE or WELTER? If so, turn to **661**. If you have neither of those keywords, turn to **724**.

835 ☐

All of the hopes, fears and uncertainties concerning the National Health Service are revealed to you in a dark, unbidden vision of things to come...

If the box above is empty, put a tick in it and turn to **730**.

If the box was already ticked, turn to **711**.

836

The Chancellor throws you a warning look. 'That's a lot to get into in a morning meeting, Prime Minister.'

For once Barkwell and he are on the same page. 'The Department for International Trade has a number of proposals to make about our future outside the single market. I'd like more time to present those properly.'

'Very well. We'll resume this discussion at a later date. Thank you, gentlemen.'

⇒ Ask the Chancellor to stay behind for a chat.
Turn to **348**

⇒ You have other urgent business to take care of.
Turn to **666**

837

You hold your own against your opponents in the debate. Towards the close, thinking you're ahead, you even start to relax. That could be a big mistake.

'Prime Minister,' says the show's compère, Martin Mugglemore, 'isn't it true that Brexit is like proposing radical surgery for an ingrown toenail? It might cure the problem, but equally well you might lose the foot. Is it, in short, a risk worth taking?'

⇒ 'Maybe it isn't just an ingrown toenail, though. What if the foot is in danger of going septic? Sometimes the biggest risk is to do nothing.' Turn to **572**

⇒ 'Don't you ever do the pools, Martin? Buy a lottery ticket? A scratch card? Maybe you don't, but millions who do know that sometimes it's worth having a flutter. Risks can pay off, you know.' Turn to **8**

838

'Of course not,' says the scientist. 'Don't you realize that even prior to leaving the EU, Britain was ranked twenty-fourth out of the twenty-eight states for the number of doctors per person? The NHS was always a political football, and Brexit was the tack that finally deflated it.'

'Surely with all the fabulous new trade deals we did there was more money to spend on research?' It's all you can do to resist asking him what year this is.

'Medical research is bloody expensive,' he says. 'And it calls for a long-range vision. When Britain pooled money with the rest of the EU we were making some real strides. After all, cancer doesn't care what nationality you are. But when everybody goes it alone it's hard to get anywhere.'

'Surely some research is still going on?'

'Of course. Each village practice is funding its own research program as part of the last prime minister's Plucky Little England initiative. I'm hoping the summer fete will raise nearly £500 for my own research into Alzheimer's.'

Abednego meets your gaze, but cannot bring himself to express the disapproval you know he must be feeling. As a child you swore to protect him, but here he is adrift in a privatized cyberpunk future that has no place for old teddy bears. Your tears leave dark patches on his scraggy fur. Turn to **368**.

839

Naturally the other ministers want to know who will get the visas. Whatever deal you reach is going to be reciprocal. Service industries often need employees to relocate to another country, even if only temporarily while a new office is being set up. And that applies as much to British workers supplying services to the continent as EU workers moving to the UK.

'What restrictions are you intending to place on visa applications?' asks the President of the Council.

⇒ 'Anyone can come to Britain as long as they have a job or a university place lined up.' Turn to **136**

⇒ 'Highly qualified workers will have no trouble getting visas, but the goal is to stop the influx of low-skilled immigrants over the next few years.' Turn to **156**

840

A nicely anodyne statement that commits you to nothing at all.

Now turn to **125**.

841

You are throwing your weight behind the campaign to press on with Brexit. After the last two years of wrangling over every detail with the EU, what else could you do?

> On your Brexit Memo Pad:
> ❖ Tick the keyword FOG.

'Focus on the fact that battle lines have been drawn,' is Thomas Tode's advice to you as he sees you crossing the lobby one morning. 'People see the EU as the "other side" now.'

'That's your considered advice, is it?' You give him a piercing stare that would shrivel anyone with a shred of sensitivity.

Tode simply returns his usual simpering smile. 'I took a few bruises in the first campaign. I think I can call myself something of an expert now.'

You turn away. 'I've had enough of experts.'

At any rate, the die is cast. Now you must hope that your personal convictions, or at least the outward appearance of conviction, will sway the voters. Look at your Brexit Memo Pad. If your Popularity score is 51% or higher, turn to **766**. If it's 50% or lower, turn to **388**.

842

'Freedom of movement was never part of the original intention of the EU,' you tell them. 'What Britain signed up to was free movement of labour. Nobody takes issue with that. That's an economic necessity, whereas untrammelled freedom of movement is a political edict.'

You note the scowls on many of their faces. 'It is well known that Britain has been resistant to the idea of ever-closer union,' says the Dutch prime minister.

'Oh come now, it's not just us. Wake up and smell the tulips, mynheer. The original treaty allowed for workers to move around the old European Economic Community. But what's happened over the last forty years is that the European Court has pushed free movement by stealth. So now you've got people coming in, saying they're looking for work, bringing in their spouses and children, applying for housing benefits...'

'Abusing the system? It's a tiny proportion of people doing that.'

'Maybe. But the voters don't perceive it that way. I'm not just talking about Britain. Different states have different attitudes and different visions of where they see the EU going. Regardless of what we decide at this summit, you're going to have to create a two-speed Europe.'

'For the benefit of the great British people we must do this?' cries the French President, flinging his arms wide in mockery.

'No. You must do it so that your union doesn't tear itself apart.'

'Even if what you say is true,' argues President Terlamen, 'it will take time. A menu of options for continental partnership? Our successors will still be discussing the terms when most of us here have retired. What do you propose in the meantime?'

⇒ 'For the time being we'll adopt a "free movement emulator", mirroring EU legislation in British law. It'll be much like it is now, only our courts will be rigorous in enforcing the rules.' Turn to **59**

⇒ 'In the meantime I intend to introduce quotas so that I can meet my promise to the British people to get immigration down below 100,000 a year.' Turn to **497**

843

'Against: abortion, same-sex marriage, immigrants, industrial controls to reverse climate change – and of course the EU. For: zero-hour contracts, fox hunting, a Conservative alliance with UKIP – and for a while he supported both the Syrian government and Dumpster Windrip, but later had second thoughts about those.'

Terri Trough turns from the white board with a fat marker pen in each hand. 'In short, Gervais Noysom-Reek's views overlap pretty strongly with the core Party member.'

'It's not all bad news,' says Ron. 'He's actually spoken against the death penalty and corporal punishment. That won't sit well with a lot of the faithful. And of course he's twenty years younger than the average member.'

'And sort of posh,' adds Terri, trying to find a marker colour to indicate that. 'Smacks a bit of the previous leadership, maybe?'

You shake your head. 'He's more incense and cassocks than

rugger and magnums of the Widow. Totally different breed of upper class. The sort the membership instinctively tug their forelocks to. Bugger it, they're going to love him.'

'Even a Starkiller Base has a weakness,' pipes up a squeaky voice from the corner.

⇒ 'What's a Starkiller Base?' Turn to **817**

⇒ 'Get this child out of here.' Turn to **278**

844

An audacious claim. Will it wash? If your Popularity score is 69% or more, turn to **12**.

If less, turn to **675**.

845

There is a resigned sigh around the table as they see you won't be dissuaded.

'What kind of referendum?' pipes up a voice from the far end.

'Who said that?'

A sheepishly grinning face leans forward. You fight the urge to get up, walk along the table and punch him.

'Tode? Are you back in Cabinet?'

'Environment Secretary,' he says. 'And thank you, Prime Minister, for the opportunity – '

'All right. I'm not Dumpster Windrip. I don't need stroking, man. Spit it out. What kinds of referendum are there? It's just yes or no, isn't it?'

'It could be,' says Tode with a goofy chuckle. 'Just Leave or Remain like last time, that's an option. Or we could drill down, give people a range of options to choose between.'

'Steady on,' says Strewel with a guffaw. 'It's the great British public, remember. Ketchup or mayo has them spinning like a top.'

'I'm not so dismissive of the average man,' says Tode huffily. 'Anyway, there's a third option, which is to hold the referendum in rounds.'

'Rounds!' cries Leslie Barkwell, sounding for all the world like Lady Bracknell.

'The French manage it. And if we're giving more than a yes/no choice, it's the best way to find out what the public really want.'

⇒ 'Who'll speak up for the simple yes/no option?'
Turn to **600**

⇒ 'A range of options, that could work.' Turn to **698**

⇒ 'Tell me more about this runoff voting idea.'
Turn to **340**

846

'You've already ruled that EU citizens currently living in the UK will not be allowed to stay,' President Terlamen reminds you.

He's right. There's no sense in saying now that you'll let free movement continue in any form. It would just make your earlier policy look confused. You'd be kicking out three million people only to let two and half million of them back in the following month.

So what will you propose?

⇒ An immigration points system allowing you to cherry-pick who gets to come to Britain. Turn to **216**

⇒ A simple quota of fifty thousand EU immigrants a year.
Turn to **369**

847

'The Druid Poet of Kernow – an official title, believe it or not – has issued a bardic statement.' The aide reads from her phone. '"There once was a Tory prime minister, whose intentions for Cornwall were sinister..."'

'How authentically Celtic. I'm sure they all danced around reciting stuff like that when they built Stonehenge. Not that the Stonehenge builders were Druids any more than the Cornish McGonagall there.'

'I wouldn't say anything like that, Prime Minister. It might come across a bit grammar school, if you know what I mean.'

'Come off it. The UKIP brigade lap that stuff up. Pig ignorant themselves, but they love the idea that you can get a proper education without being a nob. Anyway, forget the mad poet, I need a way to spin this that doesn't sound like pulling the plug on vital investment.'

'How about: "For too long EU funds have been spent on things like poetry centres and community arts projects, when what the people of Cornwall have been crying out for are jobs and roads and hospitals."'

⇒ 'Is that really what EU funds were going on?'
Turn to **86**

⇒ 'Remind me, how much of the EU funding can we guarantee?' Turn to **721**

⇒ 'Sidestep the funding issue. Find me another upside for Cornwall post-Brexit.' Turn to **258**

848

Running the country over the last few years has meant walking a tightrope. Despite the wrench to both the British and EU economies, you've managed to maintain a good relationship with your European allies. You can look forward to continued trade and cooperation on joint engineering, science and development projects.

The few dozen ultra-Brexiteers in your Parliamentary party are not at all happy about that. They wanted bridges burnt, not an enduring friendship that could eventually open the way for Britain's return to the EU. To them, and to the most strident flat earthers among the electorate, you're just another 'saboteur', an 'enemy of the people' who needs to be taken down.

In the long run the country will do better for the decisions you've made, but you'll have to watch the rivals who are waiting in the shadows of the forum. Those are daggers in their pockets and they're not pleased to see you.

Turn to **351**.

849

After leaving it a couple of weeks so as not to seem vindictive, you send her packing and pluck another ermine-collared drone from the dozing ranks of the Lords.

This time you're careful to pick someone who'll do as you say. Whatever would Cabinet meetings be like if they degenerated into actual discussion and debate? You'd never get anything done.

> Record on your Brexit Memo Pad:
> ❖ -2% Authority – your autocratic manner is breeding resentment right across the party.

Then turn to **542.**

850

Your personal standing in the party is at a low ebb. You've noticed the looks you get as you cross the lobby. Pity is the least objectionable of them, while most regard you with contempt or palpable hatred. You're seen as an ineffective bungler, a millstone around the party's neck. The architect of a Brexit that was always doomed to be unsatisfying.

'You're not the first to face this problem,' you tell yourself sternly while looking in the mirror. 'MPs have always been a contrary and unbiddable bunch. Who needs them? From now on, make your appeals directly to the mob. Polarize the electorate. Find your tribe. It doesn't matter what the 49% want, just convince the other 51% their opponents are sore losers who are trying to cheat them of victory. Reason is the enemy, but its day is done.'

Turn to **386**.

851

Your civil servants point out that, having ruled out free movement, it is impossible to reach an agreement with the EU that will give you access to the single market.

'I don't need to be *in* the single market!' you shout at them. 'I just want us to have access to it.'

'Prime Minister,' says your Parliamentary Private Secretary, 'it's the same thing.'

After an hour or two it becomes obvious that shouting at the problem isn't going to solve it. So that leaves you having to opt either for customs union like Turkey (turn to **674**) or else try to broker a completely new free trade agreement (turn to **294**).

852

Your recent comments have placed you squarely between the extreme Year Zero absolutism of Colin Fungale and the closet European federalism of Tiffany Rufus. The next round of the contest is surely going to be between you and Dennis Dent.

'This is the vote for the centre ground,' says Ron Beardsley, echoing your thoughts.

'Odd to think that advocating a rock-hard Brexit just short of trade suicide could count as "centre ground",' you say.

'It's the new centre. Everything we're doing has been gradually moving it to the right.'

Is it even right or left any more? Those models seem to belong to a quaint past of baggy football shorts and police cars that sounded like alarm clocks. The real political debate these days is more like the Allegory of the Long Spoons – whether it's better to share food with each other, or starve while jealously guarding your own plate.

Nervously you await the results of the next vote.

If your Authority is 46% or more *and* your Popularity is 41% or more, turn to **62**. Otherwise turn to **377**.

853

A bombshell explodes your dreams of effortless victory. Chloe Stoat, the Secretary of State for Business, Energy and Industrial Strategy, reveals in an interview that you told her you're secretly opposed to Brexit. Before you know what's happening, reporters are thrusting their microphones under your nose and accusing you of hypocrisy, insincerity and duplicity.

Under the merciless draining glare of camera lights, the nation waits for your response.

⇒ 'It's politics. You say what you have to say to herd this gaggle of geese in the right direction.' Turn to **96**

⇒ 'I'm opposed to an *inept* Brexit. I make no secret of that.' Turn to **449**

⇒ 'Perhaps it's time to move Mrs Stoat from Business to Arts. She certainly has a creative imagination.' Turn to **719**

854

Grilled by a crowd of reporters in Downing Street a few days later, you make a point of giving them your Palpatine stare. 'This is a time for hard decisions. Will waiting lists get longer? Will the standard of your medical care decline? Of course not. Some may try to blame Brexit for changes in the NHS, but the truth is that foreigners have been taking jobs away from British-born nursing staff.'

'From nursing staff? Really?' calls out one of the BBC pack.

'And doctors. And hospital porters. Now we're turning back that EU tide. It will be a whole new era of healthcare.'

'Privatized and unaffordable,' yells another reporter, but by then you've waved to the cameras and turned back into Number 10.

Record on your Brexit Memo Pad:
- ❖ +1% Authority – your opponents are shocked by your ruthlessness, but also a little overawed.

If you have ticked the keyword DODO, turn to **431**. Otherwise, mark the NHS as complete on your Brexit Memo Pad and then turn to **450**.

855

Your civil servants dolefully present you with your options. 'It's quite limited, I'm afraid, Prime Minister,' says the senior Treasury official. 'In the absence of bargaining chips, there's no way to secure comprehensive access to the single market.'

'The best we can hope for is a customs union,' puts in another.

You lean back in your chair with a sigh. 'Mr Barkwell would not be happy. He keeps talking about all the trade deals he's going to be making around the world, but if we're in a customs union we'll just inherit the same tariffs as the EU, yes?'

'That's true, Prime Minister,' says another of the civil servants; you can never remember their names. 'Though there's a strong argument that says the trade tariffs negotiated by the EU will be considerably more attractive than those Britain could expect on her own.'

⇒ That clinches it. You need a customs union agreement.
Turn to **674**

⇒ Forget about existing templates, start negotiating an entirely new free trade agreement with the EU.
Turn to **294**

856

The only dirty linen your team can dig up to discredit Gervais Noysom-Reek is that he once addressed a far-right organization that advocates apartheid in Britain.

'Their newsletter says that different races aren't meant to coexist,' says Terri Trough, actually holding her nose as she views the website.

'If that were true, surely their own Neanderthal ancestors would have been wiped out. And Noysom-Reek buys into this stuff?'

'To be fair, it was several years ago and he's distanced himself from them since. Claims he thought they just wanted stronger controls on immigration.'

One talk. It's not much.

⇒ Feed it to the press. Turn to **582**

⇒ Forget about dishing the dirt. Turn to **801**

857

The one thing in Britain's favour is that the EU will be wary of allowing too many firms to relocate from the City in a short space of time. Some of those investment banks measure their assets in trillions of dollars – and in the event of another crash taxpayers would need to cover the losses.

Even so, the Treasury report makes grim reading. In the best case scenario, the City will lose 100,000 jobs and £10 billion in revenue in the year following Brexit.

You toss the report to your press secretary. 'Get all the copies of this and shred them.'

> On your Brexit Memo Pad:
> ❖ -2% Economy – the haemorrhaging of financial services from the City is going to impact everyone's standard of living.

Now turn to **400.**

858

'The easiest thing would be just to say that anyone who's been living here before March 2017 can apply for residency.'

'What about CSI?'

'If I were you, I'd modify the law. Cut the bit about it knocking off your five years if you haven't got sickness insurance. In fact, I'd just say that any EU citizen living here can apply for residency as long as they have sickness insurance, either personally or through their employer. You could even waive the five year requirement. That'd be guaranteeing their rights unequivocally. You'd probably have to waive the thirty-five thousand salary requirement too – you know, for those Bulgarian corn pickers and Lithuanian baristas and so on.'

'Not barristers, obviously.'

'Oh no. Thirty-five thou is what I spend on school fees alone. Anyway, I don't think you need to prioritize the details of how it's going to be handled just yet. Assuming there's a transition phase while trade deals are finalised, we'd be carrying on pretty much as normal for few years. You wouldn't have to worry about the laws governing residence right away. You could just promise EU citizens' rights will be guaranteed and fill in the legal details later.'

'OK, thank you, that's enough for today.'

Turn to **666**.

859

Tode's watery eyes drill into you. He sees you may have insufficient fervour to be a true Brexiteer, but you might still convince him that you're calculating enough to oversee the kind of Brexit he wants.

If you have the keyword UNCTION, turn to **633**.

If not, turn to **308**.

860

You recall your surreal conversation in a deserted Whitehall office with the minister's teenage daughter, Sprezzatura.

Turn to **700.**

861

He gazes back at you through the thick glasses that make his face look permanently surprised. Not for the first time he strikes you as a strange little meerkat, always scrutinizing people for signs of ideological impurity.

And if that's the case, what's his judgement of you? Look at your Brexit Memo Pad. If you have any of the keywords BLEAK, HEMLOCK, KOALA or LEAF, turn to **436**.

If not but you have either GAZELLE or OPAL, turn to **770**.

If you have none of those keywords, turn to **75**.

862 ☐

Your guidance in the matter comes from an ineffably knowledgeable source.

If the box above is empty, put a tick in it and turn to **33**.

If the box was already ticked, turn to **170**.

863

Word comes back from the EU negotiators that it's not going to be easy. Although it's in everyone's interests to keep the close cooperation between UK and EU police forces, after Brexit that would mean EU states being liable in principle to have to extradite their own nationals to a foreign country.

'Some EU states will have to amend their constitutions to allow this,' the EU Chief Negotiator, Willy Franjeboom, remarks to you in a late-night Skype call.

'So?'

'So they may ask why, if you want a divorce, you still expect to come and sleep on the couch. I'll do what I can.'

Check your Brexit Memo Pad. If your Goodwill score is 61% or more, turn to **448**. Otherwise turn to **476**.

864

The final polls have support for Leave just in front. It's going to be a tight race. So much depends on whether younger voters bother to turn out. With their future riding on the outcome, you might think they would crawl over broken glass to vote. But it's politics, which has always been a dark and unknowable art.

Toss two coins. If both come up heads, turn to **221**. Otherwise turn to **429**.

865

The two-year fuse lit by declaring Article 50 has nearly burnt out. In less than a week Brexit will be a reality. You glance out of the back window of Number 10 at the ochre-grey dusk. Just days after Brexit the clocks are due to change.

'And now we spring forward into a new era…' you rehearse. Needs work. Better give it to the speech writers.

If Labour had won the last election their ridiculous monolith of graven promises would now stand in the back garden like something out of *Carry On Space Odysseying*. Although, ironically, there's a metaphorical stone tablet whose commandments every politician is now beholden to follow. 'Thou shalt not deny that Brexit means Brexit,' and so on.

A whiff of tobacco wafts up through the open window. Craning your neck, you see the red glimmer of Ron Beardsley's pipe as he paces the darkened terrace. In a Proustian rush of memory you're taken back to your father's study one Christmas. You must have been seven or eight. Your father was writing his sermon and disliked interruption, but this was important.

'I wish to lodge a complaint about this present, Daddy,' you told him.

He set aside his pen and studied the object you were holding. 'It appears to be the unicorn you asked for.'

'I did ask for a unicorn. This is a stuffed toy.'

'Well, after all, there are no real unicorns.'

'I was promised a unicorn.'

'You can't have what doesn't exist.'

Was it at that moment you decided on a career in politics? You sensed a world of people who wanted things that didn't exist and that couldn't be delivered. People who would reject your father's stuffy logic with the sheer force of belief. With denial, if need be.

Those are the people who have put you here. And you mean to keep making them promises just as long as they keep electing you. Each new promise coming so fast that it washes out the failure of the last. A new era of wishing, when facts and opinions and delusions will merge in a rainbow of infinite possibility.

THE END

Or – hang on, *is* it the end? Maybe you'd like to find out what kind of shape the country is in after two years with you as Prime Minister? Turn to **736** to get your score.

"Great Britain has lost an empire and has not yet found a role. The attempt to play a separate power role — that is, a role apart from Europe, a role based on a 'special relationship' with the United States, a role based on being head of a commonwealth which has no political structure, or unity, or strength — this role is about played out."

- Dean Acheson, December 1962

ABOUT THE AUTHORS

Dave Morris has an Irish grandfather but has been informed that he's a citizen of nowhere. Jamie Thomson has a degree in Political Science but is aware that the people have had enough of experts. Both have written heaps of multiple-choice gamebooks, but this is the first one where you don't get to go home with a dragon's head and a bag of treasure.

IF AT FIRST YOU DON'T SUCCEED...

Real-life politicians only get one shot at getting it right, but you have the option to go back to the beginning and try again as often as you like.

To do that, first you'll need to reset the paper computer by erasing the scores on your Brexit Memo Pad and the ticks you'll have made throughout the book. The sections with boxes that you may have ticked while playing are:

81
150 (two boxes)
162
186
200 (two boxes in the text)
203
250
300 (three boxes in the text)
350
400 (four boxes in the text)
411
450
469
556
619
658
660
666 (three boxes)
705
835
862

Brexit memo pad

Authority - how secure is your power base? ________ %

Economy - what about the country's finances? ________ %

Goodwill - how many friends do you still have in the EU? ________ %

Popularity - what do the voters think? ________ %

(all start at 52%)

Completed negotiations

- EU Trade Talks ☐
- Exit Fee ☐
- General Election ☐
- Immigration ☐
- International Trade Deals ☐
- Negotiation Strategy ☐
- The NHS ☐
- Residency Rights ☐
- Second EU Referendum ☐
- Security & Defence ☐

Keywords

- APRICITY ☐
- BLEAK ☐
- CLARION ☐
- DODO ☐
- EIGER ☐
- FOG ☐
- GAZELLE ☐
- HEMLOCK ☐
- IRIS ☐
- JEWEL ☐
- KOALA ☐
- LEAF ☐
- MAPLE ☐
- NYLON ☐
- OPAL ☐
- PEDAL ☐
- QUORUM ☐
- REGENT ☐
- SANCTION ☐
- TIGHTROPE ☐
- UNCTION ☐
- VERTIGO ☐
- WELTER ☐
- YELLOW ☐
- ZEBRA ☐